DIETRICH BONHOEFFER WORKS, VOLUME 1

Sanctorum Communio

This series is a translation of
DIETRICH BONHOEFFER WERKE
Edited by
Eberhard Bethge, Ernst Feil,
Christian Gremmels, Wolfgang Huber,
Hans Pfeifer, Albrecht Schönherr,
Heinz Eduard Tödt†, Ilse Tödt

This volume has been made possible through the generous support of the Aid Association for Lutherans, the Lilly Endowment, Inc., the Stiftung Bonhoeffer Lehrstuhl, the Bowen H. and Janice Arthur McCoy Charitable Foundation, the Trull Foundation, the Lusk-Damen Charitable Gift Fund, the National Endowment for the Humanities, and numerous friends of the International Bonhoeffer Society.

DIETRICH BONHOEFFER WORKS

General Editor
Wayne Whitson Floyd, Jr.

DIETRICH BONHOEFFER

Sanctorum Communio

A Theological Study
of the Sociology of the Church

Translated from the German Edition
Edited by
JOACHIM VON SOOSTEN

English Edition
Edited by
CLIFFORD J. GREEN

Translated by
REINHARD KRAUSS AND NANCY LUKENS

FORTRESS PRESS   MINNEAPOLIS

DIETRICH BONHOEFFER WORKS, Volume 1

Originally published in German as *Dietrich Bonhoeffer Werke,* edited by Eberhard Bethge et al., by Chr. Kaiser Verlag in 1986; *Band 1* edited by Joachim von Soosten. First English-language edition of *Dietrich Bonhoeffer Works, Volume 1,* published by Fortress Press in 1998.

Sanctorum Communio first published in German by Trowlitzsch & Sohn in 1930, and Chr. Kaiser Verlag in 1960. Original English-language edition of *The Communion of Saints* published in 1963 by William Collins Sons & Co. Ltd., London, and Harper & Row, Inc., New York. New English-language translation of *Sanctorum Communio* with new supplementary material first published in 1998 by Fortress Press as part of *Dietrich Bonhoeffer Works.*

Translation of this work was generously supported by the Inter Nationes Agency, Bonn.

Jacket design: Cheryl Watson
Cover photo: Dietrich Bonhoeffer © Bildarchiv Preussischer Kulturbesitz, Berlin, 1998. Photo of Dietrich Bonhoeffer in 1928 in Barcelona by Rotraut Forberg, Düsseldorf.
Internal design: The HK Scriptorium, Inc.

Library of Congress Cataloging-in-Publication Data

Bonhoeffer, Dietrich, 1906–1945.
    [Sanctorum communio. English]
    Sanctorum communio : a theological study of the
sociology of the church / Dietrich Bonhoeffer ;
translated from the German edition edited by Joachim
von Soosten ; English edition edited by Clifford J.
Green ; translated by Reinhard Krauss and Nancy
Lukens.
        p.   cm. — (Dietrich Bonhoeffer works ; v. 1)
    Includes bibliographical references (p. 310) and
indexes.
    ISBN 0-8006-8301-3 (alk. paper)
    1. Sociology, Christian.   I. Green, Clifford J.
II. Title.   III. Series: Bonhoeffer, Dietrich,
1906–1945. Works. English. 1996 ; v. 1.
BR45.B6513   1998 vol. 1
[BT738]
230.044 s—dc21
[261.8]   98-29640
                          CIP

The paper used in this publication meets the minimum requirements of American National Standard for Information Sciences—Permanence of Paper for Printed Library Materials, ANSI Z329.48-1984.

Manufactured in the U.S.A.   AF 1-8301
                  3   4   5   6   7   8   9   10

CONTENTS

GENERAL EDITOR'S FOREWORD
TO DIETRICH BONHOEFFER WORKS

SINCE THE TIME that the writings of Dietrich Bonhoeffer (1906–1945) first began to be available in English after World War II, they have been eagerly read both by scholars and by a wide general audience. The story of his life is compelling, set in the midst of historic events that shaped a century.

Bonhoeffer's leadership in the anti-Nazi Confessing Church and his participation in the *Abwehr* resistance circle make his works a unique source for understanding the interaction of religion, politics, and culture among those few Christians who actively opposed National Socialism. His writings provide not only an example of intellectual preparation for the reconstruction of German culture after the war but also a rare insight into the vanishing world of the old social and academic elites. Because of his participation in the resistance against the Nazi regime, Dietrich Bonhoeffer was hanged in the concentration camp at Flossenbürg on April 9, 1945.

Yet Bonhoeffer's enduring contribution is not just his moral example but his theology as well. As a student in Tübingen, Berlin, and at Union Theological Seminary in New York—where he also was associated for a time with the Abyssinian Baptist Church in Harlem—and as a participant in the European ecumenical movement, Bonhoeffer became known as one of the few figures of the 1930s with a comprehensive and nuanced grasp of both German- and English-language theology. His thought resonates with a prescience, subtlety, and maturity that continually belie the youth of the thinker.

In 1986 the Chr. Kaiser Verlag, now part of Gütersloher Verlagshaus, marked the eightieth anniversary of Bonhoeffer's birth by issuing the first of the sixteen volumes of the definitive German edition of his writings, *Dietrich Bonhoeffer Werke*. Preliminary discussions about an English-language edition started even as the German series was beginning to emerge. As a consequence, the International Bonhoeffer Society, English Language Section, formed an editorial board, initially chaired by Robin Lovin, assisted by Mark Brocker, to undertake this project. Since 1993 the *Dietrich Bonhoeffer Works* translation project has been located in the Krauth Memorial Library of the Lutheran Theological Seminary at Philadelphia, under the leadership of its general editor and project director—Wayne Whitson Floyd, Jr., who supervises the seminary's Dietrich Bonhoeffer Center—and its executive director—Clifford J. Green of Hartford Seminary.

Dietrich Bonhoeffer Works provides the English-speaking world with an entirely new, complete, and unabridged translation of the written legacy of one of the twentieth century's most notable theologians; it includes a large amount of material appearing in English for the first time. Key terms are now translated consistently throughout the corpus, with special attention being paid to accepted English equivalents of technical theological and philosophical concepts.

This authoritative English edition strives, above all, to be true to the language, the style, and—most importantly—the theology of Bonhoeffer's writings. Translators have sought, nonetheless, to present Bonhoeffer's words in a manner that is sensitive to issues of gender in the language it employs. Consequently, accurate translation has removed sexist formulations that had been introduced inadvertently or unnecessarily into earlier English versions of his works. In addition, translators and editors generally have employed gender-inclusive language, insofar as this was possible without distorting Bonhoeffer's meaning or dissociating him from his own historical location.

At times Bonhoeffer's theology sounds fresh and modern, not because the translators have made it so, but because his language still speaks with a hardy contemporaneity even after more than half a century. In other instances, Bonhoeffer sounds more remote, a product of another era, not due to any lack of facility by the translators and editors, but because his concerns and rhetoric are in certain ways bound inextricably to a time that is past.

Volumes include introductions written by the editor(s) of each volume of the English edition, footnotes provided by Bonhoeffer, editorial notes added by the German and English editors, and afterwords composed by the editors of the German edition. In addition, volumes provide tables of abbreviations used in the editorial apparatus, as well as bibliographies which list sources used by Bonhoeffer, literature consulted by the editors, and other works related to each particular volume. Finally, volumes contain pertinent chronologies, charts, and indexes of scriptural references, names, and subjects.

The layout of the English edition has retained Bonhoeffer's original paragraphing (exceptions are noted by a ¶-symbol to indicate any paragraph break added by the editors of the English edition), as well as his manner of dividing works into chapters and sections. The pagination of the German critical edition, *Dietrich Bonhoeffer Werke,* is indicated in the outer margins of the pages of the translated text. At times, for the sake of precision and clarity of translation, a word or phrase that has been translated is provided in its original language, set within square brackets at the appropriate point in the text. Biblical citations come from the New Revised Standard Version, unless otherwise noted. Where versification of the Bible used by Bonhoeffer differs from the NRSV, the verse number in the latter is noted in the text in square brackets.

Bonhoeffer's own footnotes—which are indicated in the body of the text by plain, superscripted numbers—are reproduced in precisely the same numerical sequence as they appear in the German critical edition, complete with his idiosyncrasies of documentation. In these, as in the accompanying editorial notes, existing English translations of books and articles have been substituted for their counterparts in other languages whenever available. The edition of a work that was employed by Bonhoeffer himself can be ascertained by consulting the bibliography at the end of each volume. When a work in the bibliography has no published English translation, an English equivalent of its title is provided there in parentheses; if a non-English work appears only within a footnote or editorial note, an English equivalent of its title appears at that point in the note.

The editorial notes, which are indicated in the body of the text by superscripted numbers in square brackets—except volume five where they are indicated by plain, superscripted numbers—provide information on the intellectual, ecclesiastical, social, and political context of Bonhoeffer's pursuits during the first half of the twentieth century.

These are based on the scholarship of the German critical edition; they have been supplemented by the contributions of the editors of the English edition. Where the editors or translators of the English edition have substantially augmented or revised a German editor's note, the initials of the person making the change(s) appear at the note's conclusion, and editorial material that has been added in the English edition is surrounded by square brackets. When any previously translated material is quoted within an editorial note in altered form—indicated by the notation [trans. altered]—such changes should be assumed to be the responsibility of the translator(s).

Bibliographies at the end of each volume provide the complete information for each written source that Bonhoeffer or the various editors have mentioned in the current volume. References to the archives, collections, and personal library of materials that had belonged to Bonhoeffer and that survived the war—as cataloged in the *Nachlaß Dietrich Bonhoeffer* and collected in the Staatsbibliothek zu Berlin—are indicated within *Dietrich Bonhoeffer Works* by the abbreviation *NL* followed by the corresponding reference code within that published index. The production of any individual volume of *Dietrich Bonhoeffer Works* requires the financial assistance of numerous individuals and organizations, whose support is duly noted on the verso of the half-title page. In addition, the editor's introduction of each volume acknowledges those persons who have assisted in a particular way with the production of the English edition of that text. A special note of gratitude, however, is owed to all those prior translators, editors, and publishers of various portions of Bonhoeffer's literary legacy who heretofore have made available to the English-speaking world the writings of this remarkable theologian.

The English edition depends especially upon the careful scholarship of all those who labored to produce the critical German edition, completed in April 1998, from which these translations have been made. Their work has been overseen by a board of general editors—responsible for both the concept and the content of the German edition—composed of Eberhard Bethge, Ernst Feil, Christian Gremmels, Wolfgang Huber (chair), Hans Pfeifer (ongoing liaison between the German and English editorial boards), Albrecht Schönherr, Heinz Eduard Tödt†, and Ilse Tödt.

The present English edition would be impossible without the creativity and unflagging dedication of the members of the editorial board of *Dietrich Bonhoeffer Works:* Mark Brocker, James H. Burtness, Keith W. Clements, Wayne Whitson Floyd, Jr., Barbara Green, Clifford J. Green, John W. de Gruchy, Barry A. Harvey, James Patrick Kelley, Geffrey B. Kelly, Reinhard Krauss, Robin W. Lovin, Michael Lukens, Nancy Lukens, Paul Matheny, Mary Nebelsick, and H. Martin Rumscheidt.

The deepest thanks for their support of this undertaking is owed, as well, to all the various members, friends, and benefactors of the International Bonhoeffer Society; to the National Endowment for the Humanities, which supported this project during its inception; to the Lutheran Theological Seminary at Philadelphia and its former Auxiliary who established and still help to support the Dietrich Bonhoeffer Center on its campus specifically for the purpose of facilitating these publications; and to our publisher, Fortress Press, as represented with uncommon patience and *Gemütlichkeit* by Henry French, Michael West, Rachel Riensche, Pam McClanahan, Debbie Finch Brandt, and John Turnbull. Finally, a special note of appreciation is due to two staff members whose tenure at Fortress Press ended in 1997, Marshall Johnson, Director of Publishing, and Lois Torvik, Production Editor, who together encouraged the high standards for the entire English edition and oversaw the publication of the first three volumes; and we remember with deep gratitude the careful and untiring work of Sheryl Strauss, peerless copyeditor, who died of cancer in late 1997. The privilege of collaboration with professionals such as these is fitting testimony to the spirit of Dietrich Bonhoeffer, who was himself always so attentive to the creative mystery of community—and that ever-deepening collegiality that is engendered by our social nature as human beings.

Wayne Whitson Floyd, Jr. , General Editor and Project Director
January 27, 1995
The Fiftieth Anniversary of the Liberation of Auschwitz
Second revision on August 6, 1998

ABBREVIATIONS

AB (DBWE 2)   *Act and Being* (*DBWE*, English edition)
CC   *Christ the Center* (U.K. title *Christology*)
CD   *The Cost of Discipleship*
CF (DBWE 3)   *Creation and Fall* (*DBWE*, English edition)
CS   *The Communion of Saints* (U.K. title *Sanctorum Communio*)
DBW   *Dietrich Bonhoeffer Werke,* German edition
DBWE   *Dietrich Bonhoeffer Works,* English edition
E   *Ethics*
FP   *Fiction from Prison*
GS   *Gesammelte Schriften* (Collected works)
LPP   *Letters and Papers from Prison*, 4th Edition
LT (DBWE 5)   *Life Together* (DBWE, English Edition)
LW   [Martin] *Luther's Works*, American edition
NL   *Nachlaß Dietrich Bonhoeffer*
NRS   *No Rusty Swords*
NRSV   *New Revised Standard Version*
SC (DBW 1)   *Sanctorum Communio* (*DBW,* German edition)
SC-A   The dissertation typescript of *Santorum Communio*
SC-B   *Sanctorum Communio,* first published German edition (1930)
SC-RS   Reinhold Seeberg, marginal comments in *SC-A*
TP   *True Patriotism*
WA   *Weimar Ausgabe* (Weimar edition), Martin Luther
WF   *The Way to Freedom*

CLIFFORD J. GREEN

EDITOR'S INTRODUCTION
TO THE ENGLISH EDITION

UNDERSTANDING THE THEOLOGY of Dietrich Bonhoeffer requires a thorough understanding of *Sanctorum Communio,* his doctoral dissertation and first published work. Here are found central ideas that inform all his writings—and, indeed, his life—notwithstanding theological and personal developments associated with later works such as *Discipleship, Ethics,* and *Letters and Papers from Prison.* In this formative book Bonhoeffer articulates the concept of 'person' in ethical relation to the 'other', Christian freedom as 'being-free-for' the other, the reciprocal relationship of person and community, vicarious representative action as both a christological and an anthropological-ethical concept, the exercise by individual persons of responsibility for human communities, social relations as analogies of divine-human relations, and the encounter of transcendence in human sociality. All these theological ideas characteristic of Bonhoeffer are involved in his Christocentric theology of the Christian community, the *sanctorum communio.* Ecclesiology is set in the midst of a "theology of sociality."[1]

In his preface Bonhoeffer states that the more he has investigated "the significance of the sociological category for theology, the more clearly has emerged *the social intention of all the basic Christian concepts.* 'Person', 'primal state', 'sin', and 'revelation' can be fully comprehended only in reference to sociality."[2] This is both a far-reaching programmatic statement for Bonhoeffer's theology and a specific reference to the structure of this book. After the first chapter devoted to his

---

[1.] See Clifford Green, *Bonhoeffer: A Theology of Sociality.*
[2.] Emphasis mine. See below, page 21, italics mine; cf. page 22, editorial note 5.

1

definitions of social philosophy and sociology, Bonhoeffer's argument moves into theology. Chapter 2 deals with theological anthropology, focusing on the Christian concept of 'person' both in the I-You-relation and in relation to God. Chapter 3 treats creation, the 'primal state', with a focus on persons in community. Chapter 4 addresses the effect of sin on persons-in-relation and the community-of-persons; both a critique of Augustine and Ritschl on original sin and a reconstruction of the doctrine with an "ethical collective concept of the human race"[3] are necessary to show the 'social intention' of this doctrine. Chapter 5 treats revelation by discussing the Christian community, the *communio sanctorum*. Bonhoeffer's distinctiveness here stands out by comparison with Barth (and Bultmann), who discussed revelation under the rubric of 'the word of God'. To be sure, their treatment of 'the word' is not apart from the church, just as Bonhoeffer's treatment of Christian community is not apart from word and sacrament. But the approach and emphasis are different: Bonhoeffer highlights the 'social intention' of revelation.

The European theological landscape of the 1920s was characterized by a watershed created by Karl Barth, who asserted a theology of revelation, rooted in the Reformation, over against nineteenth-century theology, which he called 'anthropocentric' and 'neo-Protestant'. Bonhoeffer stood on Karl Barth's side of the watershed. In *Sanctorum Communio* Bonhoeffer's premise is that the church is a reality in Christ, and only from an understanding of the church given in revelation (with special reference to scripture and Luther) can a sociological investigation of its nature be undertaken. Barth later praised the work highly.

> This dissertation . . . not only awakens respect for the breadth and depth of its insight as we look back to the existing situation [at that time], but makes far more instructive and stimulating and illuminating and genuinely edifying reading today than many of the more famous works which have since been written on the problem of the church. . . . I openly confess that I have misgivings whether I can even maintain the high level reached by Bonhoeffer, saying no less in my own words and context, and saying it no less forcefully, than did this young man so many years ago.[4]

In his evaluation, Reinhold Seeberg, Bonhoeffer's doctoral adviser, wrote of the allusions to Barth that he found in some terminology of

---

[3.] See below, page 114.
[4.] *Church Dogmatics* 4/2:641.

the dissertation. But Bonhoeffer's alignment with Barth was much stronger than Seeberg recognized—the dissertation displays not mere allusions to Barth but rather a fundamental commitment to the method of a theology of revelation. When Bonhoeffer, after returning from America in 1931, visited Barth for the first time, he wrote to a friend that his chief regret about his theological education was that he had not visited Barth sooner.[5] And in Tegel prison Bonhoeffer looked back and credited Barth with making a clear distinction between revelation and religion,[6] a distinction Bonhoeffer had adopted in *Sanctorum Communio*. Nevertheless, in his alignment with Barth, Bonhoeffer remained typically independent. Already in *Sanctorum Communio* he severely criticizes Barth's interpretation in *The Epistle to the Romans* of love of the neighbor, as though the neighbor were merely a cipher for God.[7] A similar criticism of Barth's interpretation of the freedom of God would appear in Bonhoeffer's next book, *Act and Being*.[8]

Bonhoeffer does not interpret the Christian community as a religious ghetto, but advances a thesis about human sociality per se. When Bonhoeffer writes in his *Ethics* that the Christian community is "a section of humanity in which Christ has really taken form,"[9] that is another way of stating the point already made in his first book, that "the church is God's new will and purpose for humanity."[10] Christ personifies the new humanity, and the Christian community is about the restoration and consummation of the created sociality of all humanity. That is why social philosophy and sociology are intrinsic to the treatment of the church.

In addressing issues of social philosophy in *Sanctorum Communio* the young theologian reveals that he is very competent in philosophy, a characteristic that is especially evident in his next work, *Act and Being*. He knows that all philosophical positions embody fundamental anthropological convictions that theology must engage, and he evaluates various philosophical positions, from Aristotle to modern Europeans, with special attention to their treatments of the relation between the

---

[5.] *NRS* 120 *(DBW* 11:19*)*.

[6.] *LPP* 286, 328.

[7.] See below, chap. 5, footnote 28. Love of neighbor, Bonhoeffer believed, was really love of the neighbor, not love of God in the neighbor.

[8.] *AB (DBWE 2)*:90f.

[9.] *E* 85.

[10.] See below, page 141.

individual person and human collectivities. Sociological theories also embody philosophical assumptions. Thus social philosophy, whether by explicit construct or tacit assumption, has a normative function in selecting and interpreting empirical data and structures. Since social philosophy is not value-neutral, Bonhoeffer seeks to identify elements of a "Christian social philosophy"[11] that are theologically valid.

His basic philosophical move is to insist that the 'social category' cannot be derived from an epistemological paradigm. Epistemology is governed by the subject-object relation, the relation of knower and known. But this cannot yield a social 'other', since agency and power in the epistemological paradigm remain with the knower. Sociality requires another paradigm of independent, willing selves who are genuinely other, over against the self. Theologically this is rooted in the conviction that to be human is to be a person before God, and that the human counterpart of this primal relation is the relation of self and other.[12] Bonhoeffer aimed to "overcome the idealist philosophy of immanent spirit . . . [to] provide a direction for Christian social philosophy."[13] The import of Bonhoeffer's philosophical critique has been highlighted by Charles Marsh. He has argued persuasively that Bonhoeffer presents a "christological description of life with others [that] offers a compelling and unexpectedly rich alternative to post-Kantian models of selfhood—to conceptions of the self as the center of all relations to others."[14]

Central to all phases of his argument—from theological anthropology to ecclesiology—is Bonhoeffer's 'Christian concept of person'. The person is constituted above all by the ethical responsibility that arises in encounter and conflict with the will of the other person.[15] This social concept of 'person' is used to interpret *Geist* (spirit), rather than interpreting 'person' by an idealist concept of *Geist*. Crucial to Bonhoeffer's Christian concept of 'person' is his description of the relation of I and

---

[11.] See below, pages 21f.

[12.] Later, this is very clearly exemplified in Bonhoeffer's exposition of the *imago Dei* as *analogia relationis* (analogy of relationship) in the theological interpretation of Genesis 1–3. See *CF (DBWE 3)*:64ff.

[13.] See below, chap. 2, editorial note 30, pages 43f.

[14.] *Reclaiming Dietrich Bonhoeffer*, vii; see also Wayne Whitson Floyd, Jr., *Theology and the Dialectics of Otherness*.

[15.] See below, chap. 2, pages 47ff.

You, in German *Ich* and *Du*. But this should not be read as the same sort of 'personalism' that one finds in Brunner, Gogarten, and others. Distinguishing Bonhoeffer from what can be called 'interpersonal personalism' is the use of 'person' as a *corporate* concept, as well as a *relational* one defined in the I-You encounter. Thus British and American readers will have to grapple with unfamiliar concepts such as 'objective spirit' and 'collective person' as ways of describing and interpreting the ethos and culture of communities, and of discussing the relation of Christ and the Holy Spirit to the church. Among other things, such language is a way of focusing ethical obligation in individual persons, not of avoiding it by transfer to a hyperpersonal, metaphysical entity.

Among English-language readers Bonhoeffer's use of the I-You-relation often calls to mind the well-known translation of Martin Buber's book, *I and Thou*.[16] It was originally published in German in 1923, four years before Bonhoeffer completed his dissertation. Indeed, some readers have assumed Buber's influence on Bonhoeffer's use of the I-You-relation. But the Buber of *Ich und Du* is nowhere to be found in *Sanctorum Communio*; his name appears only as editor of a series of sociological books. More important, the approaches of Buber and Bonhoeffer are fundamentally different. Buber's distinction of I-It and I-You relations was rooted, like Bultmann's parallel distinction, in Marburg neo-Kantianism. Bonhoeffer drew on other philosophers of the I-You-relation such as Theodor Litt, Emanuel Hirsch, and Eberhard Grisebach. The Buber scholar Walter Kaufmann points to the difference when he rightly describes "the sense of intimacy that pervades Buber's book."[17] His aim is to create a realm of intimacy between persons, overcoming the objectified I-It world. Bonhoeffer of course would agree with Buber in resisting the objectification of persons. He, however, stresses the 'other' as boundary and barrier to the self; he emphasizes ethical encounter rather than intimacy. The other transcends the self in ethical encounter—indeed, the human You is a form and analogy of the divine You in precisely this present otherness. This personal-ethical

---

[16.] The most recent translation was made by Walter Kaufmann in 1970. The first English translation in 1937, by Ronald Gregor Smith—coincidentally the translator of *Sanctorum Communio*—gave wide currency to the phrase "I-Thou relationship." Kaufmann, while retaining the original title of the translation, *I and Thou*, made his own preference plain by giving his prologue the title "I and You."

[17.] *I and Thou*, Kaufmann translation, 37.

model of transcendence, which is found throughout Bonhoeffer's theology,[18] distinguishes him clearly from Buber.

What will British and American sociologists of religion make of Bonhoeffer's "theological study of the sociology of the church"? Here they will find no statistical data or survey research. The reflections on "Church and Proletariat," stimulated partly by Troeltsch and partly by Bonhoeffer's own observations, certainly connect with discussions about the church and social class, even though Seeberg thought them "superfluous" (see below). But the definition of sociology as a systematic discipline, and Bonhoeffer's desire to relate the form of the church as a distinctive structure to a typology of social forms, is definitely foreign to contemporary Anglo-American sociology. More important, however, is Bonhoeffer's insistence that the church is a *theological community* that identifies itself by reference to *theological norms* in scripture and tradition. How does attention to these theological norms inform the way sociologists of religion construe their task? Alternatively, if these theological norms do not inform sociological analysis of church communities, what is the source and status of the norms that *are* employed? Part of the legacy of this book is that such fundamental methodological questions about the relation of theology to the sociological study of the church cannot be avoided, even by those who define sociology quite differently from Bonhoeffer.

Sanctorum Communio is a foundational work. Familiar with this book, readers of *Life Together* will discover that life at the Finkenwalde seminary of the Confessing Church was built upon its theology.[19] Not only the treatment of 'community' but also the dialectic of 'the day together' and 'the day alone' and the mutual service of 'active helpfulness' and 'bearing with others' are all ideas first set out here. In *Creation and Fall* the exposition of the image of God as an *analogy of relationship* builds on the self-other analysis of *Sanctorum Communio*, and so does the treatment of freedom as being-free-for-the-other. The *Ethics* also reaches back to *Sanctorum Communio*, especially in developing the view of individuals' responsibilities for their communities (e.g., their nation) in vicarious representative action, *Stellvertretung*. In the *Letters and Papers*

[18.] See, for example, *LPP* 381, especially, "The transcendent is . . . the neighbor who is within reach in any given situation. God in human form . . . 'the man for others,' therefore the Crucified . . ."

[19.] The very title, *Gemeinsames Leben*, recalls "Christ existing as *Gemeinde*," as church-community.

from Prison the interpretation of transcendence in terms of the self-other relation, and the christological formula, "Jesus, the man for others," are familiar themes used to address a new issue.[20] In light of the foundational role of *Sanctorum Communio*, therefore, one has to be very careful not to interpret some of Bonhoeffer's later statements as rejections of his early theological works.[21]

The Origin and Publication of the Work[22]

Bonhoeffer's decision to become a theologian was made while still in Gymnasium.[23] Plans for the doctorate took shape in 1925. Letters between Bonhoeffer and his parents that summer discuss whether he would work with Adolf von Harnack, Karl Holl, or Reinhold Seeberg, since he was studying with each of them. By September the decision was final; he would work with Seeberg on a dissertation that would be "half historical and half systematic . . . on the subject of religious community. . . ." The same letter asks for money to buy books by Hegel, Spencer, and Max Weber.[24] Less than two years later the dissertation was completed—along with his course work, seven seminar papers, and nine homiletical and catechetical outlines.[25] This documents the intensity and speed with which Bonhoeffer worked and the deft way he used his sources. It also points to his capacity for systematic thinking.

Seeberg's report in July 1927 summarizes, rather cursorily, the course of the dissertation argument and then offers the following evaluation.

> The author is not only well oriented in the discipline of theology, but also has worked his way intelligently into the field of sociology. He clearly

---

[20.] For a more detailed treatment of themes from *Sanctorum Commmunio* in Bonhoeffer's writings see Clifford Green, "Human Sociality and Christian Community" in de Gruchy, ed., *The Cambridge Companion to Dietrich Bonhoeffer*.

[21.] See Bethge, *Dietrich Bonhoeffer*, 154–56, where in letters from 1931 to 1936 Bonhoeffer speaks of "'new views' that had changed his philosophy and theology," a "dislike" for *Act and Being*, his initial view of theology as "a more academic matter," and having wandered "in a lot of theological side-tracks." See also Bonhoeffer and von Wedemeyer, *Love Letters from Cell 92*, 220. Note that Bethge frequently points out important continuities from *Sanctorum Communio* and *Act and Being* in Bonhoeffer's later works; cf. *Dietrich Bonhoeffer*, 60, 81, 99, 374–78, 793.

[22.] Much of this section summarizes material in the German editor's introduction, *SC (DBW 1)*:1–6.

[23.] Bethge, *Dietrich Bonhoeffer*, 22.

[24.] *DBW* 9:156.

[25.] *SC (DBW 1)*:1f.

possesses a great gift for systematic thinking, as demonstrated by the dialectics in the structure of his thesis as a whole, and in its detail. He is concerned to find his way independently, and is always prepared to offer skillful counter-arguments to the opinions of others. Even though one might not always be able to concur with his judgments, one will readily recognize the scholar's interest and the energy of his argumentation. Characteristic of the author's position is his strong emphasis on the Christian ethical element, which he always takes as a starting point in his many arguments with the worldview of 'idealism'. His strong skeptical tone is reminiscent of Heim, and here and there one finds references to Barth, as is seen in terminology like *an-rufen*, call, and *ant-worten*, answer. But Barth and Heim are not the only influences on Bonhoeffer's thought; one also encounters influences contrary to theirs. The presentation is generally quite skillful, though sometimes the overly strict systematizing does introduce redundancies. The dialectical proofs of the author are not always convincing. Consider the peculiar proof that an I can only come to recognize a You by first coming to know God. Likewise, I would not subscribe to everything dialectically deduced by the author about the structure of the empirical church, for example, whether in the church the 'society' [Gesellschaft] type is really a necessary complement to the 'community' [Gemeinschaft] type. Precisely in this context, incidentally, some outstanding observations are made. The author could have spared himself the historical excursus on pp. 112ff.,[26] since it offers nothing new. Likewise his critical comments on church practice, or his hopeful optimism regarding the proletariat along with his contempt for the middle class, are superfluous, since they do not arise out of the principles of the thesis but are merely subjective value judgments. Finally, it is not always possible to agree with the author's criticism of the views of others (e.g., Troeltsch!).

At the same time, all these deficiencies are part and parcel of every youthful product. Ultimately they are the obverse of the work's great strengths: its enthusiasm for Christianity, its rigorously systematic organization, the author's inner devotion to his task, his welcome independence of view, and his critical capacity to defend his views against others. On the whole the work can be regarded as a very welcome specimen of early scholarly erudition.

I therefore request that the distinguished faculty accept it as a Licentiate dissertation, and propose evaluating it with the grade I–II.[27]

[26.] See below, pages 96ff., editorial note 116.
[27.] *DBW* 9:175f., partly cited in *SC (DBW 1)*:2f.

The oral examination and public defense of the dissertation were held on December 17, 1927, in the Old Aula of the university; the "opponents" were Robert Stupperich, Walter Dreß, and Helmut Roeßler.[28] Bonhoeffer was awarded the degree Licentiate in Theology with a grade very rarely given by the Berlin theological faculty, summa cum laude. He was twenty-one years old.

Bonhoeffer received his first copy of the published version on September 2, 1930, more than three years after the dissertation had been completed. Days later he left for a year as a postdoctoral fellow at Union Theological Seminary, New York, having already completed *Act and Being* (his *Habilitationsschrift*) and his inaugural lecture during the summer.

The History of the Text

The text of *Sanctorum Communio* has a history almost as complicated as that of the *Ethics* and the *Letters and Papers from Prison*. The original text is Bonhoeffer's dissertation, which was completed in July 1927. Its title is *Sanctorum Communio: Eine dogmatische Untersuchung* (The communion of saints: A theological study). The original bound typescript of 354 pages was for many years in the possession of Eberhard Bethge; now, along with the other Bonhoeffer papers, it is housed in the manuscript department of the Staatsbibliothek in Berlin.[29] There are notes on its title page by the Dean, Prof. Arthur Titius, and by Bonhoeffer's dissertation adviser, Prof. Reinhold Seeberg, who submitted his report on July 18, 1927. Seeberg's marginal comments, which are reproduced in the editorial notes below, are also contained in this copy. The dissertation typescript contains neatly handwritten brief corrections and additions to footnotes that appear to have been made before the typescript was submitted. This copy of the dissertation was also heavily worked over by Bonhoeffer, in ink and several colors of pencil, in preparation for publication. Passages to be omitted are crossed out, additions and new transitions are written in, and abbreviations are evident.[30] A

[28.] For his annotated text of the theses argued by Bonhoeffer see *DBW* 9:476ff. (Walter Dreß married Bonhoeffer's younger sister Susanne.)

[29.] The dissertation also is available on microfiche from the Bundesarchiv in Koblenz.

[30.] Joachim von Soosten reports that the Scharper Publishing Company in Han-

couple of pages of carbon in bright blue are bound with this copy, sug-
gesting that at least one other copy was originally made; however, no
other copies have been found.[31]

The first German edition was published by Trowitzsch und Sohn,
Berlin, in 1930 in a series edited by Reinhold Seeberg. Bonhoeffer had
edited the dissertation during his year as assistant pastor in
Barcelona,[32] and estimated that he cut 20 to 25 percent of the text
prior to publishing.[33] Partly this was to reduce the cost of printing during the Depression; partly it was to please his adviser Seeberg,[34] whose
foundation, along with Bonhoeffer's own subsidy and other funding
sources, was contributing to the cost of publication. These cuts have
had lasting consequences, right up to the present volume.

Little critical attention was paid to the work when it was published,
apart from three reviews and mention by Ernst Wolf in a 1933 article in
the Barthian journal *Zwischen den Zeiten*.[35] After World War II—and
after the publication of Bonhoeffer's *Ethics* and *Letters and Papers from*

---

nover, which took over Trowitzsch in 1952–53, searched its archives but found no files
related to the printing of *Sanctorum Communio*, nor the copy of the dissertation used to
make the original publication (*SC* [*DBW 1*]:7). There is reason to consider, however,
whether the extant typescript (*SC-A*) is in fact the one used by the typesetter to create the
published text (*SC-B*). For example, some errors of incomplete italicizing in the published
version correspond exactly to page breaks in the typescript. Of itself such pieces of evidence do not necessarily identify the extant copy as the one used by the typesetter. But it
does warrant a more thorough scrutiny of evidence like this.

[31.] In the summer of 1969 Carl-Jürgen Kaltenborn reported to Eberhard Bethge that
a copy of the dissertation had been found in the library of Humboldt University, Berlin. A
search of the library and the university archives in 1998, however, failed to find any other
copy of the typescript, or any record that one had ever been deposited with the university.
A copy of the original publication itself was found in the library's collection of published
dissertations, and it may have been this copy to which Kaltenborn's report referred.

[32.] *SC (DBW 1)*:4.

[33.] *DBW* 10:102. Unlike later editions, including *SC (DBW 1)*, the table of contents of
SC-B is a revised form of the full version found in the dissertation (*SC-A*). In parts this
amounts to a concise summary of the argument. For example, section B of chapter 2 is
summarized in the following important formulation: "The human social basic-relation
corresponds to the relation of God to humanity. The holiness of the 'You' is grounded in
God. The concept of God and the concept of community are in necessary relation to each
other." The same source also shows that in *SC-A* the second half of the heading of chapter
3, section B, was "the original unbroken community" (cf. below, page 65).

[34.] Seeberg had particularly questioned whether the section on "Church and Proletariat" really belonged in the framework of the study and had placed more marginal comments and question marks beside this section than any other part of the dissertation. See
below, the editorial notes on pages 271–74.

[35.] See *SC (DBW 1)*:5, editorial note 16.

Prison aroused interest in his early writings—the work was republished by Chr. Kaiser Verlag in 1954 with a brief introduction by Ernst Wolf. This edition simply reproduced the first publication. It may have been this later edition that first came to the attention of Karl Barth, though his reference to *Sanctorum Communio* in the 1955 volume of *Church Dogmatics* 4/2 also mentioned the first publication of Bonhoeffer's dissertation in 1930.

The third German edition of *Sanctorum Communio* was published by Chr. Kaiser in 1960, and this was a genuinely new edition, for it contained in an appendix approximately half of the material that was excised from the dissertation for the 1930 publication. Important and highly interesting material became available for the first time, thirty years after the publication of its progenitor. The appendix also gave the full original version of some sections that had been abbreviated, such as the outline of the New Testament view of the church. The fourth German edition appeared in 1969 but differed from the third only by the addition of an afterword by Eberhard Bethge.

The English translation, published in 1963,[36] was made from the third German edition. It constitutes a distinct fourth redaction of the text, and therein lies its problem. The English translator naturally wished to take advantage of the material newly available in the appendix of the third German edition. But it was really impossible to make a "version [that] corresponds more closely to the original text of the author than even the latest German edition"[37] without translating the original dissertation in toto. The original manuscript, however, was not consulted by Ronald Gregor Smith. Rather, on the basis of the published German third edition, he tried to integrate into Bonhoeffer's original publication the excerpts of the excisions given in the German appendix. This resulted in several serious problems. For example, in some places Bonhoeffer's transitions written for his published version are combined with the material they were intended to replace. Similarly, some notes to chapter 1 come from the published German text and overlap as condensed versions of notes that have been restored from the German appendix. Again, in some cases the footnotes in this English

[36.] Collins published the British edition under the title *Sanctorum Communio*, while Harper called it *The Communion of Saints*; both retained the subtitle of the published German edition, "a dogmatic inquiry into the sociology of the church."

[37.] Translator's note, *CS* 14.

edition do not give all the material cited in the third German edition. Further, some material restored from the German appendix to the body of the text is not restored to its place in the original order, where that had been altered in the process of abbreviation. To remedy these problems a new English edition was required.

In 1986 the new critical edition of *Sanctorum Communio* was published in Germany, the first volume of the *Dietrich Bonhoeffer Werke*. This was the first complete publication including all the material in the dissertation typescript. Following the rule of the critical edition that works published by Bonhoeffer during his lifetime should be presented in the form in which he originally published them, the German editorial board decided not to reproduce the original dissertation. Rather, the text of the first edition was reproduced, and the editor included in one hundred pages of editorial notes—nearly one-third of the book—all the material that had been excised from the dissertation. This ranged from lengthy passages of several pages to single words. Indeed, as a critical edition, the new German publication records every change Bonhoeffer made to his dissertation. To these the editor, Joachim von Soosten, added copious notes that reveal to the reader in great detail the sources used by Bonhoeffer, his manner of working, and the theological context in which he worked. In the German edition all the editorial material, including Bonhoeffer's excised material, is printed in the back of the book, following the text that Bonhoeffer originally published in 1930.

The present English edition is based on the German critical text. Its format differs slightly, however. To assist the reader, all the editorial apparatus is printed at the bottom of the page, below Bonhoeffer's text and his own footnotes as they appeared in the 1930 published edition. This means that the reader of the English edition now is able to find Bonhoeffer's excisions at the point in the text where they originated. The problems of the earlier English translation, moreover, are avoided, for like the German edition we have kept the excised material clearly separate from the main body of the text; but now these excisions have been placed in the editorial notes at the bottom of the page, rather than as endnotes at the back of the volume as was the case in the German edition. The page numbers of the German edition are provided in the outer margin of the English text. Those page numbers beside the editorial notes—indicating their location in the German critical edition—have been set, however, in a smaller font to remind the reader that this material was placed out of sequence, as endnotes, at the back of the German critical edition.

The editorial notes at the bottom of the page, beneath Bonhoeffer's footnotes from the 1930 published edition, therefore, contain four different types of material. (1) *Normal editorial commentary related to the main body of the text.* A notation in square-brackets indicates authorship by the English-edition editor or translators, rather than the editor of the German critical edition. (2) *Bonhoeffer's excised material, typeset in a distinctive, non-serif font.* If longer than five lines, this material is indicated as an indented block-quote. (3) *Bonhoeffer's footnotes to that excised material, typeset in the same non-serif font.* They are included in-line at the point of the notes' occurrence, unnumbered but indicated by double angle-brackets. (4) *Editorial notes to that excised material, set in the same font as regular editorial commentary.* They, too, are included in-line at the point of the notes' occurrence in the excised material and are unnumbered but indicated by square-brackets, followed by the initials of the author of the note if it is not the German editor.

In matters of citation Bonhoeffer was anything but meticulous; his passion was clearly for his argument, not for fine points of documentation and presentation. Although Bonhoeffer's notes have been reproduced complete with his idiosyncratic documentation, where such errors in his citations of titles and page numbers would mislead the reader, they have been corrected by editorial notes where possible. Full and correct citations are found in the Bibliography, "Literature Used by Bonhoeffer," which includes the correct titles for all the works he references and English translations where they exist.

When Bonhoeffer quotes from German sources for which no English translations exist, we provide the translation and cite the original German source. In quoting from one of Bonhoeffer's sources that has been translated into English, we have normally followed the published English translation. Where we found it necessary to change the existing translation, this is indicated by the phrase "trans. altered" in square brackets. In chapters 1 through 4 it should be assumed, unless otherwise indicated, that the translator is Nancy Lukens, and in chapter 5 Reinhard Krauss. Where Bonhoeffer cites a source but does not give an edition (e.g., of Irenaeus's *Against Heresies*), the bibliography lists the best recent edition, and an editorial note gives the reference in an English translation where one exists.

Matters of Translation

Several words have presented special challenges. *Geist*, generally translated "spirit," is the first. Although it is used for God (as in Holy Spirit, and absolute spirit), it is mainly used in this book as an anthropological term.[38] In German it is a complex word, similar to the English phrase "the spirit of a person." Its range of meanings can include mind, intellect, imagination, personality, feeling, and responsibility. Bonhoeffer himself gives us an important clue to his own usage when he speaks of a "general metaphysical" understanding of the human person as "self-conscious and spontaneously active spirit."[39] This definition emphasizes mind and will. Accordingly, when Bonhoeffer uses *Geist*, especially in philosophical contexts, to mean mind or intellect, these terms are used to translate it. Variants on *Geist* are *Geistigkeit* and *geistig*. In distinction from *geistig*, the adjective *geistlich* is translated "spiritual." It is a theological term, never used in a secular context; its basic meaning comes from its connection with the Holy Spirit. So the adjective "spiritual" (which Bonhoeffer uses only a few times) does not mean the sort of subjective, self-referring religious piety sometimes associated with the word "spirituality."

Bonhoeffer's terms for the church, especially *Gemeinde*, have been most challenging. He uses two categories of terms—theological and sociological—to discuss the *sanctorum communio*. The main theological terms are *Kirche* and *Gemeinde*, as in the axiom "Die Kirche ist Christus als Gemeinde existierend," "the church is Christ existing as *Gemeinde*."[40] The sociological terms are *Gemeinschaft* (community), *Gesellschaft* (society), *Herrschaftsverband* (association of authentic rule), and *Genossenschaftsverband* (cooperative association). Of these terms, *Gemeinde* has a range of meanings and usages in Bonhoeffer's text and therefore presents the most complex translation problem. In Bonhoeffer's most distinctive and fundamental usage in this book, *Gemeinde* means Christ present as *sanctorum communio*. *Gemeinde* is Bonhoeffer's preferred term; its meaning provides the theological norm for 'church'.

When Bonhoeffer says, "the church [*Kirche*] is Christ existing as *Gemeinde*," this does not mean that an institution calling itself church

---

[38.] In *AB* the word *Dasein* comes to the fore as the central anthropological term, while in *CC* the term *Existenz* is central.

[39.] See below, pages 59 and 52f.

[40.] *SC (DBW 1)*:76, 86, *passim*; see below, pages 121, 141.

defines where Christ is communally present. On the contrary, it is not a church organization that defines Christ, but Christ who defines the church. In other words, it is precisely where, and only where, 'Christ-exists-as-*Gemeinde*' that we find the 'church' (*Kirche*). This point is crucial for understanding Bonhoeffer's action in the Church Struggle against National Socialism. That there was a German church organization, with its clergy, its traditions, its congregations, its laws—yes, even its scripture and its appeals to Martin Luther—does not guarantee that it is 'church'. Only Christ present in communal word and sacrament, that is, the *Gemeinde Christi*, constitutes the church. This is why Bonhoeffer says in this book that the church-of-the-people (*Volkskirche*) must always seek to become a community of people who freely confess their faith; this anticipates the Confessing Church and the Barmen Declaration of 1934. During the Church Struggle Bonhoeffer made the bold statement that those who deliberately cut themselves off from the Confessing Church cut themselves off from salvation.[41] No more than Karl Barth did Bonhoeffer believe in a sociological fundamentalism of the church as empirical institution.

If one danger, then, is to risk making the community of Christ a creature or function of the church institution, the opposite danger is to sever the *Gemeinde Christi* from the empirical, institutional church with all its faults. This Bonhoeffer refused to do. Numerous statements make this point. "In and through Christ the church [Kirche] is established in reality. It is not as if Christ could be abstracted from the church [Kirche]; rather, it is none other than Christ who 'is' the church."[42] "Community with God exists only through Christ, but Christ is present only in his *Gemeinde*, therefore *community with God exists only in the church [Kirche].*"[43] "The social significance of Christ is decisive—Christ who is present only in the church [Kirche], that is, where the Christian *Gemeinde* is united by preaching and the Lord's Supper in mutual Christian love."[44] *"The reality of the church [Kirche] is the reality of revelation, a reality that essentially must be either believed or denied. . . . There is no relation to Christ in which the relation to the church [Kirche] is not necessarily established as well.*"[45] "For the church [Kirche] is Christ existing as

---

[41.] See Bethge, *Dietrich Bonhoeffer,* 428ff. and *WF* 93f. (*DBW* 14:676).
[42.] See below, page 157.
[43.] See below, page 158.
[44.] See below, page 138.
[45.] See below, page 127.

church-community. However questionable its empirical form may be, it remains church [Kirche] in this very form, as long as Christ is present in his word."[46] Thus, Bonhoeffer is far from arguing that wherever people experience something they call 'community' they are in some way experiencing Christ. The Christian community is constituted by the communal presence of Christ in word and sacrament in the church.

Given *Gemeinde* and *Kirche* as the two theological terms for describing the *sanctorum communio*, how should they be translated? It is clear that Bonhoeffer does not regard *Gemeinde* as a theological term for a Christocentric community and *Kirche* as merely a sociological term for describing an empirical, religious institution. They need to be related as theological terms, as in the statements above. At the same time, Bonhoeffer does have two terms, and it is *Gemeinde* that is his christological term for defining *Kirche*. Further, if 'church' is the natural translation for *Kirche*, then *Gemeinde* shares with its sociological counterpart *Gemeinschaft* the idea of something common, shared, communal. This suggests that a term or phrase meaning a theologically defined community would be the appropriate solution. Whereas some translators of Bonhoeffer have used 'church' and others 'community' for *Gemeinde*, we have chosen 'church-community'. It is used as a theological term that emphasizes the communal character of the sanctorum communio and highlights the link to its sociological counterpart, *Gemeinschaft*. Simultaneously, it links by translation the words *Kirche* and *Gemeinde*, so that Bonhoeffer's intention to define and constitute the former by the latter is honored. The hyphen will repeatedly remind the reader of the theological points Bonhoeffer is making.

Other usages involving *Gemeinde* are handled as follows. We render Bonhoeffer's terms for the local Christian body, *christliche Lokalgemeinde* and *Einzelgemeinde*,[47] as "local Christian congregation" and "individual congregation," respectively. Sometimes Bonhoeffer uses *Gemeinde* alone when the context clearly indicates the local Christian body, for example, when gathered for worship; here, too, we say "congregation." It is important to remember that the communal sense of *Gemeinde* is always meant with the word "congregation"; this, not local autonomy, is the emphasis. At the other end of the spectrum, *Gesamt-*

[46.] See below, page 211.
[47.] See *SC (DBW 1)*:255.

gemeinde refers to the whole church, and is translated as "whole church-community" or "church-community as a whole."

Gemeinde is also used in several compounds and phrases, and these we indicate by hyphenating the translation. Thus *israelische Gottesgemeinde* becomes "Israel's community-of-God," the term for the disciples as Jesus' *Gemeinde der Liebe* becomes "community-of-love" (a variant of this is *Gemeinde Jesu* [community-of-Jesus]), and *Gemeinde der Heiligen* becomes "community-of-saints." Other compounds are *Ostergemeinde* (Easter-community); *Gemeinde des Kreuzes* (community-of-the-cross); *Urgemeinde* (earliest-Christian-community); *christliche Volksgemeinde* (Christian community-of-people); and *Gemeinde des Gottesreiches* (community-of-God's-Realm). Finally, *Kirchengemeinde* appears twice and points to the community of the local congregation or parish, and *kirchliche Gemeinde*—used once—refers to the community of the whole church.

Bonhoeffer translates the Latin *sanctorum communio* of his title with both *Gemeinschaft der Heiligen* and *Gemeinde der Heiligen*; the former is used nineteen times, the latter ten times. This is interesting since, while both terms overlap conceptually by alluding to something common or shared, in Bonhoeffer's usage *Gemeinschaft* (community) is a sociological term, *Gemeinde* (church-community) a theological term. Both phrases are translated here by "community of saints." The nuances of meaning in the German phrases are these: *Gemeinde der Heiligen* (church-community) refers to the group of Christian people. *Gemeinschaft*, like the English "community," can mean both a particular sort of group of people and also the quality of relationship among those people. Sometimes Bonhoeffer uses *Gemeinschaft der Heiligen* to convey both meanings; at other times his emphasis is either on the group of people, or on the quality of their relationship; this is apparent from the context. Consequently, when the emphasis is on the group of people the two terms are completely interchangeable. But in those few instances where *Gemeinschaft* unmistakably means the quality of relationship among people, the terms are not interchangeable. In such instances we considered translating *Gemeinschaft* with the traditional English word "communion." We decided against this, however, mainly because for many people this word has individualistic and sometimes mystical connotations that would distort Bonhoeffer's meaning. The context will normally indicate when the word "community" emphasizes a quality of relationship.

Volkskirche is another challenging term. It literally means "church-of-the-people" (compare *Volkswagen*), and that is what we finally decided was the most adequate translation for this book. This is not meant to convey populism but to say that in a *Volkskirche* the emphasis is on *inclusivity*, rather than nationality, ethnicity, or connection to government. In Germany, Protestant churches (whether Lutheran, Reformed, or Union) and Roman Catholic churches understand themselves as *Volkskirchen*. While the German *Freikirchen* (free churches) such as Baptists require a definite act of commitment (e.g., baptism as an adult), membership in the *Volkskirche* is virtually automatic by birth; children of parents whose names are on the roll of a *Volkskirche*, however tenuous their connection to the church, will also be baptized into membership of the *Volkskirche*. People are included unless they take a definite step to exclude themselves by having their names removed from the roll. (Hence one meaning of *Gemeinde* is both local congregation and 'parish' in the sense of local township or district.) There is no real counterpart to the *Volkskirche* in the English-speaking world. The phrase 'established church', used to describe the Church of England, is not a good description of the *Volkskirche*, notwithstanding the church tax collected by the German government, theological education within state-funded universities, and military chaplains funded by the government. For one thing, England has only one established church, Germany several *Volkskirchen*. Similarly, the "national church" of Ronald Gregor Smith's translation is misleading—not least because a reader might confuse it with the *Reichskirche* policy of the National Socialists who created the office of *Reichsbischof* and wanted to imbue the churches with the nationalistic spirit of Nazism. In *Sanctorum Communio* Bonhoeffer certainly does not use the word *Volkskirche* with the racial and nationalistic sense of the *völkisch* movement. On the contrary, the theology developed here becomes the ground for his later fight against it. In retrospect it is curious, however, that he does not address the *völkisch* ideology. If he provoked his dissertation adviser by writing about "church and proletariat," one might have expected some critique of its right-wing opposition in the *völkisch* ideology.[48]

[48.] The term *Volkskirche* derives from Schleiermacher's time when the word *Volk* referred to people in distinction from the ruling princes. But after World War I an anti-Semitic "*völkisch* movement" began with a few agitators, grew in power during the 1920s, and reached its political zenith under Hitler in the 1930s. Klaus Scholder (*The Churches*

While not a translation issue, the term "voluntarism" perhaps deserves comment. Derived from the Latin *voluntas* (will), it refers here not to volunteering but to the centrality of 'will' in Bonhoeffer's doctrine of God and theological anthropology. The 'will' of subjects is crucial to his presentation of the Christian-ethical concept of 'person' at the heart of his theology of sociality. 'Will' and 'self-consciousness' are the two terms of his 'general-metaphysical' concept of spirit (*Geist*). Further, 'will' is a key factor in his typology of social communities. Additional insight into the importance of voluntarism for Bonhoeffer's theology can be gained from his remarks on "dynamic voluntaristic" thinking in relation to Dilthey in *Act and Being*[49] and to Luther in the Union Seminary seminar paper "The Theology of Crisis and Its Attitude toward Philosophy and Science."[50]

Bibliography

The bibliography in this English edition differs from the German in several respects. The first section of the bibliography includes, in addition to books with which Bonhoeffer worked directly, other works that he cited, but may not have consulted personally, relying instead on references in secondary literature which he was reading. These are mentioned in his text and footnotes, but were not included in the bibliography compiled by the German editor. The "Literature Consulted by the Editors" was newly created for this edition and includes all works cited by the German editor in editorial notes, as well as those cited by the English editor. The section "Other Literature Related to *Sanctorum Communio*" has been updated to include publications since the German edition appeared in 1986.

Acknowledgments

The editor acknowledges with pleasure and gratitude the collegial assistance of many people in the demanding work of producing this

---

and the Third Reich, 1:74ff.) argues that this movement was the indispensable foundation for National Socialism. But *Volkskirche* did not have these associations for Bonhoeffer in *Sanctorum Communio*, nor does it have them in Germany today.

[49.] *AB (DBWE 2)*:55, footnote 26, and 127f.
[50.] *DBW* 10:440ff., written in English.

volume. Chief among these are the translators, Reinhard Krauss and Nancy Lukens, who brought linguistic expertise, theological insight, and friendly cooperation to their challenging work. Hans Pfeifer, a member of the German Editorial Board, read the whole text in manuscript and made valuable suggestions on points of translation and information. The complex bibliographical work would not have been possible without the indispensable assistance of Carolyn Sperl of Hartford Seminary Library, who provided expert and indefatigable help with interlibrary loans, as did Tina Maresco at the Dickinson College library. Stephen Crites and Peter Hodgson assisted by identifying Hegel editions and quotations, Daniel Breazeale did the same for Fichte, and Timothy Wengert helped locate translations of several Luther citations. Anthony Macro and Mary Cornog assisted with translations of Greek and Latin texts, and Judith Fentress-Williams with Hebrew. Charles Marsh read draft translations of philosophical material in the first three chapters, and Mark Brocker provided research assistance at an early stage of the work. Teri Vaughn and Colleen Kruger assisted with word processing, and Florence Leduc assisted with the indexes. Jackie Ammermann was always ready to solve computer problems. Hartford Seminary supported this work with sabbatical leave. Finally, Wayne Floyd did substantial work on the bibliography as well as numerous editorial notes, and as the General Editor of the Dietrich Bonhoeffer Works brought an eagle eye, a persistent commitment to clarity of translation and expression, a keen sense of style, and unflagging collegial friendship to his editorial work on this volume.

PREFACE

IN THIS STUDY[1] social philosophy and sociology are employed in the service of theology. Only through such an approach, it appears, can we gain a systematic understanding of the community-structure of the Christian church. This work belongs not to the discipline of sociology of religion, but to theology. The issue of a Christian social philosophy and sociology is a genuinely theological one, because it can be answered only on the basis of an understanding of the church. The more this investigation has considered the significance of the sociological category for theology, the more clearly has emerged the social intention of all the basic Christian concepts. 'Person', 'primal state', 'sin', and 'revelation' can be fully comprehended only in reference to sociality [Sozialität].[2] If genuinely theological concepts can only be recognized as established and fulfilled in a special social context, then it becomes evident that a sociological study of the church has a specifically theological character.

This work, which was written more than three years ago, could not be fully revised before publication. Only partial modifications were feasible. This is a defect in light of the course the continuing debate has taken. My justification for publishing the book in its present form is the

---

[1.] The original title of the dissertation was *Sanctorum Communio, eine dogmatische Untersuchung* (The communion of saints, a theological study). This preface was written for the published version; for the original dissertation preface, see editorial note 5 below.

[2.] The English term "sociality" derives from Latin and French and dates back to the seventeenth century. In Bonhoeffer's usage it is a complex category comprising several specific views of person, community, and social relations. Its full meaning will become clear as he develops his argument below. [CG]

basic approach I adopted in order to deal with this problem, which I continue to believe is demanded and validated by the subject matter.

I would like to express my special thanks to Privy Councillor Reinhold Seeberg,[3] who has followed this project with kindest interest from the outset. My thanks also go to the Minister of Research, Arts, and Education for assistance with printing costs. The Emergency Association for German Research,[4] as well as a grant from the Reinhold

---

[3.] "Privy Councillor" (*Geheimrat*) was an honorific title given to distinguished people, including professors like Reinhold Seeberg and Karl Bonhoeffer. The title did not confer a legal role, but such people often assumed public tasks such as chairing a special commission. [CG]

[4.] The Notgemeinschaft für Deutsche Wissenschaft was a private organization founded after World War I to help scholars deal with problems like publication costs in a time of severe inflation. [CG]

[5.] The original version of the preface, found after the table of contents in the dissertation (*SC-A*), reads as follows:

The goal of the following ecclesiological study is a dogmatic-theological reflection on the concept of the church in light of insights from social philosophy and sociology. Creating a real conceptual connection between theology and both social philosophy and sociology is the basic task and also the difficulty of this essay, whose concrete subject matter is the idea of the church as sanctorum communio. The dogmatic character of the work prevails; both disciplines of social science are to be made fruitful for theology.

Thus the basic problem can be defined as the problem of a specifically Christian social philosophy and sociology. My intention is to discuss neither a general sociology of religion, nor genetic-sociological questions; rather, I intend to show that an inherently Christian social philosophy and sociology, arising essentially out of fundamental concepts of Christian theology, is most fully articulated in the concept of the church.

The more I have focused on this problem, the more clearly I have recognized the social intention of all the fundamental Christian concepts. 'Person', 'primal state', 'sin', and 'revelation' appeared fully understandable only in relation to sociality. Only by concentrating on this characteristically Christian set of theological problems could the specifically theological character of the study be maintained. The phenomenon of the Christian church presented itself as a unity comprised of several layers of issues. The systematic goal of the work is to separate out these different layers and to rebuild them into a coherent concept, presupposing the reality of their interrelationship in the concept of the church. If, in order to reach this goal, the study at first appears unnecessarily broad, that stems from the subject itself; and it is precisely this breadth that focuses all issues ultimately on the problem of a Christian sociology, the question of the church. While the first chapter is devoted to the general definition of social philosophy and sociology as a foundation for the whole work, the second offers an epistemological introduction to the whole area of Christian social philosophy in light of the Christian concepts of person and social basic-relations. Only when one comprehends the Christian basic-relation of I and You can one understand the idea of the church as the revelation of loving hearts. The third and fourth chapters deal with sets of problems apart from which the sociological concept of the church simply cannot be understood. The essence and structure of the new humanity 'in Christ' can only be understood in contrast to humanity 'in Adam'; one must know of the general and specific social relations

201

Seeberg Foundation, made publication finally possible. For this, too, I wish to express my thanks on this occasion.[5]

July 1930

---

of humanity in order to understand the empirical phenomenon of the church sociologically in its dual character as sanctorum communio and 'religious community'. [The contrast of two modes of human being, 'being-in-Adam' and 'being-in-Christ', is developed later. The translation here follows Bonhoeffer's usage in chap. 4, footnote 1, and chap. 5—see below pages 109 and 140; also see *Act and Being*.][CG]

To be sure, there rarely has been as much talk about community and church as in the last few years. Yet it seems to me that such thinking has lacked the thoroughness of theological reflection. It is certain, however, that one can only grasp the real seriousness and difficulty of these issues through theological reflection. Furthermore, theology is not inclined to kill something living; to the contrary, it can and should bring about the most vital changes in church life. Since many disciplines are currently focusing on sociological issues, this study will provide the opportunity to think about the fruitfulness of the result of this sociological research for our discipline of theology—and also to demonstrate its limits. Thus this study clearly is meant to address contemporary issues and to contribute to the debate about them.

Finally let me say that in view of the utterly oppressive number of perspectives that could be examined this study must remain fragmentary. Nevertheless, it intends to offer a coherent treatment of the issues that it does address.

The historical research necessary to any theological study—some already available in detail—could not be laid out in its entirety here. In any case, everything important can be found in the great works of the history of doctrine and in smaller monographs listed below. Only occasionally, in particular cases of critical argument and of positive interpretation, will I refer to the history of theology and philosophy.

I hope this study will be seen as a modest contribution to a "philosophy of the church" as was recently called for by Reinhold Seeberg in his *Christliche Dogmatik* [cf. Seeberg, *Dogmatik*, 2:385], namely one which not only clarifies the nature of the church and of religious community, but which "would result in new understanding of the cohesion of the spirit of humanity, new ideas about the nature of objective spirit [objektiver Geist] and the manner in which absolute spirit is revealed in the spirit of humanity." [Bonhoeffer's dissertation manuscript contains the following handwritten sentence, which he presumably formulated for the published version but then did not include: "My [deleted: "most solemn"] wish in presenting this study is to contribute something to the understanding that our church, profoundly impoverished and helpless though it appears today, is nevertheless the *sanctorum communio*, the holy body of Christ, even Christ's very presence in the world [deleted: "that in the depths of its poverty it is rich"].

CHAPTER ONE

ON THE DEFINITION OF SOCIAL PHILOSOPHY AND SOCIOLOGY

15   SOCIAL PHILOSOPHY and sociology,[1] two disciplines[2] with different subject matters, should be strictly distinguished.[1] Otherwise the result is a

---

1. This strict differentiation was ignored by many studies, including the so-called relation-theory of von Wiese and Vierkandt. This theory is unconsciously based on an atomistic social philosophy that it wants to overcome. Persons are fixed, isolated objects that are not drawn into the social process; their particular social 'dispositions' enable and create relationships to other persons. Cf. Litt, *Individuum und Gemeinschaft*, 3d ed., 1926, 205ff., 221ff.; Vierkandt, *Gesellschaftslehre*, 51, 48; von Wiese, *Soziologie*, vol. 1, *Beziehungslehre*, 1924, 6ff.[3]

202   [1.] In the dissertation Bonhoeffer's first footnote reference number in the text follows the word "Sociology" in the chapter title; the note reads as follows: <<The term is from A[uguste] Comte, *Cours de Philosophie*, 4:185, replacing the previously used term 'social physics'.>> Cf. *The Essential Comte*, 158f. The opening paragraph is new in the published book (*SC-B*, 1930), and replaces the following opening pages in *SC-A* and their notes [CG]:

Were it the purpose of this introductory chapter to present and critique the entire spectrum of solutions to the problem at hand, it would grow into a monograph. Since the subject of this study involves sociological content rather than sociological methodology, it is not relevant to lay out the entire methodological problem. Such discussions can be found in almost all longer sociological works. <<The best historical survey of the history of sociology is by Paul Barth, *Soziologie als Philosophie der Geschichte*, 1896.>> Therefore I will only outline the problem briefly and indicate the position I have taken.

The problem was apparent at the time universities were applying to the Ministry of Education for professorships of sociology. Memoranda were requested on the aims and subject matter of the discipline, and the accounts were so diverse that it was utterly impossible to gain a coherent picture. [On this controversy about the creation of professorships in sociology, see Becker, *Gedanken zur Hochschulreform* (Leipzig, 1919); von Below, "Soziologie als Lehrfach" (1919): 271ff.; Tönnies, "Soziologie und Hochschulreform"(1920/21): 212ff.; von Wiese, "Die Soziologie als Einzelwissenschaft" (1920): 347ff.] Another symptom of the problem is that almost every new work in the enormous

hopeless confusion of concepts, though sometimes, of course, individual results may be largely correct. Sociology relates to social philosophy

[1. *cont.*] and ever-growing body of sociological scholarship strives to modify or to reformulate the goals of sociology. Indeed, in surveying the fundamental principles of the great 'classical' works of sociology, one is horrified at the confusion that still reigns in the most basic concepts. The historical and psychological reason for this, I think, is that the primary interest of most sociologists is in political, economic, and possibly historical questions; consequently, sociology is defined specifically in relation to these disciplines. However, this leads to a loss of clarity about the proper subject matter of sociology, a subject matter that is not, I think, difficult to define. Work in economic policy, history of religion, and philosophy of history all was called sociology. A word was found for an idea that was still quite unclear conceptually. But when the question was raised as to what sociology really is, ten different subjects from every discipline were mentioned, instead of finding a single one that could define its proper nature. <<Furthermore, people are not even capable of using the terms 'sociological' and 'social' correctly. 'Sociological' is to 'social' as 'psychological' is to 'psychic'. There are social and psychic phenomena, and there are sociological and psychological methods of observing them. This relationship, clear enough in itself, nevertheless is almost never considered in using the terms. [Bonhoeffer follows Vierkandt, *Gesellschaftslehre*, 10.][CG]>> Those who are quite familiar with this state of affairs will initially consider it impossible to discern any coherent pattern in this confusion. Nevertheless it is possible upon closer examination to differentiate several clearly emerging types among the major sociological works.

    In a well-known essay, Troeltsch made such a distinction between two groups. <<Troeltsch, "Zum Begriff und zur Methode der Soziologie," *Weltwirtschaftliches Archiv*, 8:259ff.; also in his *Ges. Schriften*[, vol.] 4 (Tübingen, 1925), 705ff.>> One of them is encyclopedic and uses a 'philosophy of history' approach. The other is 'analytical-formal'. The second is more recent and in general prevails as the academic sociology of the universities today. <<The expression 'formal' sociology is taken from Simmel's major work, *Soziologie: Untersuchungen über die Formen der Vergesellschaftung*, 1908.>> It is concerned with "relations [Beziehungen] and circumstances [Verhältnisse] within the group and its products." <<Vierkandt, *Gesellschaftslehre*, sec. 3, 13.>> Its subject is 'society' not as an entity made up of elements, i.e., individual persons, but rather "insofar as it is the bearer of inwardly established interactions [Wechselwirkungen] between its individual members." <<Vierkandt, ibid., 28. Compare, for example, Gustaf Steffen, *Die Grundlagen der Soziologie: Ein Programm zur Methode der Gesellschaftswissenschaft und Naturforschung*, 1912, 12: "Since the subject of sociology is nothing other than the mutual or unilateral influences between human consciousnesses, there is no choice but to classify sociology as belonging to the psychological type of discipline.">> Thus the basic category of sociological thought must be relation [Beziehung]. <<Vierkandt, *Gesellschaftslehre*, sec. 7, 47.>> More specifically, one examines both social forces and kinds of relations. <<Ibid., 14.>> Since Simmel, 'social forces' are taken to mean such socially constitutive concepts as love, subordination, secrecy, conflict, etc. 'Kinds of relations' denotes, for example, Tönnies's classic distinction between community [Gemeinschaft] and society [Gesellschaft]. <<Tönnies, *Community and Society*; [Tönnies,] *Soziologische Studien und Kritiken*, 2 vols., 1924.>> On this basis there arises the question of the products created by social formation, culture, economic life, 'materialization of objective spirit [objektiver Geist]' (see below).

    So far we have only considered the problem of the subject matter of sociology. Its significance, however, lies equally in its fundamentally new method—comparable to induction in

by building on its theoretical constructs, though naturally often unintentionally; furthermore, social philosophy provides the continuing

[1. cont.] its time—for research in historical, psychological, and political problems, which it believes to be solved only through knowledge of reciprocal relations [Wechselbeziehungen] between human beings. This method is applied to issues like language, religion, and the state. Thus it undermines the theory that all these goods were invented by individuals. Of course, sociology as a method always presupposes a particular subject matter, as a vantage point from which a given linguistic expression is to be understood. Basically, all this means is that considering societal forms is important for understanding a great number of historical problems; that is to say, sociology contributes to other disciplines as well. For this Simmel coined the term 'sociological method'. <<Cf. the above-mentioned work [Simmel, *Soziologie*]. See further his book, *The Philosophy of Money*, and the short summary in "Fundamental Problems in Sociology," 12: "The insight that human beings are determined in their whole nature and all their expressions by living in interaction with other people must lead to a new way of seeing things in all the so-called humanities [Geisteswissenschaften]." The following is very significant in its unconscious proximity to Hegel's thought: "The consciousness of social productivity, which replaces a purely individual or a transcendent view of productivity, has introduced a genetic method into all the humanistic disciplines [. . .]" (13).>> The major representatives of this analytical-formal school are Tönnies, Simmel, Vierkandt, and von Wiese in Germany <<von Wiese, *Soziologie*, vol. I, "Beziehungslehre," 1924>>, people in France like Durkheim <<Durkheim, *The Elementary Forms of the Religious Life* and *The Rules of Sociological Method*>> with his great work on totemism as a social phenomenon and Tarde <<Gabriel Tarde, *The Laws of Imitation*>> with his discovery and description of the imitative instinct in its significance for sociology, and in England McDougall. <<McDougall, *Social Psychology* 13th ed. London.>>

Comte and Spencer <<A[uguste] Comte, *Soziologie* (selections translated into German by Dorn, 1923). Cf. Tönnies, "Comte's Begriff der Soziologie," *[Soziologische] Studien und Kritiken* 2:116f.; Herbert Spencer, *The Principles of Sociology*, 3 vols., 1876–96, and *The Study of Sociology*. Cf. Tönnies, [*Soziologische Studien und Kritiken*,] 1:75ff., "Spencer's soziologisches Werk.">> are acknowledged as the fathers of the historical-philosophical school of sociology. Among their successors Schäffle, Spann, Oppenheimer, and Müller-Lyer should be mentioned. <<Schäffle, *Bau und Leben des sozialen Körpers*, 4 vols., 1875ff., and *Abriß der Soziologie*, 1906; Othmar Spann, *Gesellschaftslehre*, 1919. 'Pure universalism': he renounces the empirical-natural science doctrine of relation-theory. The subject matter remains social formation; Oppenheimer, *System der Soziologie*, vol. I; Müller-Lyer, *The History of Social Development*, 1935.>> This school aims to describe the whole historical development of the corporate life of humanity and to explain it from the perspective of a philosophy of history. In this context sociology becomes a collective term for all the humanities and thus unwittingly renders itself superfluous as an independent discipline. By attempting too much, it fails to focus on one subject matter. Thus Oppenheimer, for example, calls sociology *the* universal discipline. <<Oppenheimer, *Soziologie*, 135.>> (Troeltsch's essay, cited above, is the best source of information on this discussion.)

In contrast to this diffusion of subject matter, formal sociology identifies its subject as the 'forms' of social formation. <<I am using this concept, which Simmel leaves rather unclear, in the sense of Vierkandt and others.>> But if we approve in principle such a limitation of the subject matter of sociology to social formation, then the content must be redefined. Thus we cannot consider the problem of subject matter solved by formal sociology either. I agree with this school to the extent that it intends to deal solely with the problem

norm of sociology. Both disciplines belong to the humanities, not to the natural sciences. As independent disciplines, both social philosophy and sociology must have their distinctive subject matters.[2]

---

2. Uncertainty in answering the question about the subject matter of sociology is the reason for the prevailing lack of conceptual clarity. On the one hand,

---

[1. *cont.*] of social formation, but I disagree insofar as formal sociology posits only relations [Beziehungen] and interactions [Wechselwirkungen] as its content. I also disagree about the method it usually employs. My first disagreement consists in the fact that formal sociology builds—unexpectedly at first glance—upon the foundations of a social philosophy that I do not share, namely, those of the atomist theory of society. This is most clearly the case with von Wiese and Vierkandt, the pure representatives of relation-theory.

As might be expected, it is the concept of the person that I must dispute here. Two apparently distinct sets of ideas are involved. Assuming that social context can affect a person's behavior (for example, contrast an officer on duty and at home, a scholar in professional service and in politics, or a child faced with a stronger or a weaker child), one's first impulse is to conclude disunity in the person and to place decisive emphasis on investigating the power of circumstances: people are products of their social circumstances, to which, of course, they do contribute their small part. <<From this it follows, for example, that in order to get to know someone fully, one must have known that person in all possible situations (Vierkandt, [*Gesellschaftslehre*,] sec. 7, 51), and even then one must always be prepared to discover completely new aspects in new situations. Obviously, this is a horrendous error; while the observation of the power of circumstances might be quite correct empirically, a crucial aspect has been overlooked. A connoisseur of human beings gets to know a person in a single situation, not knowing from experience how the other person behaves in different situations, but solely by looking at that moment into the personal center from which all possible behavior springs. The whole person is in each act. Knowledge of the person is based not upon the wealth of possible ways of behaving, but upon intuitive insight into the personal center.>> The second idea runs parallel to this one. <<For the following cf. especially Litt, *Individuum und Gemeinschaft*, 3d ed., 1926, 205ff., 221ff.>> Human beings, understood as static, isolated systems, are distinguished from the "forces which, relatively independent of persons, move back and forth between them." <<Vierkandt, [ibid.,] 48.>> At first glance, this appears to be a gross contradiction, and yet we are dealing with a single viewpoint. Basically, in its whole approach this school views persons as fixed objects whose particular social 'dispositions' enable and create relations with other persons. Human beings as persons are of no interest at all; in reality only interpersonal forces are sociologically important. While these forces are capable of transforming the social sphere of the person as described above, nevertheless the personal center remains unaffected. If one then assumes such an isolated personal center, then the *whole approach is based on the atomistic-individualistic theory of society*, regardless of how passionately one is convinced of mutual influences within the social sphere. Vierkandt is much more cautious in all this than, for example, von Wiese. <<von Wiese, [ibid.,] 6ff. Cf. Vierkandt's discussion of the disunity of the person, 50ff.>> But the fundamental perspective is the same with both: many isolated ego-centers are introduced that can enter into external connection with one another if a stimulus causes them to do so.

It would be quite incorrect, however, to identify this social-philosophical individualism of social theory with the sociologically atomistic-individualistic theories of, say, the Enlighten-

16   Social philosophy deals with fundamental social relationships that
are *presupposed by* all knowledge of, and will for, empirical community. It
deals with the 'origins' of sociality in the human spirit and the intrinsic

_____

the encyclopedic-universalist group of sociologists (cf. Troeltsch, "Zum Begriff
und zur Methode der Soziologie," *Weltwirtschaftl. Archiv*, vol. 8, 259ff., and *Ges.*

[1. *cont.*] ment. The fundamental significance of human social formation for the whole life of
the human spirit [Geistesleben] has certainly been recognized throughout formal sociology,
and this knowledge has been put to use in all its positive results. But formal sociology has
not yet achieved a philosophical-metaphysical integration of the social phenomenon. *Thus it
is not the sociology that is atomistic, but the social philosophy on which it is based.* This state of
affairs has not been articulated with equal clarity by all formal sociologists. But it can be discerned wherever the fundamentals are discussed at all. <<I do not consider it appropriate
to distinguish in principle Simmel's formal sociology from von Wiese's and Vierkandt's relation-theory, as was recently done (Schumann, "Zur Grundfrage der Religionssoziologie,"
Ztschrft [für] Systematische Theologie 4 [1926–27], 662ff., note). Certainly Simmel's concept
of form is extremely vague. However, the two sociologists in question seem to me to have
interpreted him correctly, and they have reason to emphasize that they built upon Simmel's
work (Vierkandt, [ibid.,] 1). Furthermore, it seems unjustified to make the connection
between Tönnies and Oppenheimer. While they share an interest in philosophy of culture,
the interesting thing about Tönnies is that he combines this with the formal-analytic sociological method, whereas Oppenheimer proceeds in the encyclopedic-universalist fashion.
Tönnies truly deserves a special place within formal sociology. In any case, he holds his own
there.>>

207   With a deepening of insights from social philosophy the understanding of the subject matter of sociology will take a different form. But relation-theory's concept of subject matter
brings with it a *method* that I must likewise reject: the *empirical method of the natural sciences*
that seeks to enumerate and order all possible reciprocal influences [Wechselwirkungen].
The most typical example of this is von Wiese's relation-theory. This has not really produced
any sociological work but at most assembles material for such work. It has been shown that
the definition of the subject matter of sociology depends on the most profound insights of
social philosophy into the nature of person and community. Likewise, it is clear that our definition of the subject matter of social philosophy and sociology, and its method, can only be
tested during concrete discussion of the problems in this study.

The understanding of social philosophy and sociology with which we are working should
nevertheless be introduced at this point. *Both disciplines belong to the humanities, not to the
natural sciences.* Social philosophy is to sociology as number theory is to arithmetic; i.e., the
latter builds upon the results of the former, of course often unwittingly, and the former is
the enduring norm of the latter.

[2.] Bonhoeffer's differentiation of sociological theories follows approaches taken in
the introduction to Vierkandt, *Gesellschaftslehre*, 1ff., and Schumann, "Religionssoziologie." The definition of social philosophy, which arises out of the critique of relation-
theory, follows that of Litt, *Individuum und Gemeinschaft*, 226ff.; see also 8, note 1.
Regarding the sociology of the 1920s, cf. Vierkandt, *Gesellschaftslehre*, 1ff. Also see Geiger
and Stoltenberg, "Soziologie"; *Die Verhandlungen des Deutschen Soziologentages*, 1910ff.;
and the *Kölner Vierteljahreshefte für Sozialwissenschaften*, founded by von Wiese, 1921ff.

connection of sociality and spirit. Social philosophy is[6] the study of the primordial mode-of-being of sociality per se. It is a normative discipline

---

Schriften 4:705ff.; Vierkandt, *Gesellschaftslehre*, 11ff.; on the historical perspective, P[aul] Barth, *Soziologie als Philosophie der Geschichte*, 2d ed., 1920),[4] makes sociology into a term comprising all the humanities; indeed, this group wants to make it into the ultimate universal discipline, thereby unwittingly rendering sociology superfluous as an independent discipline (see, among others, Oppenheimer, *System der Soziologie*, 135). On the other hand, the formal sociologists want to investigate the forms of concrete socialization. This seems to identify an autonomous subject matter. If, however, empirical methods are used (few have gone beyond them and begun to lay the foundations of a real discipline of sociology), then the subject is not recognized in its complete autonomy, but is subsumed under historical research. Cf. Schumann, *Ztschr. f. syst. Theol.* vol. 4 (1926–27), who defines the problem very precisely; overall, there are almost as many definitions of the subject matter of sociology as there are works of sociology.[5]

[2. *cont.*] Regarding the history of sociology, see Paul Barth, *Philosophie der Geschichte*, 146ff., and Sombart, "Die Anfänge der Soziologie."

[3.] Footnote 1 (see above, page 24) is not found in *SC-A*. The concept of 'relation-theory' [*Beziehungslehre*] derives primarily from von Wiese and his major work of the same title, *Allgemeine Soziologie*, vol. 1, *Beziehungslehre*; cf. *Systematic Sociology*, 29–32. Relation-theory became the established term among those sociologists who see the task of sociology as systematizing the multiplicity of social relations and forms. See Vierkandt, *Gesellschaftslehre*, 47ff. The objection that relation-theory presupposed a social philosophy of atomism was raised above all by Litt in his *Individuum und Gemeinschaft*, 226ff. and 230f.; cf. also Schumann, "Religionssoziologie," 697 and 698, note 1.

[4.] The correct title is *Die Philosophie der Geschichte als Soziologie*. [CG]

[5.] Footnote 2 (see above, pages 27ff.) is not found in *SC-A*. 'Encyclopedic' is the term used to describe the sociological approach that attempts to base itself on the philosophy of history. The chief representatives of this school are Paul Barth (1858–1922) and Oppenheimer (1878–1943). 'Universalist' describes the sociological school that understands individuals as intrinsically members of the social whole rather than coming together by social contract. Its chief representative is Spann (1878–1950). 'Formal sociologists' refers to the representatives of the school of so-called formal sociology, whose subject matter is not particular aspects of society [e.g., religion, economics, politics, etc.][CG] but the structural principles of social forms. By thus describing itself, formal sociology wishes to be seen as an autonomous discipline that distinguishes itself from other disciplines by its own inquiry, subject matter, and method. The chief representatives are Simmel (1858–1918) and Tönnies (1855–1935). The agenda of formal sociology was deliberately expanded by Vierkandt (1867–1953) and von Wiese (1867–1969), both of whom understood formal sociology as the study of relation. In the 1920s formal sociology was the predominant school of German sociology.

[6.] Deleted in *SC-A*: thus not a theory of social values, as it has been called—at least, not primarily of social values—but rather.

insofar as its theoretical constructs are the necessary guidelines for the accurate interpretation of empirical sociological data. Sociology is the study of the structures of empirical communities. Its real subject matter is the constitutive structural principles of empirical social formations, not the laws by which they come into being. Hence sociology is not a historical discipline, but a systematic one. In principle, it is possible to do sociology without a foundation in social philosophy, as long as one remains conscious of this limitation.[7] What is meant by the structure of community can only become fully clear in the course of this investigation. Suffice to say here that there is more to this structure than relations or interactions, though of course these are bearers of its social liveliness. The concern of sociology is to trace the many complex interactions back to certain constitutive acts of spirit that comprise the distinctive characteristic of the structure. However, the personal centers of agency belong as much to the structure of community as does the unity of the group itself as a 'configuration' ['Gebilde']. All three of these determinants are necessary to comprehend fully the general structure of empirical social formation.[8]

There are methodological consequences of this view of the matter. The sociological perspective is not morphological and descriptive (as in Durkheim),[9] but humanistic [geisteswissenschaftlich]; it focuses on the essential structure of the phenomenon of the group as spirit. The method of phenomenological study[10] derives from the systematic nature of sociology. In the study of empirical behavior this method seeks to comprehend those essential acts that are sociologically constitutive.[3] [12] Only the phenomenological method can overcome the

17   genetic approach, which considers sociology a subcategory of history.

---

3. This method has been employed, at first unwittingly, as long as formal sociology has existed (Simmel, *Soziologie: Untersuchungen über die Formen der*

[7.] A paragraph break follows in *SC-A*.

[8.] [The two preceding sentences are underlined in *SC-A*.] [CG] The next sentence in *SC-A* was deleted: This makes clear that relation-theory is inadequate and, if this is not recognized, that it is false. [By "three determinants" Bonhoeffer means fundamental or 'original' social relationships, the structures of empirical communities, and the personal units who are centers of agency.][CG]

[9.] Footnote deleted in *SC-A*: <<Durkheim, *The Rules of Sociological Method*, 111.>>

[10.] Vierkandt understands his method explicitly as a phenomenological one. Cf. Vierkandt, *Gesellschaftslehre*, 15. The phenomenological method within formal sociology

To undertake sociology of religion, then, is to research phenomenologically the structural distinctiveness of religious communities.[4] In

---

Vergesellschaftung, 1908; Tönnies, *Community and Society,* first German publication 1886; [Tönnies], *Soziologische Studien und Kritiken,* 2 vols., 1924). Later, as
in Vierkandt, it was employed deliberately and explicitly. Of course, it is precisely in his work that one still sees the struggle between the genetic and the
phenomenological methods, which results in considerable unclarity. It was precisely this contradiction in his concept of sociology as relation-theory that
required the empirical method. See also Scheler, *Formalism in Ethics and Non-
Formal Ethics of Values,* 490ff., where this error can still be observed. Cf. on this
subject the publications of the phenomenological school: Edith Stein, "Individuum und Gemeinschaft," *Jahrb. f. Philos. und phänomenologische Forschung* 5
(1922), 116ff.; Gerda Walther, "Zur Ontologie der sozialen Gemeinschaften,"
[*Jahrbuch*] 6 (1923); Samuel Krakauer,[11] *Soziologie als Wissenschaft,* 1924. Cf.
also Theodor Litt, *Individuum und Gemeinschaft,* 1926.
  4. It is hard to understand how Max Weber could speak of sociology of religion where he describes the interrelationships of politics, economics, and religion—several different aspects of culture—and in the process produces historical
work.[13] (Cf. *[Gesammelte] Aufsätze zur Religionssoziologie,* 3 vols.; also the ostensi-
bly systematic essay, "Religious Groups (The Sociology of Religion)," in *Economy
and Society,* 399–634, is really only interested in historical issues. Compare the
following definition of sociology: "Sociology [. . .] is a science concerning itself
with the interpretive understanding of social action and thereby with a causal (!)
explanation of its course and consequences."[14] This explains the breadth of

---

[10. *cont.*] was further developed in the works known to Bonhoeffer that follow in the tradition of Husserl. Litt defines the phenomenological method as follows: "It is oriented
toward those phenomena of psychic reality . . . that by their nature reveal a pattern *in the
individual experience itself* that prepares the way for the analysis" (Theodor Litt, *Individuum,* 5; cf. 1ff. and 230ff.).
  [11.] The correct name is Siegfried Kracauer. [CG]
  [12.] In *SC-A,* after the superscript for footnote 3, there follows: This phenomenological
method has been employed as long as formal sociology has existed, at first unwittingly (Simmel,
Tönnies), and later deliberately and explicitly (Vierkandt, Scheler). Cf. footnote 3.
  [13.] Regarding Bonhoeffer's critique of Weber, see Vierkandt, *Gesellschaftslehre,* 9ff.,
who contends that Weber's work was not sociology of religion but history. Cf. also the
judgment about Weber by Schumann, "Religionssoziologie," 668: "Insofar as he was a historian, he was a sociologist." Regarding the definition of an independent task of sociology
of religion, cf. ibid., 700ff.
  [14.] [When quoting from Weber, *Economy and Society,* 1:4, Bonhoeffer omits after
"sociology" Weber's phrase "in the sense in which this highly ambiguous word is used
here." The parenthetical exclamation point after "causal" comes from Bonhoeffer.][CG]
These deleted sentences, quoting Weber, follow in *SC-A:* 'Action' refers to human behavior
insofar as the acting individual attaches a subjective meaning to the behavior—be it overt or
inward activity, omission or acquiescence. Action is 'social' insofar as its subjective meaning takes

18 order to avoid misunderstandings, it should be noted that this study of the sanctorum communio does not properly belong to the sociology of religion, but to theology.[18] It will be carried out on the foundation of Christian theology and will make fruitful for theology the fundamental insights that derive purely from social philosophy and sociology, as well

---

Weber's treatment of the subject. Cf. also "Basic Sociological Terms" in *Economy and Society*, 1:3–62.[15] Earlier sociology of religion had of course almost never done anything but history of religion, either from a broad historical perspective or by means of a more specific political and economic approach. (Cf., for example, Spencer, *Principles of Sociology*, 3:3–175; Schäffle, *Bau und Leben des sozialen Körpers*, 1875, 4:144ff., and more systematically in 1:689ff.; Othmar Spann, *Gesellschaftslehre*, 1919, 323–49. Here, too, an interest in the history of religion predominates.) The only exception to this trend is perhaps Durkheim in his study of totemism as the original form of human society (*The Elementary Forms of the Religious Life*). But here, too, the interest is more in ethnology and history of religion than in systematic issues. To my knowledge, Simmel in his book *Sociology of Religion* was the first to attempt a systematic approach to the sociology of religion. There he really discusses structural questions of religious social formation.[16] Troeltsch in his *Social Teachings of the Christian Churches* developed the history of Christian ideas of community with an independent type of systematic sociology. Of course, he focuses on the historically contingent social forms, not the essential social structure of Christian community. Finally, Max Scheler (*Formalism in Ethics*, see above) produced the outline of a systematic sociology combined with a strong interest in the problem of a Christian sociology—a great project with which we have yet to come to terms. If we recall the above-mentioned sophisticated essay by Schumann, who is essentially concerned to offer a systematic understanding of sociology, we see that the light is gradually dawning regarding the inadequacy of the old concept of the sociology of religion.[17]

[14. *cont.*] account of the behavior of others and is thereby oriented in its course. [Cf. Weber, *Economy and Society*, 1:4.] Such a general concept of social behavior denies sociology its essential subject matter.

[15.] This deleted sentence follows in *SC-A*: Pp. 253ff.; 265: 'Social action is human action whose subjective meaning is related to the behavior of other people.'

[16.] Deleted from *SC-A*: of course in Simmel's typically disordered breadth and generality <<Simmel, *Sociology of Religion*>>.

[17.] Deleted from *SC-A*: This simple definition has not been considered in any positive description of the sociology of religion. The text continues with the current footnote 4, originally located in the body of the dissertation.

[18.] Bonhoeffer wrote in *SC-A* ist nicht rein religionssoziologisch, sondern, wie schon oben gesagt, theologisch ("is not purely sociology of religion but, as already indicated, theological"). [CG]

as the sociology of religion. Hence our purpose is to understand the structure of the given reality of a church of Christ, as revealed in Christ, from the perspective of social philosophy and sociology. But the nature of the church can only be understood from within, *cum* ira et studio [*with* passionate zeal],[19] never by nonparticipants. Only those who take the claim of the church seriously—not relativizing it in relation to other similar claims or their own rationality, but viewing it from the standpoint of the gospel—can possibly glimpse something of its true nature.[20] Our subject will thus be approached from two, or even three, directions: theology, social philosophy, and sociology.

After showing in the next chapter that the Christian concept of the person is really exhibited only in sociality, a section on social philosophy will likewise show that human spirit[21] generally is possible and real only in sociality.[22] Only then should we consider the structures[23] of empirical communities in a purely sociological section; for only then can we give a fundamental refutation of individualistic social atomism. In turn, it is only the new insight into the nature of community that enables us to approach a conceptual understanding of Christian community, the sanctorum communio.

[19.] Variation on a saying of Tacitus, *Annals*, 1,1: "sine ira et studio" ("without passion and bias").

[20.] Deleted in *SC-A*: of its glory.

[21.] Deleted from *SC-A*: according to God's primal order of creation.

[22.] Deleted from *SC-A*: This section is therefore included under the heading of the theological concept of primal creation.

[23.] The word "structures" is added to the phrase of empirical communities in *SC-A*.

CHAPTER TWO

THE CHRISTIAN CONCEPT OF PERSON AND CONCEPTS OF SOCIAL BASIC-RELATION

A. Four Conceptual Models of Social Basic-Relation, and the Debate between These and the Christian Concepts of Person and Basic-Relation

EVERY CONCEPT of community is essentially related to a concept of person. It is impossible to say what constitutes community without asking what constitutes a person. Since the purpose of this study is to understand a particular concept of community, namely that of the sanctorum communio, in order to grasp it fully we must analyze its related concept of person. Thus the issue becomes concretely the *question of the Christian concept of person.* What one understands about person and community simultaneously makes a decisive statement about the concept of God. *The concepts of person, community, and God* are inseparably and essentially interrelated.[1] A concept of God is always conceived in relation to a concept of person and a concept of a community of persons. Whenever one thinks of a concept of God, it is done in relation to person and community of persons. In principle, in order to arrive at the essence of the Christian concept of community, we could just as well begin with the concept of God as with that of person. And in choosing to begin with the latter, we must make constant reference to the concept of God in order to come to a well-grounded view of both God and the concept of community.[2]

[1.] Deleted from *SC-A:* Not only a Christian philosophy, but the whole of German idealism confirms it.

[2.] What follows in the published version, up to "beyond the individual person" (see page 37), replaces the following in *SC-A:*

The Christian concept of person and its corresponding concept of social basic-relation will now be presented in debate with the four philo-

---

[2. *cont.*] But we must guard against the objection that, by undertaking to separate the concept of person from that of community, we are already presuming a certain definition of community, i.e., leaning toward an atomistic theory of society. In principle it certainly is conceivable that in the course of this study the concept of person will evaporate entirely, in which case the objection would be dismissed. It is senseless to argue against thinking of person and community as somehow related. The statement above asserts no more than that.

A brief overview of, and debate with, the most important types of concepts of the person, and the corresponding philosophical theories of social basic-relation, will bring us to a philosophical foundation for Christian thought.

Two lines can be traced throughout the history of philosophy from the Middle Ages to the modern period, both of which have their origin in antiquity. One begins with Aristotle, the other with Stoic-Christian ethics. I intentionally use the term 'Stoic-Christian' to indicate that this ethic does not yet include the purely Christian position. For Aristotle, human beings are 'person' to the degree that they participate in the universal reason of the species. Nous, or mind, is included in the Aristotelian concept of divinity and is thus the ideal nature of the human species, as well as the human person. Only insofar as a person participates in the species, i.e., is concretely socialized, does one approach unification with the species reason. This is the basis for Aristotle's definition of the human being as a ζῷον πολιτικόν [political animal]; what necessarily also follows is the ethical superordination of human collectives over individuals. Only in the state can human beings develop their reason; thus by definition the state is to be regarded as prior to all individual existence. Nevertheless, no one ever completely reaches an identification of the νοῦς παθητικος [passive mind] and the νοῦς ποιητικός [active mind], i.e., individual reason and universal reason, defined reason and self-defining reason. Such an identity would comprise ideal humanity. Likewise, for Plato in the *Timaeus* only the rational part of the soul, i.e., that part that rises to the universal, is immortal. <<W[ilhelm] Windelband, *A History of Philosophy*, §13.>> Thus we have a concept of person that reaches beyond the actual person. *Essential being lies beyond individual personal being.* Only by overstepping their individual limits can people participate in essential being. For Aristotle, this overstepping occurs by intellectual activity and its goal, θεωρία [intellectual vision]. The person is a transition point within a motion that transcends persons and has no ultimate significance in that motion itself. *The antithesis between human being and the destiny of human being is the antithesis between individual and universal.* Ultimate meaning is always located in the universal. Attempting to force this relationship into sociological categories, as did Aristotle himself, leads one to the antithesis of *individual and species.* Here we encounter an attempt to make these concepts philosophically and ethically fruitful. Whether it succeeded will be discussed later.

Aristotle's concept of God is intellectualist. We must resist the temptation to look for a personal concept of God in our own sense in Aristotle's concept of the essence of God as the self-consciousness of νόησις νοήσεως [thinking on thinking] [Cf. Aristotle, *Metaphysics*, 1074b, 34] [CG]. Rather, inasmuch as it is the nature of thinking to be active toward an object, it is the nature of the universal, highest form of thinking to be active in self-contemplation and thus to attain self-consciousness. Furthermore, one should not look for any fundamental voluntarism in this concept of God; instead, what we see here is a systematically developed intellectualist-monotheistic concept of God, <<Windelband, ibid.,

sophical models of social basic-relation.[3] Our concern first of all is
only with the ontic[4] basic-relations of social being, not with the question of some sort of social sphere in human beings (whether based reli-
20 giously or otherwise), or with empirical communities of will or even
with social acts.[5] The norm and limit to all empirical sociality is established in ontic basic-relations—an assertion that will be of great significance when we deal with the concept of the church. But since we are
discussing ontic basic-relations, we will not refer to the types of social
theory, but to their philosophical antecedents.

1. In Aristotle's metaphysical model, human beings only become persons insofar as they participate in the species reason. Thus the collectiv-

---

[2. *cont.*] §13, pt. 5: "The theistic character of the notion of God as described thus has not
been reconciled with Aristotle's immanence of spirit.">> which, if employed in social
philosophy, leads to the basic model of individual and species.

211   The second root of the medieval and modern concepts of person is what we call the
Stoic-Christian concept. Two important traditions of thought meet within it: the Stoic concept of the ἡγεμονικόν [ruling part of the individual soul] and the Christian concept of
God. *The Stoic school was the first to raise the concept of personality as a philosophical problem.*
<<Windelband, ibid., §27, pt. 2, 339: "The problem of personality, which emerged only with
the Stoic conception of the ἡγεμονικόν . . ." See also 161f. Also P[aul] Barth, *Die Stoa*,
1908, 2d ed.>> Their argument was based philosophically on the unity of the person
beyond all accidents. The human being does not become a person by transcending individual limits intellectually, but rather by being subordinated to a higher imperative whose commands are reflected in one's innate reason. Thus the concept of person is not understood
intellectually, but ethically. This imperative, however, is universally valid insofar as persons,
through their obedience to it, are united in a realm of reason (that extends from intimate
friendship to world order) in such a way that all souls subordinated to the imperative share
the same humanity. This similarity, and hence equal value of souls that subordinate themselves to the realm of reason, also commits them to social and political life—ὁ σοφός πολι-
τεύσεται [the wise act as citizens]. The mild-sounding Stoic idea of humanity stems from
the contrast to the severity of the coercive concept of fate. Of course, it is also a correlate
of conscious inwardness, of nurture of the personality. But here, too, that which defines the
essential person as such reaches beyond the individual person, despite the Stoics' decisive
emphasis on the ethical, 'personal' aspect.

[3.] This survey of the concepts of person and social basic-relation is largely based on
Windelband, *History of Philosophy*. Cf. 1:139ff., 152ff. on Aristotle; 167f., 171ff., 175ff. on
the Stoic School; and 173ff. on Epicurus.

[4.] By *ontisch*, "ontic," Bonhoeffer means what would nowadays be called 'ontological',
i.e., at the level of being as described normatively by social philosophy, not at the level of
empirical observation. Thus how one construes the 'ontic' basic-relation that belongs to
the essence of the being of persons-in-relation is decisive for how one interprets the social
acts and relationships in empirical communities. Cf. also pages 117f., 126, 211, 268, and
see below, page 41, editorial note 20: "the issue is the metaphysics of sociality." [CG]

[5.] On 'empirical communities of will' and on 'social acts' see below, pages 80ff.

ity, as closer to the species, is set over the individual person. The human being is a ζῷον πολιτικόν [political animal], and the state is the highest form of collectivity which, by its nature, is prior to all individuality. Individuals only partially achieve the identification of νοῦς παθητικος [passive mind] with νοῦς ποιητικός [active mind]; in the same way, according to Plato's *Timaeus*, only the rational part of the soul, i.e., that part that rises to the universal, is immortal.[1] Thus, essential being lies beyond individual-personal being. The antithesis between a human being and its essence is the antithesis of individual and universal— expressed in terms of social philosophy, of individual and species. Accordingly, the Aristotelian concept of God also is impersonal.[2] [7]

2. The Stoic school was the first in the history of philosophy to for- mulate, with its concept of the ἡγεμονικόν [ruling part of the individual soul], the concept of the ethical person. The human being becomes a person by subordination to a higher imperative. This imperative, then, is universally valid insofar as, through obedience to it, persons are united in an order of reason, whereby each soul that submits to the imperative is of like nature with eternal reason and thus also with the soul of other persons.

But here too, despite the decisive Stoic emphasis on the ethical, 'per- sonal' aspect, that which defines the essential person reaches beyond the individual person. The ethical, rational being of persons is their nature, and at the same time it negates the person as an individual.[3]

21

---

1. W[ilhelm] Windelband, *History of Philosophy*, §13.

2. We must here skip over the question of the significant social-philosophical changes that Aristotelianism underwent in the Middle Ages. These problems can be traced as far as the question of the principium individuationis [principle of individuation] in Spinoza and Leibniz.[6]

3. The patristic view of the person coincides with this Stoic view, only the personal element is expressed much more energetically by the church fathers. This is explained by their personal concept of God with its I-You relationship as the basic-relation of God and humanity, as well as by the teaching of personal life after death, which ancient philosophy did not acknowledge. Here we must

[6.] On *principium individuationis* cf. Leibniz, *Disputatio Metaphysica de Principio Indi- vidui*; Spinoza, *Short Treatise on God, Man, and His Well-Being*, 61ff., and *Ethics*, 51ff.

[7.] On the human being as ζῷον πολιτικόν [political animal], cf. Aristotle, *Politics* 1253a; on νοῦς παθητικός [passive mind] and νοῦς ποιητικός [active mind], cf. Aristotle, *De*

The first distinction of principle between Aristotelian and Stoic doctrine is that in Stoicism the I is self-sufficient in principle, and the full height of reason is reached without another being, whereas for Aristotelians only the species, as represented in the idea of the state, possesses highest reason, so that the individual is only conceivable as a part of the species. According to Aristotle, one person enters into relationship with another only on the level of the species and only in order to overcome what is individual. The species is absolutely superior to the individual and is conceptually prior. For the Stoic, nothing new in principle is introduced by the concept of the species. The realm of reason is no more than a realm of similar beings. Thus, for the Stoic, the person[9] is something by nature closed, complete, final. The realm of reason is conceived as a realm of persons. What is essential for us here is that the basic schema is not the metaphysical-intellectualist one of individual and universal; rather, the individual and the universal are closely interconnected, and the person is seen as somehow ultimate.[10] Thus the social-philosophical basic-relation is that of one ethical person to another, which is always understood as a basic-relation between the same kind of beings.[11]

3. Epicureanism begins with Democritus's theory of atoms and extends it to social and ethical life, asserting that human social formation [Vergesellschaftung] only serves to heighten the pleasure of each
22 individual. Social formations thus have a purely utilitarian basis, arising only from a συνθήκη [agreement] and so are inconceivable as natural community.[12] Every individual is fulfilled by the individual pleasure

---

limit ourselves to observing the social-philosophical model of the Stoics that results from the new concept of person.[8]

[7. *cont.*] *Anima (On the Soul)*, 430a10ff.; on Aristotle's concept of God, cf. his *Metaphysics*, 1071b3–1076a4. On Plato, cf. *Timaeus*, 89ff.

[8.] In *SC-A* this footnote appears in the body of the text. On the Stoics and their relationship to the patristic theologians, cf. Windelband, *History of Philosophy*, 238: "The essential feature of the Christian conception of the world is that it regards the person and the relations of persons to one another as the core of reality."

[9.] Here "person" replaces personality in *SC-A*.

[10.] Deleted from *SC-A*: (of course not in the sense of personal immortality).

212   [11.] Deleted from *SC-A* at the beginning of the next paragraph: A third type of social basic-relation was formed in ancient philosophy but not taken up again until the Enlightenment, namely Epicureanism.

[12.] By 'natural' community Bonhoeffer means 'original' or 'primal' community as

that divides that person from every other. Person stands over against person as alien and dissimilar,[13] because each strives toward the highest pleasure for themselves.[14] Nothing remains here of the Stoic ethos, nor of Aristotle's intellectualist philosophy [Geistphilosophie]. Not until the Enlightenment was this doctrine taken up again.[15] The Epicurean position is characterized by its deficient concept of spirit. The deficiency can be construed as a doctrine of basic-relation holding that there are no essential or meaningful relations between human beings that are grounded in the human spirit; connections to others are not intrinsic but only utilitarian. One person is fundamentally alien to the other. Status hominum naturalis est bellum omnium contra omnes [The natural human state is a war of every one against every one][16]

[12. *cont.*] discussed below in chap. 3. A utilitarian approach cannot yield *Gemeinschaft,* "community," as an end in itself, since social forms exist in that view only to serve the happiness of the individual. [CG]

[13.] Cf. Epicurus, "ΚΥΡΙΑΙ ΔΟΞΑΙ" (Principal doctrines), in *Epicurus: The Extant Remains,* ed. Cyril Bailey, 94ff., esp. 102.

[14.] Footnote deleted in *SC-A:* <<In genuine Epicureanism, Hedoné [pleasure] means ajlupiva [painlessness], the greatest freedom from pain. Thus it is far removed from indulgence.>>

[15.] Deleted in *SC-A:*

But in the context of the medieval debate about universals and in connection with the problem of the principium individuationis [principle of individuation], Arabic philosophy repristinated Aristotle's doctrine of species reason. A simple transfer of Aristotle's thought was impossible, however, because it was opposed by the Christian-Stoic concept of personality. Realism had clearly asserted that individuality has no metaphysical meaning, but that substance resides only in species concepts. This was countered by nominalism's assertion of the metaphysical significance of individuality. The Stoic-Augustinian concept of personality came to the assistance of nominalism when it was faced with the mystics' obliteration of the person; the church fathers could not ignore the Stoic-Augustinian concept, as Averroes and others had done. Thomas, put in the difficult position of having to mediate between the two views, developed the theory that the individual is identical to the species only in its pure forms (the angels), but that the species is articulated inherently in the multitude of individuals.

Arabic philosophy thus maintained the Aristotelian schema of species and individual in order to comprehend the individual realm and social basic-relations. Nominalist theory regards the basic schema as the relation of person to person. The nominalist-realist conflict regarding the question of the principium individuationis [principle of individuation] continued into modern philosophy (Spinoza, Leibniz).

The third type of ancient philosophy only came to life again with the influence of the emerging natural sciences. The French and English Enlightenment took up the atomistic social philosophy of Epicurus and developed it further.

[16.] Except for the fact that Bonhoeffer writes "*contra omnes*" rather than "*in omnes,*" his Latin citation of Hobbes follows the form found in Kant, *Religion within the Limits of*

(Hobbes).[4] This is the basis for all social forms; thus they should be interpreted as purely contractual. This and the next two chapters contain my implicit argument with this theory.[17]

4. Descartes's transformation of the metaphysical question into an epistemological one casts the concept of person into a different light from previous theories. This was realized in essence by Kant's development of the epistemological concept of person: the knowing I becomes the starting point of all philosophy.[18] Because the synthesis of transcendental apperception[19] resolves the opposition of subject and object as well as the I-You-relation in the higher unity of spirit, of intellectual intuition, a new philosophical approach is created for solving the problem of the social basic-relation as well. This enables us to demonstrate the fundamental connection between the first and the fourth types in spite of their different starting points.[20]

---

4. Even Kant adheres to this sentence (cf. *Religion within the Limits of Reason Alone*, 89), except that he considers it possible and necessary to leave the natural state behind.

[16. *cont.*] *Reason Alone*, 89. Cf. Hobbes, *Opera Latina*, 3:103: "*conditio hominum est conditio belli omnium contra omnes*" ("the human condition is a war of all against all"); see *Leviathan*, 91.

[17.] Bonhoeffer's description of Epicurean doctrine relies on the argument of Windelband (see above, page 36, editorial note 3), who pursues the Democritean-Epicurean doctrine into the Enlightenment. He sees it as achieving a 'late victory' in the contract theories of natural law. Cf. Windelband, *A History of Philosophy*, 2:432, note 2. Regarding the critique of contract theory, also see below, page 82, editorial note 68. Also see Vierkandt, *Gesellschaftslehre*, 261ff., 283, and Scheler, *Formalism in Ethics*, 480f., 522ff. In *SC-B* as in *SC-A* (point 4 above) Bonhoeffer's critique of idealist philosophy and its underlying subject-object relation, as well as the concept of the I-You-relation growing out of this critique, is taken to a great extent from Hirsch, *Die idealistische Philosophie*, esp. 66ff.; see below, page 51, editorial note 61. See also Litt, *Individuum*, 106ff.

[18.] Deleted in *SC-A*: and everything located outside this 'I' becomes an object of knowledge.

[19.] On 'transcendental apperception', cf. Kant, *Critique of Pure Reason*, 128ff., esp. 136f. (B 129ff., A 96ff., esp. A 108). Cf. also Hirsch's discussion of Kant, *Die idealistische Philosophie*, 41ff., 66ff., and 73f. For a critique of Kant, see Litt, *Individuum*, 100ff.

[20.] Instead of the preceding sentence, *SC-A* contains the following deleted passage:

This point will be developed later.

The point of this historical overview was merely to show how it was possible to arrive at interpretations of social basic-relations from different philosophical approaches, and to show which fundamental schemas were used in conceptualizing the relationship of one person to another, or to the species. I stress that this says nothing about a possible *social realm* in the human being, and thus that the subject of empirical social relations has not yet been

The metaphysical[21] schema fundamentally denies the person by sub-   23
suming the person under the universal. The epistemological subject-

---

[20. *cont.*] broached. So far the person has been considered in possible relation to other persons only in light of various purely philosophical concepts of person. We discovered four such fundamental schemas: (1) The Aristotelian metaphysical schema of the universal and the individual, the species and the individual person. (2) The Stoic-Christian schema of person and person. (3) The Democritean-Epicurean-Enlightenment schema with its atomistic theory of society. (4) Finally, the schema of German idealism that is articulated in the subject-object relationship of epistemology. It is now possible to demonstrate a fundamental connection between the first and the fourth types in spite of their different starting points.

For both types the subject finds its meaning by entering into the universal forms of reason. What the epistemological insight of idealism adds is the view that everything the subject encounters is an object of knowledge, a view that remains fundamental to Fichte's ethical idealism and Hegel's logical idealism.

But in idealism there is no ultimate opposition between subject and object, since the act of recognizing them as opposites resolves them into the unity of intellectual intuition.

This brings us to the first systematic inquiry of this study, the question of the philosophical foundation for a Christian doctrine of person and community that must be connected with a critical discussion of the basic schemas described above. In the attempt to comprehend the specifically Christian community of persons, the sanctorum communio, the necessity of developing such a concept of person becomes evident, as already noted.

The premise of this study of the Christian concepts of person and social basic-relation is that neither is abstracted from empirical social forms. Both must be conceived in general terms in order to be applied to the specific context of empirical social relations; in other   214
words, one must not confuse empirical, actual relations with social basic-relations. The former always extend to a social realm of human being, to a group of social acts. But at this stage that is not the issue at all. Instead, what is important is whether the person must necessarily be thought of in relation to an other, or whether persons can be conceived atomistically. And if the first alternative can be proved, this in turn should lead to the question, namely, which basic-relations control life between persons? This is why our historical introduction drew not upon the history of social doctrines but upon those theories that underlie the philosophical formulation of any social theory. Briefly, we are not yet dealing with the empirical fact of communities of will here, or with the specifically sociological problem of reciprocal influences [Wechselwirkungen] of wills; we are only speaking of the *ontic basic-relations* of social being in general. Thus the issue is the metaphysics of sociality.

Because from the outset we define this part of the study as theological and social-philosophical, not sociological, we push forward toward finding normative significance in these foundations for empirical sociology. *The ontic basic-relations contain the norm for all empirical sociality.* This insight will be of utmost significance for the concept of the church.

The attempt to describe social basic-relations from the standpoint of Christian doctrine does not yet make them religious; they are purely ontic, and they are seen that way only from a Christian perspective. Thus we have all the prerequisites for taking up the critical discussion and positive presentation of a philosophical foundation for the Christian doctrine of person and basic-relation. The goal is to find that schema by which to understand Christian basic-relations.

The first question is whether the schemas from the history of philosophy are inadequate, and for what reason.

[21.] Deleted from *SC-A*: as well as the epistemological.

object-relation does not advance beyond this, since it resolves the opposition of subject and object in the unity of mind, in intellectual intuition.[22] Moreover, it does not distinguish at all between a subject-object-relation and an I-You-relation; rather, the latter is subsumed under the former. Even Fichte does not in principle get beyond this Kantian understanding when he has the self-conscious I originating in the Not-I. For his Not-I is not another I, but an object. In the end, however, both are resolved in the unity of the I.[23] Hegel, too, has the I arise at the point where, drawn into objective spirit, it is returned to absolute spirit, a move that also overcomes in principle the limit of the individual person.[24] *Basically, it is the concept of spirit that connects all these systems, namely the concept of spirit as immanent*; such a concept necessarily leads to the conclusions drawn by idealism.[5] The I is person insofar as it is spirit. But for Kant, spirit is the highest formal principle that encompasses and overcomes everything material, so that the universal and spirit become identical, and the individual loses its value. Immanent spirit, as the highest formal principle, is formal law. This also is true in ethics. Every interpretation of Kant's ethical formalism that finds in it the basis for the freedom of a material ethic is incorrect.[6]

---

5. One may perhaps object to finding Kant mentioned here, without qualification, among the idealists. I am of course aware of the distance between him and all the rest; further, I will mention later that in Kant the idea of transcendence collides with that of immanence. In the context of the present discussion he is the first of a line that progresses up to Hegel.[25]

6. Cf. Heinrich Barth, "Kierkegaard, der Denker," *Zwischen den Zeiten* [4].3 (1926), 208, where the attempt is made to make Kant's ethics the basis of Kierkegaard's. What is understood as formalism here is the corollary of either radical subjectivism or a material ethic; but in doing so the concept of formal-

[22.] The phrase in intellectual intuition is added to *SC-A*.

[23.] Deleted from *SC-A*: (More later about the fact that Fichte did temporarily move beyond this point.)

[24.] Cf. Hirsch, *Die idealistische Philosophie*, 69f., 74ff., on the critique of Fichte; see also 70ff. on the critique of Hegel. And see Fichte, *The Science of Knowledge*, and Hegel, *Encyclopedia of the Philosophical Sciences in Outline*, pt. (C), "The Philosophy of Spirit."

[25.] Bonhoeffer's footnote 5 is not found in *SC-A*. [The word 'spirit' or *Geist* in this passage is used in the idealist sense of the knowing I in the subject-object relationship. Such spirit, as mind, is 'immanent' in that the object of knowledge does not constitute an independent, willing subject who encounters, and thus transcends, the knower. In *Act and Being* Bonhoeffer distinguishes the intention of Kant's 'genuine transcendental philosophy' from post-Kantian idealism; see *AB (DBWE 2): 33ff.*][CG]

Universal validity is the highest principle of action for the person governed by reason. Fichte adopts this Kantian definition of person. Much   24
as he, too, speaks of individuality, he nevertheless does not improve upon Kant. When a person's task or duty has been accomplished, the purpose of reason is fulfilled. One I is like the other. Only on the basis of this likeness is a relation of persons conceivable at all.[27] Of course, this is only true for social basic-relations; with regard to empirical social relations Kant already recognized the decisive significance of antagonism.[7] *It is the destiny of the human species to be absorbed into the realm of reason, to form a realm of completely similar and harmonious persons, defined by universal reason or by one spirit and separated only by their different activities.* Most importantly, however, this union of like beings never leads *to the concept of community, but only to the concept of sameness, of unity.* But this is not a sociological concept, and so one sees that the subject-object schema can never lead to a *sociological category.*[8] [30]

---

ism becomes meaningless. Formalism and universality are necessarily connected in Kant, and thus they have substantive weight in his ethics. Though Brunner identifies the Kantian and the Christian concepts of person in *Die Mystik und das Wort*, 331, the point of identity is elsewhere. At many points in his ethics, Kant could have broken up his epistemology. Cf. also Scheler, *Formalism*, 109, n. 88.[26]

7. "Idea for a Universal History from a Cosmopolitan Point of View," 4th Thesis.[28]

8. More seriously than anyone else, Fichte posed the problem of the 'synthesis of the world of spirits'. He was the only one to recognize as a philosophical

[26.] For a critique of Kant's ethical formalism see Scheler, *Formalism in Ethics*, 6f., 374ff. Bonhoeffer is drawing on Scheler's critique but does not adopt his agenda for a material ethic of value. Hirsch, *Die idealistische Philosophie*, 43ff., also begins his presentation of idealist philosophy with Kant; he wants to substitute the primacy of the 'ethical' for that of epistemology (cf. 83).

[27.] Deleted from *SC-A*: Every difference among rational persons is felt to be mere inade-   215
quacy.

[28.] See pages 15–16.

[29.] Bonhoeffer bases this discussion of Fichte entirely on Hirsch, to whom he has referred. Hirsch's discussion of Fichte centers on the problem of the 'synthesis of the world of spirits', though Fichte himself does not place so much weight on this concept. Cf. also Hirsch, *Die idealistische Philosophie*, 74ff., and Fichte, *Darstellung der Wissenschaftslehre*, in his *Werke*, 2:3ff., dated by Hirsch as 1801–2 (256). [Bonhoeffer's note simply says *Wissenschaftslehre*, which might mislead the reader to think he meant Fichte's *Grundlage der gesamten Wissenschaftslehre*, rather than the *Darstellung der Wissenschaftslehre*.][CG]

[30.] Deleted from *SC-A*:

With these conclusions, we have now created the presuppositions necessary to begin the positive discussion of the specifically Christian view. We intend to go beyond mere descrip-

25   *The term 'Christian*[31] *concept of person' will now be used for the concept of person that is constitutive for the concept of Christian community and is presupposed by it.* In theological terms this means not the person-concept of the primal human state, but that of the human being after the fall—the person who does not live in unbroken community with God and humanity, but who knows good and evil.[32] This Christian concept of person necessarily builds upon the fact of the human spirit, namely the structural, individual personhood of this spirit, about which we will speak later.[33] In this general concept of personal spirit we must also

---

problem the fact that other living persons were present 'in spontaneous freedom', and that the explosive power of the entire system resides in asking 'How does one person reach the other; where is their common origin?' Fichte's answers are manifold and yet very similar. (Cf. on this subject Hirsch's description, *Die idealistische Philosophie und das Christentum*, 140–290, on "Fichtes Gotteslehre [doctrine of God]," esp. 260ff.) The synthesis of the world of spirits is in God. Only because of our common origin in God can we understand each other. Where human beings meet each other in their essence, there is God, and complete unity of all in the spirit, in turn, is present in God. Apart from God, every person is alien to the other; there is only a plurality of atomistic I's. But this is not the last to be said about Fichte. In his *Wissenschaftslehre* (1801–2), Fichte recognizes the synthesis of the world of spirits as grounded in certainty. Certainty necessarily presupposes both universal and individual consciousness and is itself neither, but absorbs both into itself; universal consciousness, however, includes some synthesis of spirits, not only in epistemological, but also in ethical, reflection. Basically we already saw this thinking in Kant, in that he, too—incorrectly and with unfortunate results, as we know—connected the metaphysical category of the one and the sociological category of the species (the synthesis) in the concept of the knowledge of reason [Vernunfterkenntnis]. Thus we must also reject Fichte's position as epistemologically incorrect. Beginning from an epistemological concept, he assumes something as fact that lies beyond the grasp of all epistemology. It is impossible to progress from the idea of universal consciousness to the idea of the 'other' in the sociological sense. Thus there is no social category in Fichte's concept of social basic-relation, but rather a metaphysical one, namely the unity of nondialectical synthesis, or identity on the basis of similar natures.[29]

[30. cont.] tion and attempt to overcome the idealist philosophy of immanent spirit with a Christian philosophy of spirit. We hope thus to obtain results that will provide a direction for Christian social philosophy.

[31.] Replaces Christian-ethical in *SC-A*.

[32.] On the knowledge of good and evil breaking community with God and others, and dividing the self, see *CF (DBWE 3):* 85–93, 121–26. [CG]

[33.] See below, pages 65ff.

overcome the idealist concept and replace it with one which preserves the individual, concrete character of the person as absolute and intended by God (cf. chapter 3 on this subject). For the present, we shall deal only with the specifically Christian[34] concept of person in order to clarify how it differs from that of idealism.[35]

The attempt to derive the social from the epistemological category must be rejected as a μετάβασις εἰς ἄλλο γένος [change to a different category].[36] *It is impossible to reach the real existence of other subjects by way of the purely transcendental category of the universal.* How, then, can one arrive at the other as independent subject?[9] There is no cognitive way to reach this point, just as there is no purely cognitive way to know God. All cognitive methods of idealism are included in the realm of personal mind [Geist],   26
and the way to the transcendent is the way to the object of knowledge. I bear within me the forms of the mind to grasp this object that, for precisely that reason, remains a mere object and never becomes a subject, or 'alien I'. To be sure, a subject can also become an object of knowledge, but then it leaves the social sphere and enters the epistemological sphere. The epistemological and the social spheres can differ so greatly in principle, however, that *in spite of epistemological realism no social sphere is recognized, and on the other hand in spite of radical epistemological idealism, i.e., solipsism, the social sphere is fully recognized.* This demonstrates that neither sphere can be reduced to the other. What remains to be shown is what we mean by the social sphere.[38]

As long as my intellect is dominant, exclusively claiming universal validity, as long as all contradictions that can arise when one knows a subject as an object of knowledge are conceived as immanent to my intellect, I am not in the social sphere. But this means that I enter this sphere *only when my intellect is confronted by some fundamental barrier*

---

9. Cf. Hirsch, [*Die idealistische Philosophie,*] 66ff.; Eberhard Grisebach, *Die Grenzen des Erziehers und seine Verantwortung,* 1925.[37] See also Gogarten, *Ich glaube an den dreieinigen Gott,* though it reached me when this chapter was already complete.

[34.] Replaces Christian-ethical in *SC-A*.
[35.] Deleted from *SC-A*: The first sentence we must explain in more detail is:
[36.] Faulty logic, according to Aristotle.
[37.] The following sentence from *SC-B* is not found in *SC-A*.
[38.] The following argument is based on Grisebach, *Die Grenzen des Erziehers,* 83ff.; cf. also Litt, *Individuum,* 106ff.

[Schranke]. At first, of course, this can happen in the intellectual sphere, but not in the epistemological-transcendental sphere; idealism's 'object' is ultimately no barrier. What is important is not the nature of the barrier, but the fact that it is experienced and acknowledged as a real barrier. But what does it mean to experience and acknowledge a barrier as real? The point is the *concept of reality* that idealism did not think through thoroughly, and therefore did not think through at all.[39] Essential[40] reality for idealism is the self-knowing and self-active spirit, engaging truth and reality in the process.[41] Persons[42] have at their disposal their own ethical value. They have the dignity to be able to be ethical and, insofar as they are persons, they are obliged to be ethical.[43] The boundary between 'ought' and 'is' does not coincide with the boundary of the person as a whole; rather, idealism divides the human being down the middle.[44] Of course, to the extent that any serious imperative implies ethical transcendence, this should have been the point at which idealism could have had second thoughts. But with Kant's "You can, because you ought,"[45] the argument abandoned the realm of ethical transcendence for the immanence of a philosophy of spirit.[10] The necessary result of a one-sided epistemological philosophy

27

---

10. Only when none other than God motivates and enters into the person can one speak in Christian terms of such an identification, and then of course only from the perspective of 'faith'.

[39.] "The point is . . . think through at all" replaces the following passage in *SC-A*: Here, Christian philosophy makes a second breach in the wall of idealism, for idealism failed to think through the concept of reality exhaustively, and therefore did not conceive the concept at all.

[40.] Deleted from *SC-A*: only.

[41.] Deleted from *SC-A*: How can one expect to meet a barrier in this case? We can do so if the concept of person is not equated with the universal spirit of idealism. The ethical barrier of Kant's and Fichte's idealist philosophy was ultimately not understood as a real barrier.

[42.] Deleted from *SC-A*: of course participates in the ethical, according to Kant and Fichte; the person . . .

[43.] Deleted from *SC-A*:

This is not in the least to imply any criticism of the absolute seriousness of the ethical demand of idealism; that would be crass and confusing nonsense. But the 'ought' of idealism was the rational person's own 'ought'. Like everything, the 'ought' was absorbed into the person's reason, thus creating its own ethical value and continually heightening it.

[44.] Deleted in *SC-A*: The problem of ethics in idealism surely is not exhausted with this discussion.

[45.] On Kant's maxim, "You can because you ought," cf. Kant, *The Metaphysics of*

thus was rational persons deciding their own ethical value, having self-empowered entry into the ethical sphere, and bearing within themselves their own ethical motives as rational persons. So one came here to recognize[46] the real barrier. This recognition is possible only within the ethical sphere. This does not mean, however, that the barrier itself can have only an ethical content. Rather, as I have mentioned, it can be purely intellectual, i.e., it can be experienced in the conflict of knowledge. Only the experience of the barrier as real is a specifically ethical experience. We have not yet described what we mean by reality over against and beyond idealism's understanding. The issue here is *the problem of time.*[47]

Kant taught that continuously advancing time was a pure form of the mind's intuition. The result in Kant and in all of idealism is essentially a timeless way of thinking. In epistemology this is evident; but even in ethics, too, Kant did not consciously move beyond this. The same starting points that could have led to recognizing the real barrier could also have led to overcoming the timeless way of thinking in ethics, without diminishing the absolute ethical claim. Fichte came closer to ethical reality in his view of individual duty, but he too remained far from the necessary transformation of thinking. In spite of the emphasis on the primacy of ethics in both philosophers, we see epistemology having a continual influence on ethics.[48] *It is not my intention here to dispute the epistemological understanding of time as a pure form of intuition.* My starting point is different.[49] Like Kant and Fichte, I am emphasizing the

---

[45. *cont.*] *Morals,* 146; see also Kant's essay, "Über den Gemeinspruch: Das mag in der   216
Theorie richtig sein, taugt aber nicht für die Praxis" (On the saying: That may be right in
theory but it doesn't work in practice). Underlying Bonhoeffer's critique of Kant is
Scheler's *Formalism in Ethics,* 236ff. *passim:* Obligation and ability cannot be reduced to an
entity; they are "equally original" (237), and grounded in a special "unity of experience"
(127), the so-called "experience of being-able-to-do" (cf. 128f.). [Scheler, *Formalismus,*
148f., says "Erlebnis des 'Tunkönnens',", not "Könnenserlebnis," which is why his translators (*Formalism,* 128f.) say "being-able-to-do."][CG]

[46.] Replaces in *SC-A:* to experience, or rather to recognize philosophically . . .

[47.] This sentence replaces the following in *SC-A:* It is a good idea to begin this discussion
at the point that divides the two views most dramatically, namely the problem of time. In the following section on the problem of time and the person in a situation of responsibility, Bonhoeffer is drawing upon the insights of Grisebach, *Die Grenzen des Erziehers,* cf. 274ff. and
294ff. See also Litt, *Individuum,* 74ff. and 90ff., and Scheler's critique of Kant's concept of
subject and his idea of time in *Formalism in Ethics,* 376ff.

[48.] Deleted from *SC-A:* But idealism can also be beaten with its own weapons on this point
of the problem of time.

[49.] In *SC-A* "starting point is different" replaces "from ethics".

absoluteness of the ethical demand and now relate this to the person
28   confronted with it. At the moment of being addressed, the person
enters a state of *responsibility* or, in other words, of decision. By person I
do not mean at this point the idealists' person of mind or reason, but
the person in concrete, living individuality. This is not the person internally divided, but the one addressed as a whole person; not one existing
in timeless fullness of value and spirit, but in a state of responsibility in
the midst of time; not one existing in time's continuous flow, but in the
value-related—not value-filled—moment. *In the concept of the moment, the
concept of time and its value-relatedness [Wertbezogenheit] are co-posited.* The
moment is not the shortest span of time, a mechanically conceived
atom, as it were.[50] The 'moment' is the time of responsibility, value-
related time, or, let us say, time related to God; and, most essentially, it
is concrete time. Only in concrete time is the real claim of ethics effec-
tual; and only when I am responsible am I fully conscious of being
bound to time. It is not that I make some sort of universally valid decisions by being in full possession of a rational mind. Rather, I enter the
reality of time by relating my concrete person in time and all its particu-
larities to this imperative—by making myself ethically responsible. Just
as sound lies in different spheres of perception for musicians and physi-
cists, so it is with time for idealist epistemology and for a Christian concept of person, without the one sphere canceling the other.

Thus there follows from our concept of time an idea that is quite
meaningless for idealism, that *the person ever and again arises and passes
away in time.* The person does not exist timelessly; a person is not static,
but dynamic. The person exists always and only in ethical responsibility;
the person is re-created again and again in the perpetual flux of life.[51]
Any other concept of person fragments the *fullness of life* of the concrete
person. In the last analysis the reason why idealist philosophy fails to
understand the concept of person is that it has no *voluntaristic* concept
of God, nor a profound concept of sin (as shall be demonstrated). This
29   in turn relates to its position regarding the problem of history. The logical flaw in the formulation of the idealist concept of person is no coincidence but is deeply rooted in the system.[52] Idealism has no

---

[50.] Deleted from *SC-A*: (for philosophy, there is no time consisting of various parts); . . .

[51.] The following sentence was deleted from *SC-A*: Subjective spirit becomes eternally
significant only in relation to absolute spirit.

[52.] Deleted from *SC-A*: and its basic philosophical insights.

appreciation of movement. The movement of the dialectic of mind was abstract and metaphysical, while that of ethics is concrete. Further, idealism has no understanding of the moment in which the person feels the threat of absolute demand. The idealist ethicist knows what he ought to do, and, what is more, he can always do it precisely because he ought. Where is there room, then, for distress of conscience, for infinite anxiety [Angst] in the face of decisions?[53]

But this brings us close to the problem of reality, the problem of the real barrier, and thus that of social basic-relations. It is a Christian insight that the person as conscious being is created in the moment of being moved—in the situation of responsibility, passionate ethical struggle, confrontation by an overwhelming claim; thus the real person grows out of the concrete situation. Here, too, the encounter lies entirely in the spirit [Geist], as in idealism. Spirit here, however, has a different meaning than it does in idealism. *For Christian philosophy, the human person originates only in relation to the divine; the divine person transcends the human person,* who both resists and is overwhelmed by the divine. Idealist individualism's notion of spirit as being-for-itself [Fürsichsein] is unchristian, as it involves attributing to the human spirit absolute value that can only be ascribed to divine spirit. The Christian person originates only in the absolute duality of God and humanity; only in experiencing the barrier does the awareness of oneself as ethical person arise. The more clearly the barrier is perceived, the more deeply the person enters into the situation of responsibility.[54] The Christian person is not the bearer of highest values; rather the concept of value can be related only to personal being, i.e., to the creatureliness of the person. Every philosophy of value, even where it regards the value of

---

[53.] On the voluntarist concept of God, cf. Seeberg, *Dogmatik*, 1:73ff. Seeberg understands God as the 'original will' (75). Voluntarism also defines a specific epistemological method. In the encounter of God with human beings, the human will is subjected to that of God. In this subjection of the human to the divine will, obedience and knowledge become one. Knowledge occurs when the divine will is grasped, at first intuitively. Intellectual knowledge follows after the intuitive, and is seen by Seeberg as the foundation for every speculative, rational system, a notion he introduced in order to critique and complement Hegel. On the concept of God, the concept of sin, the problem of history, and the issue of decision, cf. Hirsch, *Die idealistische Philosophie*, 1ff. On the issues of moment and decision, cf. also Heinrich Barth, "Kierkegaard der Denker," esp. 199 and 233.

[54.] Deleted from *SC-A*: The more the barrier is obscured, the more the human being assumes the position of the one making demands, of the spirit [Geist] equipped with ethical fullness and value.

the person as the highest value (Scheler),[55] is in danger of taking away the value of persons as such, as God's creatures, and acknowledging them only insofar as the person is the 'bearer' of objective, impersonal
30   value. But in so doing it closes itself off from the possibility of understanding personal-social basic-relations.

When the concrete ethical barrier of the other person is acknowledged or, alternatively, when the person is compelled to acknowledge it, we have made a fundamental step that allows us to grasp the *social ontic-ethical basic-relations of persons.*[56]

Obviously, here the concept of barrier is decisive. Thus, its form and structure in personal experience must first be analyzed. The concept of barrier is not to be located in the relation between the individual and the universal. The person is not the individual per se, any more than the individual as such is intrinsically fallen and sinful (Schelling).[57] But *the metaphysical concept of the individual is defined without mediation, whereas the ethical concept of the person is a definition based on ethical-social interaction.* From the ethical perspective, human beings do not exist 'unmediated' qua spirit in and of themselves, but only in responsibility vis-à-vis an 'other'. In this sense we call the ethical concept of the individual the social basic-relation, since one cannot even speak of the individual without at the same time necessarily thinking of the 'other' who moves the individual into the ethical sphere. One could object that so far[58] 'other' has been understood as referring to God, whereas now a concept of social relation has suddenly been introduced, in which 'other' refers to another *human being.*[59]

[55.] According to Scheler, *Formalism in Ethics,* 476ff., the highest values are the 'personal values'; this is why he can also designate his material ethic of value, or *Wertethik,* as "a new attempt to develop a personalism" (14f.).

[56.] For Bonhoeffer the Christian understanding of person at the ontological level is always that of the person in a social and ethical encounter with the other person; this is the Christian basic-relation of I and You [*Du*], self and other. It presupposes the theological axiom that the human person always exists in relation to an Other, namely God, and that human relations are in some way analogies of this fundamental relation. [CG]

[57.] Deleted from *SC-A:* rather, it is the person as temporally determined, necessary, and individual. On this, see Schelling, *Philosophie der Offenbarung, Werke,* 6:648ff.

217   [58.] "One could object that so far" replaces in *SC-A:* We will be accused of profound confusion, since until now . . .

[59.] Deleted from *SC-A:* Apparently a false conclusion has been drawn on the basis of a quaternio terminorum. This objection plunges us into the middle of the matter. [In logic *quaternio terminorum* refers to a fourth, and therefore inadmissible, term in a syllogism.] [CG]

First of all, one should remember what was said at the beginning about the interconnection of God, community, and individual.[60] Thus the individual exists only in relation to an 'other'; individual does not mean solitary. *On the contrary, for the individual to exist, 'others' must necessarily be there.* But what is the 'other'? If I call the individual the concrete I, then the other is the *concrete* You.[61] So what does 'You' mean in philosophical terms? At first glance, every You seems to presuppose an I who is immanent to the You, and without whom a You could not even be distinguished from an object-form. Thus 'You' would be identical to 'other I'. But this is only partially correct. Beyond the limit to epistemological knowledge there is a further limit to ethical-social knowledge, or acknowledgment. The other can be experienced by the I only as You, but never directly as I, that is, in the sense of the I that has become I only through the claim of a You. The You-form is fundamentally different from the I-form in the sphere of ethical reality. But since the You, too, stands before me as a person, as a thinking and acting mind, we must understand the You as an I in the general sense, i.e., in the sense of self-consciousness, etc. (see next chapter). These two I-forms should be strictly distinguished. The You as a reality-form [Wirklichkeitsform] is by definition independent in encountering the I in this sphere.[62] In contrast to the idealist object-form, it is not immanent to the mind of the subject. The You sets the limit for the subject[63] and by its own accord activates a will that impinges upon the other in such a way that this other will becomes a You for the I. If the objection is raised that the

31

[60.] See above, pages 34 and 44.

[61.] On the I-You-relation see Hirsch, *Die idealistische Philosophie*, 66f.; Grisebach, *Die Grenzen des Erziehers*, 83ff.; and Litt, *Individuum*, 106ff. See also on this subject [Karl] Barth, *Romans*, 492ff., and Gogarten, "Protestantism and Reality: Epilogue to Martin Luther's *Bondage of the Will*," 367ff.

[62.] Deleted from *SC-A*:

I said above that there is no way of knowing the alien 'I'. This is not to question whether the I can know of other self-conscious intelligent beings in the transcendental sense of the word 'know', but only to say that I do not know their reality in the particular sense, i.e., their ethical personhood. (It will become clear later on that the sentence about the inadequacy of the person has even further significance.) Thus, in social basic-relations, too, the 'You' is an 'I' in the sense of self-consciousness, etc., to be sure, but not an 'I' in the sense of ethical I-You-relation. Among other things the You-form has autonomous character in the ethical I-You-relation.

[63.] Deleted from *SC-A*: [and] it assumes not only a reactive posture to the I, but one of effective action . . .

other is also a content of my consciousness, immanent to my mind, then what was said above about the distinctive spheres was not understood; *the transcendence of the You says nothing at all about epistemological*[64] *transcendence.*[65] This is a purely ethical transcendence, experienced only by those facing a decision; it can never be demonstrated to someone on the outside. Thus everything that can be said about the Christian concept of person can only be grasped directly by the person who is facing responsibility.

I and You are not simply interchangeable concepts,[66] but comprise specific and distinct spheres of experience. I myself can become an object of my own experience, but can never experience myself as You. Other persons can become objects of my reflection on their I-ness, but I will never get beyond the fact that I can only encounter the other as a You. I can never become a real barrier to myself, *but it is just as impossible for me to leap over the barrier to the other.* My I as a You-form can only be experienced by the other I, and my I as an I-form can only be experienced by myself; thus *in the experience of a You, the I-form of the other is never an unmediated given.* But this means that I can be confronted with barriers by a You that has not yet become an I in the sense of I-You-relations. Thus the You-form is to be defined as the other who places me before an ethical decision. And with this I-You-relation as the Christian basic-relation we move as a matter of principle beyond the epistemological subject-object-relation.[67] Likewise, it makes unnecessary the concept of the You as the other I. Whether the other is also an I in the sense of the I-You-relation is not something I can know. This is also applied to the concept of God. God is an impenetrable You whose metaphysical personhood, which presupposes absolute self-consciousness and spontaneous action, implies nothing at all about God being an I as described above.[11][68]

32

---

11. This is not the place to discuss in what respects human beings are or are not (because of sin) barriers for God.

[64.] Replaces in *SC-A* epistemological-objective.

[65.] The German critical edition reproduces an obvious error from the first edition (*SC-B*). The latter prints in italics only the last word of the sentence (*ausgesagt*). This is found on the top of page 43 of the dissertation typescript (*SC-A*); at the bottom of page 42 the preceding words of the phrase are also plainly underlined. [CG]

[66.] Deleted from *SC-A*: which, when applied one to the other, can be exchanged . . .

[67.] Deleted from *SC-A*: The two have nothing to do with one another.

[68.] In *SC-A* this footnote and the material below were in the text. The following

Doesn't the statement that the You is not necessarily an I militate against the concept of community comprised of persons? Is the person

---

[68. *cont.*] material in *SC-A* was replaced by the two preceding sentences beginning "This is also . . ." and the sentence beginning the next paragraph, "Doesn't the statement that the You is not necessarily an I . . .":

> This brings us to the decisive question of how it is possible to think of the I-You-relation along with the concept of God. Should one conceive of God as a You? I know of no philosophical system that has fully adopted the Christian I-You-relation between God and humanity. The period of classical philosophy even rejects the notion of a personal God. 'Omnis determinatio est negatio' ['every determination is a negation'] Spinoza taught, and this dictum held sway for a long time. When theology in the modern period successfully applied to the idea of God a philosophically grounded concept of person, perhaps this influenced a reaction in philosophy that now undertook the same effort, as we can see, for example, in Max Scheler. It is, however, interesting to note that, in general, wherever a personal concept of God is advanced, there is a decisive turning away from any concretely defined concept of person; we find this fairly often in theology as well. Scheler is equally explicit in emphasizing the personhood of God (on the basis of a 'sociological proof of God's existence') as he is about the impossibility of human relation to God being an I-You relation. <<*Formalism in Ethics*, 397: "God can be a person, but not an I, since for God there is neither a You nor an external world!">> Can we nevertheless maintain the I-You-relation? We know God as absolute, but also as self-conscious and spontaneously active spirit and will. This formulation expresses as pure spirit, formally defined, God's metaphysical personhood, whose image is present in every human being as a remnant of likeness to God. Such a concept of God does not conflict with one that understands God as a You whom we can experience as an ethical barrier. Further, this experience of God as You implies nothing a priori about God as I, either as individually limited or even as ethically addressed. Though God is a You for us, i.e., active will standing over against us, this does not mean that we are barriers for God. This is not the place to discuss in what respects human beings are or are not (because of sin) barriers for God. Thus we believe that the I-You-relation between God and human beings has been theologically justified.
>
> Yet we might be accused of great one-sidedness. What has become of all that can in fact be said about the philosophical concept of person? Certainly, this discussion has been limited to ethical reflection. But at this point we only intended to confront the Christian ethical concept of person and of basic-relation with that of the idealist-metaphysical concept of person. What we can appropriate from the idealist concept of person will be made clear in another context. Here, we are only asserting that the center of the Christian concept of person lies elsewhere than in idealism. The attempt of the latter to arrive at the concrete reality of the other was bound to fail, for we are dealing with two qualitatively different spheres. From the idealist perspective, with its notion of the universal, we can at best arrive at the possibility of the other. The other is a postulate, just as idealism's entire view of the historical element in Christianity is an assumption (Christology). One can never arrive at the reality of the other by means of epistemology and metaphysics. Reality is simply not deducible, but given—to be acknowledged or rejected. It can never be explained theoretically; likewise it is only given for the whole person as an ethical being. The Christian-ethical concept of person rightly presents itself as a way of viewing the whole person. In every idealist construction the concept of spirit in fact cuts through the vitality of the person. The Christian concept affirms the whole concrete person, body and soul, different from all others, as ethically relevant.

218

not completely isolated, in effect?[69] The person arises only in relation to a You, and yet the person stands in complete isolation. Persons are unique and thus fundamentally separate and distinct from one another. In other words, one person cannot know the other, but can only acknowledge and 'believe' in the other.[70] Psychology and epistemology find their limitation here; the ethical personhood of the other is neither a psychologically comprehensible fact nor an epistemological necessity.[71]

B. The Concept of God and Social Basic-Relations in Terms of the I-You-Relation[72]

Our concern here is the relationship of the person, God, and social being to each other. The I comes into being only in relation to the You; only in response to a demand does *responsibility* arise. 'You' says nothing about its own being, only about its demand. This demand is absolute.

33 What does this mean? The whole person, who is totally claimless, is claimed by this absolute demand. But this seems to make one human being the creator of the ethical person of the other, which is an intolerable thought.[73] Can it be avoided? The person-creating efficacy of the You is independent of the personhood of the You.[74] We now add that it is also independent of the will of the human You. One human being cannot of its own accord make another into an I, an ethical person conscious of responsibility.[75] *God or the Holy Spirit joins the concrete You; only*

[68. *cont.*] What form, then, will the basic-relations of persons assume? Does not our statement that the You is not necessarily an I . . .

[69.] Deleted from *SC-A*: We must acknowledge outright that this is the case.

[70.] Deleted from *SC-A*: Only later in the work when we come to the problem of the concept of the church can we explain the significance of these last sentences.

[71.] Deleted from *SC-A*: As far as empirical community is concerned, however, we will have to describe its inner brokenness later on.

219 [72.] *SC-RS*: "This section seems inconsistent with the author's definite presuppositions. The question cannot be answered in terms of 'addressing' and 'answering'. This is insufficient and unclear. At issue is the matter of personal identity despite personal resistance, so that dedication to the defining will results in dedication to the intentions of that will. This might lead to the discovery of what portion of the person is divine and what portion human." [On Seeberg's comment, see above, page 49, editorial note 53.]

[73.] Deleted from *SC-A*: to Christianity.

[74.] Deleted from *SC-A*: That is, the person can be present but need not be; in demonstrating the essential distinctness of being between the divine and the human, it should be added . . .

[75.] Deleted from *SC-A*: If the I nevertheless arises in relation to the concrete human You, there must be another factor we have not yet considered. In Christian terms that means: . . .

through God's active working does the other become a You to me from whom my I arises. In other words, every human You is an image of the divine You.[76] You-character is in fact the essential form in which the divine is experienced; every human You bears its You-character only by virtue of the divine. This is not to say that it is a borrowed attribute of God, and not really a You. Rather, the divine You creates the human You. And since the human You is created and willed by God, it is a *real, absolute, and holy You,* like the divine You. One might then speak here of the human being as the image of God with respect to the effect one person has on another (cf. the later discussion of the problem of community of spirit [Geistgemeinschaft] and how one person becomes Christ for the other). Since, however, one person's becoming You for an other fundamentally alters nothing about the You as person, that person as I is not holy; what is holy is the You of God, the absolute will, who here becomes visible in the concrete You of social life. The other person is only a 'You' insofar as God brings it about. But God can make every human being a You for us. *The claim of the other rests in God alone; for this very reason, it remains the claim of the other.*[77]

In summary, *the person is*[78] *willed by God, in concrete vitality, wholeness, and uniqueness as an ultimate unity. Social relations must be understood, then, as purely interpersonal and building on the uniqueness and separateness of persons.* The person cannot be overcome by apersonal spirit; no 'unity' can negate the plurality of persons. *The social basic category is the I-You-relation. The You of the other person is the divine You.* Thus the way to   34 the other person's You is the same as the way to the divine You, either through acknowledgment or rejection. *The individual becomes a person*

[76.] Deleted from *SC-A*: in the reality of our lives. On Bonhoeffer's grounding of the I-You-relation in the relation to God, cf. Hirsch, *Die idealistische Philosophie,* 78ff. For Hirsch the encounter with God, out of which faith is born and all genuine personality and community arises, takes place in the realm of conscience. Bonhoeffer departs from Hirsch in this respect.

[77.] Deleted from *SC-A*:

Just as human beings cannot act without God, should we assume that God cannot act without human beings? Obviously, human beings cannot be seen as prerequisite to God's action. On the one hand, it is a *Christian insight that God uses the social nature of human beings in order to act among them in every respect.* God acts in history; thus God's claim is mediated for us, essentially and primarily, by other people, and is bound to sociality. In concluding this reflection on the Christian concept of person we have arrived at an understanding of the profound relationship between God and community as regards the individual:

The following 'summary' is not included in *SC-A*.

[78.] Deleted from *SC-A*: purely as such, as a creature of God . . .

ever and again through the other, in the 'moment'. The other person presents us with the same challenge to our knowing as does God. My real
relationship to another person is oriented to my relationship to God.
*But since I know God's 'I' only in the revelation of God's love, so too with the
other person; here the concept of the church comes into play.* Then it will
become clear that the Christian person achieves his or her essential
nature only when God does not encounter the person as *You,* but *'enters
into'*[79] *the person as I.*

Consequently,[80] in some way the individual belongs essentially and
absolutely with the other, according to God's will, even though, or precisely because, the one is completely separate from the other.[12] [82]

35   One could object, finally, that our argument has not come to grips
with the real problem of idealism since (1) we did not inquire about the
essence of the person as did idealism, but appeared to digress to the
other question about the origin of the person; and since (2) when discussing content we were quite one-sidedly oriented toward the ethical
and ignored the 'human spirit' [Geistigkeit] that was at issue in idealism, as if it were not part of the person. To (1) we reply that it is no coincidence that we were led from the problem of the essence of the person

---

12. With this conclusion, one cannot help but recall certain ideas of Fichte,
the only idealist philosopher who sensed the inadequacy of idealist categories
for solving the problem of the 'other'. In connection with the quest for a synthesis of the world of spirits [Geisterwelt] (see above, pages 24f., footnote 8), Fichte
concludes that persons cannot exist at all without others to spark their personhood. Thus the realm of persons is closely tied together through this law of the
'encounter'; one person is unthinkable without the other. And yet there is a
decisive difference between Fichte's theory and that just presented. Fichte says,
"The concept of the You arises through unification of 'it' and 'I'" (Fichte's
Werke, ed. Medicus, 3:86. Cf. Hirsch, [*Die idealistische Philosophie,*] 236ff.). He
has thus most clearly articulated that he does not recognize a nonsynthetic,
original You-concept. For him, the You is identical to the other I and at the same
time exists in object form. I rejected both of these notions above.

[79.] Replaces in *SC-A*: moves in. The following paragraph from *SC-A* is deleted:

But where, from the outset, the I-You-relation to God is obscured in a mystical unity, this
obscurity is repeated in the social basic-relation as well, where the souls of individuals melt
into a 'cosmic soul'. For this reason, Christian mysticism seems to me at best to be useful
as a historical concept, but not in theology.

[80.] "Consequently" replaces the following in *SC-A*: Thus we have found this to be an
important result of the inquiry.

to that of the origin of the person. Indeed, the Christian person alone exists in ever renewed coming-into-being. To (2) we reply that human 'spirit' with its moral and religious capacities is certainly an indispensable presupposition in order for the ethical person to come to be. This assertion has already been made above and will be elaborated further in discussing the doctrine of the primal state in the next chapter.

What follows is thus to be seen as presupposed by the preceding argument.[83]

The other thinker who attempted to grasp reality concretely in his notion of the person is Kierkegaard. Our argument is close to his in its critique of the idealist concept of time and reality. I depart from Kierkegaard, however, where he speaks of the origin of the ethical person. For him, becoming a person is an act of the self-establishing I—to be sure in a state of ethical decision. Kierkegaard's ethical person, too, exists only in the concrete situation, but his is not in any necessary relation to a concrete You. His person is self-established rather than being established by the You. In the last analysis, then, Kierkegaard remained bound to the idealist position. Thus he lays the foundation for an extreme sort of individualism in which the significance of the other for the individual is no longer absolute but only relative (see below, on the sociology of pastoral care).[81]

[81.] Deleted from *SC-A*:

There is a philosophical method behind the Christian-ethical concept of basic-relation that we have indicated. If we look at this method from the perspective of a monolinear versus multilinear concept of truth, all of idealist philosophy must be classified with the former approach. From the viewpoint of intellectual intuition, whereby the individual is conceived as possessing universal spirit, a multilinear concept of truth is unthinkable. The first point at which the latter enters into the picture is when the person can be seen as connected with the other and as value-related, not value-filled, by virtue of this connection. Socrates was the first to do so. Truth is sought in the dialogue of two persons through question and answer and is possessed by neither (see below, "Sociology of the Sermon," [pages 237ff.]). Without the other a person has no value-relation. Only when one is contradicted by an other does one recognize the limits of individual insight, thus experiencing the ethical barrier in the intellectual realm. It is well known that idealist philosophy since Plato taught that the value of one person is independent of the other.

220

On Bonhoeffer's critique of Fichte, cf. Fichte, *Zweite Einleitung in die Wissenschaftslehre* (1797) in his *Werke*, 1:502. The quotation is cited from Hirsch, *Die idealistische Philosophie*, 241, note 1. In his copy Bonhoeffer marked Hirsch's comment: "The point at which my fundamental critique of Fichte begins" (ibid.). On Kierkegaard's critique of the idealist concept of time and reality, cf. *The Concept of Anxiety*, chap. 3, 81ff.; cf. also Heinrich Barth, "Kierkegaard der Denker," 104ff.; and Litt, *Individuum*, 206ff. and 207, note 1.

[82.] In *SC-A* the current footnote 12 follows in the body of the text.

[83.] The last sentence is not found in *SC-A*.

CHAPTER THREE

THE PRIMAL STATE AND THE PROBLEM OF COMMUNITY

A. Methodological Problems[1]

THE DOCTRINE of the primal state cannot offer us new theological insights. In the logic of theology as a whole it belongs with eschatology.

[1.] In *SC-B,* section A of this chapter (up to "theological character" on page 65) is the result of revisions made in Bonhoeffer's handwriting. *NL* A 17,1 contains a four-page manuscript draft that corresponds almost verbatim to this section. The original wording in *SC-A* is as follows:

The Primal State and the Problem of Community
A. Introductory Note
The doctrine of the primal state conveys three main groups of ideas. First, we shall describe the real community of God and human beings in statu integritatis [in the state of integrity] in contrast to the ethical-ontic basic-relations discussed in the previous chapter. This divine-human community is built upon individual persons endowed with spirit. Second, we will deal with the general relationship between human spirit and sociality. Third, we will investigate the essential social forms. The task here is thus divided into theological, social-philosophical, and sociological parts. While the first section will show the original image of the church before the fall, the second and third yield the criteria for understanding the sociological problem of the church. Of course, before we break through to the concept of community appropriate to the church, the primal community must be torn apart by sin and totally new ontic basic-relations must take over. [*SC-RS*: "You must clarify the meaning of 'primal state' as it is used here and how it relates to the rest of the discussion!"] These were presented partially in the previous chapter, but only to the extent that they are not directly related to the evil will and are thus still a reality in the community of the church [kirchliche Gemeinschaft]. We will then demonstrate that there are specific implications for community inherent in the concept of sin, that these are only overcome by the revelation in Christ, and yet that they still are effective in the church. *The concept of Christian community proves to be defined by an inner history.* It cannot be understood 'in itself', but only in a historical dialectic. The concept is split within itself; its inner history can be seen in the *concepts of primal state, sin, and revelation,* all of which can be fully understood only when seen as intending community. It is thus impossible to present the concept of the church without

221

Every aspect helpful to its comprehension is imparted through revelation. Nothing about it can be ascertained by pure speculation. It cannot

---

[1. *cont.*] moving it into the context of this inner dialectical history. It belongs to the essence of the church that it still bears the community of sin within itself, and is real only in constantly overcoming it.

B. The Theological Problem: The Original Community

The theological doctrine of the primal state may serve only one purpose, to articulate theological ideas about the human spirit in its original state of integrity. In fact, the only thing of interest here is the question about the religious and moral nature of humanity in its original state. If we conceive human beings as spirit, created by God, and free, then we must connect this idea with the other, namely that God created human beings in direct relation to God's own self, as oriented toward God. There should be no objection if we call this freely affirmed direction by the terms morality and religion. As a being who is created spirit, and free, the person can now be defined as the unity of self-conscious and spontaneously active spirit. <<Cf. *Christliche Dogmatik*, Reinhold Seeberg, 1:484.>> We will call this concept of person the general-metaphysical concept of spirit [allgemein-geistig-metaphysische], in contrast to the ethical one. Here, too, the person is obviously understood as a structural unity, so that no merging of the structural units is possible in sociality. We already discovered above that the person is intended by God as an ultimate unity, purely as a concrete person, absolutely unique and distinct from other persons, a creature of God. To this we can add that the metaphysical concept of person is 'structurally closed', so that we can in fact come to a pure concept of person and to an understanding of sociality as founded purely in persons. Answering the question of how sociality and person relate to each other, then, is the chief task of the social-philosophical section. But the reason why we could not define the person only in the general sense of spirit is that this definition, while necessary, is insufficient. As mentioned before, the whole preceding argument really has presupposed the person in the sense of this definition. Yet this does not make it sufficient, because in its formal generality it encompasses the primal [urständlichen], the natural, the sinful, and also the redeemed human being; that is, it is insufficient, because this definition is irrelevant from a Christian point of view and thus does not enter into the sphere of reality at all. It raises humanity above the animal world and makes it clear that human beings are not to be considered as mere 'trunks'. [By using the Latin *truncus* Bonhoeffer means that beings lacking the consciousness and free will of the human spirit would be truncated—like a headless torso, or trunk.][CG] But this definition is justified only when delimited by the Christian—and real—concept of person. It was our intention to present the concept of person that is valid within history, i.e., the situation after the fall. This intention is justified in two respects, in that (1) for us history in the proper sense only begins with sin, since we intrinsically associate the fact of mortality, which makes 'history' possible for us in the first place, with sin; and in that (2) the central issue of our study is the question of real Christian community, which cannot be grasped adequately by the concept of person just mentioned, but only on the basis of a concept of person defined by Christian content. In all of idealism there is no rupture between the primal state and the fall, and certainly nothing about the significance of such a rupture for the concepts of person and community. The fundamental difference between our position and that of idealism is this knowledge of the inner history of the concept of person in the move from the primal state to sin—in other words, the weight that we give to sin as having real and qualitative character when connected to

222

speak of the essence of human being, of nature, or of history in general terms, but only in the context of revelation that has been heard. The

[1. *cont.*] history. *For idealism, origin and telos remain in unbroken connection and are brought to synthesis in the concept of 'essence'.* Nothing in between—sin, on the one hand, and Christ, on the other—can essentially break this eternal, necessary connection. <<Hegel also seems to me to be no exception here.>> Such a view of history as an unbroken straight line basically eliminates everything specifically Christian. In this view, neither sin nor redemption alters the essence of history.

To return to the point, if one understands the metaphysical concept of the person as fulfilled by positive Christian content, that is, as oriented toward God, the result is the *concept of person in the primal state*. Is there, then, some intention toward a concept of community inherent in this concept of person? Doubtless, the person in the primal state must be understood as serving God in direct community, as is articulated in Genesis 1 and 2. It will become quite clear only when we reach the concept of the church that this unmediated community is qualitatively different and essentially more than the ontic I-You-relation. Let it be said here, at least, that community is the real bond of love between I and I. Inherent in the Christian concept of God that we know through revelation in Christ, but ultimately through Christ's church-community, is that community with God and social community belong together—another statement that will only be substantiated later. Thus we are saying that direct community with God also demands direct human community, that the latter is absolutely necessary as the corollary to community with God, and that it is no coincidence that Genesis 2:18 reads: "It is not good that the human being [Mensch] should be alone." [The *NRSV* reads: "It is not good that the man should be alone." See Bonhoeffer's theological exegesis of Genesis 1–3 in *CF* (*DBWE* 3), especially his understanding of *analogia relationis* as interpreting the *imago Dei*.][CG] Direct community with God is documented in direct human community. But what is meant by direct or unmediated community? To be in community with God obviously means, first of all, the absolute identity of purpose of the divine and human wills, within the relation of the creative to the created (i.e., obedient) will—in other words, in the relation of ruling and serving. The ideas of the community of love and the bond of authentic rule [Herrschaftsverbundenheit] merge here in archetypical anticipation of the distinction between the concepts of God's Realm and God's rule. [The word *Herrschaft* (as in *Herrschaftsverbundenheit, Herrschaftsverhältnis* and *Herrschaftsverband*) literally means "lordship" and conveys the meaning of rule. It is important to note that Bonhoeffer recognized the ambiguity of this term, and immediately defined it theologically in terms of God's love, which rules by serving. *Herrschaftsverband*, one of Bonhoeffer's sociological terms for the church, is therefore translated "association of authentic rule," to distinguish God's rule from the common mode of ruling power in the world—as is done in Mark 10:42-45.][CG] Of course, in religious terms this community is built on unmediated mutual love. But because love rules by serving, the problem of the pure 'association of authentic rule' [Herrschaftsverband] becomes more complicated; by absolute service, God rules absolutely over humanity. Insofar as God establishes this law of life for community, however, human beings serve God by fulfilling it absolutely; thus God rules over humanity. Among human beings, therefore, unmediated love must assume other forms, for here the absolute rule of a creative will over a created will disappears, and mutual service is service in common, together under the rule of God. However, since every person is created with a uniquely individual character, tension between wills cannot be avoided even in the community of love. With this concession we already recognize that

223

doctrine of the primal state is hope projected backward. Its value is twofold. It forces the methodological clarification of the structure of

[1. *cont.*] strife as such is by no means a result of the fall but arises from a common love of God. The will of every individual strives to attain the single goal of serving the divine will, that is, serving the community in its own way. Let this statement suffice for now. In the discussion of the concept of the church we will be able to set out the abundance of these interrelationships. Finally, all that has been said above is possible only because we know about the church of Jesus Christ. Thus, following the logic of a system of theology, the origin of what has just been said is to be found in the concept of the church. Within the logic of the doctrine of the primal state, however, it emerged as a necessary consequence of the moral-religious inclination of human beings toward God.

To supplement these conclusions we will attempt to offer a biblical-*exegetical proof.* This, to be sure, must not be seen as the source of the insight just described, which ultimately comes from the revelation in Christ and would be valid whether or not the exegesis proved justified.

Certainly, the main interest in the Genesis 1–3 narrative is focused on Adam's individual primal perfection. Nevertheless, we are also confident to find traits in him that can be said to point to the social basic-relations of the primal state—that is, Adam is created as the crown of creation. He is ruler of the animals and all created things. But he does not attain the full development of his spirit. Thus, woman is created to be his companion, for "it is not good that the human being should be alone." Only indirectly, through the fall, do we learn anything about the nature of community. Woman is seduced by the serpent, and man by woman, into disobedience. Scarcely has the conscious step into the act of disobedience been taken when man and woman recognize their sexual difference and are ashamed before one another. A rupture appears in their formerly unbroken, childlike community of obedience and unknowing. [On the 'innocence' and 'unknowing' of humanity before the fall, see *CF* (*DBWE* 3): 84–87.][CG] Losing unmediated community with God, they also lose unmediated human community. Between the human being and God, as between human beings, the divisive power of sin has stepped in. Later this is symbolized in the medieval representation of the fall. In the center is the tree with the serpent coiled around it, man and woman on either side, separated by the tree whose fruit they ate in disobedience. The narrator's view of sexuality as the divisive power coming between human beings later had a devastating effect on the doctrine of original sin. For our present purposes this is not significant. The important thing is *that the narrator leaves no doubt at all about the fact of separation, whatever its nature, through the fall into sin. Through the ethical act of rebellion against God's rule, the original community between God and humanity, as well as that among human beings, is lost.* And this separation is not negated in the next sentence, "The two will be one flesh." [The *NRSV* reads "they become one flesh." Bonhoeffer, with a different word order, but the same sense as Luther, says "be," which has a stronger quality than the English "become."][NL/CG] Rather, what we see here is the extremely complex dialectic of human community (more about this later). Community with God and human community are thus somehow thought by the narrator as essentially belonging together. *Since this community is destroyed by ethical violation, obviously its character is originally ethical, and the narrator considers community as belonging to being created in the image of God.* Suffice it to say that divine community and human community belong in some way to the original, ethical life of the human spirit. But this means, further, that they also are part of the future destiny of humanity, consistent with the parallelism of Adam and Christ, primal state and eschaton. This brings us to the church. [The material in footnote 1 on page 64 occupies the

224

theology as a whole; then it renders concrete and vivid the real course of things from unity through break to unity.

Thus the concepts of person and community, for example, are understood only within an intrinsically broken history, as conveyed in the concepts of primal state, sin, and reconciliation. Neither concept can be understood theologically 'in itself', but only within a real historical dialectic[2]—not a dialectic of concepts. In this respect we differ fundamentally from idealism, for which origin and telos stand in real, unbroken connection, the synthesis of which is expressed in the concept of 'essence'. There, sin and salvation are realities that do not alter the original essence of things. For us, though, the doctrine of the primal state is significant precisely because it enables us to grasp concretely the reality of sin, which infinitely alters the essence of things.

If the revelation in Christ speaks of the will of God to create from the old humanity of Adam a new humanity of Christ, i.e., the church, and if I know myself to be incorporated into this church of Christ, then it follows that we should project the idea of unbroken community with God and with human beings back to the doctrine of the primal state as well. This explains why we cannot essentially go further than what is said in teaching about the church, for example. But within the logic of the doctrine of the primal state itself, the doctrine of original community will be developed on its own terms, again just as an example.

Human beings, called by revelation to hear, know they are meant to be active centers of intellect and will.[3] This is the formal presupposi-

[1. cont.] position given in the published version; in *SC-A* it was originally located at this point.]

This brings us back to the second problem in the doctrine of the primal state, the basic question of the connection between primal, created spirit and sociality as such. No longer do we focus on the Christian-ethical fulfillment of empirical community, but rather on the meaning of the sentence that it is not good for the human being to be alone, the meaning of the creation of woman, i.e., of life in sociality. We will find that all Christian-ethical content as well as all aspects of the human spirit are only real and possible at all through sociality. Not only does this perspective give us a deeper understanding of the concepts of sin and the church, but it will pave the way for a Christian appraisal of community life.

[2.] In referring to 'real dialectic', Bonhoeffer is picking up on a concept of Grisebach that contains a critique of idealist philosophy's formal dialectic as alien to reality. 'Real dialectic' means the existential confrontation of one human being with the claims of another; cf. Grisebach, *Die Grenzen des Erziehers*, vii ff. and 275ff.

[3.] 'Will' is a key category in Bonhoeffer's theological anthropology and also in his typology of social forms. By speaking of human beings as 'willing' subjects or spirits, his emphasis is not primarily on behavior as 'voluntary', that is, uncoerced, but on decisions

tion for what has been said about the Christian concept of person and what will be said about the concept of person in the primal state.[4] At the same time it is obvious that to understand a person as nothing more than such a center of acts is inadequate, because from a Christian-ethical, that is to say social, point of view it is irrelevant and thus does not touch the sphere of reality at all. Thus this formal and general metaphysical concept of person must be thought of as having a different kind of fulfillment and purpose. The Christian concept of person should be thought of historically, i.e., in the state after the fall, for history in the true sense only begins with sin and the fate of death that is linked with it. From this it follows that the concept of person in the primal state must be understood differently, corresponding to the idea of the new humanity which, in hope, overcomes the history of sin and death. The formal and general concept of person should be thought of as fulfilled by positive Christian content, i.e., established by God and oriented toward God. Willing and thinking come from God and go toward God; that is to say, community with God is completed in love and truth. The miracle of the Christian concept of community is that love for God involves submission, but that God's love, in ruling, serves.

Community with God by definition establishes social community as well. It is not that community with God subsequently leads to social community; rather, neither exists without the other. In the following we will show that even the formal concept of person can be conceived only in terms of community. Thus unbroken social community belongs to primal being [urständliches Sein], in parallel to the eschatological hope we have for it in the church. This is expressed clearly, if only indirectly,   38 in the Genesis narrative. With their act of disobedience against God, human beings realize their sexual difference and are ashamed before one another. A rupture has come into the unbroken community. Losing direct community with God, they also lose—by definition—unmediated human community. A third power, sin, has stepped between human beings and God, as between human beings themselves. Later this is symbolized in the medieval representation of the fall. In the center is the

---

[3. *cont.*] that are intentional, purposeful, and responsible. This role of will is what he means when speaking of 'voluntarism'. See above, page 19. [CG]

[4.] On 'formal presupposition', cf. Seeberg, *Dogmatik*, 1:101ff. According to Seeberg, human beings possess a formal capacity that enables them to perceive the divine will. Only revelation, however, gives content to this formal capacity.

tree with the serpent coiled around it, man and woman on either side, separated by the tree whose fruit they ate in disobedience.[1]

Thus we have sketched the archetype of the church. While the theological problem presents little difficulty, *the methodological issues become more complicated by relating social philosophy and sociology* to the doctrine of the primal state. Here, too, it cannot be a matter of developing specu-

---

1. It has always been recognized that humanity in its primal state must be conceived as in community with God. But very little attention has been paid to the fact that this community and social community belong together.[5] In speaking of the church in Adam's time, writers were in no way thinking of any sort of relationship in community, but only of the preaching of God's word already at the beginning of human history, in the sense of Augustine's sentence, for example: "ecclesia, quae civitas dei est . . . cuius ab initio generis humani non defuit praedicatio ("[Christ's] church, which is the city of God, proclaimed from the very beginning of human history. . . .") (*De Civitate Dei*, 16, 2).[6] To my knowledge, Schleiermacher was the first to speak of relationships in community in the primal state (*The Christian Faith*, §60.2, 246). Of course, even he only goes so far as to say that original human perfection includes "the intimate union of self-consciousness with species consciousness."[7] This is intended to ensure the possibility of mutual communication, of religious relationship in community; for only in species consciousness does one human being encounter another. If this were not present, people could never enter into relationship in community. But this relationship must be an original given, since apart from community "there is no living and vigorous piety" [trans. altered]. This idea was lost in later years, however.[8] As far as I can tell, Reinhold Seeberg, in his doctrine of humanity and created spirit (*Dogmatik* 1, sec. 22,1), was the first to present the idea of sociality as an inherent component of original human nature. He thereby brought back into theology an important doctrine without which the ideas of original sin and especially the church could not be fully understood.[9]

---

225   [5.] Deleted in *SC-A*: There has always been reflection about justice, sanctity, piety, and even intelligence and science [Wissenschaft] in the case of Adam. But for a long time no thought at all has been given to the fact that these concepts belong together with that of social community.

   [6.] Augustine, *The City of God*, Bk. 16, chap. 2, 523.

   [7.] Bonhoeffer's quotation from *The Christian Faith*, §60.2, 246, is not exact. Schleiermacher wrote "die innige Vereinigung des Gattungsbewusstseins mit dem persönlichen Selbstbewusstsein" ("the inner union of species-consciousness and personal self-consciousness")[trans. altered]. [CG]

   [8.] Footnote deleted in *SC-A*: <<When von Hofmann sees the creation of woman as the beginning of salvation history, it is not the idea of community that leads him to this conclusion, but only his interest in the origins of humanity.>> Cf. von Hofmann, *Der Schriftbeweis*, 1:404ff.

   [9.] This footnote was in the text in *SC-A* in the position indicated above on pages 61–62, editorial note 1. [CG]

lative theories about the possibility of social being in the primal state not affected by evil will. Instead, methodologically, all statements are possible only on the basis of our understanding of the church, i.e., from the revelation we have heard.[10] Thus social-philosophical and sociological problems can be dealt with in the context of theology not because they can be proved generally necessary on the basis of creation, but because they are presupposed and included in revelation. Only in this perspective can they be fully understood. Of course here, too, the reversed logic of the theological system applies to the description of what is known, in that the concept of the church only appears to emerge out of the amalgam of issues worked out in the doctrine of the primal state. This view of theological method must be kept in mind throughout the study, in order to maintain its theological character.

B. The Social-Philosophical Problem: Human Spirit and Sociality

The social-philosophical problem in this section is the relation between human spirit and sociality per se.[11] It will be demonstrated that human beings, as spirit, are necessarily created in a community—that human spirit in general is woven into the web of sociality. Such knowledge is very important for our argument because it clarifies fundamentally the problematic relationship of individual and community. This knowledge gives us the correct perspective for our typology of community. Ultimately, both are necessary to clarify the problem of religious community and the church.

1. Personal Being as Structurally Open[12]

First, as a matter of principle, when in the following we speak of 'I' and 'You' and their relations, it is in a fundamentally different sense from

---

[10.] In his theological interpretation of Genesis 1–3, Bonhoeffer similarly argues that "only the church, which knows of the end, knows also of the beginning. . . . It views the creation from Christ." See *CF (DBWE 3)*: 22. [CG]

[11.] The structure of this section follows the methodology and content of Seeberg, *Dogmatik*, 1:505ff. For other examples of Bonhoeffer's dependence on Seeberg's outline, see below, page 67, editorial note 18.

[12.] The following paragraph is lacking in *SC-A*, up to "foregoing and following argument."

39

the second chapter.[13] The I is not the person called upon by You and
40 only thereby awakened to become I; the You is not the unknowable,
impenetrable, alien other. On the contrary, we are in a different sphere
altogether. It will be shown that the whole nature of human spirit
[Geistigkeit],[14] which necessarily is presupposed by the Christian concept of person and has its unifying point in self-consciousness (of which
we will also be speaking in this context), is such that it is only conceivable in sociality. Though we must show that self-consciousness only
arises in relation to the other, one must not confuse this interaction
with the Christian I-You-relation. Not every self-conscious I knows of the
ethical barrier of the You. To be sure, it does know of an alien You—this
may even be the necessary presupposition for the ethical and real experience of the You. However, it does not know the You as an utterly alien
being, as pure claim, as erecting barriers. That is to say, it does not
know the You as real, but as irrelevant in the last analysis to the I itself.
The following, then, is to be understood in this sense, as the necessary
general account of human spirit that is the presupposition of the foregoing and following argument.

There is no distinctly human empirical social relation *unless there
exists a community appropriate to its essence*; thus,[15] the typology of social
forms must also be grounded fundamentally in a phenomenology of
sociality established in spirit.[16] We will first inquire, therefore, not
about the person who exercises will in social relations but about the person as spirit and the integral tie of spirit to sociality.[17]

[13.] In his explanation of the I-You-relation Bonhoeffer is following Litt, *Individuum*,
140ff.

[14.] On human spirit, cf. Spann, *Gesellschaftslehre*, 88ff. Against that see Litt, *Individuum*, 257ff.

[15.] This first part of the sentence ("There is . . . thus,") replaces the following in *SC-A*:
The personal power of empirical-social formation is generally viewed as drive and will. Both lead
from the condition of empirical isolation to empirical social formation. We assert that no specifically human empirical social formation (here "specifically human" is decisive) apart from a community appropriate to its essence, that . . .

[16.] Deleted in *SC-A*:

Because within formal sociology this preliminary investigation was always lumped together
with the phenomenological consideration of sociological 'forms', there arose such inconsistent descriptions, as briefly shown above in the discussion of the doctrine of relation. Metaphysical atomism was taught unconsciously mixed up with empirical connectionism. We
must break with this inconsistency.

[17.] Deleted in *SC-A*: First we will offer the following statement of definition:

In terms of its form, spirit in a person is *the bond of self-consciousness and self-determination that documents its structural unity;* this spirit can be *formally defined as the principle of receptivity and activity.* In terms of its function, spirit is effective in acts of thinking, self-conscious willing, and feeling.[2] [18] We can conceive of these acts only as based upon human sociality; they arise simultaneously from, with, and in such sociality.   41 Thus, the first section *deals with the structural 'openness' of personal unity to sociality, while the second attempts to present the structural 'closedness' of personal being.*[19] *From this argument the basic-relation of person and community should become clear.*[3]

---

2. I use this outdated distinction for the sake of simplicity. It is not the issue.

3. In order to avoid misunderstandings from the outset, we offer several pairs of concepts that must be strictly distinguished and that are essential for understanding the argument: *structure and intention.*[20] The structure of the whole certainly only becomes visible in the individual intentions to action, but in principle it is independent of them. Thus the structural openness of the person is not modified by 'intimate' intentions (to adopt Scheler's term), and vice versa; i.e., structural unity does not diminish social intentions. Likewise one must distinguish between all acts that are real only within sociality, and the will to community. Such acts are acts only in consequence of will and thought, to be sure. Will, however, does not intend community as its content; rather the intention of the act bears this indirect relation to community structurally within itself. Similarly, an intimate intention does not lead one out of the structural community. The will to community, though, leads to concrete formation of ontic basic-relations; the willing of the self leads to empirical solitude. As stated above, the essential structure that becomes visible in the intentions to action is not altered thereby. That is, these distinctions basically reflect two different concepts of community. The first is purely ontological, the other empirical. It is unfortunate

[18.] On spirit's function, *materiale Geistigkeit,* and acts, cf. Scheler, *Formalism in Ethics,* 382ff. On receptivity and activity of human beings, cf. also Seeberg, *Dogmatik,* 1:209ff. [Bonhoeffer's footnote 2 mentions an "outdated distinction" he uses between *materielle* and *materiale Geistigkeit.* The former refers to what something is made up of, the latter to how it operates. We have translated these terms with "form" and "function" respectively, without thereby invoking—any more than did Bonhoeffer himself—any particular philosophical position.][NL/CG]

[19.] By 'open' Bonhoeffer means the capacity and necessity of a person to participate in sociality with others. 'Closed' refers to the unity, integrity, and irreducibility of the person; it indicates the otherness of the other, guarding against the totalization of idealist thinking. 'Openness' does not mean merged into a supra-individual unity, nor does 'closedness' mean shut off from interaction with other persons. [CG]

[20.] On the distinction between structure and intention, see Litt, *Individuum,* 213ff., as well as Scheler, *Formalism in Ethics,* 561ff.

People find themselves immersed in an infinite richness of possibilities for expression and understanding.[21] Before humanity was aware of it, a stream of spirit entered into millions of veins, and one can only notice it when standing in the middle of the stream.[22]

People know that they *understand, express themselves, and are understood.* These three experiences belong together and at least potentially are involved in every intellectual act; thus all intellectual acts are potentially bound up with sociality. In emotional life, too, where people believe they are most alone, there is a certainty that one is capable of expressing what is felt—perhaps not completely, but to a certain extent, with which the limit of any expression is given. But at the same time this means one also can be understood, and thus can understand the feelings of others. Sociality, therefore, is relevant here as well.[23]

To identify what we are talking about, one is tempted to return to the concept of basic-relations [Grundbeziehungen] and its complement, the concept of interaction [Wechselwirkung]. The danger, however, would be to confuse these terms with empiricist theories. *Only in reciprocal*

42

---

that our terminology does not have two distinct words for these concepts. Later, community [Gemeinschaft] will be given yet a third meaning as a particular social type, not as a general term for all empirical community formation. The respective meanings will be clear in each context. These distinctions must always be kept in mind, or the following might easily be misunderstood.

[21.] Deleted in *SC-A*:

People are like glass spheres that reflect the world around them; they can take everything in, and can express everything colored by their own individuality. No matter how much such a being wills to be self-contained, it remains a glass sphere that is penetrated by everything; thus it belongs to its essence to be connected with its entire environment. Such are human beings. Without willing it, things flow in countless streams and the senses receive them. No matter how little a person might want to see, it is the eyes that see, not the person; much as one might like to avoid tactile sensations, they cannot be controlled.

[22.] Deleted in *SC-A*: One naturally thinks here of Leibniz's theory of monads, with which the social philosophy being presented is closely connected.

[23.] Deleted in *SC-A*:

The nuances of expression are uncommonly sophisticated here, and yet nonetheless understandable. A nervous playing of the fingers, a slightly twisted mouth, a scarcely perceptible frown, or a word spoken with only slightly less emphasis is seen and understood immediately by one who is paying attention to meaning and who wants to understand. Gesture, tone, facial expression, and movement are used with instinctive confidence, along with language, the system of expressive possibilities that objectively allows the finest distinctions.

226

interaction with other minds is self-conscious thinking and willing possible and meaningful. This assertion must be made more certain. First of all, the *social phenomenon of language* is so closely related to thought that one may surely say that it is chiefly language that renders thought possible—hence the ordering of language before thought, and word before spirit (Hamann).[4] [25]

Language combines the *objective intention of meaning* with its attendant *subjective emotion*, ultimately enabling empirical objectification and consolidation by sound and writing. By objectifying and consolidating, spirit both acknowledges and overcomes nature through language. This affirmation of nature (i.e., the sensual realm), which alone makes communication possible between persons (see below, pages 285f., on the 'new body'), does not mean that nature constitutes the social character of expression and signification. Nature, rather, is the material that spirit forms and thus makes objectively and subjectively fruitful; the social intention of spirit, of course, is taken for granted. Spirit and nature are so closely connected that spirit is no longer conceivable without nature, nor human nature without social spirit. The phenomenon of language would be meaningless, however, were not the understand-

43

---

4. [Wilhelm von] Humboldt, too, was able to write similarly. Cf., for example, L[ouis] G[abriel] A[mbroise] de Bonald, *Essai analytique sur les lois naturelles de l'ordre social; ou, du pouvoir, du ministère et du sujet dans la société*, pseudonymously, 1800; 2d ed. 1817. P[ierre] S[imon] Ballanche, *Essai sur les institutions sociales*, 1818. De Bonald and Ballanche develop very fanciful ideas about original community and its disintegration in contemporary society. Following the traditionalist line, they teach ideas about universal reason that are reminiscent of Hegel's idea of objective spirit and lead to a glorification of the *church*.[24]

[24.] Bonhoeffer's information is largely derived from Windelband, *History of Philosophy*, 2:527f., 575f., 601f., and 648ff. Cf. Hamann, "Zwo Recensionen," in *Sämtliche Werke*, 3:13ff., and his *Schriften zur Sprache*; see also Wilhelm von Humboldt, *Schriften zur Sprachphilosophie*.

[25.] Deleted in *SC-A*:

This was taken farther with the assertion—as found in Süssmilch, de Bonald, and Ballanche—that language is a gift of God to all of humanity <<Süssmilch, *Beweis daß der Ursprung der menschlichen Sprache göttlich sei*, 1766.>> [For de Bonald and Ballanche, see above, footnote 4.] This of course only made sense insofar as Condillac's idea of the invention of language by a human being was rejected. Decisive was the insight that language, in its origin and purpose, was not intended for individuals, but that it created a totally new realm of spirit for the genus humanum [human species], and that language embraced all human sociality.

ing of the listener or reader potentially correlated to each word.[5] [27] Thus, with language, a *system of social spirit* has been built into human beings; in other words, '*objective spirit' has become effective in history*.[28]

Will at this point must not be understood as the will to community, but in a purely phenomenological-structural sense, lest grave misunderstandings result.[29]

In contrast to instinct, will is the unified activation of self-determination and self-consciousness. Will is always self-conscious; that is to say, when initiating purposeful acts I do so as a unified center of activity. We intend to demonstrate that such acts, characteristic of the individual, are possible and real only in sociality. It is our view that *there would be no self-consciousness without community–or better, that self-consciousness arises concurrently with the consciousness of existing in community. Second, we assert that will is by its nature oriented toward other wills.* The first problem has been raised frequently in modern philosophy and, we believe, essentially solved by Paul Natorp.[6] [31] How and when self-consciousness

---

5. Cf. Edmund Husserl, *Logical Investigations*, 675, "Meaning-Intention and Meaning Fulfilment." Hans Freyer, *Theorie des objektiven Geistes*, 1923, 51.[26] Fr[itz] Mauthner, *Die Sprache* vol. 9 of M[artin] Buber ed., *Gesellschaft*.

6. Cf. *Sozialpädagogik*, 1904, 2d ed., 83ff. I find that Natorp in his long and fundamental introductory chapters has gone beyond his neo-Kantian schema. Especially in the paragraphs about the three stages of will, he delves deep into a phenomenology of will and of social being in general.[30]

[26.] Footnote deleted in *SC-A*: <<Eduard Spranger, *Zur Theorie des Verstehens*.>>

[27.] Deleted in *SC-A*: Such a corollary is necessary already in primitive expressive gestures (of threatening, waving, greeting). <<In fact, the capacity to understand mimetic movement and expression is developed even by the smallest child in the first months.>>

[28.] Deleted in *SC-A*:

Here we encounter for the first time the problem that will accompany us from here on, but will only be dealt with systematically at a later point. Let us review the three characteristics elaborated so far: the senses, emotional empathy, and empirical-natural objectification. Moreover, it is recognized that human beings cannot be thinking-beings without participating in this objective spirit, that is, that they would obviously lack a decisive ingredient of human spirit. We now show the same to be true with the problem of will.

Hans Freyer distinguishes five main forms of objective spirit, one of which is the formal type called 'sign', which includes language. See Freyer, *Theorie des objektiven Geistes*, 45ff. and 51ff.; cf. his reference to Husserl's theory of expressions in the same passage.

[29.] Deleted in *SC-A*: Our first impulse is to resist an ontic view of will, but in principle nothing stands in the way of such a view.

227   [30.] Natorp, *Sozialpädagogik*, 90: "There is no self-consciousness and there can be

begins *genetically* remains an unsolved puzzle, since of course by definition one cannot investigate one's own person in this regard. Thus we can only focus on correctly *interpreting* the fact of self-conscious spirit. This seems to be possible only within the sociality of spirit. Since I know myself as 'I', I lift myself as an individual above a vegetative condition of spirit in the community. At the same time, however, in this very act the essence of the 'You' jumps up to meet me, as the other spirit that is conscious of itself. One could turn this around and say that by recognizing a You, a being of alien consciousness, as separate and distinct from myself, I recognize myself as an 'I', and so my self-consciousness awakens.[7]

44

---

7. Scheler is certainly correct in referring to self-consciousness as a 'singularizing individual act'. But precisely this expresses the intention of the I to separate itself from the You and, at the same time, to enter into relation with the You. Scheler overlooks this fact, as Litt correctly criticized him for doing. The latter writes that the I, changing places, so to speak, with the You, learns 'to see itself with another's eyes', or better, that one could observe the I 'from the outside' as well. But this creates the danger of placing the experience of the You prior to self-consciousness. This would justifiably have to be called a contradic

---

[30. *cont.*] none without opposition and, at the same time, positive relationship to another consciousness." Cf. the same passage also on language.

[31.] Deleted in *SC-A*:

We described above the I-You-relation as a reflexive determination [Reflexionsbestimmung] that is relevant for the entire social sphere. When one moves beyond the concept of the individual to the I-concept of person, this is only possible in the social sphere, that is, where 'I' is conceived in relation to the 'other I', the 'You'. <<It is appropriate here to warn against confusing concepts. In discussing the Christian-ethical concept of person, we came upon the I-You-relation as the basic category of the social sphere. In connection with the latter, we also continued to investigate its basis in social philosophy, but then moved out of the ethical into the general-metaphysical approach. Thus the paradigm of the I-You-relation is given a different meaning here. Here, the 'I' does not signify the ethically addressed, but the self-conscious and self-determining, I. It should no longer be necessary to point out that this does not imply two contradictory concepts of person; rather, both are joined in the unity of the concrete, living I, insofar as one presupposes the other. With the ethical concept of person, the You and the other I had to be kept distinct, while here the two are joined. It is only about the other's being as a Christian person that I know nothing. As now will be shown, I do know about the other's personhood as a self-conscious and self-determining being, through or in connection with my own self-consciousness. The preceding casts no doubt upon the fact that people as individuals nevertheless are able to retreat again and again into themselves and into impenetrable darkness, that psychologically one person really only knows the other very partially, and finally, that there are limits to every person's possibilities for expression and thus also for understanding.>>

Above all it is important to see that the consciousness of being an I and the consciousness that there is a You arise together and from their interaction.[33] "Thus self-consciousness in particular, and hence self-conscious willing, are developed solely in and with the community of one consciousness and the other."[8] Thus the will, too, as actively arising from self-consciousness, is possible only in sociality. One more thing needs to be said. It is in the nature of the will as activity to function in community. Will comes into being where there is 'resistance'. However, resistance in the fullest sense of the word can only be that of another spirit's will. Where it is a matter of removing a natural barrier, it is not the will per se that experiences resistance, but the natural force (or the organizational force of the will). Will itself experiences resistance only in the will of a person who wills something different. Only in strife with other wills, in subjecting these to one's own will or being subjected, is strength and richness of will developed. Such conflict occurs on a small scale everywhere that people live in the community of the I-You-rela-
45   tion. For when a person encounters a person, a will meets a will, and each one wrestles to overcome the other. Only in such encounter does the will attain its essential nature.[34] Will as an isolated phenomenon is absurd. Again, we discover the fundamental significance of sociality for the human spirit.

---

tion. If I know that one can view me from the outside, then I must obviously already possess knowledge about 'myself'. Natorp, [*Sozialpädagogik,*] 90: "How could I become a You to myself, if there were not first a You facing me in which I recognize another I?" Cf. Scheler, [*Formalism in Ethics,*] 521f. Litt, *Individuum und Gemeinschaft,* 231ff.[32]

8. Natorp, [*Sozialpädagogik,*] 93. We cannot give a more detailed philosophical foundation here for the thesis above. Cf. the works of Natorp and Litt already mentioned.

[32.] Scheler, *Formalism in Ethics,* 521f., distinguishes "social acts" from "singularizing individual acts." By contrast, see Litt, *Individuum,* 232.

[33.] Deleted in *SC-A:*

Idealism's understanding, too, rests on this knowledge—and especially that of Fichte in his persistent striving for a synthesis of spirits. Idealism and Fichte sense that self-consciousness demands a You, and yet they do not attain this goal, because they do not think of the self and the You as interrelated from the outset.

[34.] Deleted in *SC-A:* satisfaction and fulfillment. Cf. Seeberg, *Dogmatik,* 1:507ff., and the definition of resistance in Scheler, *Formalism in Ethics,* 134f.

A brief look at human emotional life shows[35] that even here, in extreme isolation, there is a certain consciousness of the possibility of, and need for, expression—for being understood by others. Furthermore, it shows that there are certain acts of shared feeling, experience, rejoicing, etc., that orient the individual life to the emotions of others. But acts of pleasure, affection, and erotic love also are intentional-social acts.

In summary, *human spirit in its entirety is woven into sociality and rests on the basic-relation of I and You. "Only in interaction with one another is the spirit of human beings ever revealed; this is the essence of spirit, to be oneself through being in the other."*[9] In infinite closeness, in mutual penetration, I and You are joined together, inseparable from one another forever, resting in one another, intimately participating in one another, empathizing, sharing experiences, bearing together the general stream of interactions of spirit. *Here is where the openness of personal being becomes evident.* But the question arises, does it still make sense to speak of I and You, if all seem to become one?[36] Does not everything that appears individual merely participate in the one, supra-individual working of spirit?

2. Personal Being as Structurally Closed

The idea of the 'openness' of the person threatens to turn into its opposite, that of apersonal spirit. As spirit comes into being, the I plunges into a sea of surrounding spirit; it awakens and finds itself standing in the midst of this spirit. It can live only in spirit, and it knows that every You that it encounters is borne by the same current. But the characteristic form in which all this happens is the You-form, that is, human beings *really know their I only in the You-relation.* Thus, they clearly are not only reservoirs or receptive organs for a certain quantity of objective spirit, but much more they are spontaneous 'bearers', active members, of the great social nexus. Otherwise there would be no I-You-relation at all—

46

9. Othmar Spann, *Gesellschaftslehre*, 103ff.

[35.] This part of the sentence replaces the following in *SC-A*: If we are to indulge ourselves further with a look at human emotional life, we must remember the above, . . .

[36.] Deleted in *SC-A*: , if each is but a wave borne up by the sea, only to sink back into it?

and thus in turn no spirit.[37] The more the individual spirit develops, the more it plunges into the stream of objective spirit,[10] the more it becomes a bearer of objective spirit, and this immersion is precisely what strengthens the individual spirit.[38]

Thus the 'openness' of the person demands 'closedness' as a correlative, or one could not speak of openness at all. In a certain sense, therefore, the question whether individual being exists, untouched by all social bonds, must be answered in the affirmative, in order not to give up the idea of the I-You-relation.[39] Otherwise by wanting, like the atomist doctrine of relation, to preserve an asocial personal core, one runs the risk of ultimately falling back into atomistic thinking.[40] But such a fundamental change would be of decisive significance for the problem of the church.

The tragedy of all idealist philosophy was that it never ultimately broke through to personal spirit.[41] However, its monumental perception, especially in Hegel, was that the principle of spirit is something objective, extending beyond everything individual—that there is an objective spirit, the spirit of sociality, which is distinct in itself from all individual spirit. Our task is to affirm the latter without denying the former, to retain the perception without committing the error.

The fact that personal unity is closed is documented[42] through the recognition that self-consciousness and self-determination are irreducibly separate from everything social; these acts are inwardly directed. The structural unity of the I is given as an experience already in the experience of the You. It cannot be constituted by acts; rather,

---

10. I will later offer a theory of objective spirit.

[37.] Deleted in *SC-A*: The goal of every I must be to give the greatest and strongest individual formation and effectiveness to this reception.

[38.] Deleted in *SC-A*: Thus it becomes increasingly clear that genuine individualism and genuine collectivism are not mutually exclusive; rather, each is necessary to the existence of the other. Cf. Seeberg, *Dogmatik*, 1:506; cf. also Spann, *Gesellschaftslehre*, 88ff.

[39.] The phrase "not to give up" replaces the following in *SC-A*: to justify, which we can only do with the greatest caution, however, since after all we recognized material spirit as real only in social fulfillment, . . .

[40.] For a critique of the doctrine of relation, see page 29, editorial note 5.

[41.] Footnote deleted in *SC-A*: <<See the discussion in chapter 2 and the exception represented by a certain complex of ideas in Fichte.>>

[42.] The word "documented" replaces in *SC-A*: guaranteed, that is, documented, proved, . . .

they presuppose it and are directed toward it. Let us recall the basic dis-   47
tinction made above[11] between structure and intention. Here the *funda-*
mental synthesis between social and individual being comes to light.
Individual personal spirit lives solely by virtue of sociality, and 'social
spirit' becomes real only in individual formation; thus genuine sociality
itself presses toward personal unity. One cannot speak of the priority of
either personal or social being.[43] We must acknowledge that besides
those acts that are only real through sociality, there are also purely
inwardly directed acts. Certainly these, too, are possible only in a person existing fully in sociality—indeed, there is no other kind of person.
Whereas in experience these acts isolate the I from the You completely,[12] the intimate act is not primarily what constitutes the person as
structurally closed. Rather, social intention is inconceivable without
structural 'closedness', because no intimate act is conceivable without
corresponding openness. On the other hand, social intention is
directed toward the openness of the person, the intimate act toward the
person's closedness. But it would be wrong to distinguish an inaccessible, utterly isolated core of the person from a completely open layer surrounding it. *The unity and closedness of the whole person is posited along with*
its sociality. The You cannot be experienced except by an I—thus, never
in the epistemological paradigm. Then, however, the only question
asked *by idealist philosophy* about I and You—namely *Fichte's question about*
the synthesis of the realm of spirit—is formulated wrongly. It starts from the
assumption that I and You can be conceived quite unrelated to one
another, and then it inquires about their point of unity, which obviously
must exist. The question of the alien psyche, the question how one   48
finds one's way to the other, is not sufficiently informed by the fact of

---

11. See above, page 67, footnote 3.

12. The criterion for such acts is certainly not immediacy. Litt ([*Individuum,*]
213) obviously is right to criticize Scheler on this point. But it seems to me that
Litt's fear is irrelevant for us when he says that by postulating intimate personal
acts one risks creating, within the I, rigid structural-substantial strata of an intimate and a social "partial person," thus destroying the essential unity of the I.
As long as one recognizes the locus of the *one* person only in sociality, its unity
cannot be diminished by inward or outward intention.

[43.] Deleted in *SC-A:* Thus our turning against idealist theory is clear; equally clear, of
course, is what we have to learn from it. Obviously there also are sufficient grounds for our
departure from any sort of theoretical individualism.

the *unity* of all activity of spirit. This question always assumes an individual conceived as fundamentally isolated, who subsequently seeks contact somehow with others.[13] Thus, we hold to our conclusion that *personal and social being have equal weight.*[45]

Does the social unit then involve more than personal interactions, and, if so, how should we conceive it? Or does the social unit consist solely of these interactions? In theological terms, does God intend by community something that absorbs the individual human being into itself, or does God intend *only the individual*? Or are community and individual both intended by God in their distinctive significance? Is objective spirit closer to God than subjective spirit? Or vice versa? Or do both stand side by side under God's will?[46]

---

13. There is no basic difference here between Fichte's earlier synthesis of the realm of spirit that was teleologically oriented and his later one oriented toward origins. (Cf. Hirsch, [*Die idealistische Philosophie,*] 140ff.) This question alone proves the idea of possible isolation of the I. We would be correct to speak not of *synthesis* but of *thesis*. At its deepest level, Fichte's position is based upon a concept of the You that unifies the 'it' and the I.[44]

[44.] See above, page 56, footnote 12.

[45.] Deleted in *SC-A*:

But is this not all too easily stated, perhaps? Is not the argumentation of Hegel, for example, quite convincing, with his notion of objective spirit, which is then elaborated by the organologists (P[aul] Barth, Schäffle, Othmar Spann)? The totality of the social unit transcends the infinite multiplicity of personal being, conditioning it and absorbing it into itself. A constancy of growth is guaranteed here, the individual participating in the social unit just like a leaf on the tree. Thus we seem to be faced with the alternative of placing the community before the person or vice versa. Or would it not be possible to maintain the equal weight of the two? We recognize that the individual only exists and is preserved in the whole. Thus our question boils down to the relation that we want to posit between the social unit and the personal unit.

[46.] Deleted in *SC-A*:

This problem has been in constant dialectical movement since the Enlightenment, or, if you will, since the beginning of all philosophical thought, and it has still not been settled. The either-or alternative was all one ever saw; one was unable to grasp that the intrinsic dialectical movement of the subject matter entailed both-and. Of course here we are still speaking of the social-philosophical foundation. On the empirical level the both-and was operative since human community came into being. Only recently has this possibility been thought through theoretically and, in my view, a solution approached via this route. The way was prepared by the investigations about the problem of understanding [Verstehen], to my knowledge first pursued systematically by Scheler, taken up by the students of the phenomenological school (see above), and then with Theodor Litt extended by discoveries of basic principles and modified. The discipline of sociology proper played little role here.

If the equal weight of social and personal being is to be maintained, what is the meaning of community as a metaphysical unit in relation to the individual person?[47] *We maintain that community can be interpreted as a collective person with the same structure as the individual person.*[48] Since Plato, the tradition has been to think of community as a large-scale human being, somewhat in the manner of modern organology,[14] with the aim of completely subordinating the individual to the whole.[50] This subordination must be rejected as contrary to the equal weight of personal and social being. But the question remains whether, besides the single individual person, there might not be an *individual*[51] collective person[52] in which the individual participates—one that transcends all individuals but would be incomprehensible without the correlate of personal, individual being.[15] All we can do here is entertain the   49

---

14. Cf. Kistiakowski, *Einzelwesen und Gesellschaft*, 1899, chaps. 1 and 2.[49]

15. Scheler (*Formalism in Ethics*, 519ff.) saw the sense of such a notion. W[illiam] Stern's conclusions (*Die menschliche Persönlichkeit*, 40ff.) agree in substance with Scheler's. E[dith] Stein (["Individuum und Gemeinschaft,"] 250ff.) modifies the idea in her debate with Scheler and Litt ([*Individuum und Gemeinschaft,*] 234ff. and 260ff.) and rejects it decisively.

[47.] Deleted in *SC-A*: The idea of objective spirit as Hegel formulated it is unacceptable to us in this form, since it represents the bridge between subjective spirit and absolute spirit and is thereby placed above subjective spirit. When we get to the concept of the church we will discuss   229
the impact of Hegel's idea.

[48.] Deleted in *SC-A*: (On the limits of this idea in concrete social formation, see below.)

[49.] The correct title is *Gesellschaft und Einzelwesen*. 'Organology' or organicism was a school of late-nineteenth-century sociology and political science for which the human body and its organs was a model or analogy for social organization. Bonhoeffer mentions Paul Barth, Albert Schäffle, and Othmar Spann as representatives, and distinguishes Paul's use of the body metaphor in the New Testament from this school of thought (cf. page 76, editorial note 45, and page 138). [CG]

[50.] See above, page 76, editorial note 44. One finds the criticism about Plato in Kistiakowski. See above, footnote 14; cf. Plato, *Republic*, 435a ff., which merely speaks of the similarity (ὅμοιος) between the state and the human being.

[51.] *SC-RS*: "concrete".

[52.] The idea of collective person is taken from Scheler, e.g., *Formalism in Ethics*, 519ff. [Bonhoeffer uses the term *Kollektivperson*, whereas Scheler uses *Gesamtperson*, which literally means 'the-whole-community-understood-as-a-single-person'; it is rendered by Scheler's translators as 'collective person'. See further on *Gesamtperson* below, page 79, editorial note 58.][CG] Within the hierarchy of collective persons the church occupies the highest and most comprehensive place; its goal is realizing the basic value of collective salvation. For Scheler, religion has "its *own* domains of value and being, its own source of experience, which is called 'grace' with regard to the individual person and 'revelation' with regard to the collective person" (*Formalism in Ethics*, 550). Bonhoeffer marked this sentence in his copy of Scheler's book and wrote "revelation" in the margin.

metaphysical possibility of such a notion; only the *idea* of equal weight, or of the monadic image[53] in sociality, is in principle to be developed here. The concrete application will follow later. My own empirical consciousness of the fact that I myself represent community resists such hypostatizing of community; such consciousness does not wish to ascribe to community any being outside myself. But this empirical view must be overcome. Social unity is experienced as a center of acts from which it operates; such unity is self-conscious and has a will of its own, though only in the form of its members. It is a typical empiricist objection to conclude from this that the collective person is an impossibility. A *community is a concrete unity*. Its members must not be viewed as separate individuals, for the center of activity lies not in each member, but in all of them together. This unity must be the starting point for a concept of community, for there is no way from the many to the one. Thus an individualistic starting point precludes understanding community.[54] It is not as if many persons, gathered together, now add up to a collective person. Rather, the person comes into being only when embedded in sociality, and the collective person comes into being together with the individual person. It is neither prior to, nor a consequence of, the individual.[55] That is, the collective person exists only where there are individual persons. But since the collective person, understood as a center of activity, is only possible as concrete community with specific goals, it is possible only where the individual person belongs to the essence of the concrete community. The question of the 'body' of this collective person, and whether it is meaningful to speak in such terms, will be addressed later.[56] Litt's objection that in speaking of interpersonal relations one cannot jump from individual persons to

50   collective persons—and that all social being is exhausted in the relations of I and You—is in my view inconclusive. For I-You-relations are also possible between a collective person and an individual person. For the collective person is, after all, also an individual person; only when collective persons are included in social intercourse can its richness be fully grasped. Thus to postulate a collective person does not mean to

---

[53.] On the monadic image, see below, page 79, editorial note 60.

[54.] *SC-RS*: "to consider the aspect of will in the objective spirit".

[55.] Cf. Scheler, *Formalism in Ethics*, 521ff.

[56.] Deleted in *SC-A*: Suffice it to say that the idea of a collective person appears quite possible and legitimate. <<Litt, [*Individuum und Gemeinschaft*,] 260ff.>>

limit the sociological basic-category of I-You-relations. Rather, one must articulate the similarity of structure of the collective person and the individual person in the eyes of the universal person of God [der Allperson Gottes]:[57] closedness and openness, mutual enrichment, social and inward intentions within this structural unity. Yet we still hesitate to *declare the reality* of the collective person [Kollektivperson]. Since the problem of reality can be solved fundamentally only from the perspective of ethics, we must first consider the degree to which ethical categories can be applied to a collective person [Gesamtperson],[58] in the sense of an ethical personhood. This will provide decisive insights for the concept of the church.

Thus the groundwork is laid for a theory of the formation of empirical forms of community. They all must be built upon these basic-relations that are given with the personhood of every human being. This net of sociality into which people are woven is prior to any will for community. Its real relations are still present even when empirical community is consciously and entirely rejected.[59] Clearly, Leibniz's *image of the monad* may serve to clarify these social basic-relations. This is an image of individual beings who are completely self-contained—'monads have no windows'—and yet conceiving, mirroring, and individually shaping all of reality, and, in so doing, discovering their being.[60]

What is the theological significance of all the insights above?[61] The universal person of God does not think of people as isolated individual

---

[57.] William Stern, *Die menschliche Persönlichkeit*, 44, speaks of the divine *Allperson*.

[58.] There is no conceptual difference for Bonhoeffer between *Kollektivperson* and *Gesamtperson*, as this paragraph illustrates; consequently both words are translated as "collective person." Nevertheless, since *Gesamtperson* literally means 'the-whole-community-understood-as-a-person', the interchangeability reinforces the point that the 'collective person' depends on all the individual members of the community, that is, the whole, and does not exist apart from them. Further, *Gesamtperson* stresses the meaning of the-whole-as-person, as when a community acts responsibly through those who represent it, following Bonhoeffer's socioethical model of 'person' and his concept of *Stellvertretung*. [CG]

[59.] Footnote deleted in *SC-A*: <<A hypothetical being standing utterly alone would be unable to rise to the level of human being. This definition ties human beings to maternal nurture longer than the animals.>>

[60.] Deleted in *SC-A*: thus no atomist theory with human dynamics, etc., despite the structural closedness of the individual. Cf. Leibniz, "The Monadology," 67f., par. 7. Litt also calls his method the "monadological principle" (cf. Litt, *Individuum*, 139; 188f., note 1; 221; and 305ff.).

[61.] Deleted in *SC-A*: First, it can be seen as contributing to the doctrine of the primal essence of human being.

beings, but in a natural state of communication with other human beings. Furthermore, in relations with others, I do not merely satisfy one side of my structurally closed being as spirit; rather, only here do I 51 discover my reality, i.e., my I-ness. God created man and woman directed to one another. God does not desire a history of individual human beings, but the history of the human *community*. However, God does not want a community that absorbs the individual into itself, but a community of *human beings*. In God's eyes, community and individual exist in the same moment and rest in one another. The collective unit and the individual unit have the same structure in God's eyes.[62] On these basic-relations rest the concepts of the religious community and the church.

C. The Sociological Problem

1. Social Community as Community of Will [63]

One cannot speak of human social formation [Vergesellschaftung] in the precise sense of pure instincts leading people together. Human

---

[62.] Deleted in *SC-A*: Thus for God, community is more than the sum of individuals, and yet community is built solely upon individuals. This insight will be useful for all that follows. The concepts of religious community and of church rest on these basic-relations.

[63.] In *SC-A* section 1 begins with the following introduction, deleted for the published version:

Empirical communities in the broad sense of the term are the social aggregates that stand out from general sociality. In the narrower sense, empirical 'communities' ['Gemein-schaften'] are those that are built upon certain social acts of will.

Animal instincts connect the most primitive forms in which human beings coexist [Beieinandersein] with animal social life. If there were no other drives toward sociality, then hunger and the sexual drive would necessarily be the first to bring human beings together. Two different experiences are inherent in these drives. The child's hunger seeks the mother 230 for the sake of milk; hunger asserts only itself—it wills matter that it can control. One hunter seeks out the other to be more certain of the catch.

The sexual impulse is structured differently. It does not actually desire something of the other person for itself, but desires the whole person, and desires to give itself as a whole person, in its bodily nature, to the other. It desires to be together with the other in bodily intimacy. It desires shared pleasure with the other. Its primary intention is not reproduction, but its own life, and by living to the utmost in intensity, it creates new life. Two types of social life in general are prefigured here in the most primitive instinctual forms. [By "two types," Bonhoeffer means *Gesellschaft*, a form of society that is a means to an end, and *Gemeinschaft*, community that is an end in itself.][CG] The parallels between animal and human social drives are extensive. The sociality of animals is highly developed; the

beings and animals share the drives of imitation, subordination, sociability, and especially of hunger and sexuality. Human community per se is only present[64] where conscious human spirit is at work, that is, where community rests upon purposeful acts of will.[65] Human community, then, does not necessarily result from acts of will; rather, its essence subsists in such acts.[16] [69] Human community is essentially community   52

---

16. Thinkers like Rousseau erred in confusing these two questions. If his idea of the social contract (written in 1754, printed in condensed form in 1762) meant to say that all specifically human community rests essentially on self-conscious being that is endowed with will, we could agree with him. His error, however, consists in the fact that (1) the conscious will of the individual is wrongly located already at the origin of organic social forms, such as the most primitive kinds of marriage; and especially that (2) this will is construed as purely contractual, so that all empirical associations [Sozialverbände] would have to be conceived as arising from such a contract. But this is sociologically untenable.[66] Sociologically, a contract is obviously unthinkable without the underlying communal ethos that treats a contract as binding (cf. Vierkandt, [*Gesellschaftslehre,*] sec. 29).[67] The interpretation of marriage as a form of economic life (Kant,

[63. *cont.*] principle of solidarity is no less present than the formation of states, with division of labor, etc., which cannot be further elaborated here. <<Cf. Espinas, *Die tierischen Gesellschaften,* 1879.>>

[64.] "Human beings and animals share the drives . . . is only present" replaces these words in *SC-A*, which appear after "leading people together": or where any purely natural social formations exist, where the community lives and grows at a pre-human level, but only there . . .>>

[65.] Footnote deleted in *SC-A*:

<<H[erbert] Spencer follows a totally different route in differentiating animal (organic) and human (supra-organic) communities. The animal is constituted by shared descent from one pair of parents; the human forms "a union among like individuals independent of one another in parentage, and approximately equal in their capacities (*The Principles of Sociology,* 1:6). This distinction is not only zoologically incorrect, as Spencer himself knows, but it is also useless for understanding problems concerning essence [Wesensprobleme]."">

[66.] Deleted in *SC-A*: Difficult though the former is to demonstrate, a healthy historical eye will refuse to recognize this theory.

[67.] Deleted in *SC-A*:

Pure drive never constitutes specifically human community, not imitation, <<G[abriel de] Tarde, *The Laws of Imitation,* in which imitation is made the fundamental constituent of sociological commitments.>> not subordination, not a drive toward sociability, and not the sexual drive. The fact of marriage cannot be derived from the purely sexual drive that goes no further than the moment. Only where the will to erotic love joins up with the urge for meaning and lasting commitment is marriage possible in its real essence. <<The

of will, and only as such does it give meaning to its own natural form. Thus it is legitimate to *define the goal of sociology as the study of the structures of communities and the acts of will that constitute them*, i.e., *as a phenomenological* and *systematic discipline. The subject matter of systematic-sociological investigation is the acts of will that are essentially operative in any community*, not the origins of the state, marriage, family, or religious community.[70] Human community is community of self-conscious beings endowed with will.[17] [72]

We must first describe the *nature of social ties as such*, and then set out the *concrete types of social acts of will and 'structures'*.[73]

---

opposed by Hegel) will never fully comprehend monogamy (Kant, *The Metaphysics of Morals*, sec. 24; *Hegel's Philosophy of Right*, sec. 161.[68]

17. It follows from this that statistical social units, such as drinkers, single people, suicides, etc., cannot be viewed as communities. These distinctions have already been dealt with by logic. Cf. Sigwart, *Logic*, 2:483ff. Further, see Kistiakowski, [*Gesellschaft und Einzelwesen*,] 111ff., 117ff.[71]

[67. *cont.*] interpretation of marriage as a form of economic life (Kant, opposed by Hegel) will never fully comprehend monogamy.>>

[68.] Deleted in *SC-A*: Here, the drive is embedded in a social spirit and will to community between two persons. [The references to Kant and Hegel at the end of Bonhoeffer's footnote are handwritten additions to the dissertation manuscript. After the Kant reference, but not printed in the German text *SC (DBW 1)*, is found the following phrase from the Kant citation about marriage: "zum lebenswierigen wechselseitigen Besitz ihrer Geschlechtseigenschaften" ("the union of two persons of different sexes for lifelong possession of each other's sexual attributes").][CG] On contract theory, see Vierkandt, *Gesellschaftslehre*, 264ff. and 389ff. On marriage, cf. Kant, *The Metaphysics of Morals*, §24, 61ff.; and see Hegel, *Philosophy of Right*, §161, 111ff.

[69.] In *SC-A* Bonhoeffer's current footnote 16 appears in the text at this point.

231   [70.] Deleted in *SC-A*:

How monogamy evolved genetically is not a specifically sociological problem, but rather a historical-ethnological one. Its existence as a natural form is not sufficient evidence that it is intrinsic to spirit. This is merely a matter of 'symbiosis', a phenomenon familiar to biologists. Marriage in the specifically human sense only exists when it is willed by the spirit. We repeat:

[71.] Kistiakowski, *Gesellschaft*, 122f.: "The aggregates of unmarried mothers, suicides, or male criminals are totally artificial notions that only demonstrate that a particular individual process has occurred so many times." See Sigwart, *Logic*, 2:483ff., as cited in Kistiakowski, [*Gesellschaft*,] 118.

[72.] Deleted in *SC-A*: Rousseau's theory is overcome a priori because of his error, that is, his confusion of genetic and specifically sociological issues. Cf. Seeberg, *Dogmatik*, 1:507ff., and Vierkandt, *Gesellschaftslehre*, 58ff.

[73.] Deleted in *SC-A*:

Characteristically, communal acts of will do not run parallel to each other toward a purpose beyond the persons themselves; rather in communities the direction of the personal wills is the same—that is, they are reciprocal.[74] One person must in some way intend and will the other, and be intended and willed by the other, whether for a pure union of persons, or for some specific purpose beyond the intended person. 'Agreement' without this reciprocal attitude is merely parallel existence, which is not overcome even by the knowledge that the other will is running the same course.[18] Agreement must prevail in the mutual willing that is directed toward the person of the other. This is the meaning of the concept of 'unity' of will: it rests upon the *separateness of persons.*   53 Thus the essence of community is not 'commonality'—although formally every community has this. Rather, reciprocal will constitutes community. Communities that are really founded only on formal agreement, on commonality (lecture halls,[77] etc.), are not communities of will, but should be considered under the sociological category of the *mass,* or public (see below).[78] *'Unity' of will thus signifies an identity of*

---

18. This is contrary to Schumann's recently delivered definition of the social unit as occurring "when every one of the souls in question *knows* that every (!)[75] other is one with it in that unity created by their own relationship to a common purpose, or, in short, one in their common will" (Schumann [, "Religionssoziologie"]).[76] Cf. also Gerda Walther, "Zur Ontologie der sozialen Gemeinschaften," 132. The reciprocal act of will is not included among the thirteen constituent aspects of community listed here.

[73. *cont.*] Every empirical human community builds on the ground of the general sociality of the human spirit. Thus, a fundamental atomism is abolished. At the same time, however, the presupposition of every possible human community is its being totally meaningful [Vollsinnigkeit] as the basis for understanding and expression, that is, for the reciprocal influence of wills.

[74.] Community, *Gemeinschaft,* is willed as an end in itself; therefore, people in community will 'reciprocally'—that is, they will each other. In a society, *Gesellschaft,* people do not will each other but rather a particular goal toward which all the members of the *Gesellschaft* are reaching; therefore, their wills are 'parallel' toward that goal—rather than 'reciprocal' toward each other. [CG]

[75.] This exclamation point in the middle of the Schumann quotation is Bonhoeffer's insertion and is found in *SC-A.* [CG]

[76.] Cf. Schumann, "Religionssoziologie," 686.

[77.] Deleted in *SC-A:* school communities, . . .

[78.] Deleted in *SC-A:* (One should not confuse here the school as an 'institution' and the concrete community of wills of its pupils, for example, with the construct here of a pure type of a school community.)

content in what is intended and willed. Here a further distinction must be made. 'Unity' must exist *absolutely* in the willing of the community, that is, as formal unity in the sense of 'agreement' above. At first it will also exist as absolute unity in regard to content, namely the purpose that is apart from the pure will to community. But in the historical development of every community, differences of opinion arise about the realization of the aim. These often lead to substantive differences in the conception of the purpose itself, so that the unity of content can only be described as *relative*.[79] Thus even the formally absolute unity of the empirical community of the church [kirchliche Gemeinschaft] is only a relative unity as regards content.

Whatever kind of unity of will exists, one must never conclude any kind of unity of the willing persons in the sense of fusion; this is impossible considering all that has been said. *Community of will and unity of will only build upon the inner separateness of I and You.* The idealist argument—that proceeds from the identity of what is willed to the similarity, and thus unity, of persons—had to be rejected earlier. The person who is united with me in common intention is structurally just as separate from me as the one who is not so united.[80] Between us lies the boundary of being created as individual persons. The Christian notion of community with God can be realized only on the basis of this interpretation of community. Otherwise, community with God becomes unification in the sense of transgressing the boundary of the I-You-relation—that is, mystical fusion.

By viewing the individual person in a primal state as an ultimate unit 54 who is created by God's will—but also by seeing individual persons as real only in sociality—we interpret their relations to one another, which are built upon their difference, as willed by God. This means, however, that strife [Kampf] is recognized as a fundamental sociological law[81] and basically is sanctified. Concretely, this implies the necessity and the justification of partisanship in every community relation. Genuine life

---

[79.] This view corresponds to that developed by Seeberg, *Dogmatik*, 1:511ff.

[80.] Deleted in *SC-A*: Another person does not become I, nor I that person.

[81.] On strife as a fundamental sociological law, cf. Vierkandt, *Gesellschaftslehre*, 103ff., 263f., and 269ff., as well as Seeberg (see below, page 000, editorial note 21).

[82.] Deleted in *SC-A*:

This is equally true of political life as well as scholarly work. <<It has already been shown that the concept of truth is also related to basic social-philosophical insights. Christian

arises only in the conflict of wills; strength unfolds only in strife.[82] This is an old[83] insight.[19]

Only since the fall[86] has there been no concrete and productive conflict in the genuine sense. Hence the very notion of such a development

---

19. Hobbes was in all likelihood the first to articulate the purely social meaning of strife. He sees the origin and significance of social formation in the bellum omnium contra omnes [war of all against all] and, with some qualification, Kant agreed with him (*Religion within the Limits of Reason Alone*, bk. 3, pt. 2, 88–89). But Hobbes only wants to describe contract theory, and the status belli omnium in omnes [condition of the war of all among all] (according to Kant's revision) is essentially pre- and extrasocial. In order to regulate it, so to speak, the social contract is made (Rousseau, see above [page 81]). Kant recognizes 'antagonism' as the principle that propels *society's spirit* (*Idea for a Universal History from a Cosmopolitan Point of View*, 4th Thesis[, 15–16].).[84] Attraction and repulsion always occur together; life, talent, and art unfold in strife. "Human beings want harmony; but nature knows better what is good for their species. It wants discord" [trans. NL] (Kant[, *Idea for a Universal History*]).[85]

[82. *cont.*] revelation is the only truth that can enter into the individual, and even that happens by means of the church. All other truth is never 'possessed' absolutely, but only in arguing with others; that is, truth remains in the midst of those engaged in discussion. This is true not only of truths rooted in differences between individuals, but also of formal truths. Only recently has mathematics cast doubt upon the most basic assertions of logic such as that of the excluded middle (Brower). [The correct name is Brouwer.][CG] The debate between philosophy and mathematics is by no means over. Cf. esp. Grisebach[, *Die Grenzen des Erziehers*].>>

[83.] Here "old" replaces ancient in *SC-A*. In *SC-A*, the current footnote 19 occurs here   232 in the body of the text.

[84.] The remainder of the Kant citation, which is deleted in *SC-A*, reads:

Antagonism in society is the means nature uses to bring about the development of all its talents, insofar as antagonism is ultimately the cause of a legitimate order among them. I understand antagonism here to mean the *unsociable sociability* of human beings, that is, their tendency to enter into society, which is perpetually associated with a resistance that constantly threatens to disrupt this society. . . . Human beings have a tendency to participate in social forms, but they also have a strong tendency to seek solitude. [trans. NL]

[85.] The continuation of the Kant quotation, deleted in *SC-A*, is as follows:

The natural motives for this, the sources of unsociability and relentless resistance that produce many evils—but that also spur one on to harness one's energies anew and to develop one's talents further—thus reveal the *ordering hand of a wise creator*, and not the hand of an evil spirit who botched up God's divine works, or jealously ruined them, as some would have it. [trans. NL]

[86.] In *SC-A* "Only since the fall" replaces Of course, since evil will began its reign . . .

has come to be condemned as evil.[87] But even in conflict that has been rendered unholy through an evil will, the most intimate social bond of the human spirit becomes visible. In conflict the other will is not ignored and negated; rather, one seeks to force it into one's own will and thus overcome it. This opposition of wills is resolved only in the cooperation of wills. That is *"the social synthesis that triumphs over all voluntary and natural antitheses,"*[88] in which "the sociality of human spirit is revealed as a primal energy. . . . It is a tremendous reality that lets us comprehend the secret of humanity and its history and to have hope for its future."20 To be sure, this is just as valid for the relation *between God and human beings* as it is for that between persons. Through conflict, the will of the sinful human being is forced into the holy will of God, and thus community is established.

Community is a community of wills, built upon the separateness and difference of persons, constituted by reciprocal acts of will, finding its unity in what is willed, and counting among its basic laws the inner conflict of individual wills. This definition remains incomplete until the theory of objective spirit is discussed. But this will be possible only after looking more closely at the content that determines the bonds between wills. Only then can we comprehend, and graphically describe, the essence of concrete community—and thus the concrete form of objective spirit.

2. Typology of Social Communities

The bonds between wills can be considered from the standpoint of the *relation between the willed goal and the will to communal formation [Vergemeinschaftung]*—that is, according to the *directional determination* of the wills.[89] The analysis of the direction of wills at the same time explains

---

20. Seeberg, *Christliche Dogmatik*, 1:513.

[87.] Deleted in *SC-A*: Though strife today has taken on morally intolerable forms, and is therefore subject to the judgment of sin, this cannot alter the fact that as a law of life for communities it is necessary, holy, and good.

[88.] Seeberg defines social synthesis as the unity of the reality of will, feeling, and thought in their mutual opposition, a 'personalism' that includes 'socialism' and must in fact promote it (*Dogmatik*, 1:515). Seeberg attaches to his view of objective spirit the notion of the progress of culture toward the Realm of God as the purpose of history.

[89.] "Communal formation" here and below is a general term covering different types of social forms, including both *Gemeinschaft* and *Gesellschaft*. Soon, building on Tönnies,

both *the closeness and the looseness of the bond.* The other way to look at bonds between wills is to consider the *relation of strength [Stärkeverhältnis]* of the wills to each other. It seems to me that one must be able to discover the essence of every bond between wills from these two or three points of view, although in any concrete case the analysis can be impeded by the combination of several types.[90]

We will begin with the first-mentioned point of view. Every will strives to reach a *goal.* There is then a double possibility of relations between the willed goal and the will to community. According to this distinction the will has a phenomenologically different form in each.[21] [92]

---

21. Tönnies distinguished between 'natural will' ['Wesenswille'] and 'rational will' ['Kürwille'] (*Community and Society,* 136). The distinction described below is not identical to that of Tönnies's because he blends a phenomenological analysis of acts of will and social structures with a genetic approach. Based on the principles developed above, we must reject this procedure as methodologically unsound. Obviously, the genesis of social structures has heuristic significance for Tönnies's phenomenological analysis, and thus he cannot get beyond it. The genetic procedure here in fact approximates the truth; nevertheless, for the concept of the church it would lead to the same consequences, for example, as those that we will demonstrate below to be erroneous in Troeltsch. Even Scheler often seems to follow a genetic approach rather than the phenomenological method he consciously strives for. To overcome this error we will hold strictly to what we consider to be the essential social acts of will and their analysis, deriving the typology of communities from this.[91]

[89. *cont.*] Bonhoeffer will differentiate specific types, depending on whether a purposeful goal is willed or whether a 'structure of meaning' is willed as an end in itself. [CG]

[90.] Vierkandt, *Gesellschaftslehre,* 179ff. and 232ff., also attempts to define the special character of social basic-relations by determining the varying degrees of connection in common human life.

[91.] In *SC-A,* footnote 21 is included in the text. Tönnies's *Gemeinschaft und Gesellschaft* first appeared in 1887 [English translation, 1957], but gained broad readership only with its second edition (1912)—in the context of the youth movement's opposition to Wilhelmine society. After World War I this pair of concepts was advanced as a popular slogan in the arsenal of conservative social criticism, quite apart from Tönnies. Of course, Tönnies prepares the way for this ideological turn, since in his work it remains unclear whether the two concepts represent sociological ideal types, antithetical notions, or a process of decline from community to society. Cf. the forewords to the individual editions in the reprint of the eighth edition (Darmstadt, 1979), xv ff. [These forewords by Tönnies himself are not included in the English translation.][CG]

[92.] Footnote deleted in *SC-A:* <<The reason for this is to be found in the attempt to isolate the 'collective person' [Gesamtperson] and to categorize the other two types of lifecommunity and society with it, so that they are negated, reconstituted, and fulfilled in the collective person. Cf. *Formalism in Ethics,* 544ff.>>

56   Wills can will 'together', 'beside', and 'against' one another. Only the first leads to empirical social formation. The second is sociologically irrelevant (see below, however, for the sociological concept of the mass). The third, when developed in completely pure form, does create real social vitality, but remains unable to create a social form [Sozialgebilde]. Thus only the first form is significant here. If wills will together with one another, then what is thus willed can be one of two things. *Being-with-one-another [Miteinander] can be willed as an end in itself* (this also includes willing-for-one-another [Füreinander-wollen]). *Being-with-one-another* can also be willed as a means to an end. The will expressed in the first case we shall call *'will to meaning'*, and the second *'rational purposive will'*. The first term was chosen because its communal form has no rationalizable material goal; what is willed and affirmed in it is not a purpose, but a meaning. The schema of a 'structure of meaning' and 'structure of purpose' corresponds to these concepts of 'will to meaning' and 'rational purposive will'. Community[93] can thus be constituted to serve as a means for the rational will that is strictly directed toward a purpose; or it can be constituted by the will to meaning that recognizes the value of community as such. *In the structure of purpose the unity of what is willed establishes the reciprocal direction of wills, whereas in the structure of meaning the unity of what is willed is itself represented in this reciprocal movement.* The latter can also set out certain purposes, only they are not constitutive of the structure. When Aristotle says in the *Politics*, "πᾶσα κοινωνία ἀγαθοῦ τινος ἕνεκα συνέστηκεν" ["every community is
57   established with a view to some good"][94] he wants to articulate the teleological character of all social forms. For obviously, ἀγαθόν here signifies the 'good', i.e., a good that lies outside the community itself. We dispute the statement in this form, since it corresponds to a eudaemonistic ethic[95] and fails to recognize the essence of the 'meaning' of community as such. Structures of meaning are not constructed toward a

---

[93.] Here, as frequently, Bonhoeffer uses the word in a general sense to comprise both the *Gemeinschaft* and *Gesellschaft* types; see the following paragraph. [CG]

[94.] Cf. Aristotle, *Politics*, 1252a. The quote appears in Freyer, *Theorie des objektiven Geistes*, 53.

[95.] Taking its name from the Greek word for happiness, a eudaemonistic ethic (such as Aristotle's) seeks personal well-being through a life governed by reason. [CG]

purpose and cannot be interpreted with reference to a purpose. This will be treated further below.[22]

According to current scholarly terminology—an ingenious discovery by Tönnies in his time—the first type would be called 'community' [Gemeinschaft] in the specific sense, and the second would be called 'society' [Gesellschaft]. We will follow his terminology. It would be tempting to identify this distinction with the genetic one between associations [Verbände] that have 'grown' and those that are 'made', between those 'previously existing' and those 'willed'.[23] Family, people [Volk], and *church* would then belong to the first category, and corporation, club, and *sect*, for example (to follow Weber and Troeltsch),[97] would belong to the second. But this identification is fundamentally false. A people is 'community' in the specific sense, not as something that has grown but only as something willed, namely willed-community—recognized as an end in itself, as a value, for all community is community of will. The task of a sociological study is not to demonstrate the thousands of motives and their many variants that lead to the *genesis* of a social structure—one might think of von Wiese's table on the intensification of relations [Beziehungsnäherung];[98] rather, its task is to study the acts of will that are *constitutive* of a social structure. Of course, associations that have grown often do coincide with the community type; but to equate the two would be methodologically and logically incorrect. In speaking of the psychological differences between life in a community and life in a society, we will discuss the *closeness and looseness* of bonds of will. We do not mean that the types are constituted by   58

---

22. Compare these definitions with those of Tönnies [*Community and Society*], secs. 1 and 19, 37ff., 64ff., where he distinguishes between the organic and real culture of the community [Gemeinschaft] and the ideal and mechanical culture of the society [Gesellschaft].[96] Freyer comes close to Aristotle's view in his *Theorie des objektiven Geistes*, 53ff.

23. Windelband, *An Introduction to Philosophy*, "voluntary communities [Willensgemeinschaften]," 256.

[96.] Cf. Tönnies, *Community and Society*, 33ff. and 64ff.
[97.] See below on 'Church and Sect', pages 267ff.
[98.] Cf. von Wiese, *Allgemeine Soziologie*, appendix: "Table of Human Relations in Sociological Perspective."

psychological differences, but that the different acts of will have different psychological consequences.

To a certain extent Scheler is correct in calling all 'communities' life-communities,[99] not because all of life necessarily runs its temporal course within them, but because human beings, intended for vital and personal existence, can 'live' in them. The first act of affirming that one belongs to a community is usually *embedded in a concrete, living, non-formal act* such as conscious participation in the work of the community. Thus even young children can sense it, for example, through an act of love, trust, or obedience. Unlike the society, a *community can support young children as well*. This is not to introduce the genetic concept of community; rather, young children in a community are *a part of their parents' will* until they can will for themselves—a thought that would be absurd in a society. This insight will be very important for the sociological concept of the church. Common feeling, common willing, and co-responsibility[100] are forces of inmost cohesion. The basic attitude is mutual *inner interest*.[101]

If a community is essentially a life-community, then a society is an association of rational action.[102] It appeals to human beings' ability to use their reason most effectively, as demonstrated in the search for the most appropriate means to a willed purpose, and in using the society itself extensively to this end. The only reason this is not called unethical is that it is based on consent and applies equally to all. Moreover, the other person must be treated with utmost consideration, precisely in

---

[99.] Cf. Scheler, *Formalism in Ethics*, 525f., which differentiates 'mass', 'life-community', 'society', and 'collective person'. [Scheler's term here is *Lebensgemeinschaft*, which Bonhoeffer later applies to the church. By saying a life-community is one people can 'live' in, Bonhoeffer means that we do not live by the utilitarian purposes and relationships of a *Gesellschaft*; these are intrumental to life. Rather, we live in communities such as family, friendship, people, and church whose relationships are meaningful in themselves.][CG]

[100.] Footnote deleted in *SC-A*: <<Scheler's statement that everyone is co-responsible is untenable. Co-responsibility is founded on self-responsibility. On this see E[dith] Stein, ["Individuum und Gemeinschaft,"] 250ff.>> According to Scheler, self-responsibility is based upon the "experience of *co-responsibility* for the willing, acting, and effecting of the whole community" (*Formalism in Ethics*, 527).

[101.] Deleted in *SC-A*:

This takes visible shape, for example, in the household community as a community of table, living space, festivities, shared culture, through tradition, custom, usage, and order; for such forms of community, memory and custom are intellectual, vital qualities of human spirit. Only in community is such education possible.

[102.] Cf. Tönnies, *Community and Society*, 64ff., and Scheler, *Formalism in Ethics*, 527ff.

order to be used to full advantage. *This is the basis for the inner self-preservation of a society.* The voluntary act of joining a society must be directly expressed and contractually secured. Everything intimately personal is excluded here. In the system of means, complete isolation of spirit goes hand in hand with communication between purposeful wills. People accept responsibility for the society only in their very own interest.[103]   59
In principle a society has no tradition. The basic attitude is expressed in mutual inner indifference, in strictest caution toward one another,[104] and thus in simultaneous reserve and personal self-assurance—and finally, insofar as it suits one's purpose, in conventional amiability. The organized structure of purpose has its basis in the contract, *which is the origin and measure of the association;* the organization then develops into an elaborate system of means and is fixed in written documents and agreements.

It becomes clear from the above that the directness of personal bonds in a community and the mediated nature of bonds in a society are manifested both in lifestyle and psychological attitude—in the form of closeness of connection in the former and looseness of connection in the latter. Of course it must be emphasized that no pure type exists in concrete form. There is no community without the connection of wills that exist in a society; but even more certainly, there is no society without the connection of wills existing in a community, because society [Gesellschaft] is essentially rooted in community [Gemeinschaft].[24]

Up to now, our discussion has centered upon the will as *determined by direction,* its intentions toward purpose and meaning. Now the question arises about the relation of strength of the wills toward one another. This can appear as a *relation of force [Gewaltverhältnis],* or a *relation of rule [Herrschaftsverhältnis].*[106] Whereas in the former the will that is

---

24. See the conclusive proof in Scheler, [*Formalism in Ethics,*] 530ff.[105] See also Vierkandt, [*Gesellschaftslehre,*] sec. 29.

[103.] Deleted in *SC-A:* Since he does not 'live' with it, neither will he 'die' with it.
[104.] Deleted in *SC-A:* or perhaps mistrust, . . .
[105.] Cf. Scheler, *Formalism in Ethics,* 531: "*No society without community* (but, to be sure, community without society in some cases). All *possible* society is necessarily *based* on community" [trans. altered].
[106.] On the relation of force [*Gewaltverhältnis*] and the relation of rule [*Herrschaftsverhältnis*] see Scheler, *Formalism in Ethics,* 529: "If, however, a society is to 'will' anything at all which is 'common' to its elements, it can only do this . . . through *illusion* and *coercion*" [trans. altered]. Cf. also Vierkandt, *Gesellschaftslehre,* 248ff. and 272ff.

dominated is brought into motion in a purely mechanical way by the will that exerts force upon it, in the latter it is presupposed that the obedient will understands the meaning of the command. Sociologically, this is significant insofar as in the association of force [Gewaltverband], community is not possible anymore. By contrast, *a genuine association of authentic rule [Herrschaftsverband] not only makes community possible, but in most cases realizes it.* These insights will be *very important for the concept of the church.*

The unequal relation of strength in an association of authentic rule corresponds to the situation in a 'cooperative association' ['Genossen-

60　schaftsverband']. This brings us to Otto von Gierke's famous distinction.[25] The concept of 'cooperative' is thus applicable only to the relation of strength and *is not identical to the concept of community.* In this sense, however, cooperative is a legal, not a sociological term, in that it expresses the legal equality of its members. It is not applicable in a living, social relation. Sociology has shown in many contexts[107] that in concrete instances there is no pure balance of power among the members of a social form. In every community that is apparently based on the dynamic coordination of wills, there exists in reality a relation of subordination. We concede this with a certain qualification, namely that in relation to the will of an absolute ruler, there is real coordination of those who are ruled. The idea of equality before the law, but also that of the rule of God, includes the coordination of those who are ruled, as will be demonstrated. But this transforms the notion of cooperative. As a necessary corollary to the idea of rule, it no longer has a sociological meaning of its own. Thus the only sociologically new structure that remains is the association of authentic rule. But with the sociological insight[108] mentioned above, it has been shown that the schema of community and society is connected to[109] the concept of an association of authentic rule. An association of authentic rule can be a community or a society.[26] Its application to the concept of the church must wait until

---

25. Von Gierke, *Das deutsche Genossenschaftsrecht*, esp. 1:12–140.

26. I cannot agree with Schumann's view (["Religionssoziologie,"] 691) that

[107.] "Sociology has shown in many contexts" replaces in *SC-A:* "Spranger [showed] in his *Lebensformen*" . . .

[108.] "with the . . . insight" replaces in *SC-A:* "with Spranger's insight" . . .

[109.] Replaces *SC-A:* **pervades.**

later.[110] Any further account of the relations between the three socio-logical types belongs in a detailed sociological investigation. Empirical social forms such as army, school, etc., are to be understood sociologi-cally as arising from such combinations.

Now there is one additional social form that does not fit into the gen-eral concept of community, and that can be called a human form only   61 because it is composed of conscious beings. I am speaking of the con-cept of the *mass*. "Mass is not yet reality" (Rosenstock).[111] In the mass there is no genuine social bonding of wills; instead, wills are seen as mechanical forces reacting to stimuli, so to speak. That is, the essence of their bonding is found not in the directional-relation or the relation of strength, but in an objectively effective stimulus that produces a nec-essary reaction, while their bonding is accidental.[112]

Thus we do not call just any arbitrary collection of people a 'mass'[27] in the sociological sense, but only the structure that is called into being through external provocation and that rests on the parallel direction of the wills of a number of persons. In the mass, the boundary of person-hood is lost, and the individual is no longer a person but only a part of

---

associations of authentic rule create no unity because A—who gives orders—intends to direct the will of B toward change, C, while B—who obeys—only wills change, C, with the result that no unified object of will is present in both par-ties. B does not want C, but wants to satisfy the will of A, who in directing B's will, insists on C.

27. Vierkandt, [*Gesellschaftslehre,*] 427; Le Bon, *The Crowd: A Study of the Popu-lar Mind,* 102f.; Simmel, *The Sociology of Georg Simmel,* 31ff.[113]

[110.] See below, pages 252ff.

[111.] Cf. Rosenstock-Huessy, *Soziologie,* 66f.

[112.] Deleted in *SC-A:*

An example of such effective stimuli is the commissioner of nutrition appearing in a time of famine before a crowd, most of whom are starving; another example is a beating on the street. In a certain sense, the sacrament, and the liturgy of the Roman Catholic churches, are such stimuli. The sociological concept of the mass, which is as old as humanity itself and no achievement of civilization, <<This contrary to Vierkandt, [*Gesellschaftslehre,*] 427.>> finds its complementary concept in that of a dynamic force that works through nature or spirit.

[113.] Deleted in *SC-A:* Contrary to Le Bon, in both his own book and also in Simmel the clarity of the sociological concept of the mass leaves something to be desired. Cf. Vierkandt, *Gesellschaftslehre,* 418ff., where one also finds the critique Bonhoeffer offers of Le Bon and Simmel.

the mass, drawn into it and directed by it. The mass is a unity, however, that is not supported by the separateness of the person and thus cannot last. It is the simplest social form and creates the most powerful experiences of unity.[28] [115]

---

28. For this reason people confuse the consciousness of mass unity and the feeling of community, as does Vierkandt in my view (cf. 202ff.), when he lists the idea of the invisible church along with edifying communities such as the theater, the literary circle, and the scholarly academy. Obviously he has overlooked the intermediate concept of the audience, which is a subconcept of the mass.[114]

234   [114.] Deleted in *SC-A*:

Vierkandt's concept of the invisible church expresses what the church has often become today, or rather what churches consider emancipated: religious theaters and lecture halls. The congregation is an audience, viewers who feel pleasantly edified by the music and the sermon. Each individual is happy to see many others who feel edified by the same spiritual food. And of course this feeling of shared joy is invisible, <<One thinks of the so-called 'invisible community' among music lovers, mountaineers, visitors to Rome, etc.>> an idea so obvious as to be superfluous if it meant nothing more. Vierkandt continues with his quotation from Goethe's *Urmeister*: "Where is society more pleasantly bound together, where else must people confess their brotherhood, than when they hang on the lips and features of a single person and are borne heavenward, all knit together in a common feeling?" [*Wilhelm Meisters theatralische Sendung* (1771), bk. 1, chap. 15. This book is commonly called the *Urmeister* because it is Goethe's earliest treatment of the material, much of which was later incorporated into the novel, *Wilhelm Meisters Lehrjahre* (1791); cf. *Wilhelm Meister's Apprenticeship*.][NL] Yet shared emotion and knowledge of it, even a sense of belonging based upon this, are not enough to make a 'community'. Community can be present, but it remains a distinct sociological category, and the audience remains a subcategory of the mass that rests upon wills of parallel direction. Everything about the other sociological forms that has to do with meaning and purpose is temporal in nature.

This gives rise to a new problem. *Do the fundamental sociological concepts developed so far express anything in relation to time or duration?* <<It is our intention to refute Schumann's recent negative answer to this query (["Religionssoziologie,"] 690). Tönnies's profound view is proved in his statement ([*Community and Society*,] 35): "Community is the lasting and genuine form of living together, society only transitory and superficial." This insight proves true phenomenologically.>> Can we find here a new ordering principle? Ultimately we are dealing here with the relation of eternity to the temporal form of community. This brings us to the heart of the problem of the social forms we are considering; it will be important for the idea of the church. We distinguished between the will to meaning and the rational purposive will, structures of meaning and structures of purpose, and hence community and society. The meaning of the term 'structure of purpose' is clear. But why do we speak of 'will to meaning' and 'structure of meaning' in reference to community? We do so because in this kind of bond the will is not self-establishing—rather, it acknowledges something established; because it is not related to purpose, but to value; because what is acknowledged is a value-form that cannot be grasped rationally or teleologically; <<This is in opposition to Freyer, *Theorie des objektiven Geistes*, 53ff.: "It is just as complex, but in principle

Having elaborated the structures of acts of will and the possible types of social formation, we can now turn our thoughts to the concept of

---

[114. *cont.*] just as plausible, to spell out the teleological meaning-structure of a moral association [Sittenverband], or a community of a people [Volksgemeinschaft], as to spell out the aesthetic meaning-structure of a symphony."> or, from another perspective, because community by its nature points to no purpose beyond itself. Unlike many sociologists, we consider it impossible—however sensitively one tries—to elaborate the telos of a community, a family, or a people. A community may have a rational telos, but its very essence is not absorbed by that telos, nor identical with it. Instead, *community* as such is characterized by value, as is history, and, as value-bearing, transcends inner historical limitations. As history by nature finds its telos at the limit of history—thinking eschatologically and supratemporally, that is, in God—so the nature of community is grounded in and willed by God. History has no rationally discernible purpose; it comes from God and goes to God. It has meaning and value as such, however broken its reflection of this origin and purpose. So, too, genuine community in marriage, family, or people exists entirely in "coming from God and going to God," who is its telos found at the boundaries of history. The concept of community thus also contains *the idea of infinite time*, whose only limit is the boundary of time. The 'duration' of community is identical with the duration of history. Of course, we speak of community as an idea, not as an empirical entity. By their very nature all communities are from God to God, whether we mean the *physical* communities of blood such as family and clan, *historical* communities such as people and nation, or *life-shaping* communities such as marriage and friendship. There is no essential difference between those given communities in which one finds oneself and those that are created, <<Linguistic usage very nearly expresses the essence of the matter here: one not only 'finds oneself' in a family, one also finds a friend.>> as long as they are communities in the sense described above.

By contrast, a society understood as a structure of purpose exists purely within history. It is constituted in history to realize its purpose. The purpose can be the sheer personal wishes of each individual (earning money, making connections), in which case the 'duration' of the society ideally comes to an end with the satisfaction of the individuals' wishes. If a society's purpose extends beyond the individual, or even a whole generation, then the duration corresponds to this purpose. If the society's purpose is the dream of many to establish the Realm of God on earth, its purpose lies, speaking purely eschatologically, at the end of history. And this is where the category of 'development' enters in, which is absent with a community. In no way does the idea of a society extend beyond the idea of its constitutive purpose. If a purposive association aspired to something beyond the temporally possible, it would cease to be such an association. Here the end of history is really an end, not a boundary. Thus the idea of a purely teleological concrete society is necessarily within history and is temporally conditioned.

It is fruitless to try to refute the above description by arguing from the empirical difference in duration. We spoke here of the idea of community, not of empirical duration. If wills have joined together for the sake of their bond, if people have said 'yes' to a community in which they find themselves, quite apart from rational purposiveness, then the intentionality inherent in these acts extends to the limits of time, that is to say, to the limits of history, to God—community is "from God to God." This is the basis of *all 'holiness' of human community life, and the basis of the relationship of friendship, marriage, and community of people to God, and thus also ideally of the indissolubility of all these life structures.*

Finally, in the sociological concept of the mass we saw that the constitutive factor was a powerful, mechanical stimulus of a majority of people. 'Stimulus' is only conceivable in the

235

236

objective spirit. This concept is of utmost significance for social philosophy and sociology and must perform an important service for us in the analysis of the concept of the church; yet, its current use is woefully unclear.[116]

[114. *cont.*] category of the temporally limited, the temporal 'moment'. *Thus if we recognize 'community' as at the limits of time [grenzzeitlich], and 'society' as limited by time [zeitbegrenzt], then the mass can be described as temporary [innerzeitlich].*

There is nothing to be said here about the association of authentic rule. It should be categorized according to whether one thinks of it as belonging to a life structure of a society or a community.

[115.] In *SC-A* the present footnote 28 follows in the text.

[116.] Deleted in *SC-A*:

Before we treat this problem, we present a brief historical excursus on the views of the Christian church fathers and of Thomas Aquinas about the naturally occurring forms of human social formation.

Historical Excursus on Social Theory in Patristic Writings and Thomas Aquinas

This question shall be treated as briefly as possible. [*SC-RS:* Couldn't the content of the excursus be worked into the above?] The problem of social formation arose early in the history of theology as a philosophical and an ethical problem. By its nature, the issue developed with regard to the community life of the state rather than the church. Is the state a consequence of the fall, that is, is it a result of sin? Or is it willed by God? <<On this whole section see Seeberg, *[Lehrbuch der] Dogmengeschichte*, 3d ed., 3:263ff., 502ff., and Troeltsch, *The Social Teachings of the Christian Churches*. See also the corrective (i.e., Catholic) response of O[tto] Schilling's *Die christlichen Soziallehren* (1926), in the series Der katholische Gedanke.>> The answer can be understood in light of the two concepts of the world <<Troeltsch, *[Social Teachings,]* 100ff., Schilling, *[Soziallehren,]* 45ff., 79ff.>> that run through early Christian literature. One approach sees the world as good, as created, the other approach as bad, degraded by evil will. Corresponding to these are the concepts of natural law as primary and as secondary, <<Schilling, *[ibid.,]* 59ff.>> as absolute and as relative, <<Troeltsch's terminology.>> or as ideal and as practical. <<Seeberg, *Dogmengeschichte*, 503. sec. 3.>> In itself the state is willed by God and good. But as a consequence of sin, punitive force and compulsion are necessary. Even in the primal state, human beings would have founded a state. What is remarkable, however, is that the state reflected in patristic literature essentially has the character of a society [Gesellschaft]. Its task is to ensure order and welfare. This concept comes nowhere near the ideals of the state in Hegel's sense. <<Schilling, *[Soziallehren,]* 58: "The law of the state is nothing other than a reasonable order, decreed by the competent power in possession of force for the protection of the whole, for the preservation of the common good; in essence this goes back as far as Tertullian.">> This dual nature is now inherent in all social formations that would all have arisen in the primal state as well, but that now all have faults. Human beings are by nature social. "Sociale quiddam est humana natura." <<Augustine, "The Good of Marriage," chap. 1.>> This is the general patristic view. The Fathers recognized the distinctness and dissimilarity of persons as a necessary presupposition for all empirical social formation, and indeed as characteristic of the primal state, not as a consequence of sin. The reason for this is that the Fathers adopted an organic conception of community. Were this possible as a solution to the problem of the church, as those following Paul's example believed it

237

3. Objective Spirit [117]   62

Mostly without realizing it,[118] people mean two different things when they speak of objective spirit:[29] (1) objectified spirit as opposed to

---

29. On this whole subject, cf. Hegel, "The Philosophy of Spirit," secs. 483ff.,[119] and Hans Freyer, [*Theorie des objektiven Geistes,*] 53ff.

[116. *cont.*] necessary to think, then it would be applicable to the primal human state. Marriage and family are the most primitive social forms and doubtless willed by God. These forms are of course depraved in the state of sin, by concupiscence and also by patriarchalism understood as punishment; they are restored to sanctity again by Christ. Originally, neither reproduction nor the idea of 'subordination' is associated with sin as constitutive forces of the family. Both are good and necessary. In particular, 'equality' is not abolished by subordination. [Here Bonhoeffer uses the German word *Subordination* in a way parallel to his use of God's *Herrschaft* (see above, page 60). In the primal state, 'subordination' to God is free obedience to the One who rules by serving, the corollary being free, self-giving love between creatures. This view of the primal state is needed to explain 'patriarchalism as punishment', where a very different form of 'rule' and 'subordination' follows from sin.][CG] The heavenly hierarchies serve as an example of this. Troeltsch's idea of equality in the primal state in the sense of absolute likeness of being does not hold true for patristic literature. <<Contra Troeltsch, see Schilling, [*Soziallehren,*] 77. The divine right of emperors, frequently cited by the Fathers, demonstrates the truth of this.>> From the idea of organic equality the philosophical-ethical justification of private property came into force in Lactantius who followed Cicero and Aristotle. <<Giles of Rome later defended private property in *The Governance of Kings and Princes.*>> [Cf. Seeberg, *Dogmengeschichte*, 3:504, note 1.] A few isolated voices argued that poverty and wealth are the consequence of sin (Ambrose). By viewing the instinct for gainful activity as natural and therefore good, and approving contracts and profits from risk, they explicitly acknowledged social activity in the sense of purposive rationality. The Fathers noted again and again that the danger of evil self-seeking lay close at hand. <<Troeltsch, [*Social Teachings,*] 127: "From the ascetic point of view it [trade] was suspect since it assumed pleasure in possessions and in gain, and from the point of view of the principle of love it was suspect because it meant taking from one to give to another, and enriching oneself at the expense of others.">> But the necessity for commercial activity was never lost to view. Thus all honorable work was fundamentally and explicitly valued as fulfilling its proper function   238
within *organic social formations.* <<Only when a formal concept of equality is applied, as in Troeltsch, is there an obstacle to including monastics in this organism.>>
   These basic ideas were essentially taken over and systematized by Thomas. <<Cf. especially Maurenbrecher, *Thomas' Stellung zu dem Wirtschaftsleben seiner Zeit,* 1898.>> Here, too, his theological system of reason and revelation is evident. Using Aristotle, and assisted by the idea of organism, Thomas grounds and acknowledges the state and the social life of Christian society in natural law. He defines the state as having essentially the same purpose as that held by the patristic view. The concept of the church provides the spiritual superstructure to which everything is related. <<Cf. Seeberg, *Dogmengeschichte*, 3d ed., 3:406ff., 501ff.>> The notion of organism, as Thomas understands it, provides the balance between individualism and 'collectivism' ['Sozialismus']. We cannot examine here whether this is systematically valid. Suffice it to say that we have seen that activity in both community and

unformed spirit, and (2) social spirit as opposed to subjective spirit. Both meanings are based on the fact that where wills unite, a 'structure' is created—that is, a third entity, previously unknown, independent of being willed or not willed by the persons who are uniting. This general recognition of the nature of objective spirit was a discovery of the qualitative thinking that became dominant in romanticism and idealism.[120] Concrete totality, which is not a matter of quantity, but is grounded in intuition and in phenomenal experience, is found only here.[121] Two wills encountering one another form a structure. A third person joining them sees not just one person connected to the other; rather, the will of the structure, as a third factor, resists the newcomer with a resistance not identical with the wills of the two individuals. Sometimes this is even more forceful than that of either individual—or than the sum of all the individuals, if this is at all conceivable. Precisely this structure is objective spirit. It not only appears as independent and autonomous to the third person, who desires admission into a bond of friendship; the objective spirit also thrusts itself as a third entity right between two who are bound together in even the most primitively formed structure. Thus the persons themselves experience their community as something real

---

[116. *cont.*] society are acknowledged as belonging to the primary ideal of natural law, and that social formation in general is willed by God. If, as Thomas argues, humanity is conceived as one person (unus homo), then social formation is necessary. <<Thomas, *Summa Theologiae*, 1a2ae, 81,1.>> Only evil will depraves the whole and brings self-seeking into organic communal life.

[117.] Bonhoeffer is guided here in his understanding of objective spirit by Seeberg, *Dogmatik*, 1:505ff., as well as Freyer, *Theorie des objektiven Geistes*. Freyer seeks to redefine the theory of objective spirit in critical differentiation from Hegel's dialectical method.

[118.] The German text should be corrected by reading in the first sentence on *SC* (*DBW* 1):62 the word *meist*, as in the dissertation typescript, instead of the second *Geist*. The typographical error derives from *SC-B* not *SC-A*. [CG/NL]

[119.] The citation here is to Hegel, *Encyclopedia of the Philosophical Sciences in Outline*, pt. (C), "The Philosophy of Spirit," section 2 of which deals with "The Objective Spirit." *SC* (*DBW* 1) cites subsections 483ff., which do not exist; this is a repetition of a typographical error in *SC-B*. The correct reference is presumably to sections 438ff., as also cited below in chap. 5, footnote 68. [CG]

[120.] Deleted in *SC-A*: This is the only way to arrive at a living concept of spirit.

[121.] Deleted in *SC-A*:

Half a sphere and half a sphere are not two half-spheres, but a whole sphere. There is no smallest unit that can be reached by logical-objective means. The idea of the indivisible unit is logically conceivable, to be sure, but it has no objective meaning epistemologically. Several boys writing in a room with a teacher in front of them are not 1, 2, 3 . . . boys added together, but a school class.

outside themselves, a community that distances itself from them without their willing it, rising above them.[122]

In a community, individuals are confronted by their objectified selves. Their own lives have flowed into the community, and now daily it stands before them as a content and form that they experience, as the regulative principle for their conduct.

Thus the law of human community is an interchange between *being that is continually moved and being that is objectified*. Time solidifies every past moment in objectivity, so that the present moment and the past resist one another. In this strife, advancing time wins out and makes *objective spirit into the historical-social turning point between past and future*. In objective spirit elements of both forward historical thrust and expansion are at work. The first is the reality of the historicity of objective spirit; the second is the reality of its sociality. *Objective spirit is thus to be regarded as the connection between historical and communal meaning, between the temporal and spatial intentions of a community. Objective spirit is will exerting itself effectively on the members of the community.* It has individual

63

[122.] Footnote deleted in *SC-A*:

<<This is what also connects the two meanings that are incisively distinguished by Kistiakowski [*Gesellschaft und Einzelwesen*] in his 'concept of universal spirit' as 'empirical totality of social feelings and strivings, and as an ethical-legal norm.' To be sure, one can trace the development from the revolutionary movement to the *law of equality*, but there is also a qualitative difference between the two. Normally, society relates to the individual as the concept of the genus to the specimen, whereas in a living movement there is a relationship of the whole to the part. In the first instance one would see the society not as a community, but as consisting of isolated individuals, whereas in the second it would be a real community. However, the norm, the law, is not the objective spirit itself; it is a form that expresses it, perhaps an especially characteristic form, but that, like any expression, has meaning only as long as it is dynamically acknowledged by the community. It thus has no real authority beyond the community, only within it. But this then eliminates what seemed to be a mutually exclusive opposition of meanings. For this reason the distinction can be of no further use to us. We agree with the view that the normative claim isolates insofar as it really is normative; yet because the laws of state reach beyond the individual, and because, as formal laws, they ideally contain an infinite variety of cases, this does not alter the fact that they have reality only in community. *Without being part of the whole, then, the individual is not concretely touched by the norm.*>> The text of *SC-A* on page 62 adds (following the phrase "rising above them": Even boys at play take oaths to their community, which may consist of only two, to carry out or avoid certain things, as if there were something real, a spirit of the community, which had the capacity to take cognizance of this oath.

It is not the other boy, but the community that demands things of him that bring him into conflict with his domestic, civic, and moral duties.

239

form.[123] It leads an individual life 'beyond' the individual persons, and yet it is real only through them. The more alive the individual persons, the more powerful the objective spirit. It interacts reciprocally with each individual and with them all. To withdraw from it is to withdraw from the community. It wills historical continuity as well as the social realization of its will.

What is objectified, however, is utterly ineradicable, whether by each individual or by all members together. An individual radically separated from the community can no longer experience the objective spirit; but even separation can do no more than this. Everyone will admit that in instances where what is objectified has been given material expression[124] the ability to experience the objective spirit is not all that can be lost. What cannot be shown, however, is that there is a fundamental distinction between objectification in a work of art (so long as it is not experienced as mere matter) and nonmaterial objectification, insofar as both are objective spirit.[125]

Objective spirit exists both in a society and in a community.[126] The wider the circle of those joined in community—and the less specialized the consciousness of norms in it—the less its inner power and the greater its outward power. It is easier to immerse oneself in the spirit of a school class than in that of a friendship. The difficulty of entering the spirit of a societal association [gesellschaftlich Verband] is generally independent of the number of members.[127] The objective spirit of a societal association bears no marks of personal vitality. What is a means 64 to an end in a society (e.g., an advertisement) is a symbol in a community. This corresponds to the difference between them; a society's actions are purposeful or goal-oriented, while those of a community are a self-presentation. The objective spirit of the society is not affirmed as a value in itself, but only as a means to an end; it is the objective struc-

---

[123.] This sentence replaces the following in *SC-A*: It exists only as long as the community has members. The effective objective spirit has individual form.

[124.] Bonhoeffer is arguing that material expressions of objective spirit—e.g., in language, music, books, folk art—can be destroyed or lost, but that, while one may not experience the objective spirit of a community, objective spirit itself is ineradicable; furthermore he is arguing that there is not a fundamental distinction between material and nonmaterial objectification. [CG]

[125.] Cf. Freyer, *Theorie des objektiven Geistes*, 51ff. Freyer distinguishes the category of the 'sign' (*Zeichen*) as a form of objective spirit from that of the 'social form' (*Sozialform*).

[126.] Deleted in *SC-A*: The distinctions will be pointed out.

[127.] The next two sentences are not found in *SC-A*.

ture of purpose. In this case the productivity of objective spirit extends to the system of means. If the society is dissolved, what remains is this system of means as a materialized form of spirit; but it has lost its inner meaning because its purpose has gone. A 'device' whose purpose is no longer understood or interesting is dead, because the objective spirit that sustained it, and that was always only a means to an end, has ceased along with that purpose.[128] A work of art, on the other hand, that intentionally (not purposefully) bears fulfillment and understandability in itself, rests in itself, because the objective spirit that sustained it was an end in itself and continues to live 'above' the will of the members.[129]

From all this it follows that a society and a community relate differently to time.[30] If we describe the temporal intention of a community as reaching the boundary of time [grenzzeitlich], that of a society would be timebound [zeitbegrenzt]. Because of the eschatological character of community, which it shares with history, the deepest significance of community is 'from God to God'.[130] This is the basis for the 'holiness' of human community life, whether we think of physical communities of blood and clan, historical communities like a nation, or life-shaping communities such as marriage and friendship. This holiness reveals the fundamental indissolubility of all these life structures. By contrast, the idea of a society never extends beyond the idea of its constitutive purpose. It remains timebound within history; for a society, the end of history is a real end, not a boundary. (As already noted, the temporal intention of the mass is relative to the moment.) This explains why only a community, and never a society, can or should become 'church'. This will be elaborated below.[131]

65

---

30. Schumann's denial of this fact, ["Religionssoziologie,"] 690, is to be refuted here. Tönnies's insight, [*Community and Society,*] 35, that "community is the lasting and genuine form of living together, society only transitory and superficial" is verified phenomenologically.

[128.] The preceding, beginning with "the objective spirit that sustained it . . . ," replaces the following in *SC-A*: its essence, which consists in its relation to a purpose, is dead.

[129.] The last clause beginning with "because . . ." replaces the following in *SC-A*: Thus the objective spirit of a community reaches to the boundary of time (see above), while that of a society is timebound.

[130.] Cf. Seeberg, *Dogmatik*, 1:140: "All things must serve for the good, for the totality of events is from God to God." Cf. Romans 11:26.

[131.] See below, pages 252ff.

The most profound difference between the two social forms is that the objective spirit of a community (but not that of a society) can be ascribed personal character.[31] It is considered an advance in sociology that it has moved beyond such metaphysical hypostatizing.[32] Basically, however, what comes through here is fear of Hegel. His idea of the spirit of a people [Volksgeist] is unsettling to individualism.[134] But as a matter of principle, we cannot accept the criticism of his idea. It is based on the empiricist notion that there would be no objective spirit were there no persons, that its existence depends on persons coming together and going apart, the former constituting objective spirit and

---

31. Cf. below, pages 125ff.

32. Litt, [*Individuum und Gemeinschaft*,] 260. "The structural principle that we called social interrelatedness precludes the assumption of a particular supra-personal center of activity, but also makes the return to such a center superfluous." Why should only the individual person have monadic being? Litt would probably answer that it is because only the individual has a body. But a community, too, has a body (see below). Thus in my opinion, the idea of the monadic image is not negated by the introduction of collective persons (see also above). Cf. Litt's superb critique of organology, 279ff. Further, see Scheler, [*Formalism in Ethics*,] 519ff., on the collective person [Gesamtperson]. Scheler's sociological argument begins with life-community as the entity that swallows up the individual. To this is added society as built upon individual selves. The highest form of social being for Scheler is then the notion of Christian community, "the unity of independent, intellectual [geistig], and individual single persons, 'in' an independent, intellectual, and individual collective person" (533).[132] Its moral law of life is solidarity (cf. *The Nature of Sympathy*, 164ff.). At the deepest level there are only two pure total collective persons: a culture's collective person and the church (668). Thus for Scheler the church is ultimately something that unfolds in the ethical world; it is an ethical, holy entity. But at best this arrives at the idea of religious community, not that of the church. As far as the sociological structure of the church is concerned, Scheler misses its deeper significance due to his insufficient understanding of the Christian concept of love.[133]

[132.] In Scheler this quote is italicized. [CG]

[133.] Cf. above, the discussion of the 'collective person', page 77, editorial note 52.

[134.] Deleted in *SC-A*: Here, as before, it is not my intention to call Hegel forth from the grave. Hegel postulates the spirit of the people [*Volksgeist*] as well as the spirits of the peoples as 'moments' in the dialectical evolution of spirit; see Hegel, *Lectures on the Philosophy of History*, 55–56, 77–78. The true spirit of a people can be the bearer of morality; cf. Hegel, *Phenomenology of Spirit*, 289, 440. Cf. also Fichte, *Addresses to the German Nation*, Eighth Address, 130ff. Litt decisively rejects this belief in 'collective beings' [*'Kollektivwesenheiten'*] (*Individuum*, 281).

240

the latter destroying it. The mutual dependence of individual and objective spirit is commonly accepted. The individual spirit lives in the objective spirit, but "it is the triumph of the subjective spirit that the objective structures that it can create out of itself, which have their own value and existence, never become totally free of it, but must always long to return to it in order to be completely real."[33] It should be unnecessary to repeat that *the genetic*[135] *dependence of objective spirit says nothing about its autonomy in the theoretical sphere.* For, as we have shown, subjective spirit, too, is dependent upon other spirits in becoming a person, yet is fundamentally[136] autonomous. Objective spirit lives its own life, but not in such a way that the lives of individuals are absorbed in it in the sense that Hegel implies when he writes that "spirit has reality, and individuals are its accidents."[34] [137]

Rather, we maintain that "in principle everyone can say adieu and go their own way."[35] Nevertheless a community has its own center of activity that experiences love, compassion, shared joy, etc., and its own way of acting, alongside other individual persons, in the sense of equal social weight and the monadic image.

Thus we are not dealing here with the conception of some spirit entity, called spirit of the people, that arises of its own natural strength from metaphysical depths. Rather, in the dialectical movement through which alone persons originate, individual collective persons come into being as well. Only with this insight does the richness of the monadic image of social life become clear. Collective persons are self-conscious and spontaneous.[138]

66

---

33. Freyer, *Theorie des objektiven Geistes*, 61.

34. [Hegel,] *Lectures on the Philosophy of Natural Right and Political Science*, sec. 156.

35. Freyer, *Theorie des objektiven Geistes*, 81.

[135.] "Genetic" here replaces in *SC-A* genetic-real.
[136.] "Fundamentally" replaces in *SC-A* metaphysically.
[137.] For Litt's critique of Hegel, cf. above, page 102, editorial note 134.
[138.] Deleted in *SC-A*:

Objective spirit operates in the social transactions of the group. If all activity in the society-type is purposive activity, then community activity is characterized by meaning, that is, it is representative action, and thus ultimately self-representation. [The translation of the previous sentence follows the dissertation manuscript, correcting *SC* (*DBW 1*) to read "so daß des gemeinschaftlichen Sinnhandeln."][CG/NL] In principle, it is the whole

But it is also clear why no personal character can be attributed to a society. Its objective spirit is seen as only a means to an end, while *a person can never be only a means to an end.*

Can we speak of *the collective person as having a body?* At the outset we must warn against confusing this with a theory of organism, which again would be close to the theory of the spirit of the people. Body is not the same as the executive function of spirit, which is a false definition in any case. 'Body' cannot be objectively measured but only subjectively experienced. Thus it must not be confused with physical body[139] ("flesh" in the Apostles' Creed).[36] A physical body has the same objective appearance whether dead or alive, but only the latter is 'body'. 'Body' exists in relation to the I; it is the physical body that the I experiences as its possession. The I is inwardly connected with the body and, to a certain extent, controls it. But it is in this same sense that a community's center of activity experiences all of its members who have affirmed the community. It takes their affirmation seriously and in this sense controls its 'body'. The idea of a community of will makes this distinction and separates the body from the idea of organism. The concept of body is important for the concept of the church, as will be shown.[140]

67

---

36. Scheler, [*Formalism in Ethics,*] 398ff., 543f.

[138. *cont.*] community that acts. The most primitive community activity is play, the least purposeful activity of all. <<Play is an excellent example of the concept of 'sociability' (cf. Simmel's excellent description of its nature in "Fundamental Problems of Sociology (Individual and Society)," *The Sociology of Georg Simmel,* 43ff. All ideas of human spirit are drawn into the motion of play. In itself sociability is neither community, nor is it society; rather, if it is genuine, it is activity as such.>> It is an activity that is purely expressive, like artistic activity, expressing itself in buildings, dances, ceremonies. But there is also representation 'before something', without that activity becoming purposive. Thus cultic activity of primitive religious communities is often pure self-representation before the deity.

What is advertising or 'sign' in a corporation, for example, is essentially *symbol* in a community, [*SC-A* correctly has *Gemeinschaft* here, not *Gesellschaft* as in *SC* (*DBW* 1).] [CG] that is, it points to the concrete form of objective spirit of the community; it is based upon itself and in principle does not extend beyond the community (flag, cross). 'Signs' are directed outward and are closely related to advertising.

Not all expression is objective spirit per se, but rather the effect of objective spirit. One can only ascribe personality to its vitality.

[139.] Here *Körper* (body) is rendered in the parenthesis as *Fleisch*, since in German the Apostles' Creed confesses belief in "the resurrection of the flesh," not "resurrection of the body" as in English. [CG]

[140.] See below, pages 178ff. and 223ff.

Anyone who has followed this line of argument will certainly object adamantly that now idealism finally has been vindicated. Has the community of will, so often emphasized, which is based upon the structural separateness and diversity of individuals, perhaps finally become unity, which, it now turns out, even has its own center of activity? How should we answer this? It is true that with the collective person a new unity does arise that is something other than the absolute and relative unity in the identity of what is willed. Yet this new unity does not abolish the specific reciprocal movement of community. Individual persons remain completely separate from one another.[141] The collective person is metaphysically autonomous in relation to the individuals, though at the same time genetically dependent. In the structure of persons the collective person has a status that is no different from that of each individual.[142] Strictly speaking, *unity* and *community* are not mutually exclusive, nor are they identical,[143] but each needs the other.[144]

The theological reason for including the above in the discussion of the doctrine of the primal state is that all the community relations that we have considered can be imagined in a state of integrity, that is, within the originally given religious and social community of love. Thus the *spirit-form [Geistform], namely this love community, and the nature-form*   68 *[Naturform], i.e., the empirical community, are created to complement each other;* this allows one to draw conclusions about the nature of empirical community.[145]

[141.] Deleted in *SC-A*:

Individual persons do not in fact melt together, but remain completely separate from one another. They also do not melt partially into the collective person. Rather, the reciprocal structure of their community as such becomes a person with its own center of activity, which exists 'beside' or 'above' the individual persons.

[142.] Deleted in *SC-A*: In this way we think we have correctly preserved the basic ideas of romantic-idealist philosophy and yet safeguarded the interest of a concrete philosophy.

[143.] *SC-A* lacks the phrase nor are they identical.

[144.] Deleted in *SC-A*:

Quite consciously this exposition has been under the doctrinal concept of the primal state. This provides a way to evaluate the idea of community in all concrete community formation. And only by recognizing this context is it possible to look ahead to the eschatology of communities. Only from this perspective can we understand and appreciate the concrete fact of the church in terms of social philosophy, and show how the *idea of the holy church*   241 *both realizes and overcomes the forms God intended for all primal community.*

[145.] The translations 'spirit-form' and 'nature-form' are used to highlight the

The following chapter will show, by the entry of sin, how (1) the spirit-form takes on a new shape, and (2) what connection exists between these altered ethical basic-relations and the nature-forms that are preserved. Only then can the idea of the collective person be interpreted fully.

[145. *cont.*] parallelism of the terms 'spirit' and 'nature' that run through all of Bonhoeffer's theological anthropology. Although the word *Geist* (spirit) may be replaced by words like *Dasein* and *Existenz* in *Act and Being, Creation and Fall,* and the 1933 Christology lectures, the conceptual structure of 'spirit' and 'nature' developed in his first work remains consistent. [CG]

SIN AND BROKEN COMMUNITY

THE WORLD OF SIN is the world of 'Adam', the old humanity. But the   69
world of Adam is the world Christ reconciled and made into a new
humanity, Christ's church. However, it is not as if Adam were completely overcome; rather, the humanity of Adam lives on in the humanity of Christ. This is why the discussion of the problem of sin is
indispensable for understanding the sanctorum communio.[1]

The essential task of this chapter is to expose the new social basic-
relations between I and You, as well as between I and humanity, that are
inherent in the concept of sin. The concept of the Christian person presented in chapter 2 will be central to this discussion. The question of
how these relations are connected to the natural forms can be treated
much more briefly.

Whereas the previous spirit-form grew out of love, the fall replaced
love with selfishness. This gave rise to the break in immediate community with God, and likewise in human community. With this change of
direction the whole spiritual orientation of humanity was altered.
Morality and religion in their proper sense[2] disappear from human
nature, and are now only formally[3] visible in the structures of legal
order and in natural religion.[4]

[1.] Bonhoeffer's presentation of "Sin and Broken Community" is based upon Seeberg,
Dogmatik, 2:1ff.

[2.] Deleted in *SC-A*: and their content.

[3.] The word "formally" replaces in *SC-A* in the forms of its nature.

[4.] Deleted in *SC-A*: and they are preserved down to the most primitive life in the form of
primal social synthesis (see above) and superstition.

Human love, instead of being directed toward the other—whether that be God or other

Whereas in the primal state the relation among human beings is one of giving, in the sinful state it is purely demanding. Every person exists in complete, voluntary isolation; everyone lives their own life, rather than all living the same life in God.[5] Now everyone has their own conscience.[6] There was no conscience in the primal state; only after the fall did Adam know what good and evil are. Conscience can just as well 70 be the ultimate prop of human self-justification as the site where Christ strikes home at one through the law. Human beings, hearing the divine law in solitude[7] and recognizing their own sinfulness, come to life again as ethical persons, albeit in ethical isolation. With sin, ethical atomism enters history. This applies essentially to the spirit-form. All natural forms of community remain, but they are corrupt in their inmost core.[8]

But the recognition by human beings of their utter solitude in responsibility before God, and the utter uniqueness of their culpability, is met with another perception that does not cancel the first, but rather intensifies it, even while appearing to contradict it completely. This second perception is based upon insight into the qualitative nature of sin, that is, knowledge that the misery of sin is infinitely great. This implies, however, that sin must have a significance that is not only individual, but also supra-individual. Sin must be conceived as both a supra-individual deed and, of course, as an individual deed; it must be simultaneously the deed of the human race[9] and of the individual. Thus

---

[4. *cont*] people—is now focused on oneself. Everything becomes a means to one's own selfishness. On morality and religion as the primal tendencies of human beings, cf. Seeberg, *Dogmatik*, 1:502ff.

[5.] *SC-RS*: "What does this mean?" ["Life in God" is the translation for *Gottesleben*, literally "life of God" or "life through God." Bonhoeffer means that sin atomizes a shared life in communion with God.][CG]

[6.] On the manifestations of religion and morality in the conscience of the human person in the natural state (as opposed to the primal state), see Seeberg, *Dogmatik*, 2:82ff.

[7.] The wording from "Conscience can just as well . . ." to "hearing the divine law in solitude" replaces the following in *SC-A*:

In the conscience we can see a remnant of humanity's disposition toward religious morality, as well as an opportunity for the will of the eternal. If conscience is moved by God, people experience the divine demand and recognize their own sinfulness in absolute solitude before God—now not the giving, but the demanding God. In this solitude they hear the divine 'You shall' . . .

[8.] The statement "they are corrupt in their inmost core" replaces in *SC-A* they have been emptied of their content.

[9.] "Human race," meaning all human beings, the whole human species, is the transla-

recognition of one's *utter solitude* leads to the other insight, namely the *broadest sense of shared sinfulness*, so that by our very nature the 'one' is led to the 'other', without whom the existence and nature of the one would be unthinkable.

Two problems surface here. How should we understand the universality of sin in terms of the logic of theology? Simply regarding it as a fact is not enough. Second, how should the empirical spread of sin throughout humanity be conceptualized?

It was in the doctrine of original sin that the idea of the social significance of sin was elaborated theologically.

A. The Doctrine of Original Sin

This doctrine, which presupposes that sin has spread through all of humanity, investigates the manner of this spreading. It then details accordingly *how human beings belong together* and are bound together in status corruptionis [state of corruption].[10] But since ideas intended to prove the universality of sin in the first place were mixed into the inquiry about the proliferation of sin, the doctrine of original sin is one of the most difficult logical problems of all theology.[1][11]

71

---

1. It would be tempting, if it would not lead too far astray, to introduce here a sociological-historical investigation of the doctrine of original sin that could be quite productive. Of special significance to social philosophy are concepts such as all humanity's 'being in Adam'; Adam, or for that matter every individual, representing the human race; imputatio [imputation]; of the collective person of the genus humanum [humankind] as the scholastics knew it (cf. Thomas Aquinas, *Summa Theologiae*, 1a2ae, 81,1 [26:5]); and a concept that has repeat-

[9. *cont.*] tion for *Geschlecht*. The phrase 'human race' in English does not have the connotations of its German cognate *Rasse* (the latter can also mean 'breed' as in pedigree and selective breeding of animals). Bonhoeffer did not use the word *Rasse*, and he opposed any racist ideology, especially in the form of anti-Semitism. His theological concern is with all humanity, not with a biological ideology of race; see below, pages 114ff. [NL/CG]

[10.] The italics in the dissertation typescript extend from the word *"how"* to the word *"corruptionis"*. [CG]

[11.] *SC-A* does not include footnote 1. In its place is the following:

Theology has found a wide variety of answers to this problem. Suffice it here to sketch briefly the biblical findings.

Scripture refers throughout to the universality of sin (Gen. 8:2; Ps. 58:5; Psalm 14; Job 14:4; Rom. 3:24), but never to original sin [Erbsünde] [The German *Erbsünde* literally

The culpability of the individual and the universality of sin should be understood together; that is, the individual culpable act and the cul-

---

edly been confounded with it, that of the human species in the biological sense, which in turn is connected to the sociological importance of infant baptism in Roman Catholicism. These concepts would all have to be clarified from the Bible to the present and examined for their theological content. We will include in the text only the most important systematic results for the present context.

[11. *cont*] means 'inherited sin'. We have employed the usual translation "original sin," noting that there are nuances of emphasis between the two terms.][CG] (not even Ps. 51:7 or Exod. 20:5; cf. Ezek. 18:2, 20; Jer. 31:29). Nor does Paul speak of a doctrine of physical original sin. The translation of Romans 5:12 ἐφ' ᾧ as in quo [in whom] is incorrect; rather, it must be rendered by 'in that' ['wobei']. [The translation of the Greek by the Latin *in quo* is found in the Vulgate, where 'in whom' refers to Adam. The *NRSV* ("because all have sinned") interprets the Greek the same as Bonhoeffer.][CG] The idea is thus as follows: through *one human being, sin enters the world*, i.e., the human race. When Adam sinned, he sinned as an individual and as the human race. From eternity, God now imposes the sentence of death [Todesverhängnis] upon the sin of Adam both as an individual and as the embodiment of the human race, i.e., upon humanity from Adam to Christ. For the one sin establishes the "objectively effective principle" (Seeberg) [Cf. *Dogmatik*, 2:44.] for all further sins of humanity. No one will act differently from Adam; that is, there is in principle a universality of sin established by this 'objectively effective principle'. Paul does not discuss what empirical form this takes; however, the doctrine of original sin [Erbsündenlehre] raises this very question. Thus Paul provides us no more than the general idea that God imputes to all human beings the *one* sin of Adam, and that this can be concluded from the fact of the universal destiny of death. Systematically, then, the question is, first, how the one person relates in principle to the entire human race, and, then, how sin is spread empirically. One should note that Paul probably had a reason for not answering the second question.

242

A brief historical survey will remind us how these two basic sociological-ethical problems have been treated in the history of theology. This will give us some starting points for the systematic presentation. <<Two preliminary remarks will suffice. The incorrect translation of Romans 5:12 ἐφ' ᾧ as in quo [in whom] has had disastrous effects in the history of doctrine. It was believed that one could find here the nucleus of a physically based doctrine of original sin, although the earlier parallel in 1 Corinthians 15:22, where 'in Adam' stands beside 'in Christ', should have proved the impossibility of this idea. Furthermore, it should be noted that Paul does not view the analogy between Adam and Christ as exhaustive. This is understood without his stating it explicitly. Adam is by nature *the human being* and as such is also the *first* human being, since he stands *within* history. His sin was the 'first' sin. But qualitatively, 'first' sins are the only kind there are (see below). Christ was human and divine; he stood within and beyond history. Insofar as Adam is *the* human being, he can be compared to Christ in limited analogy as the representative of the old humanity as opposed to the new.>> We begin with Augustine. The essence of original sin is the culpability [Schuldhaftigkeit] of the entire human race, brought about by Adam, propagated by procreation, demonstrated in humanity's nature and in concupiscence; the latter is judged as punishment for the primal sin. Sin must somehow have been committed by humanity itself,

pability of the human race must be connected conceptually. When the human race is understood by means of the biological concept of the

---

[11. *cont.*] since ethical thinking presupposes some sort of identity between the guilty and the punished. Thus it is said that, according to Romans 5:12, all human beings were 'in Adam'—though being 'in Adam' is a necessary but insufficient cause for punishment. The sins committed 'in Adam' must be 'taken into account'; this is the meaning of the concept of *imputatio* [imputation]. At the same time it implies the consequent punishment, i.e., concupiscence. However, original sin [Erbsünde] and original evil [Erbübel] are closely connected, in fact so closely that Augustine can regard original evil itself as the cause for the 'ascription' of culpability [Schuldanrechnung]; thus he calls concupiscence itself a sin, not merely a punishment, and a place where further sins can arise. Original sin and original evil are spread through procreation. This raises the question how the social basic-relations of humanity are presented in this context. It seems to me that the three significant social-philosophical concepts that shed light on this subject are: *(1) original evil, (2) the 'being in Adam' of humanity,* and *(3) imputatio [imputation].*

When Augustine considers humanity as a whole, his initial feeling is that he belongs to a species that has been struck by a terrible and overpowering fate, turned upside down in its very nature and corrupted through every fiber of its being. Terrible punishment has been imposed upon him like a catastrophe. As procreators and procreated, the members of the human race are indissolubly connected to one another, and just where they find their closest bond, there is also their utter ruin. For it is sexual concupiscence that Augustine judges in this way. But precisely because of its naturalness, the complete universality of this fate is assured. With terrific emotional intensity, Augustine subjects himself to the power of the *natura vitiata [defective nature]* of inherited evil [Erbübel]. The licentiousness of his age made him shudder at the overwhelming power of *concupiscentia [inordinate desire]* in the world. This power must have especially significant religious and metaphysical meaning, for not even the will can command it; it brings even a saint to destruction again and again, and it leaves no person untouched. In infinite inferiority, humanity must look this power in the face. Such thoughts are the devastating utterance of a person who attributes to the powers of nature a metaphysical-fatalistic significance. They lead logically to the view of the *massa perditionis [mass of ruin], the mass that is subject to a tragic fate understood as a fact of nature.* [In *SC-A* it is clear that the italic type begins with *massa.*][CG] <<This concept of the mass is not the sociological one of a social structure, but gathers a multiplicity of persons under a single viewpoint.>>

But this pessimistic, almost Manichaean, view also contains the grounds of its defeat. There is a double aspect to each person's consciousness of body that is given with sexuality: first, one is endowed with something quite personal, and yet precisely here one is a natural being quite apart from one's personhood. By thinking of the first along with the second, Augustine not only is led to associate natural corruption with personal culpability, claiming that the corruption is the punishment for the sin, but also makes concupiscence the reason for ascribing culpability, because concupiscence itself is sin. <<Seeberg, *Dogmengeschichte,* 2:504f. We cannot elaborate here on the theological obscurity in Augustine's argument.>> Concupiscence is still seen as a power, to be sure, but different from an earthquake or thunderstorm. It is connected with the bodily nature of human beings, and thus with the person; then again, it is quite independent of the person. This double aspect is clearly expressed in the image borrowed from Romans 5:12, that we were all 'in Adam', that is, in a purely biological and natural sense—although that very text intends to express

243

species, the ethical gravity of the concept of culpability is weakened. We must thus discover a Christian-ethical concept of the species. The issue

[11. *cont.*] precisely the culpability of every individual. To our way of thinking the contradiction is extreme. Augustine turns most strongly toward the purely personal spirit with the statement "we all were that Adam" (*On the Merits and Forgiveness of Sins*, 1.10–11). This is as much as to say that our will is the same as Adam's, and therefore that we ourselves have done what Adam did. This puts the emphasis on personal culpability; at the same time, however, the idea of original sin as *inherited* seems to have been suspended. Although Augustine always strove to define personal culpability as truly and strictly personal, in the end he was always led by the idea of *infant baptism* to false biological views of the human species. Nevertheless, one must acknowledge that, besides the mass, another concept has been added here that could be called that of the realm of ethical persons. The dissonance of these two ideas is most evident in the doctrine of the imputatio [imputation] of Adam's sin. It takes up a middle position between Augustine's two basic views mentioned above. It is part of the first—thinking in terms of the mass—insofar as it defines humanity as a biological unity; it is part of the second—thinking in terms of ethical persons—insofar as it tries to express the idea of personal culpability. Its problem is how to derive personal culpability from the biological unity of humanity in Adam—a problem that the doctrine of imputatio cannot solve, because the problem contains inner contradictions. In two respects Adam is conceived as progenitor and representative of humanity: first, as procreator, and second, as the one in whom lay the will of humanity as a whole—in later terms, as caput seminale and morale [the seminal and moral head]. Adam's act of will is imputed to human beings as their own. Thus biological and ethical views of humanity struggle with one another with no prospect for resolution. For Augustine, however, interest in the universality of sin prevails over interest in personal culpability, the biological over the ethical. <<Since Catholic scholasticism there were efforts to develop an ethical concept of humanity, with differing rationales. Anselm, coming from realism, sees humanity as a single substantial reality. Through the fall of the one, the one humanity was also bound to fall (*de fide Trin.*, 2). [The reference to Anselm (actually to his "On the Incarnation of the Word") is a paraphrase of Bartmann, *Lehrbuch der Dogmatik*, 1:311.] [CG] Duns Scotus traces the loss of the divine likeness to a divine decree. Thomas stresses the physical and moral unity of humanity in Adam, the physical consisting in the Adamic nature borne by human beings ("Omnes homines, qui nascuntur ex Adam possunt considerari ut unus homo, in quantum conveniunt in natura" ["All who are descended from Adam can be regarded as a single human being, since they belong together by their nature"], *Summa Theologiae* 1a2ae., 81,1 [26:9]). Thomas grounds moral unity in the fact that the members of a community [Communität] are regarded as unum corpus [one body], but the community as unus homo [one person] ("in civilibus omnes homines sunt qui unius communitatis reputantur quasi unum corpus, et tota communitas quasi unus homo . . . sic igitur multi homines ex Adam derivati sunt tanquam multa membra unius corporis" ["In political matters all belonging to one community are reckoned to be like one body, and the whole community like one person. . . . So then the many people descending from Adam are, as it were, many members of the one body"], 1a2ae., 81,1 [26:9]). The individual human person stands within the collective person of the human race. But from this point Thomas leaps to the biological image of the organism for the sake of greater clarity. The member has no free will, but must act according to the will of the head. While Anselm does not move beyond the Augustinian concept of nature, and in Duns Scotus we hear of the moral solidarity of all people, Thomas makes the head of the body again exclusively responsible. Post-Tridentine Roman Catholic theology took up the

244

is how to understand the human species in terms of the concept of sin.[12] Previously the human species appeared to be comprehensively

---

[11. cont.] problem at this point and (following Duns Scotus) developed the theory of God's decree and covenant with Adam (Busch, *Lehre von der Erbsünde bei Bellarmin und Suarez*, 70ff., 171ff., 186. [The correct title is *Das Wesen der Erbsünde nach Bellarmin und Suarez*.][CG] Cf. Ambrosius Catharinus, *De casu hominis et peccato originali*, 184: "in ipso existentes ratione simul naturae et pacti" ["Human beings have both natural and contractual relations"]. [Cf. Busch, *Lehre von der Erbsünde*, 70.] Likewise Suarez; the biblical basis is Genesis 2:16ff.). All these efforts at an ethical view of humanity were doomed to failure in conceiving humanity biologically as a species, as long as one had to defend a Catholic doctrine of infant baptism. [Bonhoeffer's note summarizes material from Bartmann, *Lehrbuch der Dogmatik*, 1:298ff. The quoted passages are found there as well.]>>

Luther then put all the weight on the ethical culpability of human beings and overcame the biological view of the species that had derived from the idea of procreation. He identifies the essence of original sin in the 'will of the ego' ['Ichwillen'], that is, in a personal ethical act. Thus he maintains that sin is simultaneously inexcusable and universal. Protestant orthodoxy did not succeed in preserving this.

Schleiermacher rediscovered the significance of original sin as a problem of social philosophy and dealt with it using a new biological approach. It seemed readily understandable to him to think of sin as something inherited, though the concept of sin then appeared misleading (*The Christian Faith*, §69, postscript, 281). Original sin, on the one hand, is that sinfulness that is present in people but grounded beyond an individual's existence ([ibid.,] §70, 282ff.); on the other hand, it is the culpability of one person toward another, and it is therefore to be regarded as both collective deed and corporate culpability of the human race ([ibid.,] §71, 285ff.). Everyone is born with sinfulness in the form of sensuality, which is actualized through free and autonomous action 'into real sins'. The first human being already had innate sinfulness as something original [Ursprüngliches] ([ibid.,] §72.5, 301ff.). Real sin increases the disposition to sin "like any skill increases a talent," [Bonhoeffer's phrase, "like any skill increases a talent" (*wie "jede Fertigkeit die Anlage [steigert]"*), is not an exact quotation of Schleiermacher, who wrote in *The Christian Faith*, §71.1, 287: ". . . as every disposition in man attains by exercise to proficiency and thereupon grows. . ." ("Allein wie jede Anlage in dem Menschen durch Ausübung Fertigkeit wird und als solche wächst. . . ." [*Der christliche Glaube*, §71.1, 275]).][CG] thus becoming 'originating original sin' [verursachende Ursünde], which incites others as well as itself to real sin (ibid., §71.1, 286f.; §72.6, 303f.). Only in the sinful act should the individual be aware of being the subject of original sin [Erbsünde]. But since sinful deeds necessarily occur, it is clear that everyone would have acted as Adam did, so that his culpability is rightly called that of everyone. *But no one can conceive of sin as something individual; rather it arises as something communal in the self-consciousness that has become the consciousness of the species.* Everyone knows that their own sinfulness is caused by others, but also that their own real sin causes the sinfulness of others. Thus, not only have all made themselves guilty, but they exist in a corporate context of guilt that both exonerates and implicates them all. Thus, on the one hand, everybody is a "representative [Repräsentant]" of the whole human race" (ibid., §71.2, 288), and, on the other hand, the concept of original sin as culpability [Erbsünde als Schuld] is correct only when it applies to "the totality of the entire human race," in which it "cannot in similar fashion be the culpability of the individual" (ibid., §71.2, 289). [Bonhoeffer writes "die Gesamtheit [totality] des ganzen Geschlechts" while Schleiermacher says "die Gesamttat [collective deed] des ganzen Geschlechts."][CG]

defined only in terms of nature. Young children, the mentally deficient, and normally developed people seemed to have to be conceived as equals. But this necessarily led to ethically indifferent views of sin, sacraments, and the church. It follows from this that the Christian concept of culpability is incompatible with a biological concept of the species. Thus the concept of the species [Gattung] should be based upon the concept of culpability, not vice versa. This would allow us to move on to an ethical collective concept of the human race [Geschlecht], which alone can do full justice to the idea of the sin of the human race. The individual is then established as the self-conscious and

---

246

[11. cont.] But this means the individual is relatively exonerated by the totality. The human race is the subject of original sin, as the individual was earlier seen in the context of the sinful act. Schleiermacher was doubtless correct in one respect, namely seeing that the concept of sin implies fulfillment in a social, collective concept. But he introduced a biological category instead of the ethical-social one, in part giving it a metaphysical basis. Sin is sensuality, inhibition of God-consciousness, thus a negative factor, but not an ethical category. The emphasis is entirely on the theory of heredity in the sense of a physical fact. Schleiermacher's efforts are thus directed at exploring precisely that aspect of the problem that is unbiblical, namely the *inheriting of sin*; this led him to lose sight of the biblical content of the concept of sin.

Ritschl formulated his doctrine of the realm of sin partly in reaction to Schleiermacher and partly in agreement with him. According to Ritschl, the subject of original sin [Erbsünde] is humanity as the sum of all individuals. (*The Christian Doctrine of Justification and Reconciliation*, 328ff.) This amounts to a rejection of the biological concept, including that of *inherited*-sin [*Erb*-Sünde]. However, it seems to me that we can replace it only with the idea of a collective person, not with Ritschl's sum of individuals (see below).

Twentieth-century theology as a whole tends to push aside the problem of inheriting sin. The Catholic philosopher Scheler, with whom we will deal briefly below, offered the latest defense of a *doctrine of inherited culpability* [*Erbschuldlehre*].

We now resume our systematic presentation in debate with the conceptual framework just presented, and we will attempt to comprehend ethically some fundamental sociological concepts such as human race [Geschlecht], ascription [Zurechnung], and collective person, which are essential to an understanding of the concept of the church.

[12.] In German and English *Sünde* and 'sin' refer to the act and condition of offense against God. In German the consequence of *Sünde* is *Schuld*, which refers both to an objective situation (e.g., owing a debt, or being judged guilty by a court) and a personal obligation, or culpability. In the vocabulary of debt, *Schuld* refers both to the debt itself and to the personal obligation to repay it. Theologically *Schuld* can refer both to the fact of sin (translated by the English "sin") and to the personal consequence of sin (translated here by "culpability" or "guilt" and their variants). Since for many people the English noun "guilt" primarily expresses a subjective feeling, whereas *Schuld* refers to an objective condition, we avoid the use of the noun "guilt." The English adjective is closer to the German— as in the legal verdict "guilty," which refers to the objective judgment of a court, not to the subjective emotion of the accused. [RK/CG]

spontaneously acting person, the prerequisite for ethical relevance, and the human race is conceived as consisting of such persons.[13]

The idea of the sin of the human race and that of the individual must be discussed from the standpoint of the Christian concept of the   72 human race, of humanity. How can one conceive of the individual culpable act and the guiltiness of the human race together without making one the reason for the other, that is, excusing one by means of the other? Augustine evidently thought of the sinful collective act [Gesamtakt] as the basis for every individual act, and Anselm and Thomas basically get no further than this.[14] Ritschl moves in just the opposite direction by going from the sum of individual sins to arrive at the concept of the kingdom of sin, thus not sufficiently grounding the universality of sin.[15] Everything obviously depends upon *finding the act of the whole in the sinful individual act*, without making the one the reason for the other. An ethical category must be related to the individual as a specific person. Precisely the social element, however, is thereby not excluded, but posited simultaneously. *The human being, by virtue of being an individual, is also the human race.* This is the definition that does justice to the human spirit in relation to the fundamental social category. When, in the sinful act, the individual spirit rises up against God,[16] thus climbing to the utmost height of spiritual individuality—since this is the individual's very own deed against God, occasioned by nothing else—the deed committed is at the same time *the deed of the human race* (no longer in the biological sense) *in the individual person*. One falls away not only from one's personal vocation but also from one's generic vocation as a member of the human race. Thus all humanity falls with each sin, and not one of us is in principle different from Adam; that is, every one is also the "first" sinner.[17] At the same time, this relationship

---

[13.] Deleted in *SC-A*: The problem of young children will be dealt with below in the context of infant baptism.

[14.] On Augustine, see Seeberg, *Dogmengeschichte,* 2:504ff. and 518 and *Dogmatik,* 2:4ff., on which Bonhoeffer is obviously basing his argument. On Anselm and Thomas, see Bartmann, *Lehrbuch der Dogmatik,* 1:289ff.; cf. Anselm of Canterbury, *The Virgin Conception and Original Sin,* and Thomas Aquinas, *Summa Theologiae,* 26:2–59 (1a2ae., 81–83). See above, page 112, Bonhoeffer's note about Catholic scholasticism.

[15.] Cf. Ritschl, *The Christian Doctrine of Justification and Reconciliation,* 327ff.

[16.] "God" replaces in *SC-A* absolute Spirit [absoluten Geist].

[17.] The next sentence was a footnote in *SC-A*.

of individuals and human race corresponds to the monadic image presented in the section on social philosophy, where each individual monad 'represents' the whole world.[18] Aware of this state of affairs, we connect consciousness of our deepest personal culpability with that of the universality of our deed.[19] Every deed is at once an individual act and one that reawakens the total sin of humanity. This, then, establishes the universality of sin as necessarily posited along with, and in, individual sin.[2]

73　　　Knowledge of the link between the individual and the human race leads to what has been called *the experience of common sinfulness.* "I am a person of unclean lips and dwell in the midst of a people of unclean lips," Isaiah proclaims[21] as he stands utterly alone in the face of God's holiness. He does not thereby exonerate himself of his personal culpability, but rather associates his own guiltiness with the consciousness that the sin of the whole people has awakened in him—that his sin stands in closest connection with that of the whole people. The experience of ethical solidarity and awareness of oneself as *peccator pessimus* [the worst sinner] belong together. This experience does not in any way

---

2. Max Scheler's recent defense of the idea of original sin begins with the correct insight that our ethical concepts have not kept pace with our social knowledge, but are one-sidedly individualistic. He argues that culpability is necessarily linked with autonomous, personal action, but that does not mean it is necessarily linked with concrete individuality; it is quite possible for a person to act culpably without individually being guilty. This argument is based upon the platonic concept of good and evil as substantial essences, a concept that then leads to the shallow concept of autonomy. For Christian thought, good and evil are qualities of will; thus, Scheler's argument collapses. We have hopefully shown that it is nevertheless not necessary to think in purely individualistic terms.[20]

[18.] On the monadic image, see above, page 79, editorial note 60.
[19.] Deleted in *SC-A*: We cannot hide behind having to bear the burden of guilt of an empirical-temporal first sin, for that would mean reverting to the biological concept of the species. Instead, we are to make the connection between our individual, generic deed and universal culpability. Thus it is clear that the burden of guilt is not decreased but increased.
[20.] In *SC-A*, footnote 2 was originally placed further below in the text; see below, page
247　 117, editorial note 22. On this subject, see Scheler, *Formalism in Ethics*, 479ff. Bonhoeffer's critique of Scheler follows Seeberg, *Dogmatik*, 2:49ff.
[21.] Isaiah 6:5. [*NRSV* reads: "I am a man of unclean lips, and I live among a people of unclean lips."][CG]

constitute sociality; rather, sociality exists before the experience and independently of it. This principle must be strictly observed (see below on 'the experience of the church', pages 272ff.). The experience of ethical solidarity is based upon the utmost singularity of the person, so that even in the awareness of the closest solidarity, the ontic-ethical separateness of individual persons caused by sin can never end, nor disappear from consciousness. One cannot avoid the boundaries of the self. Here we are faced with the I-You-relation described above but actualized in a sinful way, whose 'overcoming' ['Aufhebung'] is only possible in the concept of the church. We should add, however, that the I cannot exist without the You, nor can it exist without the human race.[22] The

---

[22.] Deleted from *SC-A*:

And furthermore, the I that has become a person is bonded by experience only with other individual egos [Ichen] who have become persons; only to such persons can a concept of community be applied. All others belong only *potentially* to this category (note how the basic lines of the concept of the church already are emerging here).

With these observations all empirical objectification of the universality of sin has been put aside, and we consciously have distanced ourselves from the Augustinian theory of original sin. [Continues in *SC-A* with the text found above, page 116, footnote 2: "Max Scheler's recent defense . . ."]

Now that we, too, must assume some sort of historical proliferation of sin, we are still faced with the question of the manner of this empirical proliferation. First of all it should be said that nothing really can be known about this. Sin in every case is unfathomable, inexcusable defiance of God, arising from free will. One can trace the psychological motivation right down to the deed, but the deed itself is something completely new, born of freedom, and psychologically inexplicable. All explanations are historicizations and excuses that weaken the fact of sin, whether they are purely on the level of the psyche or also on the level of the spirit. Thus, we place a warning sign beside the whole question. If we heed it, then basically we cannot go wrong anymore; hence, we now ask the question again and recognize its relative legitimacy. We now will attempt to trace the motivation at least down to the deed. Our exposition, above, about the social connectedness of human beings seems to be very useful in this effort. We look for the motives leading to the deed, not in sexuality, as did the tradition, but in the human spirit bound up in a net of sociality. It is to R. Seeberg's credit that he was the first to articulate this idea. <<See R[einhold] Seeberg, *Dogmatik*, 2:49ff.>> The original community of love, as mutual harmony of reciprocally directed wills, is essentially destroyed when one will changes from a loving to an egocentric direction. Then it is in the nature of things that whoever sees that everyone else is giving up the unbroken community and pursuing a self-seeking direction—seeing that their own intention toward community is 'running idle', finding no response—also will turn in this direction. This begins in the smallest circle and extends wider and wider, so that one can rightly say that it is precisely *in sociality that one should look for the basis of universal egotism*.

Should this development be identified with the transition from the community type [Gemeinschaft] to the society type [Gesellschaft]? Obviously not. For in practice both types continue to exist, though neither any longer in its pure form, but in 'relativity'. There

'experience' of the peccatorum communio [community of sinners] in its relation to the ontic basic-relations anticipates the 'experience' of the church as it will be described below.

74   **B. Ethical Collective Persons**

If the subject of sin is both the individual and the human race, then one must ask in what sociological form of unity humanity-in-Adam [Adamsmenschheit] should be conceived. This reintroduces the question of the ethical personality of collective persons that was left open above, and that should determine whether there is any meaning at all in the idea of a collective person. Is it possible to regard the collective person as an ethical person, that is, to place it in the concrete situation of being addressed by a You? If so, it would be a proven center of activity.

The meaning and the reality of such a call can be grasped only by one who has experienced it within an empirical community. It is the Israelite concept of the 'people of God', which only arose from being thus called[23] by God, by the prophets, by the course of political history, by alien peoples. The call comes not to the individual, but to the collective person. The people must do penance as the people of God. It was

---

248   [22. cont.] is no longer community without sin; but, on the other hand, a 'society' is not simply a 'sinful community'. A 'contract' as such is not evil (see above[, page 97]). Only when it involves the conscious exploitation or destruction of the other is it to be judged evil. Likewise the will for self-preservation is not evil as such. Sin, therefore, does not enter the community with the individual's will for self-preservation—indeed, community is only possible on this basis. Rather, sin enters with the will that in principle affirms as valuable only itself, and not the other, and that acknowledges the other only on its own terms. But, people will object, this is precisely the essence of a society [Gesellschaft]. That is not so. A society is not based essentially upon self-seeking, but upon the instinct for self-preservation; thus a society is no more based upon evil will than is a community. If we speak of a relative community life, this means that community is a necessary form of human activity in general and is not completely bound to the ethical content of will. Even when wills are oriented to evil, there is community, though it is hollow. The value of communal life apart from any particular purpose is still acknowledged, in contrast to a society; yet the individuals in the community move fundamentally apart, and are isolated. By contrast, evil will turns a society into an institution for the systematic exploitation of one by the other. It would be misguided to try to understand the essence of community and society in general in these terms. Rather, they imply that their essence has degenerated through sin and that this misery is only relieved in the Christian concept of community.

[23.] The use of "being called upon" [*Aufgerufensein*] is replaced here in *SC-B* by "being called" [*Angerufensein*] and the latter is consistently used in the published version.

not the individuals but the people who had fallen into sin. Thus it is the people who must be comforted (Isa. 40:1). *Where peoples are called, God's will for their purpose in history is at work*, just as where individuals are called, they experience their history. There is a will of God with a people just as with individuals. Where a people, submitting in conscience to God's will, goes to war in order to fulfill its historical purpose and mission in the world—though entering fully into the ambiguity of human sinful action—it knows it has been called upon by God, that history is to be made; here war is no longer murder.[24] However, God is concerned not only with the nations, but has a purpose for every community no matter how small, every friendship, every marriage, every family.[25] And in this sense God also has a purpose for the *church*. There is not only the culpability of individual Germans and individual Christians, but also the culpability of Germany and of the church. It is not enough for individuals to repent and be justified; Germany and the church must likewise repent and be justified. The community that is from God to God,[26] that bears within itself eternal meaning, endures   75
in God's sight and does not melt into the fate of the many. It is willed and created and has become culpable; it must seek repentance, believe in and experience justification and sanctification, and experience judgment and grace at the limits of time. Clearly, this can only happen 'in' individuals. The hearing of the call can only be concretely grasped in this way, and yet it is not individuals, but the whole community [Gesamtheit] that, in the individuals, hears, repents, and believes. The center of activity is in the whole. Thus the corporate culpability of a community is something different from culpability found in social interactions within the community.[27] If the 'people' must repent, it does not matter how many repent, and in actuality it will never be the whole people, the whole church; but God can regard the whole 'as if' all had

---

[24.] The statement "here war is no longer murder" replaces in *SC-A*: here war is more than murder. *SC-RS*: "Ambiguous!" Cf. Seeberg, *Dogmatik*, 1:515ff.

[25.] Deleted in *SC-A*: How many "Stories of a Marriage" have been written and lived out; but there is no community in which such a story would not be experienced.

[26.] This statement anticipates Bonhoeffer's quotation below (see page 282) of Leopold von Ranke's remark that "every age is in direct relationship with God" (*The Theory and Practice of History*, 53). [CG]

[27.] On the concept of corporate culpability [*Gesamtschuld*], see Scheler, *Formalism in Ethics*, 480f.

repented. "For the sake of ten I will not destroy them" (Gen. 18:32).[28] God can see the whole people in a few, as God could see and reconcile the whole of humanity in one man. Here arises the problem of vicarious representative action [Stellvertretung],[29] which will be treated later.[30] When the collective person is addressed ("Let those who have ears to hear, hear what the Spirit says to the *churches*," Revelation 2 and 3),[31] the conscience of individual persons is addressed. Each person, however, has only *one* conscience, which serves each of them as a particular member of the collective person, and as an individual. There are not two layers in human beings, one social and one intimate; a human being is a structural unity, and it is only the directional intentions that can conflict within the person. People must know themselves as inwardly integrated beings and make decisions accordingly. They must not blindly subordinate themselves to the concrete demands of the collective person, but must struggle to reach an integrated decision of their own wills. Ethical community can only be built upon such integrated people. Our conception of corporate culpability is thus not one of culpability based upon certain contents or parts of the soul; rather, *the utter culpability of the integrated person is the concrete form of corporate culpability.*

These insights must now be transferred to the concept of humanity. Humanity is the comprehensive community [Gesamtgemeinschaft] that embraces all communities. Participation in humanity's community life is demonstrated by the affirmation of community life in general. For this always exists within the collective person of humanity [Men-

76

[28.] *NRSV*: "For the sake of ten I will not destroy it." The English translation refers to the city, while Bonhoeffer's rendering emphasizes the people of the community or, by extension in this context, the church. [NL/CG]

[29.] *Stellvertretung* is one of Bonhoeffer's fundamental theological concepts throughout his writings. Literally the word means to represent in place of another—to act, advocate, intercede on behalf of another; we translate this as "vicarious representative action." As a theological concept in the strict sense it is rooted in Christology and refers to the free initiative and responsibility that Christ takes for the sake of humanity in his incarnation, crucifixion, and resurrection—it is not just a soteriological concept applied only to the cross (as "vicarious" might suggest). By anthropological analogy, *Stellvertretung* involves acting responsibly on behalf of others and on behalf of communities to which one belongs. [CG]

[30.] See below, pages 145ff. and 183ff.

[31.] Rev. 2:7, 3:6, and *passim* in the *NRSV* reads: "Let anyone who has an ear listen to what the Spirit is saying to the churches." [CG]

schheitsperson]. Like every person, the collective person of humanity is also capable of being addressed ethically, as indeed the call can be heard for *all of humanity in the story of Jesus Christ.* The collective person of humanity has one heart. Participation in its ethical nature is demonstrated by individuals through every act of repentance and recognition of culpability. Wherever individuals recognize themselves both as individuals and as the human race, and submit to the demand of God, there beats the heart of the collective person. This ensures its moral unity; insofar as every human being is Adam, the collective person really has *one conscience*. The structure of humanity-in-Adam is unique because it is both composed of many isolated individuals and yet is one, as the humanity that has sinned as a whole.[32] It is 'Adam', a collective person, who can only be superseded by the collective person 'Christ existing as church-community'.[33] Sin is the sign of belonging to the old humanity, to the first Adam; consciousness of guilt reveals to individuals their connection with all sinners. When individuals recognize that they belong to Adam's humanity, they join the peccatorum communio [community of sinners]. 'The humanity of sin' is one, *though consisting of nothing but individuals. It is a collective person, yet infinitely fragmented. It is Adam, since all individuals are themselves and Adam. This duality is its essence, and it is superseded [aufgehoben] only though the unity of the new humanity in Christ.*

[32.] *SC-RS*: "Which is the function of Adam and which of Christ?"
[33.] See below, page 198, editorial note 217.

CHAPTER FIVE

SANCTORUM COMMUNIO

77   **A. Basic Principles**

*1. Synthesis of the Previous Argument in the Concept
of the Church: Retrospect and Prospect*

THE WHOLE THEOLOGICAL reflection thus far not only leads to the discussion of the sanctorum communio,[1] but is possible and meaningful only

---

1. This word sequence is shown to be the original one by F[erdinand] Kattenbusch, *Das apostolische Symbol*, 2:928ff. The earliest source for this sequence is Jerome, Ep[istola] 17, between 374 and 397. The fact that Niceta of Remesiana (ca. 400) uses the reverse word sequence certainly deserves attention but may be explained by the syntactic structure ("De symbolo," 10; see Burn, *Niceta of Remesiana*, 48). Moreover, a few lines earlier the sentence can be found: "Ecclesia quid aliud quam sanctorum omnium congregatio?" ["What is the church but a community of all the saints?"] (Kirsch, *The Doctrine of the Communion of Saints in the Ancient Church*, 257, note 4, and 255ff.).[1]

[1.] Deleted from *SC-A*:

Concerning the question whether the concept sanctorum communio implies sancti [saints] or sancta [holy], and who might be understood by the former, see the literature on the subject: Theodor Zahn, *Das apostolische Symbolum*, 91ff.; Kattenbusch, *Apostolische Symbol*, 941f.; Harnack, *Das apostolische Symbol* [*Symbol* should read *Glaubensbekenntnis*], 32ff.; Kirsch, [*Communion of Saints*,] 261ff.; Seeberg, [*Lehrbuch der*] *Dogmengeschichte*, 2:465ff., note 4. [The correct footnote number is 2, not 4.] [CG] Without being able to substantiate my position extensively here, I think that the original form certainly had the sancti 249   [saints] in mind, but it is difficult to determine whether this meant the saints in heaven or all Christians. There is much evidence in favor of the first interpretation (Kirsch, [*Communion of Saints*,] 261f.). In our study the concept will refer to the church-community of Christ, the 'company of saints' (Seeberg). The notion of a cooperative association [Genossenschaft]

from the perspective of the sanctorum communio. Only from this vantage point are we justified to integrate philosophical considerations into the theological framework. It is not the case that the concept of the sanctorum communio would make everything that has been said about the peccatorum communio [community of sinners] irrelevant; rather, it is precisely at this point that the meaning of the peccatorum communio first becomes relevant.[2] True, the person who has been justified, who belongs to God's church-community, has 'died to sin'. "Whoever is in Christ does not commit sin." "The old has passed away, see, everything has be- come new."[3] "For as all die in Adam, so all have been made

---

[1. *cont.*] cannot be used by us, however, in view of the definition given above. We shall speak of a church-community [Gemeinde] of saints or a community [Gemeinschaft] of saints, although the meaning of both these terms will not be identical, as we shall see.

Sanctorum communio (*communionem*) is an addition to the Roman baptismal creed, the *Romanum*, from which the Apostles' Creed evolved. The origin and meaning of this addition is disputed. In one of his letters Jerome mentions a creed that he had to affirm during a stay in Chalcis (between 374 and 379), the so-called Creed of Jerome (Jerome, "Epistola 17," in Migne, *Patrologia Latina*, 22, 359ff.; the creed is found in G. Morin, ed., *Anecdota Maredsolana*, 3/3:199). Its third article reads: "Credo remissionem peccatorum in sancta ecclesia catholica, sanctorum communionem, carnis resurrectionem ad vitam aeternam" ("I believe in the forgiveness of sins in the holy catholic church, the communion of saints, the resurrection of the body to life eternal"). There exists an exposition of a creed by Niceta of Remesiana (ca. 400) with catechetical commentary by Cyril of Jerusalem (Migne, *Patrologia Latina*, 52, 871, A–B), there still mistakenly attributed to Niceta of Aquileja, which includes the following: "Ecclesia quid aliud, quam sanctorum omnium congregatio? . . . Ergo in hac una ecclesia crede te communionem consecuturum esse sanctorum" ("What is the church but the community of all the saints? . . . Believe, therefore, that in this one church you will attain the community [communionem] of saints"). The addition "sanctorum communio" ought to be understood both in a personal sense (community [*Gemeinschaft*] of saints) and a sacramental sense (community [*Gemeinschaft*] of the sacrament), according to Kattenbusch whom Bonhoeffer quotes. The faith of the early church regarded both notions, in his view, as inseparable. The meaning of *sanctorum communio* can be explained, according to Reinhold Seeberg's *Textbook of the History of Doctrines*, from the opposition of Jerome against the Novatianists. In the church sin is forgiven (anti-Novatian); nevertheless, and even because of this fact, the church is the community of saints. Seeberg further maintains that this formula entered and spread from there in the West through Augustine who called the church a *congregatio sanctorum* [community of saints] (see Seeberg, *Dogmengeschichte*, 2:465ff., note 2; Bonhoeffer largely follows this exposition). Seeberg refers to this understanding of *sanctorum communio* also in his dogmatics (*Dogmatik*, 2:333). See also Luther's exposition of the third article in his *Large Catechism* (*The Book of Concord*, 415ff.). For the state of research during Bonhoeffer's time, see Adolf von Harnack, *The Apostles' Creed*.

[2.] Deleted from *SC-A*: It is no more unimportant than sin itself is unimportant.

[3.] See Rom. 6:2, 7-9; 2 Cor. 5:17.

alive in Christ,"[4] but the life of those who have been justified, that is, the new life, is "hidden in God."[5] "I do what I do not want to do, and what I do want I do not do."[6] "Nullum unquam extitisse pii hominis opus, quod si severo dei judicio examinaretur, non esset damnabile" ["There never existed any work of a pious human being which, if examined by God's stern judgment, would not deserve condemnation" (trans. altered)].[2] The reality of sin and the communio peccatorum remain even in God's church-community; Adam has really been replaced by Christ only eschatologically, ἐπ' ἐλπίδι (in spe) [in hope].[3] So long as sin remains, the whole of sinful humanity also remains in every human being. In the concept of the church, therefore, all lines of thought pursued thus far converge; in this concept they are carried to their logical conclusion and are transcended.[9]

Until now we have been pursuing two, or rather three, different lines of thought that must now be integrated conceptually—or better, we must reflect upon their union that already exists in the reality of the church. On the one hand, there was the line of thought about the ontic basic-relatedness of human beings to one another as persons. On the other hand, there was the discovery of the pre-volitional sociality of the human spirit, and the subsequent investigation of the forms of empirically existing communal relations, which always require intentional

---

2. Calvin, *Institutio* (1536), 3.14,11.[7]

3. *WA* 2:457.[8]

[4.] 1 Cor. 15:22. [*NRSV* reads "will be made alive," whereas Bonhoeffer's German reads "have been made alive" (*lebendig geworden*); like the English, the 1911 Luther *Bibel* reads "alle lebendig gemacht werden" ("all will be made alive").][CG]

[5.] Cf. 2 Cor. 4:3. [Cf. Col. 3:3.][CG]

[6.] Cf. Rom. 7:19. [*NRSV* reads: "For I do not do the good I want, but the evil I do not want is what I do."][CG]

[7.] *Institutes of the Christian Religion* 3.14.11, 778f. Bonhoeffer cited the 1536 edition of the *Institutes* but the quotation comes from the 1559 edition.

[8.] Footnote 3 was added to *SC-A*. See Rom. 4:18, 5:2ff., and 8:20ff. Bonhoeffer's citation of Luther's "Lectures on Galatians" (*WA* 2:457) is not the correct reference. Compare instead Luther's *Vorlesung über den Römerbrief 1515/1516* (Lectures on Romans 1515–16) in the Ficker edition used by Bonhoeffer, 1/2:105, lines 18–24, which corresponds to *WA* 56:269, lines 25–30 (*LW* 25:258); cf. also *WA* 56:272, lines 17–21 (*LW* 25:260) and *WA* 1:149, line 9.

[9.] Deleted from *SC-A*: In it they are both preserved and 'superseded' [in doppeltem Sinne 'aufgehoben'].

social acts in order to manifest themselves as personal social relations. The ontic-ethical basic-relations in the state of sin not only are fundamental for all personal social relations, but also condition even their empirical formation. When they are modified, or re-created, in the concept of the church, the concrete form of the community must change as well; indeed this provides the possibility and necessity of developing a unique empirical form of community. Since we recognized certain basic forms as belonging to the created order, we now must ask about the extent to which the church as a social form participates in them, and even whether in it the synthesis of them all might be found. However, only later can this be discussed.

Sin remains even when the ethical basic-relations have changed, which means also that the old ontic relationships are not completely abolished; therefore every empirical formation is subject to the ambiguity of all human action. However, what is unprecedentedly novel is that the new basic-relations have their own unique form, that their sole function, as it were, is to produce such a form. In this we perceive a special   79
will of God that we may not brush aside by condemning everything that has taken form as a merely human product. *Formally speaking, the necessary bond between the basic-relations and the empirical form of community, understood as a unique structure, constitutes the essence of the church.*

There are basically *two ways to misunderstand the church, one historicizing and the other religious; the former confuses the church with the religious community, the latter with the Realm of God.* The former overlooks the fact that the new basic-relations established by God actually are real, and points instead to the "religious motives" that in fact lead to empirical community (the missionary impulse, the need to communicate, etc.).[10] This view, however, plainly is condemned by the saying in John's Gospel that "You did not choose me, but I chose you" (John 15:16). The second misunderstanding does not take seriously the fact that human beings are bound by history; this means that historicity either is objectified and deified, as in Catholicism,[11] or simply is regarded as accidental, as sub-

---

[10.] For the "historicizing misunderstanding," see below, pages 252ff.

[11.] Regarding the objection against Roman Catholicism, see the literature by Catholics that Bonhoeffer consulted: Bartmann, *Lehrbuch der Dogmatik*, 2:128ff. and 195ff.; Adam, *The Spirit of Catholicism*, esp. 47ff. Concerning the Roman Catholic concept of the church, see also ["Catechismus Romanus" (1566),] *Catechism of the Council of Trent*, pt. 1, chap. 10, 90ff., and "'Pastor aeternus' de Ecclesia Christi," translated as "Dogmatic

ject to the law of death and sin. Doing so, however, does not accept, but
circumvents, God's will that all God's revelation, both in Christ and in
the church, be concealed under the form of historical life. To put it differently, the much discussed 'seriousness' is carried so far that it loses
its real character and becomes formalistic.[12] It is almost impossible to
avoid the first misunderstanding in a historical or sociological
approach—a misunderstanding that is equally at home, however, in the
religious-romantic circles[13] of the Youth Movement.[14] The second is
found in theology. Both are dangerous, since both can be nourished by
religious pathos and seriousness. Neither of them, however, understands the reality of the church, which is simultaneously a historical
community and one established by God. Thus, the concept of the
church, in our view, justifies and synthesizes the lines of thought that
we have pursued thus far. The new ontic basic-relations are the foundation of a social entity that, viewed from the outside, can only be called a
'religious community'. Now it is certainly possible to focus on the
80   empirical phenomenon 'church' qua 'religious community' or religious
society, to analyze it as a 'public corporation' and *to develop a sociological
morphology* of it. In that case all theological reflection would be superfluous; or—and this is the other possibility—the claim of the church to
be God's church is taken seriously. In this case one must focus on what
this church acknowledges as constitutive, namely the fact of Christ, or
the 'Word'. It will also be necessary to delineate the new social basic-
relations, which are established by the fact of Christ, as constitutive in
the deepest sense for a social body like the church. One premise, however, will not have to be justified further, namely that we take the claim
of the church seriously, i.e., not as being historically comprehensible,

----

[11. *cont.*] Constitution 1 on the Church of Christ" (Denzinger, *The Sources of Catholic
Dogma*, 451–57).

[12.] Deleted from *SC-A*: Every beginning of the 'new life' not only takes place in history, but
also is subject to history. With the term 'seriousness' Bonhoeffer alludes to the controversy
over the self-understanding of Protestant theology between Erik Peterson and Karl Barth
(see Peterson, "Was ist Theologie?" and the reply by Barth, "Church and Theology," in
Theology and Church: Shorter Writings, 1920–1928, 286–306). Peterson accuses Barth of
bypassing the concrete revelation with his theology; he charges that the "seriousness" of
Barth's theology is only "apparent seriousness" (5). In his early articles Barth indeed
spoke quite frequently about "seriousness" (see, e.g., Barth, "The Need and Promise of
Christian Preaching," in *The Word of God and the Word of Man*, 97ff.).

[13.] Replaced in *SC-A*: religious circles.

[14.] On the Youth Movement, see below, pages 276ff.

but as being grounded in the reality of God and God's revelation. We do not want to employ external criteria for judging the church. Rather, the church can be understood fully only from within, on the basis of its own claim; only on this basis can we develop appropriately critical criteria for judging it.

With this, however, right from the very beginning we seem to fall into logical inconsistencies. We said we were taking seriously the claim of the church to be God's church; but naturally that does not mean, first of all, that we could assert this claim without examination. At issue is only the question, by which criteria do we examine the meaning of the assertion? In principle it is indeed possible to take the course of finding external criteria, which means deducing the truth of the proposition from the outside. This course basically does not lead beyond the category of *possibility*. From there one then necessarily arrives at the *concept of religious community*. The concept of the church is conceivable only in the sphere of reality established by God; this means it cannot be deduced. *The reality of the church is a reality of revelation, a reality that essentially must be* either believed or denied.[15] Thus an adequate criterion for judging the claim of the church to be God's church-community can be found only by stepping inside it,[16] by bowing in faith to its claim. Now, admittedly, faith is not a possible method by which to gain academic knowledge; rather, by acknowledging the claim of revelation, faith is the given prerequisite for positive theological knowledge. It would also be completely wrong to 'deduce' faith in the church, as a conceptual necessity, from faith in Christ. *Whatever is necessary conceptually is not thereby already real. Rather there is no relation to Christ in which the relation to the church is not necessarily established as well. The church, therefore, logically establishes its own foundation in itself;* like all revelations, it can be judged only by itself. What is to be found is presupposed. Knowledge and acknowledgment of its reality must exist before one can speak about the church. Precisely in this regard it proves itself to be a reality of revelation—not to an external observer, but to the person who believes its claim. The legitimacy of this theological method can be

81

[15.] See Seeberg, *Dogmatik*, regarding the notion of the church as a reality of revelation (1:152ff.) and the connection between faith and church (2:345). Concerning positive theological cognition, see above, page 49, editorial note 53.

[16.] Deleted from *SC-A*: not in some kind of emotional way that 'understands' each claim, however presumptuous it may be, as having its origin in religious enthusiasm, but . . .

acknowledged only by someone who already stands inside the church; then, however, the objective external position already has been surrendered. The logical stumbling block for the entire question of the church lies at this very point. People ask whether religious community— which is then also called church-community—is a necessary consequence of the Christian religion, or whether Christianity is essentially individualistic. They attempt to deduce a power that generates community from a concept of the 'holy', or they endeavor to prove from Christian ethics that human beings are ethically dependent upon one another. Or they try to infer a sociological category from the nature of a religion of revelation. But in no case is the starting point sought by acknowledging the reality of God's church-community as a revealed reality. And so it is certain from the outset that the concept of the church will not be reached. It becomes evident, further, in my view, that it is impossible to deduce from a general concept of religion, as a necessary consequence, the notion of a religious community. Two outstanding examples from the most recent Protestant and Catholic works on the philosophy of religion may illustrate this.

In his "ethics of values" Max Scheler[4] develops a hierarchy of values in which the highest rank is awarded to the religious value of the 'holy'. Now there are certain essential a priori principles that govern the hierarchy of values, one of which can be expressed in the proposition: "The higher the values, the less divisible they are."[17] If several people wish to participate in a sensory pleasure, then the value of the sensory object—a loaf of bread for example—is divided by the number of persons. Half a loaf of bread has half the value of a whole loaf. However, the situation is quite different with works of art, for example, which are in principle indivisible. The most pronounced contrast, however, is represented by the value of the holy, which is "in principle proper to every being," but that by its nature does not even allow for a material bearer.[18] As the sensory value divides the participants, so the spiritual value functions to unite them to an eminent degree. The deduction sounds very plausible, but it is devised in a thoroughly formalistic way.

---

4. *Formalism in Ethics*, 93f.

[17.] [Bonhoeffer states Scheler's point, but does not quote exactly.][CG] See *Formalism in Ethics*, 93: "There is also no question about the fact that values are 'higher' *the less they are 'divisible.'*"

[18.] See Scheler, *Formalism*, 94.

True, the idea of a sensory pleasure does imply that one can experience the pleasure itself only as a whole. But what does Scheler mean by 'unifying'? Evidently he means the possibility of gathering several people around one object at the same time. For neither the empirical gathering of several people, nor community in the strict sense, can be meant here, since both these ideas would obviously be wrong (cf. the phenomenon of the mass and egocentric mysticism). To say that the 'realm of the spirit' ['das Geistige'], or the 'holy', would by nature be more likely than the sensory sphere to provide such a possibility is correct, but devoid of content. For one could just as well say that the value of the unholy, of the diabolical, is a value with an eminently unifying power. Likewise, Scheler would be unable to demonstrate any difference in principle between the unifying effect of the holy and, for example, that of the beautiful or the true. The truth of the deduction lies in the recognition of the essential unity of the immaterial value, above everything material; this unity, however, only *potentially* guarantees a certain greater participation in that value. It is an application of the logical proposition: "the smaller the content of a concept, the wider its range."[19] The flaw in Scheler's argument lies in the fact that in the idea of the holy he proceeds from a metaphysical notion of value that in its absoluteness always remains inaccessible to us. Instead he should have argued from the historically positive revelation of the holy in Christ, the "material bearer of value," and he should have arrived at the reality of the community that is based on the holy by proceeding from the specific contents of revelation (which are not merely 'symbols').[20] Only on the basis of the concrete revelation can one overcome the empty concept and potentiality, arriving at *real* community relations that exist by virtue of the 'historical' reality of the holy.[5]

83

---

5. Luther, from whom Scheler could have learned here, had already made this point in *WA* 4:401: "quia spiritualia habent hanc naturam, ut non possint dividi in diversa, sed diversos et divisos colligunt in unum." ["For spiritual things have this nature, that they cannot be divided in different things, but they gather into one those who are different and divided" (*LW* 11:540).][21]

[19.] The rule of the content and range of a concept was formulated in the so-called Port Royal logic; see Antoine Arnauld and Pierre Nicole, *Logic, or, the Art of Thinking.*

[20.] Regarding "symbol," see above, pages 103ff., editorial note 138. Regarding Scheler's concept of the church, see his *Formalism in Ethics*, 547ff., 554ff.

[21.] See Luther, "First Lectures on the Psalms" (1513), *LW* 11:540ff. [*WA* 4:401].   251

Precisely this seems to have been attempted by Heinrich Scholz.[6] By proceeding from the idea of revelation, he seeks to arrive indirectly at the concept of community. Religion is, first, one of the essential components of the human spirit and is, second, not a priori but revealed, these being mutually exclusive concepts. From this follows the necessity of education in religion. However, education in a revealed religion is possible only on the basis of a tradition that, in turn, is inconceivable without *community*. First, we contest the absolute opposition of the categories a priori and revelation in the sense in which Scholz uses the concept of revelation, namely as synonymous with consciousness of revelation. We ask, further, what educating someone in revelation is supposed to mean. Obviously, only the body of religious knowledge can be transmitted. But this does not yet seem to be specifically an education in or toward religion; and the agent carrying out this education—the community that preserves the tradition—has as such no qualification to be a specifically religious community, let alone a church. The nature of academic inquiry equally implies such essential 'sociological categories'. Scholz basically does not tell us anything more than that religion is able to be imparted to others (and even here he is unable to prove that this is necessary in principle—one only has to think of mysticism) and thereby exerts certain social effects. This, however, is nothing new or distinctive about religion, but something that is historically self-evident.

84   Our problem has been to discern to what extent the reality of God's revelation in Jesus Christ simultaneously establishes the church as a reality of revelation. We see a decisive difference between the community as the guardian of Christian tradition and the Christian church-community. Scholz at least should have asked why religion is handed down, whether such a phenomenon has more significance in the case of religion than in the case of scholarship, and whether community is grounded in his general concept of religion or derives from the accidental inclination of human beings. Scheler thought too formally; Scholz seeks to think more concretely, but falls into a historicizing empiricism. He admits that he does not deduce the concept of community directly from the nature of religion, and he doubts whether such a deduction is possible at all.[22] There is in fact only *one* religion in which

---

6. H[einrich] Scholz, *Religionsphilosophie*, 2d ed., esp. 115ff.

[22.] See Scholz, *Religionsphilosophie*, 292ff.

the idea of community is an integral element of its nature, and that is Christianity.[23] Thus the two approaches just outlined are in our view

---

[23.] Deleted from *SC-A*:

A brief attempt in this direction shall be made in the following. We point out the fact that this problem is not discussed within the framework of the church, but on the general level of philosophy of religion. Therefore only the main ideas can be examined.

The topics to be discussed are, first of all, the general relation between religion and community, i.e., the concept of religious community, and, second, a typology of religious communities. Our first proposition is that *from the perspective of their origin all religious concepts are derived from the social sphere*: if humans were not social beings, we would not have religion.

It is also valid for religion that there is no life of the human spirit that does not have at least its indirect cause in social formation. The I-You-relation between deity and human being, or between deity and religious community [Gemeinde], which is as old as religion itself, is conceivable from a *psychological* perspective only where the meaning of such a relation has been experienced in social life. <<Very perceptive observations on this point are made by G[eorg] Simmel, *Sociology of Religion*, 11ff.>> But there is no religious content whatsoever without its counterpart in the ordinary social process, ranging from total dependence to free action, from struggle with God to peace, from rebellion to its overcoming, from remorse to reconciliation, from mistrust to the most heartfelt trust, from shamelessness to reverence (pietas! [piety!]), from the greatest remoteness from God to mystical union; demanding and obeying, giving and receiving—everything has its place here. All spirit presupposes community, but this means that the primal community cannot itself be derived from spirit. We acknowledge that for the sake of communication God makes us conceive of religious concepts on the model of social life. But this causal and imitative connection between religion and community does not yet say anything about a social impulse toward community in religion. What is certain is only the impulse of the community toward the deity, without which there is no religion. Religion here is defined as the touching of the human will by the divine will, and as the overcoming of the former by the latter to enable free action. <<At first sight this definition does not seem to include the primitive religions, but this really is not the case. See R[einhold] Seeberg, *Dogmatik*, 1:70–77. It seems appropriate to me that our definition does not include genuine Buddhism. Its development into a religion takes place only with the deification of the Buddha.>> A community would then be called a religious community when it made itself the object of divine action and was itself an agent in community action. This shows that an impulse toward religious community is not in principle entailed in religion, and this must be so; the value of the holy is not exclusively actualized in a social context as, for example, the value of justice, or love, or equality, and so on, but also in solitary communion [Gemeinschaft] with God. The mystics too were religious. Our second conclusion, therefore, is that the general concept of religion does not necessitate social community—*neither its empirical form nor its general collective basis*—but only permits it. In the following these two concepts of community must be strictly distinguished.

It is nevertheless a fact that religion is a social phenomenon. It may be uncertain whether religion begins as a slow dawning of an 'other' in the most primitive stirrings (horror, fear, terror, longing, sexual desire) in the individual soul, or whether the biological communal forms [Vergemeinschaftungsform] like the family, the clan, are primarily seen as the subject of religion. What is certain is that wherever we find worship of divine or demonic

252

unable to deduce the nature and necessity of religious community, let alone the necessity of the church. Of course, this does not mean that

---

[23. *cont.*] beings, however primitive, it is carried out by a community that, so to speak, 'keeps' this private god from whom it expects the protection of its communal life. It is also certain that very early in cultic behavior there are, besides the acts carried out by individuals (patriarch, sorcerer, priest), also communal rituals like the cultic dance, the cultic song, and the cultic prayer—that is either a chaotic mass prayer or a responsive prayer alternating between an individual and the congregation. <<Friedrich Heiler, *Prayer*, 12ff.>> In this category, further, belong the sacred meals, <<See Durkheim, *The Elementary Forms of the Religious Life*. Here Durkheim attempts to prove that totemism was the sole source of all social life, and especially religious social life. The fraternization associated with the common meal of a cultic animal, which established common rights and duties, later led to an animal being regarded as the symbol of a community, and this certainly came to have a considerable influence on sexual, family, and economic life. But the extent of this influence was not as great as Durkheim supposes.>> the sexual orgies of the fertility cults, and sacred prostitution—since the orgy, "the social form of ecstasy," can be regarded as the original form of religious community formation. <<See Max Weber, *Economy and Society*, 1:401.>> These two observations prove religion from its very origin to be closely tied to social life. This is so because the subject of religion is basically seen to be the community with the individual as its member, and also because the community itself as a whole is religiously active.

But even if there is in principle no essential connection between religion and community, as has been shown, most concrete forms of religion must, nevertheless, have a certain affinity with the concept of community in both senses. What is the nature of this affinity?

253

There are four different modes of relation between religion and community formation. *First,* a radical rejection of outward and inward community, as is characteristic of mysticism. *Second,* there are free religious communities that are held together purely *on the basis of and in order to achieve a purpose,* and solely through a common religious practice as a means for accomplishing a purpose. Their internal structure is individualistic; they are cultic societies and have the character of a voluntary association (see below). To be distinguished from these are, *third,* the religious formations of community that are based on *physical communities.* In this category the family, the clan, etc., are so firmly regarded as the subject of religion that the individual is active in religious practice (cult) only as a part of the whole, and this constitutes a pronounced collectivism. In this category also belong the *historically conditioned religious communities.* The people of Israel, or the 'children' of Israel, combine both types. Admittedly, the collective basis can also break up in these communities and become individualistic. Such a case would fall into the second category. Finally, as a *fourth* category, there are free communities that are held together by meetings for worship, without which each individual would wither religiously; these consider the communal element in particular as constituting an aspect of the meaning of religion.

From this survey several motives may be discerned that lead to the formation of empirical communities. Utilitarian considerations, including the system of needs (need to communicate, etc.), the power of an idea or of an experience that has a concrete communal impulse—all lead to formation of religious community; religion regulates and sanctions common bonds, both natural and historical. This, however, shows that the motives for empirical community formation are accidental and diverse. Not only is it impossible to prove that the connection between religion and community is intrinsically necessary, but it is equally impossible to prove that it is psychologically necessary. One can take up Schleiermacher's notion of the need of the individual to communicate, or one could speak, with the problem in philosophy of religion concerning the relationship between religion and community would be dismissed as such. In order to solve it, however, more distinctions are needed.

The general concept of religion has no intrinsic social implications. The idea of the holy in its general sense as religious category is actualized not in social interaction, but in the solitude of the soul with God. The mystic, too, is religious. If it is nevertheless a fact that religion is for the most part social in character, primarily due to psychological causes that are more or less accidental (the need to communicate, as in Schleiermacher, the receptive-active human nature, as in Seeberg).[24] These causes demonstrate the possibility, but not the necessity, of religious community. This directs us back from the general concept of religion to the concrete form of religion, which for us means the concept of the church. But here it is not possible to demonstrate that the communal form of the church is a general necessity; rather, such a demonstration is possible only where the Christian revelation is believed, that

---

[23. *cont.*] Seeberg, of the receptive-active nature of the human spirit. But first, these approaches do not prove community to be psychologically necessary, and second, a community based solely on the need of its members to communicate would be a religious voluntary association designed in a purely individualistic fashion. A collective basis and a corresponding motivation for empirical community formation can be demonstrated only in concrete religions, since *the general concept of religion does not contain specifically social impulses*. Only observation of the concrete characteristics of the religions can discern their possible affinity to community. Now it is not the task of the sociology of religion to study the genesis of religious communities, since problems of genesis are by definition not sociological problems; rather, the sociology of religion has to explore the general structures of religious communities. But this cannot be our task here. We can indicate only briefly that such an investigation would, in our view, also discover the two basic types of community, one being the free, charismatic community characterized by the "sorcerer," and the other being the regulated, uncharismatic community characterized by the priest; both of these kinds of community are surpassed by a third type of specifically religious community characterized by the prophet. <<See Max Weber, [*Economy and Society*,] 439ff., and R. Seeberg, *Dogmatik*, 1:52ff.>>

We recognize that only by starting from the concrete religious form can we come to an understanding of the concept of community that may be connected with it; this throws us back from the foregoing inquiry based on the general philosophy of religion to the problem of the church. From the contents of the Christian faith it is possible to deduce certain impulses toward community that become visible in the empirical formation of community; but this still does not lead to the concept of the church (Schleiermacher even thought he could deduce the concept of the church from the general concept of religion). The concept of the church can, however, be reached only where the Christian revelation is believed, that is, taken seriously.

[24.] Regarding Schleiermacher and Seeberg, see above page 64, footnote 1.

254

is, taken seriously. *Only the concept of revelation can lead to the Christian*
85 *concept of the church.* Once the claim of the church has been accepted,
however, it is as superfluous as it is impossible to prove its necessity on
general grounds. The situation here is not different from the case of the
christological efforts that seek to demonstrate the necessity of redemption *after its reality has already been grasped.*[25] Only when faith accepts
the meaning of redemption does it become clear what makes this reality
necessary. *In doctrinal theology necessity can be deduced only from reality.*
This follows from the concept of revelation.

When works of doctrinal theology end by presenting the concept of
the church as a necessary consequence of the Protestant[26] faith, this
must not imply anything other than the inner connection between the
reality of the church and the entire reality of revelation.[27] Only if the
concept of God is understood to be comprehensible when exclusively
connected to the concept of the church is it permitted, for technical reasons of presentation, to 'derive' the latter from the former. In order to
establish clarity about the inner logic of theological construction, it
would be good for once if a presentation of doctrinal theology were to
start not with the doctrine of God but with the doctrine of the
church.[28]

Now in order to stand on firm ground in the positive exposition, we
will give a brief outline of the New Testament teaching on the concept
of the church, especially as a social phenomenon.

2. Major Themes in the New Testament View of the Church [29]

1. The Christian concept of ἐκκλησία [church] is the fulfillment of the
Jewish concept of קָהָל [assembly]. Paul, whose understanding of the

---

[25.] Regarding the christological model to which Bonhoeffer refers, see, for example,
Anselm of Canterbury, *Why God Became Man.*

[26.] Going back to a Reformation sense of the gospel (*euangelion*), Bonhoeffer used
evangelisch rather than *protestantisch*; in this, his usage is like Barth's. We translate this
term as "Protestant," aware of the problems of this word, only because the ambiguities of
the word "evangelical" in the English-speaking world are at least as great. [CG]

[27.] *SC-RS*: "as realization".

[28.] Deleted from *SC-A*: These logical-theological premises are fundamental for all that
follows.

[29.] The section of eight themes that follows in the main text is from *SC-B*, replacing
the detailed outline of the New Testament understanding of the church originally in *SC-A*
and given here:

church is outlined in the following, thinks of a church-community established by God as a whole [Gott gestiftete Gesamtgemeinde] that

---

[29. *cont.*]
2. Brief Outline of the New Testament View of the Church
The picture can be outlined only in its main aspects. Two different concepts of the church can be found in the New Testament, one developed in Jerusalem and the other by Paul. <<Holl, "Kirchenbegriff des Paulus in seinem Verhältnis zu dem der Urgemeinde," in *Sitz. Ber. d. preuss. Akad.*, 1921, 920ff.>> The former is the prototype of the Roman Catholic, the latter of the Lutheran, concept of the church. The former is characteristic of Jewish Christians, the latter of gentile Christians. In the first type of church there existed "a regular hierarchy from the very beginning, a divinely established order, a divine church law, a church as a compulsory organization into which individuals are admitted. A clearly defined group, the 'apostles,' i.e., James and the Twelve, possesses a permanent, divine preeminence unattainable by anybody else, and is therefore entitled to exercise leadership." <<Holl, ["Kirchenbegriff,"] 932.>> Paul overcame this concept of the church on the basis of his understanding of the gospel. His views of the church will be briefly outlined. In the Septuagint ἐκκλησία [assembly] <<See esp. Cremer, "Ekklesia," in *Biblisch-theologisches Wörterbuch*, 480; Scheel, *Kirche*, 13; Sohm, *Kirchenrecht*, 16ff.; Köstlin, "Kirche," in *Protestantische Realenzyklopädie*, 3d ed.; Traugott Schmidt, *Der Leib Christi*, 113ff.; Kattenbusch, "Quellort der Kirchenidee," in *Harnack Festg.*, 1921, 143ff.>> is the translation for קָהָל [assembly] [This Hebrew word is misspelled in SC (*DBW* 1).][CG] and in Paul also for עֵדָה [congregation, assembly], which is usually translated as συναγωγή [synagogue, assembly]. The term ἐκκλησία originally means gathering and assembly of the people [Volksgemeinde] [Here the sense is a community meeting like the German public use of *Gemeinde* to refer to a civil division of a small political unit.][CG], and is not significantly different from συναγωγή. Later συναγωγή denotes the individual Jewish congregation, while ἐκκλησία denotes the religious community as a whole. The Jews retain ἐκκλησία as a self-description; the adoption of this term by Christians was especially opportune in that it was already an established term in the Greek language, although exclusively in the sense of a political assembly. The Christian community-of-people [Volksgemeinde], ecclesia, transcends all national and political boundaries; it is universal and yet 'one people'. It is, besides Gentiles and Jews, the 'third people'. <<See Harnack, *The Mission and Expansion of Christianity in the First Three Centuries*, 266–78.>> To help the Greeks understand this, Paul speaks of the ἐκκλησία τοῦ θεοῦ [assembly of God], <<Schmidt, [*Der Leib Christi*,] 120.>> although in most cases to designate the church-community as a whole [Gesamtgemeinde] (1 Cor. 10:32; 15:9; Gal. 1:13). But ecclesia is also used by Paul to describe the local Christian congregation [Lokalgemeinde] (1 Cor. 1:2; 2 Cor. 1:1; 1 Thess. 2:14; Gal. 1:2; in the plural 1 Cor. 16:1, et passim). This is justified theologically as well as linguistically; the individual congregation [Einzelgemeinde] is the concrete form of the whole church-community [Gesamtgemeinde] of God (1 Cor. 1:2). But it is also itself God's church-community. It is "the manifestation of the whole church [Gesamtkirche] in a specific place." [Cf. Holl, "Der Kirchenbegriff des Paulus," 944.] The church-community as a whole is real only in the individual congregation. For Paul, therefore, ecclesia always means a reality established by God on earth, even where he speaks of the individual congregation. The church <<See A[ugust] Dorner, *Grundriss der Dogmengeschichte*, 1899, 40; B[ernhard] Weiss, *Biblical Theology of the New Testament*, 2:112-18; Beyschlag, *Neutestamentliche Theologie*, 2:226ff.; Gloel, *Der heilige Geist*, 303ff.; Holtzmann, *Neutestamentliche Theologie*, 2:191ff.; Feine, *Theologie des neuen Testaments*, 446ff.; Alfr[ed] Krauß, *Dogma [von] der unsichtbaren Kirche*, 124ff.>>

becomes concrete in the individual congregations—that is, concrete in its totality in each individual congregation (1 Cor. 1:2).[30]

[29. cont.] exists through the work of Christ and the work of the Holy Spirit, which have to be clearly distinguished. In Christ the church-community has been elected from eternity (Eph. 1:4ff.; 2 Thess. 2:13; John 15:16, according to the text of the Diatessaron). The new humanity, created by Christ's death (Eph. 2:15), lives in Christ, who is the second, the new Adam (1 Cor. 15:45). The redemption of the human race is truly real in Christ, who laid down his life *for the church* (Eph. 5:25), and the building of the church is the actualization of what has already been accomplished in Christ. In the church Christ is, on the one hand, the foundation (1 Cor. 3:11; Rom. 15:20), the cornerstone (Eph. 2:20ff.; 1 Peter 2:4), the pioneer of a new humanity (1 Cor. 15:27) [This does not appear to be the correct reference; 1 Cor. 15:20ff., as in the next line, seems more appropriate. Bonhoeffer may also be thinking of Hebrews 12:2 where Jesus is described as the *Anfänger* (lit. 'beginner') in the Luther Bible.][CG], the firstborn among a very large family (Rom. 8:29; 1 Cor. 15:20; Col. 1:15, 18; Heb. 1:6; Rev. 1:5). On the other hand, the church is the body of Christ, and individual persons are members of this body (1 Cor. 12:2ff.; Rom.

256 12:4ff.; Eph. 1:23, 4:15f.; Col. 1:18) or of Christ himself (1 Cor. 6:15; Rom. 6:13, 19). These are two different ways in which the relation of Christ to the church is expressed; yet doctrinally they are consistent. There follow designations of Christ as head of the body, as head of the church-community (Eph. 1:22, 4:15, 5:23; Col. 1:18, 2:19). Finally, the thought of Christ as head leads to the thought of marriage, where the husband is the head of the wife, and the relationship of Christ to the church-community is then depicted, analogous to the Old Testament model of Yahweh and Israel, by using the image of marriage (Eph. 5:23ff.). *Christ's relation to the church fundamentally is twofold. Christ is the creator of the whole of its life, which rests on Christ, the master builder of the church. Christ is also, however, a real presence in Christ's church at all times*; since the church is Christ's body, Christ governs it as the head governs the body. *The body, however, is governed by the Holy Spirit* (1 Cor. 12:13; Eph. 2:18, 4:4), although the Spirit of Christ and the Holy Spirit must be clearly distinguished since their manner of operation is not identical. <<See Seeberg, *Dogmatik*, 2:320ff., whom I follow here.>> *What Christ is for the church as a whole, the Holy Spirit is for the individual.* The Holy Spirit impels individuals to Christ, brings Christ to them (Rom. 8:14; Eph. 2:22), and establishes community among them (2 Cor. 13:13; Phil. 2:1). <<I interpret these passages in this way in agreement with Schmidt, [*Der Leib Christi*,] 135.>> That is, the Holy Spirit's work applies to the social life of human beings and uses their social bonds and their social will, whereas the Spirit of Christ aims at the historical nature of human life as a whole. [A variation and development of this idea is found in *CC* where Bonhoeffer writes that Christ as word, sacrament, and church-community (*Gemeinde*) is the center and mediator of human existence, history, and nature.][CG] If we now reflect on the church, not in terms of how it is structured, but as a unit, then this reflection necessarily connects with the image of the body of Christ. What does this mean specifically? Christ is at work in the church-community, Christ's instrument, and is present in it. Just like the Holy Spirit in relation to the individual, Christ makes himself present in the community of saints [Gemeinde der Heiligen]. <<This does not deny that the Holy Spirit instills Christ into the heart of the individual (Gal. 2:20; Phil. 1:21), nor that the Holy Spirit is at work in the church-community.>> The notion of the body, if taken seriously, in effect means that this 'image' intends to identify Christ and the church, as Paul himself clearly does (1 Cor. 12:12; 6:15), since where my body is, there am I. <<Von Hoffman, commentary on 1 Cor. 12:12, "Christ is the I of the church-community that is his body.">> In the case of a division within

2. The church-community exists through Christ's action. It is elected in Christ from eternity (Eph. 1:4ff.; 2 Thess. 2:13). It is the new human-

[29. *cont.*] a congregation, Paul can therefore ask "μεμέρισται ὁ Χριστός ["has Christ been divided"] (1 Cor. 1:13)? On the basis of this conviction that Christ himself is the church-community, there follows, from the image of the organism of the body, the thought of an organic life in the church-community in accordance with the will of Christ. It is only too obvious, however, that the former concept, as well as the latter, clashes with the reality of sinfulness; this problem still needs to be tackled in a systematic way. Thus Christ is really present only in the church-community. [In *CC* 43, 28, and 62ff. Bonhoeffer argues that Christ is present and known in the church, and present but not recognized in the world (the "hidden center").][CG] The church-community is in Christ and Christ is in the church-community (1 Cor. 1:30; 3:16; 2 Cor. 6:16; 13:5; Col. 3:9; 2:17), and *"to be in Christ" is synonymous with "to be in the church-community."* <<See Kattenbusch, "Quellort der Kirchenidee," in *Harnack Festg.*, 1921, 143ff., who, together with Schmidt, *Der Leib Christi,* comes to similar conclusions. Christ and church are identified, without, however (contra Schmidt), connecting any mystical notions with this idea. While Schmidt (154) still hesitates to make the equation, after the example of Bousset (2 Cor. 5:17 et passim), between 'in Christ' and 'in the church', Kattenbusch approves of it: "ἐνδύσασθαι τὸν Χριστόν [putting on Christ] means merging into the church. For Paul it thus means the same thing whether a person lives ἐν Χριστῷ [in Christ] or ἐν ἐκκλησίᾳ [in the church]. Never does ἐν Ἰησοῦ [in Jesus] occur as a mystical expression" (157). See Deissmann, *[Die neutestamentliche Formel] In Christus-Jesus,* vi.>>

This touches on another thought. To the image of Christ's body Schmidt quite rightly   257
adds the notion of the collective personality [Gesamtpersönlichkeit] of the church. The church becomes a person insofar as it is in Christ (Gal. 3:28). In Col. 3:11 Christ is even said to be τὰ πάντα [all things] in the church-community, thus the identification between Christ and the church-community is made once again (similarly in Eph. 1:23). <<Here πλήρωμα means 'vessel'.>> In this context belong all expressions about "putting on the new self" (Col. 3:10; Eph. 4:24)—which can also be expressed as "putting on the Lord Jesus Christ" (Rom. 13:14; Gal. 3:27)—and also the sayings about 'a new creation' (2 Cor. 5:17, Gal. 6:15), and further Eph. 2:15; 4:13. And yet one point still remains unclear, namely why the direct identification between Christ and ecclesia is made so rarely (1 Cor. 1:13; 12:12; 6:15; Col. 3:11; Rom. 13:14), and why quite often the collective personality of the church and Christ are thought of as being in some kind of relation, and therefore as not identical. Schmidt's interpretation, which refers to Paul's mysticism, is not satisfactory. <<Schmidt [*Leib Christi,*] 154: "When the church-community is incorporated into Christ, it is not only governed by his person, but it really fuses with him and merges into him." Feine speaks of the "mystical depth" of the idea of the church ([*Theologie,*] 447). Holtzmann introduces the doctrine of the church under the title "Mysterious Matters"; he speaks of "mystical association" ["mystisches Vereinswesen"], and then coins the happy phrase, "the social miracle." The reference to mysticism in the idea of the church is ancient and owes much to the concept of the corpus mysticum [mystical body] taken from Eph. 5:32.>> The collective person [Gesamtperson] of the church-community can be conceived of only in Christ, that is, in his person. But Paul does not want to make the complete identification, because for him also Christ is with God. He has ascended into heaven (Eph. 4:8ff.; 1 Thess. 4:16; 1 Cor. 15:23). We await his coming (Phil. 3:20). Paul himself did not tackle this doctrinal problem. It is also not discussed by Schmidt, Kattenbusch, and others.

The problem becomes even more complicated if we include the indispensable *notion of pneuma* [spirit]. For in the creation of the church-community the Holy Spirit evidently is at

ity in the new Adam (1 Cor. 15:22 and 45; Rom. 5:12f. and 19f.). It has
been created in a real sense only by the death of Christ (Eph. 2:15 and

[29. *cont.*] work as a personal agent. The Spirit establishes community (see above) and is
presumably also the principle of unity (1 Cor. 12:4ff., esp. 11–13; Eph. 4:4; in Paul this admittedly remains somewhat unclear, for the body as such is also a unity). The church-community is the body of Christ, but only under the gathering and unifying work of the Holy Spirit.
Thus the identification between Christ and church-community is further complicated; and
yet it has to be made, and it is made.

258   The social significance of Christ is decisive—Christ who is present only in the church,
that is, where the Christian church-community is united by preaching and the Lord's Supper
in mutual Christian love. The real presence of Christ also is decisive. The problem of the
relation of the scripture and preaching to this real presence is only hinted at in Paul. The
sole content of the church is in any case God's revelation in Christ. Christ is present to the
church in his word, by which it is constituted ever anew. *The church is the presence of Christ
in the same way that Christ is the presence of God.*

    The doctrinal difficulties involved here must be discussed later. One must not think of a
second incarnation of Christ (for instance, in the individual human being, see below), but
rather of a form of revelation that may be called 'Christ existing as church-community'.
Only if this is understood can one comprehend how Paul can say in the indicative: "You are
the body of Christ" (1 Cor. 3:16; 6:19; 12:2; 2 Cor. 6:16; Eph. 5:30). He means that the
actual local congregation is the body of Christ—precisely that one whose "reputation is
not good" (1 Cor. 5:6) because of an incestuous person in its midst. [The Luther Bible
translates the Greek καύχημα by *Ruhm*, reputation, whereas the *NRSV* renders it by
"boasting."][CG] Christ is present to this visible congregation. The fundamental error of
the views of both the pietist and the religious socialist is that they consider the earliest-
Christian-community as actually 'pure'. In fact, there never has been a Realm of God on
earth of which one could have said, "Look, here it is" (Luke 17:21). In history the church-
community is, was, and remains ecclesia militans [church militant], not triumphans [tri-
umphant]. The theological meaning of Paul's indicatives is not exhausted in the description
of empirical facts—even when they are viewed with good will in an idealized way; rather,
the meaning is contained in the hard *contradiction between the actuality and the reality of
human holiness.* <<See P[aul] Althaus, *Die letzten Dinge,* 1926, 155 and 169ff. See Augustine
Ep[istola] 208, 2ff.>> Every misunderstanding of this idea of earliest Christianity has always
led to a sectarian ideal of holiness in the process of building the Realm of God on earth.

    The body of Christ has a community life according to the laws of *organic* life (1 Corinthi-
ans 12). The body is attached to the head, and the whole is held together by ligaments and
joints; but the bond of communal action is love (Eph. 4:16 and Col. 2:19). Paul's notion of
organism is neither the Roman Catholic nor the biological; and it is not that of organologi-
cal political philosophy. [See page 77, editorial note 49.][CG] In all of these views the
empirical community as a whole is ranked higher in value than individuals, who become
part of a collective body, losing their identity to it. Paul speaks of the *church of God.* As such
it is God's reality of revelation, and the individual is really only a part of it—a part, however,
as a whole person, as someone elected by God within the church-community. As a purely
empirical community, however, the church in principle can make no absolute claim on the
individual, otherwise this would amount to the Roman Catholic view of the church. With
the notion of the organism, therefore, Paul wants to express, on the one hand, that all
belong to the body of Christ, who is the unity of all members; Paul wants to express
belonging to God's church community, in which alone the individual can live. But, on the
259   other hand, from this membership there follows the demand, or rather the obvious

5:25). The relation of Christ to the church is twofold. Christ is the foundation, the cornerstone, the pioneer, the master builder. But Christ is 86 also at all times a real presence for the church, for it is Christ's body, and the people are members of this body (1 Cor. 12:2ff.; Rom. 12:4ff.; Eph. 1:23, 4:15f.; Col. 1:18), or members of Christ himself (1 Cor. 6:15; Rom. 6:13 and 19). This means that the church is at once already completed[31] and still in the process of growing. The actualization is accomplished by the spirit of Christ and by the Holy Spirit. What the former is for the church as a whole, the latter is for the individual. The Holy Spirit brings Christ to individuals· (Rom. 8:14; Eph. 2:22) and establishes community among them (2 Cor. 13:13; Phil. 2.1). Whereas the Holy Spirit uses the social nature of people; the spirit of Christ deals with the historical becoming of the life of the church as a whole.[7]

---

7. See Seeberg, *Dogmatik*, 2:320ff.[32]

[29. *cont.*] consequence, of cooperating with the whole. It is not the empirical church as such that is an organism (the empirical-sociological concept of organism is sociologically untenable if it attempts to be more than a partially appropriate image, and superfluous if it does not attempt to be more), <<See Kistiakowski, *Gesellschaft und Einzelwesen*, 1898, chaps. 1 and 2.>> but the church-community of God. The Spirit of Christ functions to make the church-community an organism; that is, it is the 'body of Christ' in the sense described above and according to the notion of the body of a collective person [Gesamtperson]. From here it also becomes comprehensible how Paul can say that we are the body that is governed by the head. 'Body' is in each case a functional concept (see below), and, conversely, Christ is truly present where Christ governs human wills. Christ is 'body'—'Christ existing as church-community'. From all that has been said it follows that in the sociological structure of the church according to the view of the New Testament, plurality of persons, community, and unity are understood as belonging together, analogous to the structure of all communities of will.

[30.] See Holl, "Kirchenbegriff," 942ff., which Bonhoeffer follows largely in his outline of Paul's concept of the church. Holl's article is aimed especially against the proposition of Rudolph Sohm, who states that the nature of church law and the nature of the church are in contradiction with each other (see Sohm, *Kirchenrecht*, 1:16ff. and 700). This position is refuted, according to Holl, by Paul's concept of the church, which gained full acceptance only through Luther (see Holl, ["Kirchenbegriff,"] 947).

[31.] By "completed" (*vollendet*) Bonhoeffer means that the church, as established by God in Christ, is eternally and at all times complete, consummated, and fulfilled; this corresponds to his idea that in Christ the church is *realisiert*, realized. He also holds that the church is 'actualized' in time by the Holy Spirit, i.e., it grows in history, and thus the *vollendete Kirche* takes on empirical form. No single word in German or English fully captures the meaning Bonhoeffer intends. In using "completed" for *vollendet* we mean to convey both the eschatological character of the church (as "consummated" would express) and to indicate that it is not the result of a temporal process, but is a divine reality. [CG/RK]

[32.] Cf. Traugott Schmidt, *Der Leib Christi*, 81ff.

3. Paul repeatedly identifies Christ and the church-community (1 Cor. 12:12, 6:15, 1:13). Where the body of Christ is, there Christ truly is. Christ is in the church-community, as the church-community is in Christ (1 Cor. 1:30, 3:16; 2 Cor. 6:16; Col. 2:17, 3:11). 'To be in Christ' is synonymous with 'to be in the church-community'.[8]

4. Connected with this thought is the idea of the church-community as a collective personality [Gesamtpersönlichkeit], which again can be called Christ (Gal. 3:28; Col. 3:10f.; similarly Eph. 1:23). In this context, too, belongs "[clothe] yourselves with the new self," which can also be expressed by the phrase "put on the Lord Jesus Christ" (Col. 3:10; Eph. 4:24; Rom. 13:14; Gal. 3:27). A complete identification between Christ and the church-community cannot be made, since Christ has ascended into heaven and is now with God, and we still await Christ's coming (Eph. 4:8ff.; 1 Thess. 4:16; Phil. 3:20; 1 Cor. 15:23). This is a problem that remains unsolved.[34]

87   5. The church is the presence of Christ in the same way that Christ is

---

8. Kattenbusch, "Quellort der Kirchenidee," in *Harnack Festgabe*, 143ff., comes to similar conclusions on this point, as does Traugott Schmidt, *Der Leib Christi*. Christ and church are identified without, however (contra Schmidt), connecting any mystical notions with this idea. While Schmidt, after the example of Bousset (2 Cor. 5:17 et passim), still hesitates to equate 'in Christ' and 'in the church-community' (154), Kattenbusch approves of it: ἐνδύσασθαι τὸν Χριστόν [putting on Christ] (157) is merging into the church-community. For Paul it thus means the same thing whether a person lives ἐν Χριστῷ [in Christ] or ἐν ἐκκλησίᾳ [in the church] but ἐν Ἰησοῦ [in Jesus] never occurs as a mystical expression.[33] See Deissmann, *[Die neutestamentliche Formel] In Christus-Jesus*, vi.

[33.] See Kattenbusch, "Kirchenidee," 157, note 1: "It is thus also the *same thing* for Paul whether a person lives ἐν Χριστῷ [in Christ] or ἐν ἐκκλησίᾳ [in the church]. He never spoke of a person as living ἐν Ἰησοῦ [in Jesus]! But only this would be 'mysticism!'" The article by Kattenbusch is, like Holl's article, aimed against Rudolph Sohm (see above, page 139, editorial note 30). Kattenbusch intends to prove that what the "Apology of the Augsburg Confession" formulates as a pair of opposites—"societas fidei et spiritus sancti in cordibus" ["community of faith and of the Holy Spirit in people's hearts"] and "societas externarum rerum ac rituum" ["community of external things and rites"] (*The Book of Concord*, 169)—is originally a unity, already found in the New Testament.

[34.] For the idea of the church as a collective personality [*Gesamtpersönlichkeit*] see Traugott Schmidt, *Der Leib Christi*, 142ff. and 147ff. Kattenbusch, "Kirchenidee," 157, calls the church, conceived of as a collective personality, 'collective individual' [*Kollektivindividuum*]. [On the 'unsolved problem' in Paul just mentioned, see "Promotion Thesis 2," *DBW* 9:477, and *AB (DBWE 2)* 112, footnote 39.][CG]

the presence of God. The New Testament knows a form of revelation, 'Christ existing as church-community'.[35]

6. This is the meaning of Paul's indicative, "you are the body of Christ" (1 Cor. 3:16; 6:19; 12:27; 2 Cor. 6:16; Eph. 5:30), which refers to the concrete, individual congregation (see 1 Cor. 5:6!). Even the church-community of the New Testament was never actually 'pure' (Luke 17:21)—it was so only eschatologically, that is, as God's church-community, as the body of Christ. A misunderstanding on this point necessarily leads to perfectionist sectarianism.

7. The church is visible as a corporate social body in worship and in working-for-each-other [Füreinanderwirken]. It is invisible as an eschatological entity, as the 'body of Christ'.

8. Paul takes the idea of organism from Greek tradition, but reworks it. Its original sense, thus, is not important for the concept of the church. 1 Cor. 12:12ff. and Rom. 12:5ff. speak of Christ's church, the body of Christ as such, as a body that does not become visible in the empirical church, but that is believed, and that as the body of Christ exists only through Christ 'above' and 'before' all individuals. The theory of organism in Roman Catholicism, biology, or the philosophy of the state ranks the collective above the individual. For Paul, only Christ exists 'before' and 'above' the individuals. He looks at the church from the perspective of the collective person [Gesamtperson], that of 'Christ existing as church-community'. In speaking of our being Christ's body, we need to remember the definition of the body as a functional concept; that is, we are governed by Christ in the same way that I govern my body. But the Christ who governs us leads us to serve each other [Dienst aneinander]. From this it follows that applying the idea of organism to the church is misleading and should therefore be avoided.

B. Positive Presentation: Introduction to the Basic Problems and Their Exposition

The church is God's new will and purpose for humanity. God's will is always directed toward the concrete, historical human being. But this means that it begins to be implemented *in history*. God's will must become visible and comprehensible at some point in history. But at the   88

[35.] Regarding the concept 'Christ existing as church-community' [*Christus als Gemeinde existierend*], see below page 198, editorial note 217.

same point it must already be completed. Therefore, it must be revealed. Revelation of God's will is necessary because the primal community, where God speaks and the word becomes deed and history through human beings, is broken. Therefore God must personally speak and act, and at the same time accomplish a new creation of human beings, since God's word is always deed. *Thus the church is already completed in Christ, just as in Christ its beginning is established.* Christ is the cornerstone and the foundation of the building, and yet the church, composed of all its parts, is also Christ's body. Christ is the firstborn among many sisters and brothers, and yet all are one in Christ; see Eph. 1:4f.: "Καθὼς ἐξελέξατο ἡμᾶς ἐν αὐτῷ πρὸ καταβολῆς κόσμου, εἶναι ἡμᾶς ἁγίους καὶ ἀμώμους κατενώπιον αὐτοῦ, ἐν ἀγάπῃ προορίσας ἡμᾶς εἰς υἱοθεσίαν διὰ Ἰησοῦ Χριστοῦ εἰς αὐτόν"; v. 11: "ἐν ᾧ καὶ ἐκληρώθημεν προορισθέντες κατὰ πρόθεσιν τοῦ τὰ πάντα ἐνεργοῦντος" [1:4f.: "just as he chose us in Christ before the foundation of the world to be holy and blameless before him. In love he destined us for adoption as his children through Jesus Christ"; 1:11: "in whom we have also become heirs, predestined by the decision which was made before by him, who works all things."] (cf. 2 Tim. 1:9; John 15:16 in the Diatessaron).[36] To be noted is the use of ἐν [in] throughout—"we are reconciled not only by him, but *in him*. Hence to understand his person and history properly is to understand our reconciliation properly."[9] If we, the members of the Christian church-community, are to believe that in Christ we are reconciled with God, then the mediator of this reconciliation must represent not only the reconciling divine love, but also at the same time the humanity that is to be reconciled, the humanity of the new Adam.[10]

---

9. See Hofmann, *Erste Schutzschrift* [Schutzschriften], [1:]19; see also his *Schriftbeweis*, chap. 6.[37]

10. A[lbrecht] Ritschl, *A Critical History of the Christian Doctrine of Justification and Reconciliation*, 546f.[38]

[36.] Bonhoeffer's Greek quotation does not contain the full three verses, and his punctuation of the Greek varies from the *NRSV*, which reads ". . . holy and blameless before him in love." John 15:16 ("You did not choose me but I chose you") is in Tatian's *Diatessaron*, 46:32 in the English translation, which is numbered differently from the German edition. [CG]

[37.] This quote is also to be found in Ritschl, *A Critical History*, 546.

[38.] This sentence is quoted verbatim from Ritschl, *A Critical History*, 546, where Ritschl summarizes a thought from the theology of Hofmann.

In order for the church, which already is completed in Christ, to build itself up in time, the will of God must be actualized ever anew, now no longer in a fundamental way for all people, but in the personal appropriation of the individual. This is possible only on the basis of God's act in Christ. It also presupposes both being in the church, which is already completed in Christ, and the individual who is brought into the church—that is, into the humanity of Christ—only by the act of appropriation. The opposition of the concepts of revelation and time, completion and becoming,[39] cannot be overcome logically. Revelation enters into time not just apparently but actually, and precisely by so doing it bursts the form of time. If, however, for this reason one regarded revelation only as beginning (potentiality), and not at the same time also as completion (reality), this would take away what is decisive about the revelation of God, namely that God's word became history.[40]

In order to build the church as the community-of-God [Gemeinde Gottes] in time, God reveals God's own self as *Holy Spirit*. The Holy Spirit is the will of God that gathers individuals together to be the church-community, maintains it, and is at work only within it. We experience our election only in the church-community, which is already established in Christ, by personally appropriating it through the Holy Spirit, by standing in the actualized church.

Thus the line of argument falls naturally into the following parts. *First*, we have to inquire into the church-community established in Christ and already completed by God's act, the community-of-God; or, to express it in terms used earlier, we have to inquire into the life-principle of the new basic-relations of social existence.[41] What we are dealing with is thus analogous to the basic-relations established in Adam and

89

[39.] Added to *SC-A*: completeness and becoming.

[40.] See Seeberg, *Dogmatik*, 2:346. According to Seeberg, the historical-empirical church forms a unity with the 'essential' church, that is, the church that is realized by Christ. This unity corresponds to the unity of possibility and reality, "insofar as this possibility only exists for the sake of this reality, and insofar as this reality would not come about without this possibility" (ibid.). See also Schleiermacher, *The Christian Faith*, §54.2, 212–14. Regarding the relationship between possibility and reality, see Aristotle, *Metaphysics*, 1045b27ff. and 1071b3ff., and Hegel, *Hegel's Science of Logic*, 529ff. Regarding the redefinition of the relationship, see Kierkegaard, *Philosophical Fragments*, 89ff.; Barth, *Romans*, esp. 229ff.; and Bultmann, "What Does It Mean to Speak of God?" in *Faith and Understanding*, 53ff.

[41.] See below, pages 145ff.

their preservation [Aufhebung]. These basic-relations are already completely established in Christ, not ideally but in reality. Humanity is new
in Christ, that is, from the perspective of eternity; but it also becomes
new in time. *Second,* we have to reflect on the work of the Holy Spirit as
the will of God for the historical actualization of the church of Jesus
Christ.[42] But we must pay strict attention to the fact that here the counterpart of *actualization by the Holy Spirit is not potentiality in Christ, but the
reality of revelation in Christ.* This is the foundation for the entire understanding of the problem of the church. The 'possibility' of the church
not being actualized by the Holy Spirit simply no longer exists; the
church that is established in Christ and already completed in reality
must necessarily be actualized. Using the category of potentiality in
Christ might seem very natural here. But this category virtually destroys
the reality-character of redemption. For faith, the reconciliation and
justification of the world are established in reality in the revelation in
90　　Christ, though faith is possible only within the actualized church. The
church does not first become real when it assumes empirical form,
when the Holy Spirit does God's work. The reality of the church of the
Holy Spirit is just as much a revelational reality; the only thing that matters is to believe this revelational reality in the empirical form. As Christ
and the new humanity now necessarily belong together, so the Holy
Spirit must be understood as being at work only in this new humanity. It
is evidently a mistake, therefore, to attempt to reflect on the objective
work of the Holy Spirit independently of the church-community. The
Spirit is only in the church-community, and the church-community is
only in the Spirit. "Ubi enim ecclesia ibi et spiritus; et ubi spiritus dei,
illic ecclesia et omnis gratia" ["For where the church is there is the
Spirit; and where the Spirit of God is, there is the church and every kind
of grace"].[11] But Troeltsch still thought it necessary to maintain that
what matters in the Protestant concept of the church is not the church
as community, but solely the word—that is, precisely the objective work
of the Spirit. He maintained that where the word is, there is the church,
even if there is no one to hear it.[44] This is a complete misconception of

---

11. Irenaeus, *Against Heresies*, 3.24.1[43]

[42.] See below, pages 157ff.
[43.] Irenaeus, *Sources chrétiennes*, vol. 211, bk. 3.24.1.
[44.] See Troeltsch, *Social Teachings*, 477. Bonhoeffer probably refers to the dictum:

the Protestant tenet of the importance of the word, which is still to be discussed.

It will then be necessary, *third*, to determine the relationship between the Holy Spirit of the church-community and the human spirit of the community that is brought about by the former. This then raises the problem of the empirical church. In this context the difference between the idealist and the Christian concept of objective spirit also will become clear.[45]

1. The Church Established in and through Christ—Its Realization

The reality of sin, we found, places the individual in a state of utmost solitude, a state of radical separation from God and other human beings. It places the individual in the isolated position of the person who confesses to committing the 'first' sin, confesses to being the one in whom all humanity fell. But the reality of sin places the individual at the same time, both subjectively and objectively, into the deepest, most immediate bond with humanity, precisely because everybody has become guilty. As a bond of those who are guilty it cannot take on empirical form; it is nevertheless experienced in each concrete relation. Now since in the individual guilty act it is precisely the humanity of human beings that has been affirmed, humanity has to be considered a community. As such it is also a collective person, but a collective person that has the same nature as each of its members. In Christ this tension between isolation from, and bondage to, each other is abolished in reality. The cord between God and human beings that was cut by the first Adam is tied anew by God, by revealing God's own love in Christ, by no longer approaching us in demand and summons, purely as You, but instead by *giving God's own self as an I, opening God's own heart. The church is founded on the revelation of God's heart.*[46] But since destroying the primal community with God also destroyed human community, so likewise when God restores community between human beings and God's own self, community among us also is restored once again, in

91

[44. *cont.*] "The church would still exist even if there were nothing left save the word" (*Social Teachings*, 480). See also the criticism of Troeltsch by Holl, *Luther*, 297, note 3.

[45.] See below, pages 208ff.

[46.] The image of God's heart being opened in love comes from Luther. [CG]

accordance with our proposition about the essential interrelation of our community with God and human community.[47]

In Christ humanity really is drawn into community with God, just as in Adam humanity fell. And even though in the one Adam there are many Adams, yet there is only one Christ.[48] For Adam is 'representative human being' ['der Mensch'], but Christ is the Lord of his new humanity. Thus everyone becomes guilty by their own strength and fault, because they themselves are Adam; each person, however, is reconciled apart from their own strength and merit, because they themselves are not Christ. While the old humanity consists of countless isolated units—each one an Adam—that are perceived as a comprehensive unity only through each individual, the new humanity is entirely concentrated in the one single historical point, Jesus Christ, and only in Christ is it perceived as a whole. For in Christ, as the foundation and the body of the building called Christ's church-community, the work of God takes place and is completed. In this work Christ has a function that sheds the clearest light on the fundamental difference between Adam and Christ, namely *the function of vicarious representative [Stellvertreter]* (this will be discussed extensively later). Adam does not intentionally act as a vicarious representative; on the contrary, Adam's action is extremely egocentric. That its effect closely resembles a deliberately vicarious representative action must not obscure the *entirely different*

92 *basic premises.* In the old humanity the whole of humanity falls anew, so to speak, with every person who sins; in Christ, however, humanity has been brought once and for all—this is essential to *real* vicarious representative action [Stellvertretung]—into community with God.[49]

Since death as the wages of sin (Rom. 6:23) first constitutes *history*, so *life that abides in love* breaks the continuity of the historical process—not empirically, but objectively. Death can still completely separate past and future for our eyes, but not for the life that abides in the love of Christ. *This is why the principle of vicarious representative action* can become fundamental for the church-community of God in and through Christ. Not 'solidarity',[12] which is never possible between Christ and human beings,

---

12. This is the position held by Scheler, *Formalism in Ethics*, 533ff.

[47.] See above, chap. 2, page 34. [CG]

[48.] Cf. Rom. 5:12ff. [CG]

[49.] Seeberg places *Stellvertretung* (vicarious representative action) in the center of "the redemptive work of Jesus Christ" (*Dogmatik*, 2:242ff.).

but vicarious representative action is the life-principle of the new humanity. True, I know myself to be in a guilty solidarity with the other person, but my service to the other person springs[50] from the life-principle of vicarious representative action.

Now by encompassing the new life-principle of Christ's church-community in himself, Christ is at the same time established as the Lord of the church-community, which means his relation to the church-community is both 'communal' and 'governing'.[51]

Because, however, the entire new humanity is established in reality in Jesus Christ, *he represents the whole history of humanity in his historical life.* Christ's history is marked by the fact that in it humanity-in-Adam is transformed into humanity-in-Christ. As the human body of Jesus Christ became the resurrection body, so the corpus Adae [body of Adam] became the corpus Christi [body of Christ]. The former as well as the latter leads through death and resurrection; the human body—the corpus Adae—has to be broken, in order for the body of the resurrection—the corpus Christi—to be created. The history of Jesus Christ, however, is closed to us without his word.[52] Only if we take both together will it be possible to read the past and the future of humanity in Christ's history.[53]

Jesus Christ places his life under the law (Gal. 4:4); he takes his place within Israel's community-of-God [Gottesgemeinde].[54] The baptism (Matt. 3:15) is the clearest example of this. What was Israel's community-of-God?[55] It was the people, as a collective person, whom God had   93

[50.] Deleted from *SC-A*: in the deepest sense.

[51.] *SC-A* does not begin a new paragraph here.

[52.] The text "Because, however, . . . word" reads in *SC-A*:

But because the entire new humanity is really established in Jesus Christ, *Christ's own historical life represents the whole history of humanity* from Adam until the church. Christ is both the criterion as regards content and the foundation of the church; Christ's history, therefore, can tell us how the new humanity is created out of the old, and only through Christ's own history does Christ become the life principle of the church. This history is closed to us without Christ's word.

[53.] *SC-A* does not begin a new paragraph here.

[54.] Here *israelitischen Gottesgemeinde* is a parallel construction to *christliche Gemeinde.* On the following pages Bonhoeffer contracts it to *israelitische Gemeinde,* then *Gottesgemeinde,* and finally simply to *Gemeinde.* [RK/CG]

[55.] The text that follows, up to ". . . history of the community [*Gemeinde*]-of-Israel," reads in *SC-A*:

chosen; it was constituted by God's law. The law of God for Israel is the calling properly heard. Law and calling belong together. Fulfillment of the law is the obedient realization of the calling. Because the people are called as a collective person, the fulfillment of the law is fulfillment of God's call to be a people, a holy community-of-God. Both ideas of God's call and of God's law, therefore, point toward community. To play off God's call against God's law—which means to invert the meaning of law and thus not to fulfill it—shatters the very core of the community that is constituted by the true correlation of calling and law. When taken under human control, the law becomes a claim of each individual on the God who calls. But at the same time the law reveals itself as a living force, becoming a power of wrath to those who misuse it, showing them the irreparable rift in the community, and isolating them completely. That, in brief, is the history of the community-of-Israel.

By placing himself within this community-of-Israel, Christ does not declare his solidarity with it, but in vicarious representative action for all he fulfills the law by love, thereby overcoming the Jewish understanding of the law. Whereas formerly only the willful transgressor of the law was excluded from the community-of-Israel, Jesus now declares the whole community-of-Israel to have essentially fallen away from God. Far from being the community-of-God itself, it belongs to the humanity-of-Adam, and must be reconciled with God. That is, it must be re-created into a new community [Gemeinde]. Whereas formerly each individual in the community faced the law in isolation, the person of Christ must now unite all individuals in himself, and act before God as their vicarious representative.[56] The transformation into a new

---

[55. *cont.*] It [the community-of-Israel] was the people that God had chosen as a collective person; they were simultaneously a historical and a religious entity. It was constituted by God's law—by which it also foundered. It thus belongs to the humanity-of-Adam; however, it continues to have the revelation of God in the law, which places it above all peoples, but that at the same time subjects it to the most severe judgment of God: "You only have I known of all the families of the earth; *therefore* I will punish you for all your iniquities" (Amos 3:2, *NRSV*). In the people of Israel, God's will that there should be history and that a community should be built both become visible.

[Bonhoeffer's German version of the Amos quote reads 'peoples' (*Völkern*), rather than 'families'; emphasis his.][CG]

[56.] "Whereas . . . as their vicarious representative" reads in *SC-A*: Whereas formerly each individual in the community faced the will of God alone, the person of Christ must unite them in Christ's own self, and stand before God as their vicarious representative.

[57.] Missing in *SC-A*: ultimate.

community-of-God is possible only if the deficiency of the old is recognized. To bring this about, Jesus calls to repentance, which means he reveals God's ultimate[57] claim and subjects the human past and present to its reality. Recognizing that we are guilty makes us solitary before God; we begin to recognize what has long been the case objectively, namely that we are in a state of[58] isolation. With this recognition the old community-of-God [Gottesgemeinde], whose norm and constituting power is the law, is broken up. The law does not establish community [Gemeinschaft] but solitude—as a consequence of human sin, of course—for the law is holy and good and was meant to be the norm and pattern of life of a holy *people* of God. The law can only be fulfilled in spirit through the spirit, that is, an unbroken will to obey God, i.e., through perfect love.[59] With the recognition that the strength to do this is lacking, the way is cleared for the gift Jesus gives, for the message of God's love and royal rule in God's Realm. Thus out of utter isolation arises concrete community, for the preaching of God's love speaks of the community into which God *has* entered with each and every person—with all those who in utter solitude know themselves separated from God and other human beings and who believe this message.[60] It would not do, however, for Jesus to re-create the community-of-God during his lifetime.[61] His love had to become complete by fulfilling the law—that is, the claim of God and of human beings—even to death. The

94

[58.] Deleted from *SC-A*: ethical.

[59.] "that is, . . . love" reads in *SC-A*: that is, out of an unbroken, childlike will to obey God.

[60.] *SC-A* begins a new paragraph here.

[61.] The text that follows, up to "community-of-love" in the next sentence, reads in *SC-A*:

Only when the work of obedience was completed was God's love fully revealed. Jesus could not found the Christian church, which is characterized by his spiritual presence. True, the foundation of the church-community was laid at the moment when Simon said: "You are the Christ"; for if faith in the love of God in Christ, faith in the community, existed, then the church of God automatically existed with it. God's rule created its own Realm. Faith and church are related to each other not as a sequence, nor as a logical consequence; rather, both are by inner necessity established together—so closely together that the former can really be regarded as an expression of the latter. Faith is an expression of community with God, and that implies human beings' community with each other, just as community with God is an expression of faith. We admittedly said that God's empirical church-community is constituted only through the work of the Holy Spirit; but evidently the Holy Spirit is present only after Christ's death. The community-of-Jesus [Gemeinde Jesu], therefore, before it finally could be established as the church [Kirche] of Jesus Christ, had to pass through the death of Christ, it had to fall, it . . .

revealed community-of-love[62] had to be broken up one more time by its founder's own action, though not before Jesus had tied them tightly together with a close bond at the very last hour. This happened in the Last Supper. Jesus says: just as I break this bread, so my body will be broken tomorrow, and as all of you eat and are filled from *one* loaf, so too will all of you be saved and united in me alone. The Lord of the disciple-community [Gemeinde] grants his disciples community with him and thus with each other. With considerable plausibility this event has been considered the point where the church was founded (Kattenbusch).[63] Jesus has now openly expressed his will for the church-community [Gemeinde] to exist; yet theologically the moment of the church's birth is to be sought in another event.

Serving the law leads Jesus to the cross, truly leads him into the most profound solitude that the curse of the law brings upon human beings.[64] When Jesus is arrested all the disciples forsake him, and on the cross Jesus is quite alone. The disciple-community[65] seems to be broken up. This has a meaning that is theologically significant[66] and is not simply to be dismissed as the weakness or disloyalty of the disciples. It is an event with an objective meaning; it had to happen in this way, "so that everything would be fulfilled",[67] one would like to add. In the death of Jesus on the cross God's judgment and wrath are carried out on all the self-centeredness of humanity,[68] which had distorted the meaning of the law. This distortion[69] brought the Son of God to the cross. With this the burden[70] becomes unbearably heavy. Each individual is Adam; everyone is entirely responsible. Here each person stands alone before God. Here all hope is gone; the disciple-community existed only as long as one knew that Jesus was alive. But, in going to

95

[62.] *Gemeinde der Liebe* [community-of-love], i.e., the disciples. [CG]

[63.] See Kattenbusch, "Kirchenidee," 166 and 169. See Mark 14:22ff. and parallels.

[64.] Deleted from *SC-A*: The church-community is to be constituted by his death; Jesus was right, and yet what happens is totally different from what one should expect.

[65.] Here, as above and also below, Bonhoeffer is referring to the community-of-love between Jesus and the disciples. The church will also be described as a community of love (*Liebesgemeinschaft*); see below, pages 178ff. [CG]

[66.] *SC-A* reads: This has a profound meaning . . .

[67.] Cf. John 19:28.

[68.] *SC-A* reads: the whole sinful humanity.

[69.] *SC-A* reads: Human sin.

[70.] *SC-A* reads: its weight.

the cross,[71] in submitting to the law, in taking the curse of the law upon himself on our behalf, Jesus himself had apparently accepted that the world was right. The old 'community-of-God' seemed to have won. Because he was made sin for us, and because he was accursed by the law for us, Jesus died in solitude.[13] Therefore the disciples, for whom the present had no future, had to be alone too. To us, for whom Easter also lies in the past, the death of Christ is conceivable only in the light of the victory of love over law, of life over death. The absolutely contemporary character of the death of Jesus is no longer available to us. This results for us in *the paradoxical reality of a community-of-the-cross*, which contains within itself the contradiction of simultaneously representing utmost solitude and closest community. *And this is the specifically Christian church-community.* But a community-of-the-cross exists only through the Easter message. In the resurrection of Jesus Christ his death is revealed as the death of death itself, and with this the boundary of history

96

---

13. Schleiermacher, too, gives a theological interpretation of this scattering of the disciples. "After the death of Christ we find the disciples about to scatter, and until his ascension we find the continuity of their group interrupted and diminished to a total formlessness. During the lifetime of Jesus, however, it could only be the case that each person was mainly attached to him and wanted to receive from him, without anyone regarding himself mature enough for free self-directed activity in the Realm of God which was to be built" (*The Christian Faith*, §122.2, 566f.)[trans. RK]. Jesus had appealed to the receptivity of the disciples; they were totally attached to him. Only the Holy Spirit brings about self-directed activity and reunion. To this it has to be objected that (1) Schleiermacher identifies the events of Ascension Day and Pentecost (§§122.1 and 122.2, 565–67); before Pentecost, however—that is, before the imparting of the Holy Spirit—the community was assembled in prayer and supplication with one accord (Acts 1:14–2:1); and that (2) Schleiermacher's separation of receptivity and self-directed activity is theologically questionable, as he himself is aware (§122.3, 567ff.). Where Christ is at work, Christ makes us both fully receptive and fully self-directed. Schleiermacher concedes as much, but the self-directed activity became, according to him, a truly 'joint' activity only after Christ's departure and could manifest itself only then as Holy Spirit.

[71.] The following, up to "had to be alone too," reads in *SC-A*:

. . . Jesus had completely entered into the old community-of-God and placed himself under the law. He had let himself be crucified as a blasphemer; the law had celebrated its greatest victory—it had defeated God's love. But where the law is, there is solitude. Because Jesus 'was put under the law', he died in solitude; and therefore the disciples had to be alone too. For them, to whom the present had no future, it had to be this way.

marked by death is abolished,[72] the human body becomes the resurrec-
tion-body, and the humanity-of-Adam has become the church of Christ.
To be sure, the church could be created only in an empirical form by the
Holy Spirit. In the resurrection it is 'created' only insofar as it has now
run the course of its dialectical history. It is realized, but not actualized.
In the resurrection the heart of God has broken through sin[73] and
death; it has really conquered God's new humanity and subjected it to
God's rule.[74]

Admittedly, the existing empirical community cannot be the actualized church, since Christ has not yet ascended. The time between the
resurrection and the ascension and the time after Pentecost are different insofar as in the first case the disciple-community lives in Christ as
its Lord and life-principle, whereas in the second case Christ lives in the
community. Formerly the disciple-community 'represented' Christ; now
it possesses him as revelation, as Spirit.[75] *Thus the day of the founding of
the actualized church remains Pentecost.* Since human community was
formed only when it became a community of will and spirit, and since
human spirit is operative only in sociality, *the church originates with the
outpouring of the Holy Spirit, and so too the Holy Spirit is the spirit of the
church-community of Christ. But if the Spirit is operative only within the
church-community, then the genesis of the latter cannot be deduced from the
spirits of individuals.* In the perspective of systematic sociology, the problem of the church therefore cannot consist in the question of the empirical association of people and their psychological motivation. It can
consist only in *exhibiting the essential structure of the social entity,* its volitional acts, and its objective form in connection with the concept of
spirit—consistent with the definition of sociology given above.

Now the relationship of Christ to the church can be stated by saying
that in essence Jesus Christ was no more the founder of the Christian
religious community than the founder of a religion. The credit for both
97   of these belongs to the earliest church, i.e., to the apostles. This is why

[72.] "and with this . . . abolished" reads in *SC-A*: and this also provides the meaning of a
new church-community-of-God which, in its fullness, is established in Christ . . .

[73.] Here *Schuld* is translated 'sin' because it is parallel to death as an objective power,
and its meaning is not a subjective emotion. [CG]

[74.] *SC-A* does not begin a new paragraph here.

[75.] On the sense in which the church-community possesses Christ, see the important
passage in *AB* (*DBWE* 2) 90f. [CG]

the question whether Jesus founded a church is so ambiguous. He brought, established, and proclaimed the reality of the new humanity. The circle of disciples around him was not the church; its history prefigured the inner dialectic of the church. It is not a new religion recruiting followers—this is the picture of a later time. Rather, God established the reality of the church, of humanity pardoned in Jesus Christ—not religion, but revelation, *not religious community, but church.*[76] This is what the reality of Jesus Christ means.

¶And yet there is a necessary connection between revelation and religion as well as between religious community and the church. Nowadays this is often overlooked.[77] And yet only because of this connection can Paul call Jesus the foundation and the cornerstone of the building of the church. As pioneer and model, Jesus also is founder of a religious community, though not of the Christian church (for it indeed exists only after Pentecost—Matt. 16:18 and the scene of the Last Supper express this).[78] And, after the resurrection, Christ himself restores both forms of community that had been broken: with Peter through Christ's appearance to him as presumably the first to whom this was granted (1 Cor. 15:5), perhaps with an express conferral of office (John 21:15ff.); and after that with the Twelve through an appearance in their midst (1 Cor. 15:5; John 20:19). Christ is thus the sole foundation upon which the building of the church rests, the reality from which the historical 'collective life'[79] originated.

¶The relationship of Jesus Christ to the Christian church is thus to be understood in a dual sense. (1) *The church is already completed in Christ, time is suspended.* (2) *The church is to be built within time upon Christ as the firm foundation. Christ is the historical principle of the church.* Time belongs

---

[76.] Regarding the relationship between religion and revelation, religious community and church, see Ritschl, *Justification and Reconciliation*, 1ff., 8ff., and 399ff.; esp. 414 and 543ff. Also see Troeltsch, *Social Teachings*, 69f., and Barth, *Romans*, 229ff. and 330ff., 391ff.

[77.] Deleted from *SC-A*: but this implies a lack of seriousness toward the historical facts. Cf. above, page 126, editorial note 2.

[78.] See above, page 150, editorial note 63.

[79.] In *The Christian Faith* Schleiermacher speaks of the church as the new 'collective life' [*Gesamtleben*] established by Christ. Cf. also his organization of the doctrine of the church, which falls into three main sections: the origin of the church (§§115 & 116, 532–36), existence of the church in the world (§126, 582–85), and the perfection of the church (§157ff., 696ff.).

to him, the vertical direction, as it were.[14][81] These statements correspond to the well-known New Testament view concerning the Realm of God as present and still to come, but they are not identical with it; for the church is not the same as the Realm of God. The church is not the Realm of God any more than the Christian, who is iustus-peccator [justified-sinner],[82] is actually already completed, even though in reality the Christian is just that. The Realm of God is a strictly eschatological concept, which from God's point of view is present in the church at every moment, but which for us remains an object of hope, while the church is an actually present object of faith. The church is identical with the realm of Christ, but the realm of Christ is the Realm of God that has been realized in history since the coming of Christ.[15]

What is the *principle*, then, upon which the *efficacy of Christ* rests with regard to the new social basic conditions? The crucified and risen Christ is recognized by the church-community as God's incarnate love for us—as God's will to renew the covenant, to establish God's rule, and thus to create community. Two things are still opposed to this, *time* and the *will to do evil*. The second is self-evident; the first means that what has happened cannot be undone. This is the gravity of time that became a burden for us since sin and death appeared.[85] If human

---

14. As the temporal nature of the church is given in Jesus Christ, so *the work of the Holy Spirit falls within its spatial impulse.*[80]

15. See 1 Cor. 15:24. See also Luther's exegesis, *E[rlangen] A[usgabe] [Sämtliche Werke]* 51:159,[83] and the discussion on this point by Karl Barth, *The Resurrection of the Dead*, 176f.[84]

[80.] Deleted from *SC-A*: i.e., as the former works on the historical level, the latter does in the social sphere (this will be discussed in the next chapter). [In using the metaphor 'vertical direction' for time, Bonhoeffer appears to have in mind the earlier image of a building rising upwards.] [RK]

[81.] In *SC-A* footnote 14 is to be found at a later point in the text, at the end of the present paragraph.

[82.] Bonhoeffer's variation on the familiar phrase of Luther, "simul iustus et peccator," "at the same time justified and a sinner." [CG]

[83.] Cf. Luther, "The Fifteenth Chapter of St. Paul's First Letter to the Corinthians" (1534), *LW* 28:124 [*WA* 36:568f.].

[84.] Bonhoeffer, who normally cites the Weimar edition, takes his reference here from Karl Barth's citation of the Erlangen edition of Luther in *The Resurrection of the Dead*, 177. [CG]

[85.] An allusion to Romans 5:12, "sin came into the world . . . and death came through sin . . ."; see above, chap. 4, page 110, editorial note 11, where Bonhoeffer cites this verse.

beings are to have community with God, then both of these must somehow be removed: their sin must be forgiven, and what has been done
must be judged undone by God's sovereign decree. Now human sin cannot be viewed by the true God 'as if it did not exist'; it must truly be
'undone', that is, it must be wiped out. This occurs not by reversing
time, but through divine punishment and re-creating the will to do
good. God does not 'overlook' sin; that would mean not taking human
beings seriously as personal beings in their very culpability; and that
would mean no re-creation of the person, and therefore no re-creation
of community.[86] But God does take human beings seriously in their
culpability, and therefore only punishment and the overcoming of sin
can remedy the matter. Both of these have to take place within concrete
time, and in Jesus Christ that occurs in a way that is valid for all time.
He takes the punishment upon himself, accomplishes forgiveness of sin,
and, to use Seeberg's expression, stands as surety for the renewal of
human beings.[16] *Christ's action as vicarious representative* can thus be   99
understood from the situation itself. It is simultaneously 'within concrete time' and the 'for all times'. Vicarious representative action for sin
does take place. Here the one requires the other, for 'punishment' obviously does not mean taking the consequences of sin upon oneself, but
considering these consequences as 'punishment'. The punitive character of the suffering of Jesus has frequently been denied. But Luther
placed all the emphasis especially on this very idea.[87] To take the consequences of sin upon oneself is conceivable in the framework of ethical behavior in civic life. But what characterizes the Christian notion of
vicarious representative action is that it is vicariously representative
strictly with respect to sin and punishment.[88] Though innocent, Jesus
takes the sin of others upon himself, and by dying as a criminal he is

---

16. Seeberg, *Dogmatik*, 2:271ff.

[86.] Missing from *SC-A*: and therefore no re-creation of community.

[87.] According to Ritschl the notion of punishment originated in the context of a legal
relationship and is therefore to be rejected for use in the Christian religion (see Ritschl,
Justification and Reconciliation, 364f. and 472ff.). Concerning Bonhoeffer's judgment of
Luther, cf. Seeberg, *Dogmatik*, 2:268; concerning Bonhoeffer's criticism of Ritschl, cf. Seeberg, *Dogmatik*, 2:307ff.

[88.] Bonhoeffer follows Seeberg not only in taking the concept of vicarious representative action as the sum and substance of Christology, but also in defining it as vicariously
representative with respect to culpability and punishment.

accursed, for he bears the sins of the world and is punished for them. However, vicarious representative love triumphs on the criminal's cross, obedience to God triumphs over sin, and thereby sin is actually punished and overcome. So much for a brief sketch of Christ's vicarious representative action. It contains profound implications for social philosophy.[89]

Is this Christian view of vicarious representative action for sin ethically tenable? As ethical persons we clearly wish, after all, to accept responsibility ourselves before God for our good and evil deeds. How can we lay our fault upon another person and ourselves go free? It is true, the doctrine of vicarious representative action includes more than our ethical posture, but we *ought* to let our sin be taken from us, for we are not able to carry it by ourselves; we *ought not* reject this gift of God. It is God's love that offers it to us, and only for the sake of this love ought we abandon our ethical position of responsibility for ourselves—a position that counts for nothing before God—thereby demonstrating precisely the necessity for vicarious representative action. The idea of vicarious representative action is therefore possible only so long as it is based on an offer by God; this means it is in force only in Christ and Christ's church-community. *It is not an ethical possibility or standard,*[90] *but solely the reality of the divine love for the church-community; it is not an ethical, but a theological concept.*[17] Through the Christian principle of 100   vicarious representative action the new humanity is made whole and sustained. This principle gives Christian basic-relations their substan-

---

17. There is, however, also an ethical concept of vicarious representative action; it signifies the voluntary assumption of an evil in another person's stead. It does not remove the self-responsibility of the other person, and remains as an act of human heroic love (for one's country, friend, etc.) even within the bounds of the highest ethical obligation. In acknowledging it we do not put our ethical person as a whole at stake, but only as much as we owe (body, honor, money) to the person who acted vicariously on our behalf; we acknowledge Christ, however, as vicarious representative for our person as a whole, and thus owe everything to him.[91]

[89.] Deleted from *SC-A*: The difference from Adam's action has already been described. All of humanity is viewed as being concentrated in a single point and this point actually exists only once.

[90.] Concerning the concept of vicarious representative action as an ethical possibility, see Ritschl, *Justification and Reconciliation,* 446ff.

[91.] In *SC-A* footnote 17 is part of the main text.

tive uniqueness. We will discuss later the extent to which this principle not only unites the new humanity with Christ, but also links its members to each other in community. It is certain, however, that human community comes into being where community with God is a reality.

Thus the church is established in and through Christ in the three basic sociological relationships known to us:[92] his death isolates the *individuals*—all of them bear their own culpability and have their own conscience; in the light of the resurrection the community of the cross is justified and sanctified in Christ as *one*. The new humanity is seen synoptically in *one* point, in Christ. And since the love of God, in Christ's vicarious representative action, restores the community between God and human beings, so the *community of human beings with each other has also become a reality in love once again.*[93]

2. The Holy Spirit and the Church of Jesus Christ: The Actualization of the Essential Church

In and through Christ the church is established in reality. It is not as if Christ could be abstracted from the church; rather, it is none other than Christ who 'is' the church. Christ does not represent it; only what is not present can be represented. In God's eyes, however, the church is present in Christ. Christ did not merely make the church possible, but rather realized it for eternity. If this is so, then the significance of Christ must be made the focal point in the temporal actualization of the church. This is accomplished by the Spirit-impelled word of the crucified and risen Lord of the church. The Spirit can work only through this word. If there were an unmediated work of the Spirit, then the idea of the church would be individualistically dissolved from the outset. But   101

[92.] Regarding the three basic sociological relationships, see Hegel, *Lectures on the Philosophy of Religion*, 3:133: "The singularity of the divine idea, the divine idea as *one* human being, is first brought to completion in actuality to the extent that initially it has *many* single individuals confronting it, whom it brings back into the unity of spirit, into the *community*, and therein it is [present] as actual, universal self-consciousness." [In Hegel's *Lectures on the Philosophy of Religion* the translators have consistently translated *Gemeinde* with "community"; in contrast, Bonhoeffer is both more christological and ecclesial.][CG] Concerning the function of the same schematism in Hegel's logic, see the passage on 'the syllogism of existence' in *Hegel's Science of Logic*, 666ff.

[93.] Deleted from *SC-A*: These basic-relations emerge as discernible for us only in the actualization by the Holy Spirit of the church that is established in Christ.   263

in the word the most profound social nexus is established from the beginning.[94] The word is social in character, not only in its origin but also in its aim. Tying the Spirit to the word means that the Spirit aims at a plurality of hearers and establishes a visible sign by which the actualization is to take place.[95]

The word, however, is qualified by being the very word of Christ;[96] it is effectively brought to the heart of the hearers by the Spirit. Christ himself is in the word;[97] the Christ in whom the church-community is already completed seeks to win the heart by his Spirit in order to incorporate it into the actualized community of Christ. But in the word of Christ the actualized church-community is also present, as every word of Christ comes out of that community and exists only in it. If one asks how the actualized church-community could have been present at the time of the first sermons, before individuals who were moved joined together to form the church, then one forgets what has been said earlier,[98] that the Spirit is solely the Spirit of the church, of the church-community, and therefore, that there were no individuals moved by the Spirit before the church-community existed. Community with God exists only through Christ, but Christ is present only in his church-community, and therefore *community with God exists only in the church.* Every individualistic concept of the church breaks down because of this fact. The individual and the church have the following mutually conditioned relationship: the Holy Spirit is at work only in the church as in the community of saints; thus every person who is really moved by the

---

[94.] Deleted from *SC-A*: We recall what has been said concerning language.

[95.] "and establishes a visible . . . is to take place" replaces the following in *SC-A*:

Just as Christ, as the Word of God, bore in himself the word of demand and redemption that had become manifest, that is, the new humanity, so the word, impelled by the Holy Spirit, is to actualize the new humanity; that is, the word is to gather and move it by bringing Christ to it. The word in its clarity and distinctness is necessarily directed at every individual, demanding to be heard. With this a visible sign is established by which the actualization is to take place. However, it is important to recognize that the existence of the word establishes sociality only in general, but not yet community as such in the strict sense.

Concerning the relationship among the Holy Spirit, preaching, and sociality, see Seeberg, *Dogmatik*, 2:322ff.

[96.] "The word . . . very word of Christ" reads in *SC-A*: The word is not merely message, but by being the very word of Christ . . .

[97.] *SC-RS*: "Not 'address,' but δύναμις θεοῦ."

[98.] See above, page 145.

Spirit has to be within the church-community already; but, on the other hand, no one is in the church-community who has not already been moved by the Spirit. It follows that *in moving the elect who are part of the church-community established in Christ, the Holy Spirit simultaneously leads them into the actualized church-community*. Faith is based on entry into the church-community, just as entry into the church-community is based on faith.[18] [104]

___

18. Schleiermacher, for example, did not recognize this connection. In his work two conflicting trains of thought on the nature[99] of the church can be found. See Seeberg, *Begriff der christlichen Kirche*, 202ff.; Krauß, [*Dogma von der unsichtbaren Kirche*,] 103ff.; Ritschl, [*Critical History*,] 445ff., 475f. This can be shown briefly. "The Christian Church is formed through regenerate individuals coming together for mutual interaction and cooperation in an orderly way" (*The Christian Faith*, §115, 532 [trans. altered]). "Once there is religion, it must necessarily also be social. . . . You must admit that it is highly unnatural for people to lock up in themselves what they have created and worked out" (*On Religion*, Fourth Speech, 163 [trans. altered]).[100] The reason for the formation of religious community lies in the need of the individuals to communicate. The church is the satisfaction of a need; it is constructed individualistically.[101] The famous statement in *The Christian Faith* (§24, 103), that Protestantism makes the relationship of individuals to the church dependent upon their relationship to Christ, points in the same direction; here the individual's community with Christ is obviously conceived of as being independent of the church. In conflict with this view there is the concept of the church as the entity that exists before any individual, outside of which there is no religious self-consciousness (§113, 525), and the whole doctrine of the collective life of sin and grace, of the holy spirit of the community [heiliger Gemeingeist] that absorbs the individual. This contradiction has already been pointed out by Ritschl who interprets it as ultimately giving priority to the individual dimension over the communal by granting the latter only a historical, preparatory significance for the development of the former ([*The Christian Faith*,] §113.2, 526f.; §122.3, 567ff.). Admittedly, the community always precedes the individuals temporally; but the individuals, by their very nature, "would have cooperated in the founding of such a community if it had not been there already" ([*The Christian Faith*,] §6.2, 27 [trans. altered]). So the church is created anew at every moment through the need of the individuals. Were this not so Schleiermacher could not have said that the relation of an individual to the church was established only through that individual's life-com-

[99.] Deleted from *SC-A*: or origin.
[100.] Deleted from *SC-A* is the title of this speech: "On the Social Aspect in Religion or on Church and Priesthood." In his copy Bonhoeffer has underlined and marked this sentence in the margin.
[101.] For Bonhoeffer's own understanding of *Lebensgemeinschaft*, see above, chap. 3, page 90; also see his reflections later in his life in *LT* (*DBWE* 5). [CG]

102   The church does not come into being by people coming together (genetic sociology),[105] rather its *existence is sustained* by the Spirit who is a reality within the church-community;[106] therefore, it cannot be derived from individual wills, since an individual will can at most be an expression of belonging to the church. Thus the individual is possible only as a member of the church-community, and this is not merely a preparation for higher individual life, but *personal* life is possible only

munity [Lebensgemeinschaft][102] with Christ; and only in this way can he claim the individual's need to communicate to be the basic sociological structure of the church. In his thinking, an individualism derived from social philosophy—which, however, is not a 'personalism', although occasionally it seems to become such, as, for instance, in the very concept of the individual's life-community with Christ—meets with a monism of spirit, a pantheism, which should, I think, ultimately even be interpreted as a result of such a concept of person. Only on this basis is it possible to find an explanation for such divergent assessments as that of P[aul] Althaus, *Das Erlebnis der Kirche*, 8: "Schleiermacher proceeds from the individual and in this way justifies the church as a religious community. Human beings have to communicate . . . thus the church is formed as a free association," and that of A[lfred] Krauß, [*Dogma von der unsichtbaren Kirche*,] 103: "Schleiermacher, therefore, completely ignores the proposition that had been held as axiomatic up to then, namely that in defining the church one would have to proceed from the individual human beings who make up the 'coetus' ['assembly']. He instead proceeds from the quality of the spirit that manifests its power in them."[103]

[102.] The following footnote was deleted from *SC-A*:

<<Schleiermacher also describes the state of mutual communication in *The Christian Faith*, and in the course of his description develops a concept that later gained importance in sociological literature, namely 'imitation' [Nachbildung] (§6.2, 27). The states of mind of one person are not only perceived, but by dint of the species-consciousness are actually reproduced in another. In his famous work, *Les lois de l'imitation*, G[abriel de] Tarde has taught us to understand imitation as a fundamental sociological phenomenon and has found almost unanimous acceptance of this view (see Vierkandt, *Gesellschaftslehre*, 127ff.). This is mentioned to point out Schleiermacher's sociological acumen.>>

[103.] In his criticism of Schleiermacher, including the references to *The Christian Faith*, Bonhoeffer largely follows Ritschl's discussion of Schleiermacher in *A Critical History*, 1:474ff. In Bonhoeffer's copy of Ritschl's work the passage on Schleiermacher has numerous markings. Regarding the social-philosophical individualism and the monism of spirit in Schleiermacher's work, see Seeberg, *Der Begriff der christlichen Kirche*, 204, and Hirsch, *Die idealistische Philosophie*, 102ff., and *Die Reich-Gottes-Begriffe*, 25f.

[104.] In *SC-A* footnote 18 is part of the main text.

[105.] The phrase "(genetic sociology)" reads in *SC-A*: (as the horde is not yet human sociality).

[106.] Deleted from *SC-A*: (or in the sociality).

within the church-community. A person who is not in the church has no real living-community [Lebensgemeinschaft] with Christ; but a person who is in Christ, is also in the church-community, that is, in both the completed and the actualized church. A person is in Christ, however, through the word of the church-community. Therefore, in the word that comes to the individual both the already completed community of saints and the community of saints developing in time are present; for Christ and the Holy Spirit are at work in this word; and both are insepa-rably linked—the Holy Spirit has no other content than the fact of Christ. Christ is the criterion and the aim of the work of the Holy Spirit, and to this extent Christ himself also participates in building the church in time, although only through the work of the Holy Spirit.

The word is active in three different modes of operation. That is, the   103
church-community of the Holy Spirit is acted upon in a threefold way by the Spirit. This is analogous to the three sociological[107] basic-relations that we saw were in force in the church established in Christ: plurality of spirit, community of spirit, and unity of spirit. This work of the Holy Spirit is thus analogous also to the basic sociological realities that we recognized as the essential structure of every community. Both analo-gies are of the utmost importance.

a) Plurality of Spirit

The Holy Spirit of the church-community is directed as a personal will toward personal wills, addressing each person *as a single individual, lead-ing that person into 'solitude'*.[108] The members of the Holy Spirit's

---

[107.] Word added to *SC-A*: sociological.

[108.] Deleted from *SC-A*:

As long as human beings are simul iustus et peccator [at the same time justified and sinful], this solitude exists in the solitude of the *conscience*, where the Holy Spirit is experienced in   264
maiestate sua [its majesty]. <<Luther, *Disp.*, ed. Drews, 268, 294, 298 passim.>> Here the ethical social basic-relations described earlier are alive. The I-You-relation (in the above sense) between God and us and within sociality still continues to exist, even though God has revealed God's own self (God's 'I'), and even though within the church the other has become an 'I', that is, has been revealed as love. Sin, the law, and the wrath of God still exist; the *cross* of Jesus still stands in the center of the church-community, which remains 'the community-of-the-cross' (in the above sense); and thus the I-You-relation also still remains. This ethical solitude [Einsamkeit] present in our own decisions of conscience must be confused neither with the structural unity of the created person, on which it is of course based, nor with the intentional 'isolation' ['Alleinsein'] of the sinner.

church-community are led by the Spirit into solitude. This results not only from the Spirit's claim but also from the Spirit's gift. Everyone believes and experiences their justification and sanctification in solitude, everyone prays in solitude, everyone breaks through to the certainty of their own eternal election in solitude, everyone 'possesses' the Holy Spirit and Christ completely 'for themselves'. This solitude, however, is not something done by faith,[19] but is willed by God.[20] It is the solitude of the individual that is a structure of the created order, and it continues to exist everywhere.[110]

The recognition that a person is an individual both in a structural sense as creature and also ethically[111] is expressed in that concept of the church that takes as its point of departure the deepest Christian insight concerning the individual, namely the *concept of the church based on predestination*. From an outside perspective this concept of the church seems to result in the dissolution of the church-community into a number of predestined individuals. Scheler[21] is quite right when he

104

---

19. E[rnst] Lohmeyer, *Zum [Vom] Begriff der religiösen Gemeinschaft*, 42ff., 44: "The possibility of withdrawing becomes an obligation for faith."

20. Kierkegaard, who like few others knew how to speak of the burden of solitude, comes to reject the concept of the church on that basis (see *Fear and Trembling*, 188). "As soon as the single individual has entered the paradox, he does not arrive at the idea of the church" (*Furcht und Zittern*, 106).[109]

21. Scheler, [*Formalism in Ethics*,] 563: "The notion, however, that individual persons must grasp the idea of solidarity solely and exclusively on the ground of their own solitary relationship with God, that is, only via this necessary detour, would be a doctrine amounting to a denial of the very concept of the church itself" [trans. RK].[112] Scheler's footnote to this reads: "This denial has many

---

[109.] The correct citation is *Furcht und Zittern*, 67 (*Fear and Trembling*, 74), not 106 as cited. The other reference is actually to *Repetition*, the second part of the same volume that contains *Fear and Trembling*.

[110.] Deleted from *SC-A*: In the concept of the church, therefore, 'solitude' [Einsamkeit] has the double meaning of the singular personal being of the creature and the social solitude of the I-You-relation, the latter being overcome in the church only in faith and in the beginning of sanctification; only in the Realm of God will it be overcome in actuality. [The word that has been translated "sanctification" should read *Heiligung*, following the dissertation typescript, not *Heilung*.][CG]

[111.] "The recognition . . . also ethically" reads in *SC-A*: This individuality of the person.

says that from this viewpoint the intercourse of the innermost person with God is the basic 'way to God'. It would seem that this idea has a persistent corrosive effect on the concept of the church, for individual persons perceive themselves as ultimate in God's sight; every community seems to be fragmented into the components of individual persons, and the will of God appears to be directed only toward these.[113]

Viewed logically, one might say that such an individualistic dissolution of the concept of the church implies a *delimitation of its extent*, namely in the concept of the *numerus praedestinatorum* [number of the predestined].[114] But this concept has no content (it is the counterpart of our concept of humanity expressed through the concept of sin). On the other hand, it is indeed not possible to give any other definition of the extent of the church,[22] whence it follows that nothing essential   105

---

forms. Historically, for example, it is just as much implied in the strict doctrine of election by grace as in the doctrine of justification by faith. For the community of love and salvation in its solidarity is, according to both of these doctrines, not an equally basic nor equally necessary intercourse with God as the immediate intercourse of the innermost person with God. Both seem to be derived only from this intimate relationship" [trans. RK]. In simply identifying the doctrine of election by grace with the doctrine of justification in this context, Scheler is overlooking the entire problem of the word.

22. Thomas Aquinas, though, does give another definition of the extent of the church. According to him, the church also has members who are not predestined: *Summa Theologiae*, 3a. 8,3: "ecclesia constituitur ex hominibus qui fuerunt a principio mundi usque ad finem ipsius . . . sic igitur membra corporis mystici accipiuntur non solum secundum quod sunt in actu, sed etiam secundum quod sunt in potentia . . . qui in potentia sunt ei uniti, quae nunquam reducetur ad actum, sicut homines in hoc mundo viventes qui non sunt praedestinati" ["The church consists of the people of all times who have been from the beginning of the world until its end. . . . Therefore one considers as members of the mystical

[112.] Bonhoeffer omits Scheler's parenthetical word "unjustified," *unberechtigten*, [112. *cont.*] before the word "denial," then omits Scheler's emphasis on the word "essential" before the phrase "concept of the church," as well as several other details of emphasis and punctuation. [CG]

[113.] Deleted from *SC-A*: A human being stands completely alone before God; in the face of eternity the community seems to dissolve.

[114.] The concept of the *numerus praedestinatorum* [number of the predestined] that Bonhoeffer uses in this context is derived from the theology of Augustine. By linking the idea of election with the concept of the church, Augustine has abandoned, according to Holl, not only the notion of a visible church, but also the notion of the church as 'one'. See Holl, *Augustins innere Entwicklung*, 41.

about the concept of the church can be expressed by such a definition; and this follows from the individualistic starting point.[23] The problem takes a completely different turn, however, if the notion of predestination is understood not as a human question about election, but as a way from God to us. In this case the attention is no doubt also directed toward the individual, but insofar as it is *the word about Christ* that actualizes the predestination in us, the individual is always meant and

---

body not only those who are actually members, but also those who are potentially members . . . those who are united in him as in a potentiality that never becomes actuality; they are the people living in this world who are not predestined" (*Summa Theologiae*, vol. 49)].[115] This we cannot accept. See *LW* 39:76: "For a head must be joined to the body, . . . [hence] Christ cannot be the head of some evil community."[116] The use of the doctrine of predestination for the concept of the church was already initiated by the early church, by Augustine. But it is erroneous to think that Augustine's doctrine of predestination is the sum total of his idea of the sanctorum communio (Holl, *Augustins innere Entwicklung*, 41ff.). Quite the contrary is true. His concept of the sanctorum communio was only disturbed by the notion of predestination; he developed a tremendously rich view of the sanctorum communio that can match that of Luther. See R[einhold] Seeberg, *Dogmengeschichte*, 2:464ff., and his *Begriff der christlichen Kirche*, 38ff. Wycliffe (*Trialogus*, bk. 4.22) is the first to hold a purely predestinarian concept of the church. He is joined by Hus (*The Church*, esp. chaps. 1–7), and later by Zwingli, who openly divides the concept of the church into three parts (predestined church, individual congregation, universal church), which only brings the predicament to light. The definition of the extent of the church does not tell anything about its nature. Krauß, [*Dogma von der unsichtbaren Kirche,*] 16: "The definition 'praedestinatorum universitas' [company of the predestined] is no answer at all to the question of the nature and concept of the church. We first have to have the concept of the whole as such, before we are can reflect on the individual parts."[117]

23. See J[ulius] Kaftan, *Dogmatik*, 4th ed., sec. 63, 597.

[115.] On Thomas Aquinas, see also Krauß, *Dogma von der unsichtbaren Kirche*, 8ff., and Holl, who in this context also refers to the passage by Thomas Aquinas (*Luther*, 293ff.; see 294, note 5).

[116.] The reference to Luther, "On the Papacy in Rome, against the Most Celebrated Romanist in Leipzig" (1520), *LW* 39:76 (*WA* 6:302), is found in Holl, *Luther*, 299, note 1. Here Holl compares Luther's concept of the church with the views of scholasticism and Augustine.

[117.] Regarding Wycliffe, Hus, and Zwingli, see Krauß, whose discussion (*Dogma von der unsichtbaren Kirche*, 10ff., 12ff., and 19ff.) is summarized by Bonhoeffer. Here Krauß also mentions the works that Bonhoeffer quotes.

elected only as a member of the church-community. And in this sense the notion of predestination is most certainly the necessary foundation for any concept of the church; God sees the church-community of Christ and the individual in a *single act*. God therefore really sees the individual, and God's election really applies to the individual. This is why recent theology recognizes the concept of predestination as necessary for the concept of the church,[24] and why Luther had already embraced this concept.[25] *The predestinarian concept of the church is consequently only a part of the whole concept of the church, and is meaningful and Christian only in connection with the whole.* It needs supplementing, and this derives as much from the work of the Holy Spirit as does the predestinarian concept of the church.[119]   106

b) Community of Spirit

In the word the Holy Spirit brings to human hearts God's love, which has been revealed in the cross and resurrection of Christ. The Holy Spirit brings us into community with God. But in Christ himself the church is already established. When Christ comes 'into' us through the Holy Spirit, the church comes 'into' us. The Holy Spirit, however, moves us by putting Christ in our hearts, creating faith and hope. But this faith in Christ generated by the Holy Spirit includes faith in the church-community in which Christ reigns; love, however, as the love or the heart of Christ in us, is given to us as a new heart, as the will for good. *Faith acknowledges God's rule and embraces it; love actualizes the Realm of God.* Love is therefore not an actualization of the metaphysical social-relation [metaphysischen Sozialbeziehungen], but rather of the ethical social-affiliation. But, as we saw, in the state of sin this ethical social-affiliation exists only in a broken form, which became intelligible when we considered the reality of the ethical personality and of sin. As a theological proposition it is founded on the doctrine of the primal

---

24. Seeberg, *Dogmatik*, 2:339f. Ritschl, [*Justification and Reconciliation*,] 320: "If God eternally loves the community-of-God's-Kingdom (Eph. 1:4f.), then God also loves already those who are to be joined together in it, insofar as God intends to bring them into that Kingdom" [trans. RK].

25. Holl, *Luther*, 293, note 3.[118]

[118.] The correct citation is Holl, *Luther*, 293, note 9.
[119.] Deleted from *SC-A*: because it is based on the work of the Holy Spirit.

state. Every human social formation is an actualization of the metaphysical social-relations. What is unique about the actualization effected by the Holy Spirit is that it links both basic-relations.[120] In every previous social formation the ethical-basic-relations continue to exist in their brokenness. *Here they are renewed and as such actualized, thereby producing a*

107 *concrete form of community.* The person living in the community of the I-You-relationship is given the assurance of being loved, and through faith in Christ receives the power to love also, in that this person, who in Christ is already in the church, is led into the church.[121] For that person the other member of the church-community is essentially no longer claim but gift, revelation of God's love and heart. Thus the You is to the I no longer law but gospel, and hence an object of love. The fact that my claim is met by the other I who loves me—which means, of course, by Christ—fulfills me, humbles me, frees me from bondage to myself, and enables me—again, of course, only through the power of faith in Christ—to love the other, to completely give and reveal myself to the other.

This clearly shows that new social relations have been created, and that the breach of sin has been closed, both of which came about through the revelation of God's heart in Christ, and through God implanting God's own heart, God's will and Spirit, in human beings, thus realizing God's will for the church-community to exist. The main problem now is to grasp how 'love' can entail this social significance, and what is evidently expressed in the Christian concept of agape and what is meant by the Christian concept of agape. This will of necessity make evident the Christian concept of community as it exists in the relation with God as well as in the relations of human beings with each other.[122]

It is remarkable to see how divergent are the views concerning this decisive concept of Christian love,[26] which prevents a consensus on the

---

26. For all that follows, I draw attention to *Communio sanctorum* (1929), by P[aul] Althaus. Unfortunately it was published so late that I was not able to analyze it fully but had to confine myself to occasional references. I was neverthe-

[120.] By "both" Bonhoeffer means the metaphysical and the social-ethical basic-relations. For these concepts, see above, chaps. 2 and 3. [CG]

265 [121.] *SC-A*, which does not begin a new paragraph here, continues: **This clearly shows that new social relations . . .** , which in the present text comes as the start of the next paragraph below.

[122.] *SC-A* does not begin a new paragraph here.

concept of community. It will be wise in this case to hold firmly to the New Testament; otherwise it will scarcely be possible to avoid the greatest danger, namely to argue from the idea of humanitarianism and to make the fateful mistake of confusing eros and agape.[124]

We have two infallible points of reference for what the New Testament calls love: the first, defined positively, is the *love of God* revealed in Christ; the second, defined negatively, is our *self-love.* Thus our starting point must not be our love for God or for other human beings. Nor do we really know what love is from the dangers of war, the sacrificial death of our brothers,[125] or from personal experiences of love shown to us; we know love solely from the love of God that manifests itself in the cross of Christ, in our justification, and in the founding of the church-community, and even, indeed, in our egotistical attitude toward ourselves. Whereas the former shows us the foundation, depth, and meaning of love, so the latter discloses love's crude intensity as directed toward ourselves.[126] The ethical command to love is not specifically Christian,[127] but the reality of love is nevertheless present only in Christ and in his church-community; thus the Christian concept of love must presumably have a special meaning. And this assumption proves to be correct.

1. *Christian love is not a human possibility.*[128] Initially, it has nothing to

108

---

less delighted, of course, to find that to a large degree this work illustrates important parts of my study with Luther's thought.[123]

[123.] Footnote 26 is added to the text of *SC-A.* [Hans Pfeifer, who himself has written on Bonhoeffer's understanding of the church, reports that Bonhoeffer found little confirmation in Althaus's book—which was published in 1926, not 1929—and that the veiled meaning of the note is that Althaus is in fact one of the "divergent views" alluded to here.] [CG]

[124.] With the distinction between *eros* and *agape* Bonhoeffer follows Barth, *Romans,* 450ff., who draws on Kierkegaard's distinction between 'natural love' and 'spiritual love' (see *Works of Love,* 44ff.).

[125.] Bonhoeffer's brother Walter was killed in World War I; see Bethge, *Dietrich Bonhoeffer,* 15f. [CG]

[126.] The German is obscure. There is a clear contrast between the love of God in the cross of Christ and an "egotistical attitude toward ourselves." But the description of the latter as, literally, a "brutal force" (*Härte*) directed against oneself is not explained by Bonhoeffer. The sense may be the relentless persistence of egotism's focus on the self. [CG]

[127.] Deleted from *SC-A:* —one only has to read rabbinic literature and Stoic works—...

[128.] This expression draws on the language of Barth, for whom love is merely a 'relative' human possibility; see *Romans,* 450ff.

do with the idea of humanitarianism, with feelings of sympathy, with eroticism, or compassion.[129]

2. *It is possible only through faith* in Christ and through the work of the Holy Spirit. It is based on obedience to the word of Christ, who, in meeting our claims, demands that we should give up all claims whatsoever on God or on our neighbor. But this abandoning of our claims, this giving up of our own will to God's will, is possible only through faith in Christ; apart from Christ all love is self-love. Only through faith in Christ do we understand our love to be the love of God given to our hearts by the Holy Spirit,[130] and our will as conquered by God and obedient to God's will for our neighbor.

3. *Love, as a volitional act, is purposeful.* It is not unfounded affection, but, though possessing the capacity to relinquish all claims,[131] it is a matter of rational reflection as well as human empathy. The purpose of love is exclusively determined by God's will for the other person, namely, to subject the other to God's rule. This requires an infinite variety of means that cannot be formulated as a general principle. Perceiving these means is up to, or rather the duty of, each person. We must dedicate ourselves entirely and with all our strength to become a means to this end. At this point we seem to be caught up in general definitions of purpose that can never be a conscious motive of active love. But the good Samaritan[132] does not help 'the one who has fallen among thieves' in order to accomplish the purpose of subjecting him to God's rule, but rather he helps because he sees a need.[133] He really helps his neighbor out of *love for him*. It cannot be said of Christian love, therefore, that "in everything it does it only loves in others, the dormant or

---

[129.] Paragraph 2 that follows reads in *SC-A*:

It is possible only as a continuous determination of the human will by the Holy Spirit, which means it is based on freely giving up my own will to the divine will that is at work in me. It demands the whole person, our whole will. Once our will is given up to the divine will, we have lost all claims before God, but also before other human beings. We have experienced our boundary (see above); by standing in obedience before God we give up our will to our 'neighbor', which means that we direct our will that obediently loves God toward the purpose that God intends for our neighbor. This brings us to matters of content.

[130.] Cf. Rom. 5:5. [CG]

[131.] Deleted from *SC-A*: and of self-denial.

[132.] Bonhoeffer uses the standard German translation that refers to the "compassionate Samaritan." [RK]

[133.] Luke 10:25ff.; see Kierkegaard, *Works of Love*, 21f.

dawning possibility, that they will become members of its own (the Christian) community; but it does not love the reality of the You."[27] Just the contrary is true.

4. *It loves the real neighbor*, not because it would derive pleasure from that person's individuality, but because the neighbor as a human being calls on me as the other who experiences God's claim in this You of the neighbor. And yet here I do not love God in the 'neighbor', but I love the concrete You; I love the You by placing myself, my entire will, in the service of the You. The ethical basic-relations outlined above only revealed the barrier, that is, the neighbor's claim; love provides the power to really meet this claim through the Spirit, which means, 'to overcome' it. Is love that loves only the neighbor, therefore, purely spontaneous and not goal determined? It is both. The person who loves God must, by God's will, really love the neighbor.[28] But love is nothing other

---

27. Lohmeyer, [*Vom Begriff der religiösen Gemeinschaft*,] 62.

28. See K[arl] Barth, *Romans*, esp. 451ff., 492ff. I cannot concur with the exegesis of the command to love presented here, nor with the concept of community it entails. "As the 'incomprehensible way'[134] (1 Cor. 12:31) love is the eternal meaning of all of our comprehensible ways. The realization of their highest peak, the religious human possibility as God's possibility, is thus and to that degree 'the fulfillment of the law'" (493f.). "The neighbor visibly poses the question of God that must be visibly answered" (452). That is certainly a legitimate way of putting it. "Finally and ultimately this poses for us the riddle of 'nature's primal state,' that 'person faces person'. . . , that through the singularity of others we are reminded of our own singularity, that is, of our createdness, our forlornness, our sin, and our death" (494). This we can also still accept.[135] But now we are told that the essence of love for our neighbor is "to hear in the other the voice of the One" (454, 494).[136] We must acknowledge that "our radically challenged I and the You that confronts it form a unity that transcends all thought" (494f.). Through Christ I am "not only one with God, but (because of and by being one with God!) also one with my neighbor" (495). "The relation with the other is a relation with the origin" (454), and yet all acts of love do not

---

[134.] Barth's rendering of the ὑπερβολὴν ὁδὸν deviates from both the standard German translation, *besseren Weg*, and the English rendering, "more excellent way." Barth's translator, accordingly, modified the 1885 English Revised Version to read "still more excellent (incomprehensible) way." All further translations of Karl Barth in this footnote are by RK. [CG]

[135.] Deleted from *SC-A*: insofar as individuality means self-centered destruction of community.

[136.] Bonhoeffer paraphrases Barth here, rather than quoting him exactly. [CG]

110 than realizing the purpose of establishing God's rule over humanity; not that human beings could bring about God's rule *by means of* their active love—this sidelong glance would only sap the action's strength— but by God achieving God's own will by using the obedience *embodied in* our love for the neighbor. But this implies

5. *that Christian love knows no limits.* It seeks to realize God's rule in each and every place. It only has its limits where God has set them. Where we know that God has condemned we are not allowed to love. "Even if I could save the whole world in one day, if this were not God's will, I nevertheless shouldn't do it" (Luther).[138] The hard saying in

---

aim at a result, but are a pure sacrifice, obedience toward the one who "as sovereign God does not depend on it" (452). While we can agree with the last statement, we hold that love really does love the other, not the One in the other—who perhaps does not even exist (double predestination! Barth, 452)— that precisely this love for the other as other is meant "to glorify God" (453). Who gives Barth the right to say that the other is "as such infinitely unimportant" (452), when God commands us to love precisely that person? God has made the 'neighbor as such' infinitely important, and there isn't any other 'neighbor as such' for us. The other is not merely "parable of the wholly other," a "proxy of the unknown God" (452); rather, the other is infinitely important as such, precisely because God takes the other person seriously. Should I after all ultimately be alone with God in the world? Should not the other through God's command be infinitely affirmed as a concrete human being? We are not talking about an 'eternal soul of the other', but about God's willing of the other, and we believe that we can take God's will seriously only in the concrete form of the other. See R[udolf] Bultmann, *Jesus and the Word*, 115: "Whatever of kindness, pity, mercy, I show my neighbor is not something that I do for God . . . ; the neighbor is not a sort of tool, by means of which I practice the love of God. . . . As I can love my neighbor only when I surrender my will completely to God's will, so I can love God only while I will what [God] wills, while I really love my neighbor." The second difference between Barth and us consists in our understanding of the concept of *communio*. "To be one" with God and with the neighbor is something entirely different from being in community with them. Barth, however, uses both expressions synonymously. But where only the one is loved in the other no communio is possible, and there the danger of romanticism[137] ultimately creeps in. Regarding the entire argument see Kierkegaard, *Works of Love.*

[137.] *SC-A* substitutes "romanticism" for the danger of an ultimately affirmed romanticism.
[138.] See Luther, "Second Sunday after Epiphany." In Lenker, ed., *Luther's Epistle Sermons*, 8:46 ["Fastenpostille" (1525), WA 17/2:53]. This statement of Luther is quoted by Barth in *Romans*, 454.

1 John 5:16 goes even further, by warning us not to intercede where God *might* have condemned. It sees human weakness clash with divine severity and warns about the danger. But we do not know where God condemns, and the command to love our neighbor, that is, to obey, is given without restrictions, and therefore love has no limits.[29] *Love for* 111 *our neighbor is our will to embrace God's will for the other person*; God's will for the other person is defined for us in the unrestricted command to surrender[139] our self-centered will to our neighbor, which neither means to love the other instead of God, nor to love God in the other, but to put the other in our own place and to love the neighbor instead of ourselves; "homo diligit se ipsum perverse et solum quae perversitas non potest dirigi nisi loco suo ponat proximum" ("People love themselves in a corrupt and exclusive way. This corruption cannot be cured unless they put their neighbor in their own place").[30] This attitude, however, is not within our means, but is "poured out by the Holy Spirit into our hearts."[140] As the will for the concrete other, love by its intentional nature seeks to form community, i.e., to awaken love in return. All christological thinking deriving from Abelard was already unconsciously based on this insight.[141] Most recently it has been repeatedly examined 112

---

29. Schleiermacher explains the motive for loving all people as follows: "Nobody can be conscious of the divine spirit, except as they are simultaneously conscious that the entire human race belongs to this spirit. The difference between individuals is merely temporal, namely that some already have the pneuma hagion [Holy Spirit] while others do not yet have it" (*Christliche Sitte*, ed. Jonas, vol. 7, pt. 2, 514). This line of argument is *methodologically* impossible, since *apocatastasis* [the salvation of all] can at most be the very last word in eschatological reflection, but not the self-evident point of departure for any theological argument. *Materially*, we have rejected *the biological understanding of the concept of humanity*, as well as the anthropological understanding of the notion of pneuma [spirit].

30. Luther, *[Vorlesung über den] Römerbrief*, ed. Ficker (1925), 1:18 [cf. Luther, *Lectures on Romans*, *LW* 25:111, n. 10].

[139.] "Surrender" here and in the following passages is a translation for *Hingabe*, which means surrender not in the sense of being defeated or compelled by a stronger force, but giving up something that is voluntarily offered to another. This 'giving up' includes a sense of sacrificing what is one's own to another, but can also include giving up what one wrongly claims for oneself. *Hingabe* carries the connotation of dedication to someone or something, and also describes the free self-surrender of sexual love. [RK]

[140.] See Rom. 5:5.

[141.] The reference to Abelard is an allusion to the description of Schleiermacher's

and clearly outlined by Scheler.[31] Even though love does not aim at love in return, it implicitly aspires to it. In order to carry out God's will toward the neighbor, there necessarily has to be a community of spirit, i.e., a community of understanding and expression, into which both the one who loves and the one who is loved must enter, regardless of the attitude of the latter; this community of spirit has to be distinguished from the community of love [Liebesgemeinschaft] to which love implicitly aspires. Most misunderstandings can be explained as a result of a confusion between the two, including presumably Schleiermacher's definition of love as the "tendency to unite with others and to seek to be in others."[32] Here looms the last vestige of egotism. The fact that love also leads to community of love does not make this definition any more correct.[33]

Does all we have said also hold true with respect to the reality of God's love in Christ? God loves human beings and, therefore, God would have to become a means in their service. But since God's will is an end in itself, there seems to be a contradiction here. Actually, however, the very meaning of the Christ event is "that God organizes the

---

31. *The Nature of Sympathy*, see above [page 102, footnote 32].[142]

32. *The Christian Faith*, 165.1, 726f. Against this see Ritschl, [*Justification and Reconciliation*,] 277f. Love is a persistent will in which "my will of love incorporates the other as an end in itself into my own being as an end in itself" [trans. RK].[143] This concept of purpose was necessary as soon as love was understood voluntaristically. Häring, for example, attempts a synthesis without making the necessary distinction: "Love is a seeking of community [. . .] in order to realize common purposes" (*The Christian Faith*, 340).[144] Seeberg aptly defines love as the community of purpose [Zweckgemeinschaft] in which loving persons make themselves the means of the purposes of others (*Dogmatik*, 1:322).[145]

33. Is it merely chance that 1 Corinthians 13 does not speak about love's will for community?

[141. *cont.*] theology made by Ritschl, who regarded Schleiermacher's approach as a renewal of Abelard's theology. See Ritschl, *A Critical History*, 440ff.

[142.] See Scheler, *Formalism in Ethics*, 517ff., which explains the context to which Bonhoeffer referred; the reference to *The Nature of Sympathy* is also found there (e.g., 520, note 165).

[143.] *SC-RS*: "Cf. Thomas Aquinas?"

[144.] The Häring quotation is not found in *Der christliche Glaube*, 216; rather, it is an abbreviated form of a statement on page 266. [CG]

[145.] Regarding this see Ritschl, *Justification and Reconciliation*, 284, and Seeberg, *Dogmatik*, 1:321ff., 2:522ff.

divine work as a means to achieve God's own purpose."[34] In Christ God
loves human beings and opens the divine heart; and in giving God's
own self to sinful human beings God renews them at the same time and
thus makes the new community possible and real; but this means that
God's love wills community. Again, there is the danger of this contradiction: in speaking about love for the neighbor we said that love gives
itself up to the other unrestrictedly, seeking nothing for itself. But to   113
surrender oneself to the other means obeying God; it is based on surrender to God's will. *God's love, therefore, is at the same time self-surrender
and will for community.* The question of the nature of God's community
of love with humanity, and of this community of love as such, is connected with the problem of the word. Only in the word of Christ do we
have community with God. All conscious community, however, is community of will. It is based on the separateness of persons. Hence community is never 'oneness', neither is it an ultimate 'being one' in the
sense of mystical fusion;[146] it is only real when constantly created anew
by wills. It can be affirmed as an end in itself or it can be organized
merely to achieve a purpose. Community of love is based on unrestrictedly surrendering to the other. *Human beings can unreservedly surrender
to God because God unreservedly surrenders to them.* God wills them and
therefore they can will God: *community is an end in itself.* God wants
God's own will with human beings—this is the only reason God wants
community; and human beings embrace God's will as the purpose of
community, so that it is even possible for them, in order to satisfy this
will, not to want community with God anymore, which means to want
their damnation, should this be God's will: *community is not an end in
itself.* But precisely in wanting this, our community with God becomes
indissolubly firm. The deepest reason for this lies exclusively in the fact
that *God simply wants community for its own sake, which really means for
God's sake.* God wills community; and the human will, which surrenders
completely, is in community, precisely because this surrender of ourselves is enabled only through God's own surrender.

Now as new human beings who are drawn into community with God,
we are hidden not only to the world, but even to ourselves.[35] Thus only

---

34. Seeberg, *Dogmatik,* 2:324.
35. Luther, *Disp.*, ed. Drews, 450–51: "christianus est persona, quae iam

[146.] The words in the sense of mystical fusion are added to *SC-A.*

114   through faith are we in community with God, that is, only through the
word. We do not 'see' our 'new selves' manifested in a will for good, but
we *believe our will to be good*, because God says so, that is, because Christ
has fulfilled for us what we would never have been able to fulfill;[149] this
is the Protestant position as opposed to the Roman Catholic view of the
signa praesentis gratiae.[150] This does not deny the reality of the 'experience' of justification and sanctification, that is, of being given a new
will. But this reality is exclusively *secured* in the 'objective' event brought
about by the word and the faith generated by God. We thus come to the
fundamentally important conclusion that *community with God for us exists
only in faith*, that it is not experienced like the sort of community of
spirit found in friendship or shared experience. It is an article of faith

---

sepulta est cum christo in morte eius, mortuus peccato, legi, morti . . . sed hoc
ipsum non cernitur, sed est absconditum in mundo, non apparet, non occurit in
oculos nostros . . . in praesenti saeculo non vivit, mortuus est, versatur in alia
vita longe supra hac posita, coelesti . . . sed e contra christianus in quantum
miles et in militia versatur, hic etiam sentit et expetit quotidie militiam carnis
suae" ("Christians are persons who are already buried with Christ in his death,
who have died to sin, to the law, and to death. . . . But this does not manifest
itself, it is hidden to the world; it does not appear, nor become visible to our
eyes. . . . They do not live in the present age, but have died. They are in another
life, far superior to this one, namely a heavenly one. . . . Christians, however, are
like soldiers in military service who also daily desire and seek to offer their bodies in service"); cf. [Luther, *Disp.*, ed. Drews,] 452. Also see *WA* 1:54: "hec vita
non habet experientiam sui, sed fidem; nemo enim scit se vivere aut experitur
se esse iustificatum sed credit et sperat" ("This life has no experiential knowledge of him, but we have faith. For no one knows that they have life or feels that
they are justified; but they believe and hope.")[147] Also see [Luther, "Lectures
on Galatians" (1519),] *WA* 2:457.[148]

266   [147.] The correct source of this quote is Luther, *Vorlesung über den Römerbrief
1515-1516*, ed. Ficker (1925), 1:54 (cf. *LW* 25:52), not *WA* 1:54, as cited in Bonhoeffer's
footnote. This reference to Ficker's edition of the *Römerbrief* (1925) is cited in Holl, *Luther*,
139, note 1.
        [148.] The reference to *WA* 2:457 is erroneous. See above, page 124, editorial note 8,
referring to the same error and a possible correct reference.
        [149.] Added to *SC-A*: that is . . . to fulfill.
        [150.] Regarding the idea of the *signa praesentis gratiae* [signs of present grace], see
Holl, *Luther*, 139f. Luther regarded the Thomist and Scotist doctrine of the 'signs of present grace'—derived from Thomas Aquinas and Duns Scotus—as an error, since in his view
the justified life is not an object of experience. Also see above, the final quotation in footnote 35.

that God through Christ has entered into a community of love with us. And this faith itself is again only belief that true faith created by God is present.[36] Therefore, it cannot after all be a proof from experience of the existing community.

But from this follows the second, equally important, conclusion, namely that my community of love with my neighbor can also exist only by having faith in God, who in Christ has fulfilled the law for me and loved my neighbor, who draws me into the church-community, which means into the love of Christ, and creates a bond between myself and my neighbor. Only this faith allows me to understand as love what I do to the other and calls me to believe in our community as the Christian community of love.[152]

It still remains to be examined whether the church-community [Gemeinde], in which God's love is at work, is really 'community' [Gemeinschaft]. It was Augustine's great insight to portray the community of saints, the core of the church, as the community of loving persons who, touched by God's Spirit, radiate love and grace. Forgiveness of sin does not come from the organized church and the office, but from the community of saints.[37] Whoever has received the sacraments must still be pulled into this life-stream of spirit; all that is promised to

115

---

36. *WA* 5:164: "Oportet enim non modo credere, sperare, diligere, sed etiam scire et certum esse se credere, sperare, diligere" ("One ought not only believe, hope, and love, but also know and be certain that one believes, hopes and loves").[151] Cf. O[tto] Piper, *Theologie und reine Lehre*, 5: "We can always only believe in faith that God has given genuine faith into our heart. . . ."

37. Cf. Seeberg, *[Lehrbuch der] Dogmengeschichte*, 2:464ff., and his *Begriff der [christlichen] Kirche*, 38ff. Augustine's teaching on the sanctorum communio is already foreshadowed to a certain degree by earlier Christian writers; see Augustine, *[De] Bapt[ismo contra Donatistas]* 5:21–29: "Sacramentum gratiae dat deus etiam per malos, ipsam vero gratiam non nisi per se ipsum vel per sanctos suos" ("God gives the sacrament of grace even through the hands of the wicked, but the grace itself is given only by God or through God's saints" [*On Baptism, against the Donatists*, 474 (trans. altered)]).[153]

[151.] Luther, "Operationes in Psalmos" (1519–20), *WA* 5:165. See Holl, *Luther*, 139f., note 3.

[152.] The preceding passage, "But from this . . . Christian community of love," is added to *SC-A*.

[153.] The reference to this saying of Augustine (Migne, *Patrologia Latina*, 43.9, 191) is found in Seeberg, *Der Begriff der christlichen Kirche*, 40f., note 7, and *Dogmengeschichte*, 2:450.

the church is promised to the community of saints. It has the power of the keys, it can forgive sins, and only through it is everything the official church does endowed with God's Spirit. This provides the paradigm for all ideas about the sanctorum communio. Christian community of love between human beings means unrestrictedly surrendering to the other out of obedience to God's will. This is possible only through the work of the Holy Spirit. When several persons are genuinely committed to surrendering to each other, the constitutive element of the idea of community, namely the mutual affirmation of community as an end in itself, is already present. And yet community as such is not consciously intended; rather the You is willed while giving up the I. But this is precisely what proves and establishes the new I in accordance with the will of God.[154] Therefore, it is precisely in several persons unrestrictedly surrendering to each other that their new person becomes real, and thus a *"community of new persons." Love finds community without seeking it, or precisely because it does not seek it.* Those who want to lose their lives will save them.[155] This is the only way in which surrendering myself to what God wills for my neighbor really leads to the community of *the sanctorum communio established by God*; to realize this each person serves as an instrument of God. Thus we find that the Christian community of love has a unique sociological structure: the mutual love of the saints does indeed constitute 'community' as an end in itself, that is, community in the strict sense of the word. But this brings us again to the problem
116   derived from the thought that the community is, after all, not an end in itself insofar as it seeks only to realize God's will. However, since God wills precisely this community of saints, the problem is solved; it is therefore not the case that community in the strict sense would still have an end outside itself—a case that would be sociologically possible— but community (in the broader sense) is actually organized for a single purpose, namely to accomplish God's will. *But since this realization of God's will consists in the community itself, it is an end in itself.*[38] This is a

---

38. Cf. Althaus, *Erlebnis der Kirche*, 16: "To the eternal God only the church that worships and loves is an end in itself in the full sense; it is God's goal for the world."

[154.] Deleted from *SC-A*: All who humble themselves will be exalted. See Matt. 23:12, 18:4, and parallels.
[155.] Cf. Luke 17:33 and parallels. [CG]

completely novel sociological structure.[39] In order to come to a full understanding we still have to consider that the community of saints knows that its structure is organized according to the principle of authority [herrschaftlich]. It is community only because of the divine will ruling in it. This association of authentic rule[157] between God and us in revelation is paradoxical because God rules by serving; this is what the concept of the love of God entails. God commands, and, in commanding, God's very own self—and this is what distinguishes the association of authentic rule from the association of force [Gewaltsverband], since the latter implies an idea of divine revelation that is not simply paradoxical but even incomprehensible[158]—puts the will to obey and the understanding of what is commanded into our hearts; but this means that God establishes community among human beings and between them and God. God's will to rule is the will to love God's church-community. This is how intimately the concepts of God's rule and of God's Realm are interconnected; and yet they must be distinguished logically, materially, and, as we can now add, sociologically.[159]

117

---

39. Recent sociological works have asserted that the concept of the sanctorum communio is based on an indirect, mediated, communal bond. See Spann, [*Gesellschaftslehre*,] 144f.: "Community of saints: in it, if I understand it correctly, the saints are thought of as seeing only God *directly*, but as being connected with each other only through their identical connection with the divine being . . . as this itself is meant to be a holy and secluded rather than a social state." Even in the greatest theological work using sociological method, we find the proposition that the saints are connected only in God, and are thus only indirectly connected with each other. See Troeltsch, *Social Teachings*, 56: "It (the Christian idea of community) consists ultimately in the fact that those who sanctify themselves for God, meet in the common goal, that is in God" [trans. altered]. Cf. Scheler, *Formalism in Ethics*, 498f.[156]

[156.] In his *Formalism in Ethics*, 498, Scheler regards love of other and love of self as equally original, both as based on God's love. In his copy Bonhoeffer marked this passage in the margin and underlined "of equal value" ["*gleichwertig*"], a word not quoted here. [The phrase within parentheses in the Troeltsch quote was inserted by Bonhoeffer.] [CG]

[157.] See above, chap. 3, page 60, editorial note 1, on *Herrschaftsverband*. [CG]

[158.] *SC-A* contains the addition that is then struck out: an idea that is to be found in dialectical theology.

[159.] Deleted from *SC-A*: If one were to use here the term 'company [Genossenschaft] of saints' (Seeberg, *Dogmatik*, 2:333), it would, to be precise, only express that, formally speaking, all

And since we use the term 'community' in this context—and we are quite justified in doing so—we would already like to indicate that this concept will have to give way to an even deeper understanding (see below, pages 260f.).

We must now ask what these concrete acts are in which the community of saints acts as a community of love. This means we are not concerned with every function of the church-community, such as preaching, sacraments, etc. (these will be discussed in another context), but only with the social acts that constitute the community of love and that disclose in more detail the structure and nature of the Christian church.

This can be summarized in two groups of thought: (1) *Church-community and church member being structurally 'with-each-other' [Miteinander] as appointed by God* and (2) *the members' active 'being-for-each-other' [Füreinander] and the principle of vicarious representative action [Stellvertretung].*[160]

In reality, however, one is possible only through the other; they depend on each other.

The church-community is so structured that wherever one of its members is, there too is the church-community in its power, which means in the power of Christ and the Holy Spirit. It is conceived of as a single life to such an extent that none of its members could be imagined apart from it. But in the church-community every member is moved by the Holy Spirit; all have their divinely appointed place and their wills moved by the Spirit. Whoever lives in love is Christ in relation to the neighbor—but, of course, always only in this respect. "We are God through the love that makes us charitable toward our neighbor."[40] Chris-

---

40. *WA* 10/1:100; *LW* 11:412 [*WA* 4:280]. Holl, *What Did Luther Understand by Religion?* 100f.[161]

[159. *cont.*] are absolutely equal vis-à-vis the divine will to rule. Everything else would already be expressed in the concept of community.

[160.] The section that follows below is almost completely based on Luther's sermon, "The Blessed Sacrament of the Holy and True Body of Christ, and the Brotherhoods" (1519), *LW* 35/1:738ff. [*WA* 2:738ff.]. (See also below, 217, editorial note 285.) See Holl, *Luther*, 320ff. A note by Bonhoeffer in the margin of Ritschl, *Justification and Reconciliation*, 288f., shows how significant this sermon was for him. Ritschl criticizes Luther and Reformation theology with respect to their inadequate concept of the "community of moral action motivated by love" [trans. altered]. Bonhoeffer noted the title of Luther's sermon in the margin.

[161.] See Luther, "Second Christmas Sermon," *Sermons of Martin Luther*, 6:146

267

tians can and ought to act like Christ; they ought to bear the burdens and sufferings of the neighbor. "You must open your heart to the weaknesses and needs of others as if they were your own, and offer your means as if they were theirs, just as Christ does for you in the sacrament."[41] This is what Luther then calls "being changed into one another 118 through love."[42] Without implying any mystical notions of blurring the boundaries of the concrete reality of I and You,[43] [164] Luther is simply

---

41. *LW* 35:62 [*WA* 2:750]. "The Blessed Sacrament of the Holy and True Body of Christ, and the Brotherhoods" (1519). Here Luther expresses wonderful and profound thoughts on this question.

42. ["The Blessed Sacrament,"] *LW* 35:59 [*WA* 2:749]: "So truly are we also drawn and changed into the spiritual body, that is, into community with Christ and all saints. . . ." [trans. altered]. *LW* 35:62 [*WA* 2:750]: "This is what it means to be changed into one another through love." Baader expresses this by saying "that the sacrificial blood of Christ" also made the lifeblood of every individual human being fluid and thus free once again, which freed and saved humanity from the paralysis of self-centeredness (*Schriften zur Gesellschaftsphilosophie*, 781).[162]

43. Lohmeyer, [*Religiösen Gemeinschaft*,] 83: ". . . this expression of a fusion, which no longer knows the boundaries of I and You, because out of religious exuberance it overlooks, and is bound to overlook, the basic fact of the singularity of the I . . ."[163]

[161. *cont.*] ["Epistel in der Früh-Christmess. Tit. 3:4-7. Kirchenpostille 1522," *WA* 10/1:100f.]: "We are God's children through faith that constitutes us heirs of all divine blessings. But we are also 'gods' through love that makes us beneficent toward our neighbor. The divine nature is simply pure beneficence . . ." [trans. altered]; and *Dictata super Psalterium* (1513–16), *WA* 4:280: "Eodem modo quilibet Christianus debet se agnoscere magnum esse, quia propter fidem Christi, qui habitat in ipso, est deus, dei filius et infinitus, eo quod iam deus in ipso sit" ("In the same way any Christian should acknowledge himself to be great, because, on account of faith in Christ who dwells in him, he is God, a son of God and infinite, since God is now in him") [*First Lectures on the Psalms* (1513–16), *LW* 11:412]. Both references to Luther are found in Holl, *What Did Luther Understand by Religion?*, 100, note 71.

[162.] The citation of Franz von Baader, *Schriften zur Gesellschaftsphilosophie*, 781, is a reference mentioned by Johannes Sauter, editor of von Baader's *Schriften*. The phrase related by Sauter is found in von Baader's *Sätze aus einer erotischen Philosophie* (*Sämtliche Werke*, 4:173).

[163.] The complete sentence in Lohmeyer reads: "It is only against this background that this expression of a fusion—which no longer knows the boundaries of I and You, because out of religious exuberance it overlooks, and is bound to overlook, the basic fact of the singularity of the I—was incorporated into the opposite sphere of the love-language of all countries and nations that had been Christianized or had been touched in some way by Christianity." [CG]

[164.] Deleted from *SC-A*: of one soul sinking into the other.

saying that now I no longer want anything but the You, that the person loving me does not want anything but me, and that the positions resulting from sin are, as it were, exchanged, or transformed. It must come to the point that the weaknesses, needs, and sins of my neighbor afflict me as if they were my own, in the same way as Christ was afflicted by our sins.[44] "Behold, if you bear them all, they, in turn, will all bear you, and everything, good and evil, is shared."[45] Bear one another's burdens (Gal. 6:2). The possibility of this 'being-with-one-another' does not rest on human will. It exists only in the community of saints, and goes beyond the ordinary sense of 'being-with-one-another'. It belongs to the sociological structure of the church-community. In the *Tesseradecas*[46] Luther expounds his thoughts on this point with incomparable beauty. My burden is borne by the others, their strength is my strength, in my fear and trembling the faith of the church comes to my aid. And even when I come to die, I should be confident that not I, or at least not I alone, am dying, but that Christ and the community of saints are suffering and dying with me. We walk the path of suffering and death accompanied by the whole church.[47] "If I should die, I am not alone in death,

119

---

44. *LW* 35:59 [*WA* 2:749]: "Thus our sins assail him, while his righteousness protects us."

45. Ibid., 55 [*WA* 2:745].

46. *Tesseradecas consolatoria pro laborantibus et oneratis* (1520), *WA* 6:130ff.; 131: "onus meum portant alii, illorum virtus mea est, [. . .] meae libidinis tentationem suffert, aliorum ieiunia, mea lucra sunt, alterius oratio pro me sollicita est[. . . .] Atque ita vere congloriari possum in aliorum bonis, tanquam meis propriis, atque tunc vere et mea sunt, sic gratulor et congaudeo eis . . . eorum merita [!] meis medebuntur peccatis" ("Thus others bear my burden, and their strength is my strength, . . . and [they] endure the temptation of my flesh; the fastings of others are my gain, the prayer of another pleads for me. Consequently I can actually glory in the blessings of others as though they were my very own. They are truly mine when I am grateful and joyful with the others. . . . My sins are healed by their merits")["Fourteen Consolations for Those Who Labor and Are Heavy Laden" (1520), *LW* 42:161f.].

47. ["Fourteen Consolations,"] *WA* 6:132: "quare si dolemus, si patimur, si morimur, huc feratur intutus, et fortiter credamus ac certi simus, quod non nos aut non soli, sed Christus et ecclesia nobiscum dolet, patitur, moritur . . . comite tota ecclesia viam passionis et mortis ingredimur" ("Therefore, when we feel pain, when we suffer, when we die, let us turn to this, firmly believing and certain that it is not we alone, but Christ and the church who are in pain and are suffering and dying with us. . . . We set out upon the road of suffering and death accompanied by the entire church") [*LW* 42:163].

if I suffer, they suffer with me";[165] namely Christ "with all holy angels and the blessed in heaven and godly people on earth" [trans. altered].[48] In contrast to this we quote the well-known words of Luther's sermon to the people of Wittenberg: "[T]he summons of death comes to us all, and no one can die for another, but every one must battle with death on their own. We can shout into another's ears, but every one of us must be prepared for the time of death, for I will not be with you then, nor you with me."[49] Is one of these statements perhaps only a daring hyperbole?[167] We must try to understand what Luther intends to say with the idea of the church-community here. First, he does not seek to give out the dubious platitude that a sorrow shared is a sorrow halved, a joy shared a joy doubled. He rather seeks to depict the community of saints as the foundation and strength of all individual Christian life, because it is the object of God's will. The individual, however, is the object of God's will only as a member of the church. In death and suffering the individual does in fact face God singly and alone. One's faith and prayer takes place in this singularity and solitude. The whole seriousness of the relation with God is not taken from the individual's shoulders. Nevertheless, this individual still remains within the church-community, and in every situation and problem of life *the church-community is with this individual.* For the church-community is also wherever its individual member is, provided this person is a member, and wherever the church is, there the individual member is also. Thus Luther can say that the church-community dies[50] and suffers 'with' each member. He is not necessarily thinking that even one member of the church is aware that another member is suffering and dying, is tempted and lusting. But it is also, by virtue of being a church-community, 120

---

48. *LW* 35:54f. [*WA* 2:745].

49. *LW* 51:70 [*WA* 10/3:1] (March 9, 1522).[166]

50. This expression, "the church dies 'with' each member," makes any *psychological interpretation* impossible.

[165.] The following footnote was deleted from *SC-A*: <<(See the verse "Wenn ich einmal soll scheiden" ["When I shall one day depart"], by [Paul] Gerhard; here the idea of the church-community has disappeared completely.) See *LW* 35:53f. [*WA* 2:745].>> See *Evangelisches Kirchengesangbuch,* no. 63, verse 9.

[166.] "The First Sermon: Invocavit Sunday."

[167.] Deleted from *SC-A*: For the latter seems to say exactly the opposite of the statements quoted earlier.

present as a whole—even without being aware of it—wherever one of its members is. Obviously, Luther is also thinking of a conscious and active sharing of suffering, joy, sin, and grief even unto death; and this empirical life of the church-community must be practiced.[51] This, however, is merely the consequence of being the church-community, not what constitutes it. Now where the church-community is, there is Christ. All of Luther's statements are possible only on this foundation. "I am the head, I want to be the first to give myself for you, I want to share your suffering and adversity and bear them for you, so that you in turn will also do likewise for me and among each other, and share everything in me and with me."[52] This is the meaning of the sacrament of the body of Christ. The church-community could not bear anything, were it not borne by Christ. Thus only in view of the *meritum Christi* [merit of Christ] can Luther speak of the other's *merita* [merits] that help me. But as Christ is in every place where tribulation and death place individuals alone before God, so the church-community is there also. True, the solitude that God imposes on them is not abolished; they remain created as individuals, and as individuals, as persons, must live their own life and die their own death. But the solitude of the ethical basic-relation is overcome in faith, though not in sight, and here the solitary state of the sinner is also overcome. And thus the church-community is present. But where the church-community is, there is God's will and purpose, there is community with God. Even if the individual does not feel anything of this, it is nevertheless really the case,[53] and therefore the Christian ought to believe it, and, being truly a member of the church-community, will believe it.

This *being-with-each-other* of the church-community and its members through Christ already entails their *being-for-each-other*. This active being-for-each-other has two defining aspects: Christ is the measure and

---

51. *LW* 35:55f. [*WA* 2:746].[168]

52. "The Blessed Sacrament" (1519), *LW* 35:738ff. [*WA* 2:738ff.].[169]

53. *WA* 6:131: "nam etsi non sentiatur vere tamen ita agitur, immo quis non sentiat?" ("Even if it is not perceived, it is still true. But who could fail to perceive it?" [*LW* 42:162]).[170]

[168.] The correct page reference is *LW* 35:57 [*WA* 2:747].
[169.] The correct page reference is *LW* 35:55 [*WA* 2:745f.].
[170.] "Fourteen Consolations."

standard of our conduct (John 13:15, 34f.; 1 John 3:10); and our actions 121
are the actions of members of the body of Christ, that is, they possess
the power of the love of Christ, through which each may and ought to
become a Christ to the other (1 Cor. 12:12; Rom. 12:4ff.; Eph. 4:4, 12ff.;
Col. 3:15). Since I as a Christian cannot live without the church, since I
owe my life to the church and now belong to it, so my merits are also no
longer my own, but belong to the church. Only because the church lives
one life in Christ, as it were, can I as a Christian say that the chastity of
others helps me when my desires tempt me, that the fasting of others
benefits me, and that the prayer of my neighbors is offered in my stead.
But do we not come alarmingly close here to the Roman Catholic teaching of the treasury of merits that stands at the center of all more recent
Roman Catholic views on the sanctorum communio?[171] We are indeed,
and do so quite consciously. With Luther we want to be sure that the
sound core, which is in danger of being lost, is preserved in Protestant
theology. The decisive difference lies in the fact that we do not acknowledge any person as having overflowing merits that could be used on
behalf of another. The 'treasury of merits' is God's love that in Christ
created the church-community; it is nothing else. The Roman Catholic
doctrine of the treasury of merits is a rationalization, moralization, and
anthropomorphization of the irrational fact that human beings can
never do more than they ought, and that within the church-community
God nevertheless lets each person 'enjoy'[54] the other. This in turn is

---

54. *LW* 35:67f. [*WA* 2:754].[172]

[171.] This assertion is probably a slight exaggeration. See Bartmann, *Lehrbuch der Dog-* 268
matik, 2:196ff., esp. 198. In his copy Bonhoeffer underlined the sentence: "In Protestant
thinking the doctrine of the community of saints cannot gain full expression, since the
invisibility of the church and its being a community are mutually exclusive. This is why
the attendant belief in Christian intercession, the invocation of saints, and the conferral
of merits to others is missing there" (203). In the margin Bonhoeffer notes: "Precisely
because there are no merits." Regarding Luther's view of the doctrine of the *thesaurus
meritorum* [treasury of merits], see Holl, *Luther*, 310, 312, and 320ff.
[172.] "The Blessed Sacrament": "The fruit of this sacrament is community and love by
which we are strengthened against death and all evil. This community is twofold: one,
that we partake of Christ and all saints, and the other, that we permit all Christians to be
partakers of us in whatever way they and we are able. This means that all self-seeking love
is eradicated by means of this sacrament and gives way to the love that seeks the common
good of all. The transformation of love thus creates one bread, one drink, one body, one
church-community; this is true Christian unity" [trans. altered].

due to the fact that Christ died for the church-community so that it may live *one* life, *with each other* and *for each other*.

This being-for-each-other must now be actualized through acts of love. *Three great, positive possibilities of acting for each other* in the community of saints present themselves: *self-renouncing, active work for the neighbor; intercessory prayer; and, finally, the mutual forgiveness of sins* in God's name.[173] All of these involve giving up the self 'for' my neighbor's benefit, with the readiness to do and bear everything in the neighbor's place, indeed, if necessary, to sacrifice myself, standing as a *substitute* for my neighbor. Even if a purely vicarious action is rarely actualized, it is intended in every genuine act of love.[174]

It is apparent that in self-renouncing work for the neighbor I give up happiness. We are called to advocate vicariously for the other in everyday matters, to give up possessions, honor, even our whole lives. With the whole strength that we owe to the church-community we ought to work in it. The 'strong' do not have their abilities for themselves, in order to consider themselves superior to the church-community; they have them 'for the common good' (1 Cor. 12:7). Every material, intellectual, or spiritual gift fulfills its purpose only when used in the church-community. Love demands that we give up our own advantage. This may even include our community with God itself. Here we see the love that voluntarily seeks to submit itself to God's wrath on behalf of the other members of the community, which wishes God's wrath for itself in order that they may have community with God, which takes their place, as Christ took our place. The two great examples are Exod. 32:32 and Rom. 9:1ff. Moses wants to be blotted out from the book of life together with his people.[55] Paul wants to be accursed and separated

---

55. Symeon the New Theologian, *The Discourses*, 8.2: "I also know such a person who so fervently desired the salvation of his people that often he beseeched God with burning tears that either they be saved as well, or that he too should experience the torment."[175]

[173.] *SC-RS*: "sanctification?"

[174.] Deleted from *SC-A*: All of this is of interest here only in the context of the new social basic-relations as *community of saints*; hence the brevity of the following discussion.

[175.] Bonhoeffer quotes from Nikolaus Arsenev, *Die Kirche des Morgenlandes*, 88. Arsenev refers to Symeon in the context of his discussion of the Eucharist and the church. Bonhoeffer's copy is marked in the margin of page 87f. [The slightly fuller text of the

from Christ, not in order to be damned with his people, but to win community with God for them; he wants to be damned instead of them. Love for God gives rise to this paradox that almost exceeds what we can fathom: Paul loves his people, but he loves God above all else. Moses' stance was heroic. He asks God to accept or condemn him together with his people. This is still rationally comprehensible. But Paul seeks to win for the people he loves community with God that he loves above all else, and he curses himself out of community with God and from his people to the place of damnation, where they are, precisely because he truly loves both community with God and his people, which means, because he is obedient to the command that we should unreservedly surrender ourselves to the neighbor. But precisely for this very reason, he remains where he wishes God to ban him from, namely in the most intimate community with God. At the point where the most terrible conflict with God seems to rage, the most profound peace is established. Thus we must not consider this as a moment of weakness on Paul's part. It is not the expression of a "religious-ethical impossibility,"[56] rather his act constitutes the most complete obedience, not disobedience. This very case thus provides clear proof that love ultimately does not seek community, but wants to affirm the 'other' as such, and that the less it seeks, the more certainly it finds.

123

This basically describes the abyss into which *intercession* can lead the individual. The problem of the social structure now consists in the question of what kind of relation we have to assume between those praying for each other. Here the basis for everything must be sought in the fact that the church-community leads *a single life*, and that the individual has community with God only by participating in this life, that one does not stand before God alone, but in the community of saints, where even the most personal prayer no longer belongs to the individual, but to the church that gave birth to this person and through which this individual lives. "Nobody is saved alone; whoever is saved is saved in the church, as its member in unity with the other members. Does any-

---

56. See Lipsius, *Römerkommentar [Hand-Commentar]*, 2d ed., on this passage.[176]

[175. *cont.*] English translation (*The Discourses*, 144) is based on the critical Greek text, edited by Archbishop Basile Krivocheine in 1963.] [CG]

[176.] Richard Lipsius, "Briefe an die Galater, Römer, Philipper," 145.

body have faith? He is in the community of faith. Does anybody love? He is in the community of love. Does anybody pray? He is in the community of prayer. . . . Do not say: What prayer can benefit the living or the dead, since my prayer is not even sufficient for myself alone? Since you do not know how to pray anyway, what is the purpose of praying for yourself? It is the Spirit of love who prays within you. . . . If you are a member of the church, then your prayer is necessary for all its members. . . . The blood of the church is prayer for each other."[57]

Each intercession potentially draws the one for whom it is offered into the church-community; the ancient intercessory formula 'for all people'[58] necessarily does this as well. Where there is no possibility for that person to be incorporated into the church-community, intercession is futile and sacrilegious. Like love for our neighbor, it has its limit in our love for God. Doubt as to whether intercession is meaningful fades away before a consideration like Khomiakov's, even though, of course, it does not explain the miracle of the church-community. It is a mistaken individualism to rely exclusively on one's own prayer, as if God could not take an intercession as seriously as any other kind of prayer; this only demonstrates the perception of prayer as a pious work of the individual, and no understanding of the idea that the church-community leads a *single* life in Christ. God's will is sovereign also over prayer, which thus remains a "waiting for God to draw near" (Nietzsche).[179] To the extent we doubt the value of intercession, to that degree we are still filled with self-righteousness. Nevertheless, it is not meaningless and unimportant who prays. For the positive form of intercession has a positive meaning: intercession must be viewed from two angles, namely *as human action and as divine will*. The first makes it manifest that the members of the church-community belong together. A third person is drawn into my solitary relation with God, or rather, in intercession I

124

---

57. A[lekse] Khomiakov, *Gesammelte Werke* (Russian ed.), 2:18ff.[177]

58. See 1 Tim. 2:1 and "The Martyrdom of Polycarp," 5:1–8:1. Cf. Matt. 5:44, Luke 23:4, Rom. 12:14. Luther, *LW* 44:64f. [*WA* 6:237], calls for prayer "for all the needs of all men, foe and friend alike."[178]

[177.] Bonhoeffer's source for this citation and quotation is Nikolaus Arsenev, *Die Kirche des Morgenlandes*, 87f.

[178.] "Treatise on Good Works" (1520).

[179.] Nietzsche, *Beyond Good and Evil*, Aphorism 58, 63ff.

step into the other's place and my prayer, even though it remains my own, is nonetheless prayed out of the other's affliction and need. I really enter into the other, into the other's sin and affliction; I am afflicted by the other person's sins and weaknesses. It is not as if I, through my gift for empathy, would have to share or reproduce in myself what hurts the other. If this were necessary, intercession for all people as a whole would not be possible, of course, and especially I could not pray for a person living in complete isolation. Here, all psychologism has to vanish. The sins of the unknown sailor, for whom intercession is offered in the pastoral prayer following the sermon, afflict me no less than those of my closest friend. For the affliction springs from the recognition of my own culpability for the sins of the world, or, what is the same thing, my own culpability for the death of   125 Christ. Once this culpability is recognized, a person can act upon humanity as a Christian, that is by praying for it. In our intercession we can become a Christ to our neighbor. In intercession we are thus not given the cold comfort that others are also in the same situation, but that, if God wants it and we accept it, our debts are canceled, our sin is forgiven (James 5:15, 16; 1 John 5:16a). Our sins, however, are borne by the church-community—by Christ. The words of the psalm are only partially true, "Truly no one can redeem a brother, nor reconcile him—it costs too much to redeem their souls; it must be postponed eternally."[59] Like any other form of prayer, intercession does not compel God, but, if God does the final work, then one member of the community can redeem another, in the power of the church. This conclusively eliminates ethical self-confidence of one human being toward another. As Christians, we cannot boast about our solitary relationship with God. Our strength comes to us from the church-community, and we will never know how much our own prayer accomplished, and what we gained through the fervent intercession of people unknown to us. We

---

59. Ps. 49:8f. Following the M[asoretic] T[ext] I read "ach."[180]

[180.] Bonhoeffer quotes the Luther translation (revised, 1912), which follows the Masoretic Text. It reads אח (brother), which many modern scholars change to אך (truly, surely). Thus Bonhoeffer does not accept the modern critical version of the text. The *NRSV* (vv. 7-9), following the modern emendation, reads: "Truly, no ransom avails for one's life, there is no price one can give to God for it. For the ransom of life is costly, and can never suffice that one should live on forever and never see the grave." [CG]

know that we owe infinite gratitude not only to God, but also to the church-community, which prayed for us and still continues to do so. If our ethical self-confidence vis-à-vis God begins to break down before the vicarious representative love of Christ on the cross, then it completely dies when we consider intercession, i.e., the church-community.[181]

If we now look at intercession from God's standpoint, then it appears as individuals organizing themselves to realize the divine will for others, to serve the realization of God's rule in the church-community. This idea, when thought through, contains the meaning and power of the corporate prayer of the church, as Luther discusses it in the "Treatise on Good Works."[60] It is God's most powerful means for organizing the entire church-community toward God's own purpose; in it the church-community recognizes itself as an instrument of God's will, and accordingly organizes itself in active obedience. This is, therefore, the point of its major thrust,[61] and the devil is more afraid of a thatched roof under which a congregation prays, than of a magnificent cathedral in which many masses are said.[62] For the church it is thus critically important to assign corporate prayer the central place it deserves. Leading a *single* life, the church must also have and practice one *common* prayer. In this prayer it takes upon itself the burden of the many individuals who already or still belong to it, and carries it to God. In the church each one bears the other's burden[183] and only by recognizing that intercession is *a God-given means for realizing God's purpose can we*

126

---

60. *LW* 44:65ff. [*WA* 6:238ff.].

61. *LW* 44:66 [*WA* 6:239]: "For indeed, the Christian church on earth has no greater power or work against everything that may oppose it than such common prayer. Prayer is 'unconquerable.'"

62. *LW* 44:66 [*WA* 6:239.][182]

[181.] "If our . . . church-community" reads in *SC-A*: While our ethical self-confidence vis-à-vis God breaks down in the face of the vicarious representative love of Christ on the cross, it dies vis-à-vis our neighbor when we consider intercession, i.e., the church-community.

[182.] "Treatise on Good Works," *LW* 44:66: "For when prayer is flagging, nobody wrests anything from the devil, and nobody resists him. But if the devil realizes that we are prepared to practice this prayer, even under a thatched roof or in a pigsty, he would not tolerate it for an instant, but would fear such a pigsty far more than all the high, great, and lovely churches, towers, and bells that ever were if such prayer were not in them" [trans. altered] [*WA* 6:239 ("Sermon von den guten Werken" [1520])].

[183.] Cf. Gal. 6:2; see above, page 180. [CG]

acknowledge and practice it as something meaningful. In intercession the nature of Christian love again proves to be to work 'with', 'for', and ultimately 'in place of' our neighbor, thereby drawing the neighbor deeper and deeper into the church-community. Thus, when one person intercedes in the name of Christ on behalf of the other, the whole church-community—which actually means 'Christ existing as church-community', to use a modification of the Hegelian concept[184]—participates in that person's prayer.

This has already brought us to the final problem, which *provides the deepest insight into the miracle of the church-community, namely that one person can forgive another's sins with priestly authority.* It was Augustine who maintained that this is possible[185] only[186] in the community of saints.[187] It alone is given the promise in John 20:23, for it alone has the Spirit. Nobody can forgive sins but the person who takes them upon himself, bears them, and wipes them out. Thus only Christ can do it, which for us means his church as the sanctorum communio. The individual Christian can do it only by virtue of membership in the church-community, and in that capacity ought to do it. The Christian takes sin from the others' conscience and bears it; but clearly one can do that only by laying it in turn on Christ. Such action is thus possible only within the church-community. However, this does not mean that its effectiveness is dependent on any one of its members, but that it is nevertheless possible only because a church-community exists in the   127 first place (see below). Luther revived Augustine's idea that it is the sanctorum communio that bears the sins of its members. However, later in the same sentence he adds that it is Christ who bears them.[63] "The

---

63. *WA* 6:131: "quis ergo queat desperare in peccatis? quis non gaudeat in penis, qui sua peccata et penas jam neque portat aut si portat non solus portat, adiutus tot sanctis filiis dei, ipso denique Christo? Tanta res est communio sanctorum et ecclesia Christi" ("Who could then despair over their sins? Who would not rejoice in their sorrows, since they no longer bear their own sins and punishment, or if they do, they do not bear them alone, but are supported by so

[184.] Added to *SC-A*: to use a modification of the Hegelian concept. [Bonhoeffer's modification provides a more christological emphasis; Hegel wrote 'God', which Bonhoeffer changed to 'Christ'.][CG]
[185.] Reads in *SC-A*: real.
[186.] *SC-RS*: "Only? The word obviously contains more effects than that."
[187.] See above, page 175, footnote 37.

immeasurable grace and mercy of God are given us, in this sacrament (of the Lord's Supper), to the end that we might put from us all misery and tribulation [Anfechtung] and lay it upon the church-community, and especially upon Christ . . . ; all my misfortune is shared with Christ and the saints" [trans. altered].[64] The church-community is thus able to bear the sins that none of its members can bear alone; it is able to bear more than all of its members combined. As such, it must be a spiritual reality that is more than the sum of all the individuals. Not all the individuals, but the church-community as a whole is in Christ, is the 'body of Christ';[190] it is *'Christ existing as church-community'*.[191] It bears the sins by receiving forgiveness through the word and seeing its sins wiped out on the cross. It indeed lives *by the word* alone, but in doing so it has the Spirit. It is bearer of the word, its steward and instrument. It has authority, provided it has faith in the authority of the word; it can take the sins of individuals upon itself, if it builds itself on the word of the cross, and knows itself reconciled and justified in the cross of Jesus. It has itself died and risen with Christ, and is now the nova creatura [new creation][65] in Christ. It is not merely *a means to an end but also an end in itself. It is the present Christ himself, and this is why 'being in Christ' and 'being in the church-community' is the same thing*; it is why Christ himself bears the sins of the individuals, which are laid upon the church-community.

Summarized briefly, the new social basic-relations appear as follows: the ethical basic-relations that were severed in the corpus peccati [body of sin] (Bernard)[192] are renewed by the Holy Spirit. Community is constituted by the complete self-forgetfulness of love. I and You face

128   each other no longer essentially in a demanding, but in a giving way,

---

many holy children of God, yes, by Christ himself; so great a thing is the community of saints in the church of Christ") [*LW* 42:162 (trans. altered)].[188]

    64. *LW* 35:53f. [*WA* 2:745].[189]

    65. *LW* 42:160 [*WA* 6:130], where Luther calls the church a *nova creatura* [new creation].

[188.] "Fourteen Consolations."
[189.] "The Blessed Sacrament" (1519).
[190.] Deleted from *SC-A*: is where the Spirit lives.
[191.] Deleted from *SC-A*: (to use a modification of Hegel's concept). See below, page 198, editorial note 217.
[192.] See Bernard of Clairvaux, "In dedicatione ecclesiae: Sermo Primus."

revealing their hearts that have been conquered by God's will. However, the ethical social basic-relations between I and You in the former sense remain a fact as long as there is conscience, law, and God's wrath, as long as we do not walk by sight, but by faith.[193] A Christian comes into being and exists only in Christ's church-community and is dependent on it, which means on the other human being. One person bears the other in active love, intercession, and forgiveness of sins, acting completely vicariously. This is possible only in the church-community of Christ, and that itself rests, as a whole, on the principle of vicarious representation, i.e., on the love of God. But all are borne by the church-community, which consists precisely in this being-for-each-other of its members. The structural being-with-each-other [Miteinander] of church-community and its member, and the members acting-for-each-other [Füreinander] as vicarious representatives in the power of the church-community, is what constitutes the specific sociological nature of the community of love [Liebesgemeinschaft]. In all of this the singularity and solitude of each member is not abolished. My prayer, and my whole posture of obedience, is my very own responsibility and something I must win through struggle again and again. My sin is either entirely my own or not my own at all; I cannot foist part of it on the other. Either I still bear it, or I have laid it on the church-community, and that means 'Christ existing as church-community' is bearing it now. This discussion thus leads us to the problem of the 'unity' of the church-community, in which plurality of persons and community of persons acquire their comprehensive meaning. *The concept of the church as numerus praedestinatorum [number of predestined]* and *as sanctorum commu-*

[193.] Deleted from *SC-A*:

The Christian community of love [Liebesgemeinschaft] combines in itself the model of community [Gemeinschaft] and society [Gesellschaft] with the model of association of authentic rule [Herrschaftsverband] and cooperative association [Genossenschafts-verband] (in the above sense). It does so both by being an end in itself and a means to an end, by being the realization of God's rule, and, nonetheless, the Realm of Christ, the community of saints. This structure is so unique because the community of love comes into being precisely where it is least sought, by human beings unrestrictedly surrendering to the will of God. This paradox is resolved in God's will to have community with human beings, and for human beings, who are in community with God, to have community with each other.

[The biblical allusion just before the editorial note is to 2 Cor. 5:7.] [CG]

nio–in the sense of community [Gemeinschaft], which sociologically still must be more precisely defined[194]*–is still incomplete.*

c) The unity of spirit of the church-community—the collective person

The unity of spirit of the church-community is a fundamental synthesis willed by God; it is not a relation that must be produced, but one that is already established (iustitia passiva! [passive righteousness]),[195] and that remains[196] hidden from our eyes. Neither unanimity, uniformity, nor congeniality makes it possible, nor is it to be confused with unity of mood.[197] Rather, it is a reality precisely where the seemingly sharpest outward antitheses prevail, where each person really leads an individual

129 life; and it is perhaps missing just where it seems to prevail most. It is thrown into much sharper relief where wills clash than where they agree. When one person clashes with another, it might very well lead them to remember the One who is over them both, and in whom both of them are one. Precisely where Jew and Greek clash, out of their completely different psychological dispositions, their intuitive and intellectual perceptions, there unity is established through God's will; "here, there is neither Jew nor Greek, neither slave nor free, neither man nor woman: for you are all one in Christ Jesus" (Gal. 3:28). Christ has created, out of two, a single new person in himself, and has made peace (Eph. 2:15); but this continues to be a peace that passes all understanding.[198] For the contrasts remain, they even become more acute; in the community all are led to carry their individual viewpoints to the limit, to be really serious about it, in keeping with the basic sociological laws of social vitality.[199] But—to put it paradoxically—the more powerfully the dissimilarity manifests itself in the struggle, the stronger the objective unity. The decisive passages in the New Testament do not say: *one*

[194.] "in the sense . . . precisely defined" reads in *SC-A*: in the strict sense of community [Gemeinschaft].

[195.] See Luther's exposition of Romans 1:17f. in his *Vorlesung über den Römerbrief 1515-1516*, Ficker (1925), 1:14ff. [cf. *Lectures on Romans, LW* 25:9ff.] [CG], and the "Preface to the Complete Edition of Luther's Latin Writings," *LW* 34:327ff., esp. 336f. [*WA* 54:179ff., esp. 185f.].

[196.] Deleted from *SC-A*: completely.

[197.] The following words have been replaced in *SC-A*: unity of mood or will.

[198.] Cf. Phil. 4:7. [CG]

[199.] "in the community . . . of social vitality" reads in *SC-A*: since each person is led to carry their individual understanding to the limit, to be really serious about it.

theology and *one* rite, *one* opinion on all matters public and private, and *one* kind of conduct.[66] Instead they say: *one* body and *one* Spirit, *one* Lord, *one* faith, *one* baptism, *one* God and father of us all (Eph. 4:4ff.; 1 Cor. 12:13; Rom. 12:5); various gifts—*one* Spirit, various offices—*one* Lord, various powers—*one* God (1 Cor. 12:4ff.). The point is not "unanimity in spirit" ["Einigkeit im Geist"], but the "unity of the Spirit" ["Einheit des Geistes"], as Luther puts it in his exposition of Eph. 4:3;[67] this means the objective principle sovereignly establishes unity, unites the plurality of persons into a single collective person [Gesamtperson] without obliterating either their singularity or the community of persons. *Rather, unity of spirit, community of spirit, and plurality of spirit are*   130 *intrinsically linked to each other through their subject matter.* This has already been demonstrated in our discussion of the social-philosophical foundations.

Idealist philosophy failed to understand this for reasons that lie at its very heart;[200] here the fundamental lack of a concrete concept of the person becomes evident once again.[201] [68]

---

66. See *Confessio Augustana*, VII [*Die Bekenntnisschriften der evangelisch-lutherischen Kirche*, 61]: "nec necesse est ubique esse similes traditiones humanas seu ritus aut ceremonias ab hominibus institutas" ("It is not necessary that human traditions or rites and ceremonies, instituted by men, should be alike everywhere") [Augsburg Confession 7, "The Church," in *The Book of Concord*, 32]. 1 Cor. 1:10 refers to the destructive, evil will, not to theological views. Cf. Phil. 2:2–3:16.

67. Quoted by Traugott Schmidt, [*Der Leib Christi*,] 136.

68. The issue here basically is the same as in Schleiermacher, Fichte, Hegel, and also in Kant. Schleiermacher's central concept is the biological concept of the species. Personality is constituted by the "whole system of mental and physical organization that the spirit assumes" (*Christliche Sitte*, 510) and without which the person disintegrates.[202] A human being is a specimen of a species

---

[200.] "Idealist philosophy . . . at its very heart" reads in *SC-A*: It is a basic error of idealist philosophy that.

[201.] Deleted from *SC-A*: According to our theory, genuine idealism, i.e., idealism based on concrete personhood, exists only in a social context; and, on the other hand, there is no social philosophy that is not based on personhood. In *SC-A* footnote 68 follows here in the text.

[202.] Footnote deleted from *SC-A*:

<<Hirsch, [*Die idealistische Philosophie*,] 110, charges that Brunner in his *Die Mystik und das Wort* (278ff.) artificially undermines the sincerity of Schleiermacher's statement about the continued existence of the individual after death (*The Christian Faith*, §158). Schleiermacher clearly states, according to Hirsch, that for a Christian a continued personal existence is

131   Everywhere we find the same picture. The spirit is one, eternally
       identical, transpersonal, immanent in humanity; it destroys the con-

---

([*Christliche Sitte*,] 558)[203] and an individual remarkably differentiated in itself;
the individual being is "organ and symbol" of the species (*Ethik*, sec. 157).[204]
"The spirit is one and the same in all individuals and, considered as such, does
not contain the personality, regardless of whether we view the spirit as πνεῦμα
ἅγιον [Holy Spirit] or as κοινὸς λόγος [shared word](*Christliche Sitte*, 510; also
see *The Christian Faith*, §123, 3.)[205] The first statement concerning the unity of
the spirit appears acceptable to us. To the question as to the nature of the Holy
Spirit, Schleiermacher gives the characteristic reply of identifying the Holy
Spirit and the spirit of the community. Consciousness of the Holy Spirit is considered the same as consciousness of the community. The Christian spirit of the
community has the natural tendency to become the 'spirit of the species'. Thus
the *Holy Spirit is apparently nothing but the consciousness of the species*. The apersonal character of this concept of spirit and community is finally evident in the
definition of the Holy Spirit as the "union of the divine essence with human
nature in the form of the spirit of the community that animates the corporate
life of the believers." But this union, unlike that with Christ, cannot be considered as personal (*The Christian Faith*, §123.3), and the Holy Spirit operates
"without any regard for particular personal attributes of any person" (ibid.).
Given this situation, it cannot salvage anything to call the spirit of the community a "moral person" ([ibid.,] §121.2). As the one in all individuality the Holy
Spirit effects a "true unity" (ibid.) in such a way that it grows stronger and
stronger through "co-operative activity and reciprocal influence" ([ibid.,] §121,
thesis); the Spirit takes possession of the individual on behalf of the community
in order that through that person the best work for the whole is accomplished
([ibid.,] §123.3).[206] The unity of the spirit of the community is thus constantly

---

[202. *cont.*] certain, because this is what Jesus ascribed to himself. This certainly provides a
glimpse of Schleiermacher, the human being; it is plain, however, that the entire design of his
The Christian Faith points beyond the idea of a continued personal existence after death.>>

[203.] Footnote deleted from *SC-A*: <<Every human being is on the one hand a specimen of
the human species, and on the other hand a uniquely determined and uniquely self-determining
270   being, an individual.>>

[204.] Bonhoeffer means Schleiermacher, *Entwurf eines Systems der Sittenlehre*, sec. 157.

[205.] Deleted from *SC-A*:

As we have already stated earlier, each person attains the new life only in and through the
community. In the same way, no one shares in the Holy Spirit through their personal
self-consciousness considered as such, but only insofar as that person is conscious of being
part of this whole, i.e., as common consciousness [Gemeinbewusstsein] of the community.

[206.] Deleted from *SC-A*:

[Schleiermacher,] *Christliche Sitte*, 517, . . . that the divine Spirit is one and the same in all
and for all, and that all individuals are merely the Spirit's instruments; so that each person

crete person, and thus prevents any concrete concept of community,

---

moving toward itself, or better, is constantly growing ([ibid.,] §121); in this process the individuals (specimens) are used by the spirit of the community.[207] Schleiermacher correctly recognizes a life of an individual only for and within the community—that the work of Christ and the Holy Spirit is primarily aimed at the church, at the corporate life ([ibid.,] §121.2; biblical basis in John 16:7ff.; Acts 1:7ff., 2:4; John 20:22f.). This is, of course, only one aspect of Schleiermacher's thinking, as was demonstrated earlier. But he gained this view at the expense of serious errors: (1) the disastrous identification of the Holy Spirit and spirit of the species; (2) the individual must become a tool, which means for Schleiermacher that the individual must be extinguished as a person; (3) Schleiermacher thus missed his chance to understand true community of spirit, as well as true unity of spirit. By being applied to the species, the concept of spirit becomes an anthropological-biological category; this is due to the underlying doctrine of apocatastasis [universal salvation]. Spirit becomes a category of the psychology of peoples and species. The final claim on God is granted to the species, exactly because it is the species. It is the 'value' God wants, which is to be realized and to which the individual is sacrificed. It is obvious that this approach fails to understand the New Testament. *The biological concept of species has no place in a theological inquiry of the church* (see above). If we, too, describe the Holy Spirit as the Spirit of the church-community, then we mean something quite different, as has already been shown and will further be shown.

If the spirit of the community swallows up the individual spirit, dissolving the personality, then the possibility of a social concept of community is ruled out from the beginning. For, in that case, community must become 'unity', which already became clear at the beginning. But this implies a misunderstanding of the essential structure of all communities, including the church. Moreover, Schleiermacher's concept of unity is not theological, but psychological, and therefore profoundly mistaken. It is based on an *identification of 'religious*

[206. *cont.*] has the Spirit completely only insofar as the consciousness that all the others are equally instruments of the divine Spirit, has become that person's self-consciousness. . . . This intrinsic need of the self-consciousness of separate personalities to continually flow together is the essence of Christian love.

[207.] Deleted from *SC-A*:

In the *Speeches* the concept of the universe takes the place of the concept of the species. Individuals tend to immerse themselves into the universe, to recognize themselves as a manifestation of the infinite diversity of the whole, and to enjoy the other. For only through the union of all individualities does the entire divine nature of the universe reveal itself. "Among themselves they are a choir of friends. Each has the knowledge of being a part and product of the universe. . . . They thus consider themselves worthy objects of observation for the others—indeed, why should they hide anything from each other? Among each other they are a band of brothers, or do you have a more intimate expression for the complete blending of their natures?" [trans. altered] [Schleiermacher, *On Religion*, 188]

instead replacing it with the immanent unity of spirit;[219] with this one

---

community' and 'church' ([ibid.,] §121.3). The unity of the former is psychological; that of the church transcends psychological categories, it is divinely established, objective. Had Schleiermacher understood this basic difference, he never would have thought of identifying the Holy Spirit with the consciousness of the species. The former is present in principle only in the church. The latter is part of any community as such. True, when viewed from the outside, the church is a religious community, but this is precisely an untheological perspective.[208]

In summary, we have to say that Schleiermacher not only fails to understand social community, and thus the essence of social 'unity', but that, in spite of his efforts to develop the concepts of the corporate life and the union of humanity, he does not reach the social sphere at all. It is thus just as incorrect to call him a collectivist, as it is to call him an individualist. He is a metaphysician of the spirit, and as such founders on the concept of sociality.[209] This is characteristic of idealist philosophy as a whole. Even Hegel, who among the idealist philosophers says the most about community, does not overcome this limitation. The natural wonder about the reality of the other human being has disappeared, or, as they think, it has been 'overcome'. We will now briefly outline the idealist concept of community (see esp. Hirsch, [*Die idealistische Philosophie,*] 66ff. and 29ff.).[210]

[208.] "True, when viewed . . . perspective" reads in *SC-A*:

True, when viewed empirically, the church is only a religious community; but the *perspectives* are entirely different, in one case *looking down from above* and, *in the other, the reverse.* [The following is deleted from *SC-A*:] These two trains of thought actually converge for Schleiermacher in the concept of *instrument;* for us, however, this happens primarily in the concept of the *word.* Of course, we too acknowledge that the individual is an instrument, but with the difference that (1) this does not eliminate, but perfects the individual's personality; that (2) the unity of the church cannot be constituted by human instruments (because the human 'will for good' always remains a mere beginning, and because the visible external unity that has been attained does not yet guarantee that it is what God intends), but rather that unity must already exist 'before' or 'while' the human will is set in motion (iustitia passiva [passive righteousness]); and (3) that the *community of spirit* [Geistgemeinschaft], which is based on the separateness of the persons, is constituted ever anew by the will for good that the Holy Spirit creates through the word.

[209.] Deleted from *SC-A*:

Further proof of an inconsistency is the vacillation in the concept of the church, indicated above, where Schleiermacher is unable to combine the idea of free will with the concept of spirit. He does not take seriously the ethical-ontic basic-relation between I and You and, precisely for this reason, remains *completely outside the actual sphere of person and community.*

271   [210.] Concerning criticism of Schleiermacher, see also Hirsch, *Die idealistische Philosophie,* 103ff.

has fallen victim to the danger of "simplistically assuming the commu-

---

It is based on the common nature and equal value of individuals. These are ensured by participation in universal reason (Kant-Fichte), or in objective and absolute spirit (Hegel). There are many I's, but there is no I-You-relation. Kant, who introduces the concept of the ethically responsible person in his idea of the kingdom of God (*Religion within the Limits of Reason Alone*, 87ff., 91ff. [3.1.1, 3.1.4])—or rather, who develops the latter out of the former—nevertheless does not grasp the idea of concrete community, since his concept of person ultimately remains apersonal as well.[211] And yet it is Kant who came closest to the Christian concept of community (Hirsch, *Die Reich-Gottes-Begriffe des neueren europäischen Denkens*, 1921, 20ff., 25).[212] Fichte's concept of community can best be examined in his theory of the state (*Rechtslehre*, ed. H[ans] Schulz, 1920).[213] The community is a "great self," a collective person, to which individual persons have to surrender completely; but they dissolve into this 'unity' (see what we said above concerning Fichte's concept of synthesis).[214] Hegel has kept a clear sense for concrete individual life, but he too considers it to be merely a form of universal spirit; all individual life is thus destined to be absorbed into the corporate spirit.[215] This corporate spirit is by nature beyond individuality; it is the "objective spirit" (*Elements of the Philosophy of Right*[216] and "Philosophy of Spirit," secs. 438ff.), which has entered the life of human history and community, or "the reason of the life of the human species." According to Windelband, "Through and in the particularity of my finitude I have my personality . . ., the relation to the other persons springs from the inner relation of the free personality to the *unity* of the unconditional" (*Geschichte der neueren Philosophie*, 343ff.). (Brunstäd, "Vorrede" zur *Geschichtsphilosophie* [Hegel, *Vorlesungen über die Philosophie der Geschichte*], 27.) Everywhere we encounter the concept of unity. This is ultimately due to the immanentist concept of God or the identification of human and divine spirit. (The state, for example, is given divine titles of honor as in *Elements of the Philosophy of Right*, sec. 258: "this real God"; cf. Hobbes.)[217] This basic tendency again clearly emerges in Hegel's concept of

[211.] Deleted from *SC-A*: This is due not only to his epistemology, but also to the methodological starting point of his ethical formalism.

[212.] The reference to the citation in Kant, *Religion within the Limits of Reason Alone*, is found in Hirsch, *Die Reich-Gottes-Begriffe*, 22, note 70.

[213.] The reference to Fichte is found in Hirsch, *Die Reich-Gottes-Begriffe*, 23, note 72. See Fichte, *Das System der Rechtslehre* (*Werke*, 10:493ff., esp. 500ff.).

[214.] See above, page 56, footnote 12.

[215.] The reference to Hegel is found in Hirsch, *Die Reich-Gottes-Begriffe*, 26, note 79.

[216.] Deleted from *SC-A*: which deals with the problems of current social philosophies.

[217.] Deleted from *SC-A*:

<<Leviathan, ch. 17: "multitudo illa una persona est et vocatur et civitas et respublica. Atque haec est generatio magni illius leviathan vel ut dignius loquar, mortalis dei." ("The multitude, so united in one person, is called a commonwealth, in latin civitas [state]. This is

nity to be a unity."[69] We concur with the unanimous emphasis on the
132   idea of 'community', the recognition that individual life is real only
within the corporate life. However, we understand the terms 'corporate
life'[220] and 'real' in a significantly different sense. We understand both
as ethical categories, whereas in idealist philosophy they are partly
biological, and partly general metaphysical categories.

The unity of the Christian church is *not based on human unanimity of*
133   *spirit*, but on *divine unity of Spirit*, and the two are *not* identical from the
outset. In discussing the sociological community-type we found its

---

the Christian church community. Once the human spirit had become aware in
Christ of its identity with the divine Spirit, and through the death of death itself
finitude had been destroyed, what has become manifest in Christ must now be
realized effective in the church. (*Philosophy of Religion*, "Kingdom of Spirit,"
3:328ff. [*Religionsphilosophie*, ed. Marheineke, 1832, II: "Reich des Geistes."])
"*God existing as community*" (*Lectures on the Philosophy of Religion* 3:331)[218] brings
the "many individuals back into the unity of the spirit, into the community,"
and lives in the community as the "actual, universal self-consciousness" (ibid.,
3:133). Faith is the awareness of the spirit and the unity. Through faith "sensible
history constitutes the point of departure for spirit," and in it the spirit returns
to itself (ibid., 3:229). In spite of recent objections, it seems certain, I think, that
Hegel simply identifies the Holy Spirit with the corporate spirit of the church.
The Lord's Supper must, in Hegel's view, form the center of any Christian doctrine of the unity of the spirit and of the community. For in the Lord's Supper
the awareness of being reconciled with God, of the Spirit entering and
indwelling us, attains its clearest manifestation and reality (ibid., see 3:337–39).
    69. Hirsch, *Die idealistische Philosophie*, 73.

[217. *cont.*] the generation of the great Leviathan, or rather (to speak more reverently) of
that mortal god. . . .") [*Leviathan*, 120.]>> See Thomas Hobbes, *Leviathan* (*Opera Latina*, ed.
G[ulielmi] Molesworth, 3:131).

[218.] Concerning the formula "God existing as church-community [Gemeinde]," see
the discussion of Hegel's philosophy of religion by Seeberg in his *Dogmatik*, 2:298ff.; the
formula is explicitly mentioned on page 299.

[219.] "The Spirit is . . . unity of spirit" reads in *SC-A*: The unity of spirit is grounded
immanently; it thus destroys concrete personhood and prevents any concrete concept of community.

[220.] 'Corporate life' [*Gesamtleben*] is a term used for the church by Schleiermacher in
The Christian Faith; see above, page 153, editorial note 79.

ultimate unity to be its existence as a collective person. This insight must be applied to the Christian religious community as well as to the concept of the church. In the first case the presentation would proceed from below upwards, whereas in the case of the concept of the church it moves from above downwards.[221] *The personal unity of the church [Kirche] is 'Christ existing as church-community [Gemeinde]'*;[222] Paul could also speak of Christ himself being the church.[223]

Being in Christ means being in the church.[70] The unity of the church as a structure *is* established 'before' any knowing and willing of the members; it is not ideal, but real. It is a reality as truly as the church is the church of Christ, and as truly as the body of Christ never becomes fully manifest in history. In Christ all are one, differences no longer exist; there is not even a plurality any more. They are all *one*, "one loaf,"[71] to use Luther's phrase. Only all members together can possess Christ entirely, and yet every person possesses him entirely too. This unity is based on the fact that Christ is "the one beyond every other"

134

---

70. One might ask whether it might be most appropriate to regard the personality of the church as the Holy Spirit. In the Bible it is indeed the Spirit who is declared the principle of unity (see above). But the cooperation between Christ and Spirit is precisely what is distinctive about the subject matter; also the Holy Spirit is never conceived as the bearer of a 'body'. Seeberg (*Dogmatik*, 2:328) raises the question of an incarnation of the Holy Spirit in the church, meaning whether the Spirit becomes incarnate in the individuals. He rightly rejects this, pointing to the sinfulness of all people.[224]

71. *WA* 12:488: "So wyr denn mit Christo eyn kuche sind, so wirkt dasselbige soviel, dass wyr auch untereinander ein ding werden"[225] ("Since we are one loaf with Christ, this has such a strong effect that we also become one thing among each other"). See also *LW* 11:540 [*WA* 4:400].[226]

[221.] Bonhoeffer regularly uses spatial metaphors for theological ideas. Here "below" refers to human agency, "above" to God's revelation and action. They are not institutional or organizational terms. [CG]

[222.] Regarding the formula 'Christ existing as church-community', see above, page 198, editorial note 217.

[223.] Regarding Bonhoeffer's understanding of Pauline ecclesiology, see above his "Major Themes in the New Testament View of the Church," pages 134ff. *SC-A* does not begin a new paragraph here.

[224.] In *SC-A* footnote 70 is part of the main text.

[225.] "Ein Sermon am grünen Donnerstage."

[226.] *First Lectures on the Psalms* (1513), the complete text of which is found in *LW* 10 and *LW* 11.

(Barth).[227] It must be believed, and will always remain invisible to our eyes. This unity does not exist because the members of the body have the same intentions; rather, if they have the same intentions at all, they have them only as members of the body of Christ; for obviously they remain members, even when they sin (cf. the indicative sense of 1 Cor. 6:15). But there is no divine will for human beings that would not be realized at least to some small extent in them. In this way the objective unity already existing in Christ is realized in the persons, and only in this realization is it this objective unity.[228]

Eph. 4:5 not only mentions the "one Lord" but also "one faith" through which the Lord is revealed and in which Christ is present. *The unity of faith* is such that "without it no unity, be it that of city, time, persons, work, or whatever else it may be, can create the whole of Christianity [Christenheit]."[72] Viewed from below, it is in fact the constitutive element of the unity of the church, and this has important consequences with regard to the necessity for a creed in congregational worship.[230] It is not possible for the church-community to assemble without coming before God as a unity, without affirming in its faith the divinely established unity of Spirit of the church of Christ beyond our sight, the 'Christ existing as church-community'.[231] If God's will that there be one Spirit, one Lord, one God is the ordained constitution of the church (constitutio-cives [constitution-citizens], see below, pages 265f.), then the creed is the Yes of the church-community to this constitution. Indeed, viewed purely from the outside, it is the constitution itself, in which the religious 'community' summarizes what its objective

---

72. *LW* 39:65 [*WA* 6:293].[229]

[227.] See Barth, *Romans*, 440ff., esp. 443: "Community is communio . . .–that *oneness* which both requires the 'otherness' of each individual and makes sense of it. Community is the one that lies beyond every 'other'" [trans. altered].

[228.] *SC-A* does not begin a new paragraph here.

[229.] "On the Papacy at Rome" (1520).

[230.] The passage that follows, up to "unifying congregations" (page 202), is taken from the deleted section "The Individual Form of the Objective Spirit in the Church Today. 2. Concerning the Sociology of Worship and Pastoral Care" (see below, pages 274ff., editorial note 430). *SC-A* continues instead with The Christian community is usually called a 'community of faith'. . . (see below, page 202).

[231.] "It is not possible . . . as church community" reads in *SC-A*: It is not possible for the Christian community to disperse without having come before God as a unity, without affirming with its faith the invisible, divinely established unity of spirit. In the church, community and unity necessarily belong together.

spirit knows about its own foundation, meaning, and purpose, by which it is held together. It is quite a different question, which cannot be discussed here, whether the Apostles' Creed really measures up to this standard of a confession of faith for the Christian church-community.[232]

As the church-community that understands itself as subject to the unity of the Spirit and as living from the *one* life, it now also prays the great pastoral prayer following the sermon, and bows to pray the Lord's Prayer that, according to ancient tradition (Luke 11:1ff.), the Lord gave to his church.[73] At the present time we have to experience again and again how little the worshiping congregation understands that it is praying as the church-community. This is something we have realized recently that must not be taken lightly.[234] We must make every effort to have our congregations learn again how to pray; it is precisely corporate congregational prayer, as Luther never wearies of saying,[235] that is

135

---

73. Sociologists too have recognized the sociological significance of the Lord's Prayer.[233]

[232.] "It is quite . . . Christian church-community" reads in *SC-A*: A different question is whether the Apostles' Creed measures up to the standard of the Christian church-community's confession of faith. I would emphatically deny this, without being able to substantiate this view here. The text of the note that originally followed here can be found below, page 276, end-note 430, beginning "see only the most recent literature. . . ." *SC-RS*: "Where is the creed to be placed now?" Bonhoeffer here refers to the dispute over the Apostles' Creed that from 1892 on revolved around Adolf Harnack. See Harnack's *Das apostolische Glaubens-bekenntnis* (and his two encyclopedia articles in English listed in the bibliography), and the documents in Ernst Huber and Wolfgang Huber, *Staat und Kirche*, 3:666ff.

[233.] Deleted from *SC-A*: 'From a sociological perspective, it is not possible to conceive of a more genuine formulation of religion.' Schäffle, *Bau und Leben*, 1:182. The pastoral prayer following the sermon in a German Protestant service—the prayer of intercession or prayers of the people—comes at the end of the service of the word; it is prayed by the minister or an elder, after which the congregation joins together in the Lord's Prayer. [CG]

[234.] Starting at the beginning of the paragraph, "As the church-community . . . be taken lightly" reads in *SC-A*:

As the church-community that leads one life, it prays the great pastoral prayer and the Lord's Prayer: it gives thanks for the gift received, beseeches the Lord of the church for protection, and in priestly authority petitions God's grace for all people. To summarize all this, it bows to pray the prayer that, according to ancient tradition (Luke 11:1ff.), the Lord gave to his church, the 'Our Father'. This is one of the most painful observations in our days.

[235.] For example, see Luther's "Treatise on Good Works" (*LW* 44:15ff. [*WA* 6:196ff.]), especially the exposition of the third commandment (*LW* 44:54ff. [*WA* 6:229ff.]); also see above, pages 185ff.

one of the major sources for strengthening, gathering, and unifying congregations.[236] The Christian church is usually called a community of faith. Sociologically, this is at least an abbreviated way of saying it. The Christian community rests solely on the fact of faith, i.e., the acceptance of God's Spirit. Considered as a concrete community, however, it is not a community of faith, but rather a community of love and of spirit. Faith is not identical to community, any more than God's rule is the same as God's Realm. Faith is acceptance of God's sovereign will, submission to the divine truth.[237] Love is the application, effected by the Spirit, of this faith. Faith, by its nature, is exclusively directing oneself to God; and so several believers—considered solely as believers—have only the unity of faith in common. Even if faith in God includes faith in God's being at work in the church-community, nevertheless the community is only indirectly an object of this faith.[238] Faith is possible only in the church-community, within its unity; it is in fact the practice of this unity. Christian community in the strict sense, however, is generated only by love that acts through faith. Thus, on the one hand, we have *unity of faith correlated to the concept of God's rule, and, on the other hand, community of love correlated to the concept of God's Realm.* Both belong inseparably together, but must be distinguished sociologically. Concretely, however, the positive unity of faith is sustained by the community of love. Unity has to be won, insofar as it does not exist. But the weapon of the Christian church-community is love. It will thus always be the work and demand of *Christian* love to press toward unity. We must not forget Augustine's great notion that caritas [love] is the *bond* of the unity of the church.[239] But this notion presupposes the unity established by God, and human action as meaningful only on this basis.

136

[236.] The preceding text replaces in *SC-A*: one of the major sources for the church community.

[237.] The phrase "submission to the divine truth" reads in *SC-A*: the acknowledgment of the divine truth.

[238.] "nevertheless . . . this faith" reads in *SC-A*: this faith does not yet establish participation in the community.

[239.] See, for example, *Saint Augustine on the Psalms*, 29: "Charity [caritas] on the contrary produces coherence, coherence achieves unity, unity preserves charity, and charity attains to glory" [*Enarrationes in Psalmos*, in *Corpus Christianorum: Series Latina* 38:203]. See also the exposition of Augustine's concept of the church by Seeberg, *History of Doctrines*, 1:312ff.

We live in a time when there is much talk of unifying the churches.[74] In such a time it is particularly important not to forget that unification from below is not identical with unity given from above;[240] further, we must also remember that the will to unify should be practiced, first of all, in the smaller and even the smallest congregation. The way toward unification, however, is fraught with the fiercest resistance; for the stronger the will, the more partisan individuals behave. However, there will presumably be a basic goal that can be built upon and that provides a relative unity. And this common goal may be assumed in the church even where it cannot yet be formulated, but a conceptual expression is still being sought.[241] In spite of recognizing that we can never achieve the absolute unanimity that would correspond to the unity of Spirit, the will seeking the greatest possible realization of unanimity will be alive in the church, and will take comfort from the prayer of Jesus "that they may all be one, just as you Father are in me and I am in you" (John 17:21). And it will be the honor of the church-community to praise through its unity the glory of Jesus before the world (v. 23).

With all this the contrast to the idealist concept of unity is sharply defined: (1) The immanent unity of spirit is only the initial actualization of the transcendent unity of Spirit that is in reality established in Christ. (2) Identifying the spirit of the religious community with the Holy Spirit of the church is not possible. (3) The human being moved by the Spirit becomes and remains a full person even if immanent unity were completely actualized. Even where in Christ all are one, we must not think that the personality intended by God is eliminated, but rather have to conceive of it as reaching its highest perfection at this very point. The unity is complete, but it is full of tension; and this points to an eschatological solution that is still hidden from us (see below, "The Church and Eschatology").[242]

The fact that personal being is fundamentally indissoluble brings us to a problem that sheds still more light on the peculiarity of the social

---

74. See, as a good representative, René Wallau, *Die Einigung der Kirchen vom evangelischen Glauben aus*, 1925.

[240.] "that unification . . . from above" reads in *SC-A*: that unification is not identical with unity.

[241.] Deleted from *SC-A*: The original absolute unity of the goal has broken up in the course of history into a 'relative' unity, yet it still seeks to direct the relative unity as much as possible.

[242.] See below, pages 282ff.

137

273

structure of the Christian church community, namely, *the problem of equality*. The concept of equality[75] presupposes a plurality of persons who are equal with respect to a certain value, whether a material value or a value of spirit. 'Equality before the law' is not a material statement about the relation of people to each other, but strictly refers to the value of 'law'. The Christian idea of equality, in the same way, does not say anything about interpersonal relations, but merely places everybody before God's eyes by, first of all, stating the absolute distance separating not only the creature from the creator, but even more so the sinner from the holy: the equality of human beings consists in their universal sinfulness (Rom. 3:23), which also means their universal need for redemption and an equal share in God's grace. This becomes evident in the death of Jesus on the cross. In God's eyes it is not the outward appearance that counts, but the heart (Acts 10:34; 15:8; Gal. 2:6 et passim).[243] Before God there is no longer either Jew or Gentile, with their mutual claims upon each other. Nobody has any claim. Each must live by grace. That is their equality.[76] Is it then possible, after all, to assert

---

75. Troeltsch, [*Social Teachings,*] 70–76.

76. The modern philosophy of value[244] rejects any absolute concept of equality. Where the "uncovering of our deepest personality, this liberation of the soul from all that is not itself, this self-realization according to the law of the ego" (Simmel, *Sociology of Religion*, 59ff. [trans. altered here and below]) is interpreted as obedience to God's will, and where everything depends on "demystifying the value contained in the soul," there equality can consist only in the fact that "each individual soul has allowed its own essence to become entangled with all kinds of external matters." The absolute "communist idea of equality" must be rejected. Equality before God and before the law are basically the same; the latter does not mean that "before the law, a person breaking a police regulation is equal to a robber and murderer," but that only factors that are legally relevant are taken into consideration and that everything else is insignificant. From a theological perspective, this implies a quite superficial concept of sin. Before God, one sinner is as sinner in fact equal to any other; the community is actually destroyed. God does indeed disregard our differences in value; before God there are no differentiations, but only obedience or disobedience. The Christian idea of equality cannot be overcome by the concept of value.

[243.] Deleted from *SC-A*: Here, consequently, lies the essence of the concept of cooperative association (see above 92f.).

[244.] Simmel's *Sociology of Religion*, to which Bonhoeffer refers here, mentions the *value* of the individual soul. This by itself does not necessarily make Simmel a representative of the *modern philosophy of value*.

that God's church community is built upon ultimately equal human   138
beings? As far as everyone's relation to God is concerned, this is certainly true. This formal equality extends to all. However, placed and
addressed by God in the concrete situation of life, each human being as
a person is totally unlike every other. Nevertheless does it not seem as if
the equality of all persons were the more fundamental reality, and
space and time were the principia individuationis [principles of individ-
uation] causing insignificant differences? But this is not the case,
because equality before God cannot be perceived or demonstrated in
any way, nor is it discernible as 'uniformity'.[245] It is ultimately based on
the fact that *God is always the same.* Equality has nothing to do with affinity of souls, where a person only has to look within to know the other
person. Rather, it is really visible only to God. For us, however, it
remains completely invisible because of our dissimilarity. But it is proclaimed most clearly by the cross of Christ, in which the same judgment
and the same grace is declared to the whole world.[246] It is based on the

---

[245.] "But this is not . . . as 'uniformity'" reads in *SC-A*: This is not the case because
equality before God is strictly a formal category that does not say anything about interpersonal
relations.

[246.] The passage that follows in the published version, up to "concept of the church"
at the end of the paragraph, reads in *SC-A*:

The concept of equality has gained unique sociological significance. It has become the structural foundation of the Christian church-community; the priesthood of all believers is based
on it. No one is religiously superior to any other. However, the equality remains invisible; all
egalitarianism (the communist idea of equality) goes against God's order. This means not
only that nobody may be hindered in their dealings with God, but it also says nothing at all
sociologically about the form of church government, e.g., a democratic model. Rather, what
was created unequal must be accepted as such, and this, in turn, sanctions and introduces
the idea of patriarchalism (the same Paul wrote Gal. 3:28 and 1 Cor. 14:23). [The second
reference should presumably be 1 Cor. 14:34.][CG] Thus we find that the Christian
idea of equality does not lead to the idealist concept of unity, but to the dialectical Christian
idea of the unity of the church.

In our discussion we dealt with only the concept of unity within the social structure of
the church-community. In a standard ecclesiology the 'unity of the church' is usually understood simply as something like the uniting bond. That concept has gained a special importance in Roman Catholicism; first recognized by Cyprian, it was never again forgotten. Thus
proper Roman Catholic doctrine on the unity of the church <<See the encyclicals on "The
Unity of the Church" by Pius IX (1864) and Leo XIII (1896) ["Satis cognitum."]; see also
Bartmann, *Lehrbuch der Dogmatik*, vol. 2, sec. 149.>> differentiates between, on the one
hand, unitas fidei [unity of faith], unitas cultus [unity of worship], and unitas sacramentorum
liturgica [unity of the liturgy of the sacraments], and, on the other hand, unitas societas
[unity of association], unitas regiminis [unity of governance], and unitas caritatis [unity of
love]. This means the interest focuses on the principle that unites the empirical church

unity of spirit of the church that is beyond our perception. It is simply the dialectical relation between plurality and unity that repeats itself here. The concept of equality, thus understood, does not allow for any schematizing; rather, it includes the concrete dissimilarity of all people. It is quite possible, and even necessary, to acknowledge that, from a Christian perspective, there are some who are strong and others who are weak, some who are honorable and others who are dishonorable, some who are, from an ethical and religious perspective, exemplary and others who are inferior; and then, of course, there are the obvious social dissimilarities. But this insight can exist only within the confines of the very idea of equality before God that is beyond our perception. This equality must now also be realized within the framework of what is possible in principle, in that strength and weakness, honor and disgrace, morality and immorality, piety and impiety exist together and not just in isolation. Thus the idea of equality leads us again into the very idea of community. This duality in the idea of equality now also finds expression in the Lutheran doctrine of the priesthood of all believers. The equality, by which every Christian is a priest, is as such invisible. It becomes 'visible' only for faith—and can never be deduced without it!—through the unity of the gift in word and sacrament. As the

139

[246. *cont.*] (papal primacy). <<["Pastor aeternus"] *Vatic. sess. IV. const. dogm. I. de ecclesia,* July 18, 1870. Peter and the Pope together constitute the perpetuum utriusque unitatis principium ac visibile fundamentum [perpetual principle of unity and its visible foundation]. See, e.g., Adam, *The Spirit of Catholicism,* 39ff. "The Pope is the visible expression and the abiding guarantee of this unity.">> The intention is to use the unity of the church also as the basis from which to derive its uniqueness. <<καθολικὴ ἐκκλησία [catholic church], as in Ignatius, "To the Smyrnaeans," 8:2, originally meant una sola [singularity], not universalis [universality].>>

274   In the Russian-Orthodox church the idea of unity plays a particularly prominent role, and it has been discussed in an incomparable fashion by Khomiakov. <<*The Church Is One,* translated into German by Hans Ehrenberg as "Die Einheit der Kirche" in *Östliches Christentum,* vol. 2; it essentially deals with the unity of the church. This work is among the most thought-provoking texts ever written on the church. See also Arsenev, *Die Kirche des Morgenlandes,* 1926, 79ff.>> He is far from any externalizing; "scripture and tradition are external, and the work is external: but what is internal in them is only the Spirit of God." <<Khomiakov, quoted by Arsenev, [*Die Kirche des Morgenlandes,*] 91.>> God's Spirit, as the Spirit of love, is the bearer of unity. "Through the inner knowledge of faith the church and its members know of the unity and immutability of its spirit, which is the Spirit of God." The problem of unity is always related to the problem of community. Our intention so far has been *to delineate in their mutual relationships the concepts of unity, community, and individuality in the church as facts brought about by the Spirit, and thus to contribute to the morphology of the social form of the church as sanctorum communio.*

whole church now rests on the unity in Christ, on the fact of 'Christ existing as church-community', so all Christian community rests on the equality of all established by God. All this must be said with respect to the perspective from above. But, on the other hand, the priesthood of all believers now also means precisely affirming the concrete dissimilarity of individuals; it becomes part of mutual service, through which one becomes in practice a priest for the other. Thus all we have said above about community of spirit applies here too. If this is kept in mind, then the possible connection between the priesthood of all believers and patriarchalism becomes immediately apparent. The Christian idea of equality does not allow for an egalitarianism but indeed only for the acknowledgment of the particular circumstances. And this is where Paul's patriarchalism, for example, finds its justification. This is the basic difference between the Christian and all socialist as well as idealist ideas of equality. And this in turn points back to the Christian concept of unity of spirit, as it appears in a theological concept of the church.[77]

---

77. When discussing the unity of the church as a 'distinctive attribute', standard Protestant works on doctrinal theology understand it merely as something like the uniting bond. In Roman Catholic doctrine this concept plays a much more significant role (see the encyclical by Pius IX [1864] and the letter by Leo XIII [1896] in Denzinger, *The Sources of Catholic Dogma*, 428–29 and 494–96; also Bartmann, *Lehrbuch der Dogmatik*, vol. 2, sec. 149).[247] Catholic doctrine distinguishes between unitas fidei, unitas cultus, sacramentorum, and liturgica [unity of faith, worship, sacraments, and liturgy] on the one hand, and unitas societatis, regiminis, and caritatis [unity of association, governance, and love] on the other. This means that it is primarily interested in the uniting principle of the empirical church (Papal primacy, see ["'Pastor aeternus' de Ecclesia Christi"] Vatican I, Session IV, "Dogmatic Constitution I on the Church of Christ," July 18, 1870, which describes Peter and the Pope as the "perpetuum utriusque unitatis principium ac visibile fundamentum" ["perpetual principle of unity and its visible foundation"]. Cf., e.g., Adam, *The Spirit of Catholicism*, 39ff.) and seeks to use the unity of the church as the basis from which to derive its uniqueness (katholiké originally meant una sola [one only]). An unusually

---

[247.] In this note Bonhoeffer summarizes Bartmann, *Lehrbuch*, 2:186, which contains the discussion of the concept of the unity of the church in Roman Catholicism, including the reference to a letter by Pius IX, "officii ad episcopos Angliae," and an encyclical by Leo XIII, "Satis cognitum" (Denzinger, *The Sources of Catholic Dogma*, 428–29 and 494–96). The reference to Vatican Council I, Session IV, is to "Pastor aeternus," or "Dogmatic Constitution I on the Church of Christ" (Denzinger, *The Sources of Catholic Dogma*, 451–57).

140   Our intention in everything so far has been to present the church as consisting of *unity, community,* and *individuality;* to describe how these three realities are established by the Spirit in their mutual relations; and thus to contribute to the morphology of the social form of the church as sanctorum communio.

3. The Empirical Form of the Church

a) The objective spirit of the church-community
and the Holy Spirit[249]

The church of Jesus Christ that is actualized by the Holy Spirit is really the church here and now. The community of saints we have outlined is "in the midst of us."[250] This sentence points to the problem of the empirical church involved in the double question of 'history and the community of saints' and the 'communio peccatorum [community of sinners] within the sanctorum communio'.[251]

The empirical church is the organized 'institution' of salvation. Its center is the cult, consisting of preaching and sacrament or, sociologically speaking, the 'assembly' [Versammlung] of its members.[252] This empirical church is a legal body, and restricts its benefits to those who participate in the liturgical ordinances it has laid down. It admits everyone who accepts these rules and thus cannot be sure about the inner disposition of its members; as soon as it is sanctioned by public

---

strong emphasis is placed on the idea of unity in the Russian Orthodox church. The study by Khomiakov, *The Church Is One,* which primarily speaks about the unity of the church, is one of the most powerful and profound texts ever written on the church (see also Arsenev, *Die Kirche des Morgenlands,* 1926, 79ff.).[248] But it, too, really only speaks about the uniting spirit of love.

[248.] This section deals with "The Great Community: Eucharist and Church." [CG]

[249.] On the relation of Holy Spirit and objective spirit, see Seeberg, *Dogmatik,* 2:325ff.

[250.] Cf. Luke 17:21.

[251.] A footnote written into *SC-A* but not printed in *SC-B:* <<It is here within the entire problem of the empirical church that the normative character of basic-relations, which we discussed at the beginning, now becomes evident.>>

[252.] Concerning the term compulsory organization, *Anstalt,* see below, page 253; regarding the concept of church discussed here, see The Augsburg Confession, Article 7 (*The Book of Concord,* 32).

opinion, and perhaps has even become a political force within the state, it must necessarily reckon with the fact that it will also include 'dead members'. It is the "historical result of the work of Jesus Christ" (Seeberg);[253] as such, it manifests the church-community's objective spirit in its being and becoming, in transmitted forms and structures, and in current vitality and activity. We recognized earlier that the *objective spirit* is the new spirit-principle generated by social formation.[254] It has an active will of its own that orders and guides the wills of the members who constitute it and participate in it, and that takes shape in specific forms, thereby providing visible evidence that it has a life of its own; further, it is defined by two dimensions, namely, that of time and that of space, that is, its historical and social effects. It is the bearer of historical tradition and acts by repeatedly incorporating the same and also new individuals into its activity.[255] It would now seem as if this sociological structure, the empirical church, would have to be viewed and analyzed as one type of religious community among others. And yet, from the outset, this approach would totally preclude any understanding of the issue. The empirical church is not at all identical with religious community. Rather, as a concrete historical community, in the relativity of its forms and in its imperfect and modest appearance, it is the body of Christ, Christ's presence on earth, for it has his word. An understanding of the empirical church is possible only in a movement from above to below, or from inner to outer, but not vice versa. Once this has been grasped, however, it is in principle possible once again to define the church as a religious community, namely as a religious community that has really been established by God. If what has been said above about objective spirit is now applied to the church, then we con-

141

[253.] See Seeberg, *Dogmatik*, 2:319f.

[254.] See above, pages 97ff.

[255.] The following passage, up to the end of the paragraph, ". . . impact of the Holy Spirit," reads in *SC-A*:

If we apply this to the church, then we must speak of the dual quality of the objective spirit as bearer of the historical development whose foundation and goal is Christ, and as bearer of the social impact of the church that is effected by the Holy Spirit. The actual church in history claims to possess the Holy Spirit, and to administer effectively the word of God and the sacraments. All this opens up three extensive problem areas: (1) How does the Christ-Spirit of the church act? (2) Is there a logical and material unity of the concepts of the empirical and the essential church? (3) What is the meaning of the Christian 'assembly' for worship; how does effective preaching of the gospel come about?

275

clude that the objective spirit of the church is the bearer of the historical impact of Jesus Christ and of the social impact of the Holy Spirit.[78]

The real church existing in history claims to possess the Holy Spirit, and to administer effectively the word of God and the sacraments. This claim immediately opens up the first major complex of questions: how is the spirit of Christ[256] and the Holy Spirit of the sanctorum communio related to the objective spirit of the empirical church-community?[257]

The sanctorum communio that is moved by the Holy Spirit has to be continually actualized in a struggle against two impediments: human imperfection and sin. To rashly equate these two, either giving imperfection the weight of sin, or regarding sin as mere imperfection, means in both cases avoiding the seriousness of the Christian concept of sin. Related to the problem of the church this would leave only two options. Either one considers the entire sociologically accessible, empirical form of the church as sin,[258] or one regards the empirical church, in Kant's fashion,[79] merely as a manifestation of the nonreal, ideal church of the

142

---

78. See Seeberg, *Dogmatik*, 2:400.

79. *Religion [within the Limits of Reason Alone]*, bk. 3, sec. 4, 91f.: "The sublime, yet never wholly attainable, idea of an ethical commonwealth dwindles markedly under human hands. It becomes an institution which, at best capable of representing only the pure form of such a commonwealth, is, by the conditions of sensuous human nature, greatly circumscribed in its means for establishing such a whole. How indeed can one expect something perfectly straight to be framed out of such crooked wood?" (!) Kant's idealistic scheme had a great impact on theology and has only now been overcome. Cf. Rückert, *Ein Büchlein von [der] Kirche*, 1857, 162f.; Hase, *Gnosis*, 3d ed., 1869, sec. 159; Biedermann, *Christliche Dogmatik*, 1884, volume 2, sec. 935: "The Protestant distinction between ecclesia visibilis and invisibilis [visible and invisible church] . . . actually expresses the contrast between the finite manifestation and the idea of the church." Seeberg's recent use of the concepts of essence and phenomenon of the church (*Dogmatik*, 2:345ff.) is not based on this Kantian scheme; in his view the essence is what is real in the phenomenon, while the phenomenon represents only what is possible. Cf. 346: "The historical church is thus church

---

[256.] The German *Christus-Geist*, literally "Christ-Spirit," is unusual but clearly expresses the parallelism Bonhoeffer intends with *heilige Geist*, the Holy Spirit. [RK]

[257.] *SC-A* contains a subheading that is deleted: The Objective Spirit of the Church and the Holy Spirit.

[258.] See above, page 126, editorial note 12.

future, or shows that the real church is unattainable in this world. Neither of these views does justice to the genuinely historical nature of the empirical church. The first is mistaken because Christ entered history;[80] the church is therefore his presence in history. *The history of the church is the hidden center of world history,*[261] and not the history of one educational institution among others.[262] For the church is Christ existing as church-community [Kirche ist Christus als Gemeinde existierend]. However questionable[263] its empirical form may be, it remains church in this very form, as long as Christ is present in his word. But this means to acknowledge that God intends the nature of the church to be historical, in the sense that it grows to perfection. *The body of Christ is a real presence in history, and at the same time the norm for its own history.* This takes us back to what we said at the beginning of this study about the normative character of the ontic basic-relations. In the sphere   143

---

insofar as it makes it possible for the true or essential church to exist; and the essential church is church because it turns this possibility into reality." Here Kant's view has been completely overcome.[259]

80. Cf. the saying of Tyconius: "If someone believes the Word became flesh, why does he persecute the Word in the flesh?" (*The Book of Rules*, 112f. [trans. altered]).[260]

[259.] The reference to Kant is also found in Krauß, *Dogma von der unsichtbaren Kirche*, 101, where mention is also made of Rückert and Hase. [The parenthetical exclamation point after the Kant quote is from Bonhoeffer.][CG]

[260.] "Liber de septem regulis," Regula VI: "Si credit verbum carnem factum: quid persequitur in carne, *verbum caro factum*" (Migne, *Patrologia Latina*, 18, 54 D). [Tyconius was a Donatist theologian; this explains the context of his question.][CG]

[261.] Added to *SC-A*: "hidden". See Barth, *Romans*, 57: "All history of religion and of the church takes place completely and entirely within the world. So-called 'salvation history' is merely the continuous crisis of all history, not a separate history *within* or *apart from* history. There are no saints among the unholy" [trans. altered]. [See also *CC* 59ff. (*DBW* 12:306ff.), where Bonhoeffer develops the idea of Christ as the center of human existence, history, and nature, and as the hidden center of the *universitas litterarum* (entirety of learning) (281).][CG]

[262.] Deleted from *SC-A*:

In it the synthesis of religious community and sanctorum communio has become a historical reality, and in this respect it is a 'paradox'. It is peculiar to see how the theology of the paradox can argue so unparadoxically at this point. <<See Barth, *Romans*, 341f.>> It apparently fails to recognize that the general paradox between time and eternity formally remains, that real paradox appears only *within* the concrete historical form, not merely *attached to it.*

[263.] *SC-A* reads: imperfect.

of Christian ethics it is not Ought that effects Is, but Is that effects Ought.

This brings us to the obvious flaw in the Kantian concept of the church. The church is not merely ideally, but actually present in history. And yet the church is not only imperfect, but also sinful. Kant, whose concept of 'radical evil' had expressed an insight of Lutheran provenance that led beyond the confines of idealist philosophy, did not make use of this concept in his view of the church. Even though the members of the commonwealth of virtue are imperfect, they are basically good. The Lutheran idea of the *iustus peccator* [justified sinner] remained foreign to Kant.[264]

1. For the Lutheran concept of the church it is crucial that the sanctorum communio always has been a community of sinners and remains so. This fact is ultimately the reason why the Hegelian theory is untenable.[265] Absolute spirit does not simply enter into the subjective spirits, gathering them up into the objective spirit;[81] rather, the Christian church is the church of the word, that is, of faith. Real sanctification is only a precursor of the last things. Here we still walk in faith,[266] which means we can see nothing but our sin, and accept our holiness in faith.[82] The 'word' is the rock upon which the idealist spirit-monism founders; for the word implies that sin still exists, that the absolute spirit has to fight for its rule,[267] that the church remains a church of sinners. These ideas have been brought home to us by modern Luther research as well

---

81. Rosenstock[-Huessy], *Soziologie*, 1925, 1:55: "No genius, no office, no spirit of the people [Volksgeist], and no party spirit in art and science, in competition and politics, has anything directly to do with God's Spirit. *This* spirit is not God. All sociology begins with this bitter insight." Here a problem is tackled that is foreign to the usual kind of sociology.

82. "Preface to the Revelation of St. John (II)," *LW* 35:411 [*WA* 7:421]: "Christians are even hidden from themselves; they do not see their holiness and virtue, but only their unholiness and vice" [trans. altered].

[264.] See Kant, *Religion*, 15ff.

[265.] Regarding Hegel, see above pages 193ff., footnote 68.

[266.] Deleted from *SC-A*: in God's gracious *judgment* of our actions; the focus here is on justification, not sanctification (even though the former is not real without the beginnings of the latter); . . .

[267.] Footnote deleted from *SC-A*: <<This thought has been given special prominence by Heim in his *Leitfaden der Dogmatik*, pt. 2, 38, 55, and often.>>

as the most recent change of direction in theology.[268] They must now be applied to the picture of the sanctorum communio we have sketched thus far.

The difficulty in defining the relation between objective spirit and Holy Spirit springs from the concept of the community of love [Liebesgemeinschaft].[269] This concept shows that it is an illusion to regard the individual and the community as pure instruments of the Holy Spirit. For community with God and human community is broken and renewed over and over again.[270] Among human beings there is no such thing as a pure, organic community life. The peccatorum communio [community of sin] continues to coexist within the sanctorum communio. The Adamic humanity is still present in actuality even though it has already been overcome in reality. Those who are justified have trouble with even the very first steps of the new life.[271] The other is still experienced as a 'You', that is as alien, and as making demands; only in faith in the community of saints is this condition overcome. And it is only the beginning of the new life, an eschatological prolepsis, where the You reveals itself to the I as another I, as heart, as love, as Christ.[272]

Thus the sanctorum communio continues to fall again and again, it comes into being anew, passes away, and comes into being once more, as is the nature of any ethical person as we saw earlier. Yet for the sanctorum communio this movement, its repentance and faith, revolves around a fixed point:[273] the word is what causes the church to break up into the community-of-the-cross, and through the word it is 'built up' to

144

[268.] Regarding "modern Luther research," see Holl, *Luther*, particularly the article "Die Entstehung von Luthers Kirchenbegriff," 288ff., upon which Bonhoeffer relies throughout for his understanding of Luther. The "most recent change of direction in theology" refers primarily to the theology of Karl Barth; see Barth's *Romans*, as well as the collection of his early essays in *The Word of God and the Word of Man*, acquired by Bonhoeffer in the winter of 1924–25 (see Bethge, *Dietrich Bonhoeffer*, 50f.). [See also Bonhoeffer's summer 1925 seminar paper written for Seeberg, "Lässt sich eine historische und pneumatische Auslegung der Schrift unterscheiden, und wie stellt sich die Dogmatik hierzu?" *DBW* 9:305–23.][CG]

[269.] "The difficulty . . . community of love" reads in *SC-A*: The difficulty springs from the concept of the community of love.

[270.] Deleted from *SC-A*: (to a 'society' [Gesellschaft] such a 'history' is foreign).

[271.] "Those . . . life" reads in *SC-A*: The individuals remain egotists; they do not even get beyond the very first beginnings of the new life.

[272.] Added to *SC-A*: an eschatological prolepsis.

[273.] "Yet for the sanctorum . . . point" reads in *SC-A*: Though the sanctorum communio continues to fall again and again, yet its repentance and faith revolve around a fixed point.

276

become the Easter-community. The community of saints as the community of penitent sinners is held together by the unity of the body of Christ. In the church, as in any other community, people repent both for their own sin and for that of the collective person of the community. Now, is this collective person perhaps 'Christ existing as church-community', the body of Christ? Only insofar as God's own self is at work in the act of repentance. It is not the community of sinners but instead the holiness of this very church-community which is 'Christ existing as church-community'. The very fact that as a sinful community the church is nevertheless still holy, or rather that in this world it is never holy without also being sinful—this is what Christ's presence in it means. It is precisely as such a community that is holy in its sinfulness that the church is 'Christ existing as church-community'. If one were to say that sin must be ascribed to the individual but not to the objective spirit of the church, then this would be correct to the extent that the sum total of all wills in the church now has a new direction. But this does not mean that wherever the empirical church-community acts as 'a whole', its action would be an action of the Holy Spirit. This would amount to the Hegelian position, and to adopt it would mean to abandon our monadic social theory.[274] A council is not holier than an individual alone. It was thus not merely imperfection that was a part of the objective spirit of each particular time, but also a great deal of intentional evil; and many times the saying of Augustine seemed to be true that "the church has frequently existed only within a single individual or family."[83] The concept of the objective spirit cannot be developed without sin as a constitutive element. *The reality of sin makes it clear that it is impossible to equate the objective spirit of the church as collective person with the Holy Spirit.* There is, however, a second equally compelling reason.

2. The empirical church lives in history. Just as the individual spirit, as a member of the church, has particular tasks at particular times, so the *objective spirit of the church has an individual character; that is, it is different at any given time.* It gets its character from the historical con-

---

83. *St. Augustine, Enarr[ationes] in Ps[almos]*, 128, 2.[275]

[274.] See above, pages 77ff. and 79, editorial note 60.
[275.] Bonhoeffer here summarizes, rather than quotes, Augustine's position in *Enarrationes in Psalmos*, 128.2, page 1882.

text.[276] But the fact that the objective spirit is part of history necessarily implies that it is fallible and imperfect as far as its understanding and will are concerned.[277] The particular forms the objective spirit assumed in the churches of the past are proof of its individuality, contingency, and imperfection, which cannot be equated with the Spirit of Christ or the Holy Spirit.

3. The objective spirit of the church has perhaps[278] many participants who are not predestined, and they have both creative and hindering roles. This fact seems the most compelling proof that objective spirit and Holy Spirit cannot be equated. For those who are not predestined do not belong to the church; and yet the Holy Spirit is able, through the objective spirit, to use them too as creative instruments, although they remain only instruments, of course, and never become themselves objects of the Spirit's work. The difference between objective spirit and Holy Spirit has thus become quite clear. And yet we must assume that there is a link between them.

The historical impact of the Spirit of Christ is at work in the form of the objective spirit in spite of all the sinfulness, historical contingency, and fallibility of the church; likewise the Holy Spirit uses the objective spirit as a vehicle for its gathering and sustaining social activity in spite of all the sinfulness and imperfection of the individuals and of the whole. All this happens according to what we said earlier about the rule of Christ and the Holy Spirit in the temporal and the spatial spheres. Both assure the church of their presence through nothing else but the word. Here it becomes clear that in order to build the empirical church both Christ and the Holy Spirit make use of the forms of the life of the objective spirit as they exist historically. Thus the objective spirit of the church-community does have its special functions in this service, as we shall see.

Thus we have, on the one hand, the ever-changing, imperfect, sinful, objective human spirit; on the other hand we have the Holy Spirit who bears this human spirit, and is[279] eternally one and perfect, and we

146

[276.] Deleted from *SC-A*: Country, culture, and the particular age will be among the shaping factors.

[277.] Deleted from *SC-A*: though not from the perspective of an eschatological resolution, but as long as there is history.

[278.] *SC-A* reads: certainly.

[279.] *SC-A* reads: the Holy Spirit which is eternally superior; the final word in this phrase was originally 'moving'.

have 'Christ existing as church-community'. The objective spirit is subject to the historical ambiguity of all profane communities, of all socalled ideal associations with all their vanity, eccentricity, and mendacity. But this objective spirit claims and is certain that it is nevertheless Christ's church, that in spite of everything it stands within a church that is built and borne by the Holy Spirit.[280] It is a certainty that is in danger of foundering again and again precisely because of this similarity to other 'religious communities'. Here we have on the one hand the purely historical collective person of the church, and on the other the person of Christ as the presence of God within the church-community; on one side the human 'religious community', and on the other the church-community of the Spirit. And insofar as the former, in spite of all appearances to the contrary and fully aware of its situation, *believes* it is identical with the latter, it believes in the church, the community of saints (see below about 'faith in the church').[281] Thus this identity cannot be historically verifiable. It is 'invisible' and will be visible only in the eschaton; and yet it already has its actual beginning in the present. The objective spirit is bearer and instrument of the spirit of the church of Christ; it has certain visible forms that the Holy Spirit produced and implanted into it. The Holy Spirit thus stands behind the objective spirit as the guarantor of the efficacy of these forms; these forms are preaching and the celebration of the sacraments. But the objective spirit does not bear these forms as one would carry a sack on one's back; rather it is itself sanctified through the load, *it carries it in its heart*. This is of course true only insofar as the Holy Spirit does the carrying within it, for the objective spirit is not the Holy Spirit. But the objective spirit is, according to our earlier definition of the community of love, *both instrument and end in itself*. It is both the object and the means of the Holy Spirit's work, in an interrelated fashion that was described above. This then clearly shows that the objective spirit and the Holy Spirit cannot be equated.

b) The logical relation between the empirical
and the essential church

Our basis for determining the *material* relation between the empirical form of the church and its form in the Spirit was the relation between

147

[280.] *SC-A* reads: a church that is moved by the Holy Spirit.
[281.] See below, pages 272ff.

the objective spirit and the Holy Spirit, or Spirit of Christ. Does what we have found still allow us to speak of the church as one? Can a single concept comprehend the empirical and the essential church both logically and sociologically?[282]

This question first of all establishes the proper relation of the concept of the essential church to that of the Realm of God.[84]

1. Both concepts comprise essentially only those who are predestined[283] (the problem of the donum perseverantiae [gift of perseverance][284] does require a separate theological study and has no great significance here).

2. The material content of both these concepts is identical, namely the subjection of humanity to God's ruling and redeeming will.[85] The

---

84. See Dorner, *Kirche und Reich Gottes*, 1883, and Seeberg, [*Dogmatik*,] 2:334ff.

85. Ritschl's well-known distinction between the Kingdom of God and the church (*Justification and Reconciliation*, 284ff.) is theologically and sociologically untenable. See 285: "Those who believe in Christ, therefore, constitute the church insofar as they express in prayer their faith in God the Father, or are human beings who through Christ are well pleasing in God's sight. The same believers in Christ constitute the Kingdom of God insofar as—forgetting distinctions of sex, rank, or nationality—they act reciprocally from love, and thus call into existence that community of moral disposition and moral value that extends throughout the whole human race" [trans. altered]. How is it possible to separate these two? Is not the new morality possible only in conjunction with prayer? Does faith not already imply action? Is the community of love not inseparable from unity in faith, and the Kingdom of God from God's rule? The Kingdom of God on earth, i.e., the church, is the community that has been placed under the word. It consists of those who repent, pray for one another, and love. As such it is the body of Christ in its entire existence. Ritschl's distinction thus severs two things that belong together.[285]

[282.] *SC-A* reads: materially.

[283.] See Seeberg, *Dogmatik*, 2:340ff.

[284.] God's election includes, according to Augustine, the *donum perseverantiae* [gift of perseverance]. This concept has since been used to denote an individual's assurance of salvation. Also see below, page 279.

[285.] Deleted from *SC-A*: If it is an essential feature of the 'religious community' to incorporate the divine will into human community, then the dual direction, i.e., the vertical and the horizontal, God's rule and God's Realm, remain inseparable in everything that happens within the religious community. Ritschl assumes that his view is backed up by Reformation theology; Bonhoeffer challenges that assumption. His copy of Ritschl's study on Luther, for example, contains the note "Sermon on the Holy Body of Christ 1519" (see above, page 178,

purpose of God's rule is the Realm of God. This Realm includes all those who are predestined; the church, in contrast, includes only those who are elected in Christ as church-community (Eph. 1:4; 1 Peter 1:20). Thus the former exists from eternity to eternity, while the latter has its beginning in history. To speak of a church in the Old Testament would make sense only if this would be understood as the community of those who were expecting Christ.[86] But such parlance would nevertheless be misleading and unnecessarily stretch the concept of the church. "The church is the Realm of God, but in the form ordained for the period between Jesus' ascension and second coming."[87] "The church is the Realm of God which actualizes itself on earth under the constitution of the new covenant."[88] In its visible historical form it comprises many more members than the Realm of God, but in its essence not a single member more. (Rather, a lot fewer members; against the view represented by Hofmann,[89] for example, we assume this to be the case also for the period since Christ.) We prefer to call the church the realm of Christ (see above).[90] [288]

148

---

86. See von Hofmann, *Schriftbeweis*, 1855, 2:2, 67: "Abram's faith through which he became the forefather of the church-community . . ."; also see [*Schriftbeweis*, 2:]97: "What creates community in the Old Testament is the promise that is tied to the people of the law." Cf. [*Schriftbeweis*, 2:]130.[286]

87. Von Hofmann, [*Schriftbeweis*, 2:]125.

88. Seeberg, [*Dogmatik*,] 2:348.

89. Von Hofmann, [*Schriftbeweis*, 2:]128: "[O]nly those who live in the flesh belong to" the church; hence those who have died in faith are not in the church. "Between the ascension and the second coming, the Kingdom of God on earth is present only in the form of the Christian church"—it is an open question, however, whether God sees the Christian church even where we do not see it.[287]

90. See Ritschl, [*Justification and Reconciliation*,] 286ff. and Krauß, [*Dogma von der unsichtbaren Kirche*,] 107f.

[285. *cont.*] editorial note 160). The same criticism of Ritschl also is found in Seeberg, *Begriff der Kirche*, 232ff.

[286.] See the positive assessment of von Hofmann's concept of the church in Seeberg, *Begriff der Kirche*, 226.

[287.] Also quoted in Krauß, *Dogma von der unsichtbaren Kirche*, 107.

[288.] The passage that follows, up to ". . . impurity and imperfection too" (see below, page 222), reads in *SC-A*:

It belongs to the 'essence' of the church to be a historical entity, and it belongs to the 'essence' of every historical community to include not only genuine but also merely

But this realm of Christ, or the church, now exists for us in a con-   149
crete, historical form, and specifically in such a form that is likely to
include nominal members. It exists, in other words, as a *church-of-the-
people* [*Volkskirche*], not as a voluntary church [Freiwilligkeitskirche].
How can a church, which as a human community is by its very nature a
community of wills, be a church for all people at the same time? This is
the sociological way of putting the problem of the empirical church. We
find the solution by reflecting upon the nature of the 'word'. In the

---

[288. *cont.*] nominal members. Does the 'essence' of the church then include evil and dead
members? [Here follows the section that has been converted into footnote 91, page
220: "Roman Catholic theology . . . that was not Protestant."] We must reject such a
view. To have nominal members is not part of the essence of the church-community, but
simply a normal feature of it being a historical entity; it is just like weeds growing in every
field of wheat (Matthew 13) without this being a part of its essence, or just like a white
dress becoming soiled by the dust of the road. Indeed, it is a given that the church as an
empirical phenomenon can be conceived only in this disfigured form; and yet in its essence
it is without any spot or wrinkle (Eph. 5:27).

But in what way do these two churches constitute a unity? The unity is established   277
through word and sacrament. This was Luther's great discovery, <<Seeberg, *Begriff der
Kirche*, takes a consciously Lutheran position when he declares the means of grace to be
the criteria for evaluating different concepts of the church.>> which led him beyond Augustine and allowed him to become the founder of the Protestant concept of the church. The
word that works in history builds "the bridge between the invisible and the visible church."
<<Holl, *Luther*, 305; cf. 299.>> [The note that followed the one citing Holl is preserved
in the published version as footnote 92, pages 220f.] In the word, the gospel is offered
to all those gathered. All have the potential to be struck by the word; all are vocati [called].
But preaching brings about a division within the church. On the one side are those who are
not awakened and remain dead; on the other side are those who are truly moved, the electi
[elect]. The logical point of unity between the empirical and the essential church is thus the
formal unity between possibility and reality that is contained in the word. This is not to say
that all those who potentially belong to the essential church would also in reality belong to
it; those in whom the potential never becomes reality are of course not members of the
body of Christ (against Thomas Aquinas). It belongs to the essential church's nature to
preach and offer the gospel to all; but this is why those who resist, the hypocrites, etc., are
not part of its essential membership. We thus find a logical as well as a material point of
unity between the empirical and the essential church, namely that the latter works through
the former. It follows, therefore, that the latter must not merely accept the fact that it is
tied to a composite entity and regard this as an inevitable fate; rather, it must consider this
fact as its *greatest opportunity*. For the potential is what becomes reality, and the empirical
church ought to be the place where the essential church can shine. This argument provides
the theological justification of the *church-of-the-people* [*Volkskirche*], but also the goal of that
church to move beyond itself and become a voluntary church [Freiwilligkeitskirche] (see
below). *All the historical strength of the church lies in its empirical form*. This is what is overlooked by the despisers of the church's historical nature. Genuine love for the church will
bear and love its inconspicuousness and imperfection too.

preaching of the word, which it carries out and by which it is borne, the sanctorum communio extends beyond itself and addresses all those who might belong to it even potentially; this is part of its nature. From this it does not follow of course that the dead members also belong to the body of Christ.[91] The second argument for a church of the people is the fact that here in history the wheat cannot yet be separated from the chaff; that separation will be evident only on the day of judgment, and is now only being prepared in secret. However, in going beyond itself, the sanctorum communio is at the same time following an impulse back toward the 'real' church, toward the becoming real of what is potential.[290] This means the sanctorum communio, which by its nature presents itself as a church-of-the-people, also calls for the voluntary church and continually establishes itself as such; that is, the sanctorum communio bears the others, so to speak, who have the latent potential to become 'real' members of the church by virtue of the word that is both the author of the church and of the message it preaches. But a potential can be assumed only as long as a person has not consciously rejected it; and even this the church will not necessarily consider as final, so that it will never be possible to ascertain the absence of this potential. The logical and sociological unity of the voluntary church and the church-of-

150   the-people, the essential and the empirical, 'invisible' and 'visible'[92]

----

91. Roman Catholic theology has stated that they do (see quotations from Thomas Aquinas above, pages 163f.). Dead members, according to this view, correspond to the necessary bad parts in the human body. Protestant theology came close to this position when it considered all who had been baptized as members of the essential church. However it did so at the price of introducing an understanding of the sacrament that was not Protestant (Löhe, *Three Books Concerning the Church* [German ed. 1845]; Delitzsch, *Vier Bücher von der Kirche*, 1847; Kliefoth, *Acht Bücher von der Kirche*, 1854; Vilmar, *Dogmatik*, 1874; Stahl, *Kirchenverfassung nach Lehre und Recht der Protestanten*, 2d ed., 1862.)[289]

92. The content of all these pairs is ultimately identical. This is not the place to explore the much-discussed problem of the visibility and invisibility of the church. Recent theology has come to a consensus to eliminate both these con-

----

[289.] The authors mentioned by Bonhoeffer are discussed in Seeberg, *Begriff der Kirche*, 221ff. The view of baptism to which Bonhoeffer refers is found, for example, in August Münchmeyer, *Das Dogma*, 175, and Bonhoeffer's criticism of this position largely follows Ritschl, "Über die Begriffe," 97ff.

[290.] See Seeberg, *Dogmatik*, 2:342ff.

church is thus established by the word; this is a genuinely Lutheran insight.[294] Now, for the church there exists a point in time when it may no longer be a church-of-the-people; this point is reached when it can no longer recognize its 'popular' form as the means to become a voluntary church. But such a step would then be based on practical church politics, not on theological reasons. This shows, however, that the church is in its nature essentially a voluntary church. And yet the historical form of the church as a church-of-the-people is to be counted among its greatest strengths. This is overlooked by the despisers of its

---

cepts in order to avoid misunderstandings.[291] The concept of the invisibility of the church is dangerous mainly because it implies that the visible, i.e., the empirical church, is not church; however, the term invisible is in fact not used here as the opposite of what is visible to the eyes, but to describe the essence of an object, whether it be visually perceptible or an object of thought. The 'essential' church becomes literally visible in the empirical church. Its members are very concretely visible, but only faith sees them in their capacity as members. It makes no sense to speak, as is quite frequently done, of the invisible church becoming visible. The 'invisible' church is visible from the outset. It is proper only to speak of the empirical form corresponding to a greater or lesser degree to the essence. The invisible and the visible church are one single church. Luther says they form a unity like that of body and soul (*LW* 39:70f. [*WA* 6:297]).[292] Such an analogy is acceptable provided it does not lead us to the grave misunderstanding[293] that considers the invisible element to be the souls of the individual believers who are united in the church. The question as to what extent the church is an object of faith will be discussed later. On this point, see Ritschl, "Über die Begriffe sichtbare und unsichtbare Kirche," *Stud. und Krit.*, vol. 32, 1859; "Die Begründung des Kirchenrechts im evangelischen Begriff von der Kirche," *Ztschr. f. Kirchenrecht*, 8, 1869, 220ff.

[291.] "Recent theology" here refers mainly to Seeberg, *Dogmatik*, 2:345ff. Seeberg replaces the concept of the 'invisible' church with the expression of the 'essence' of the church (ibid.). See also Ritschl, "Über die Begriffe," whose views Bonhoeffer largely adopts.

[292.] "On the Papacy at Rome against the Most Celebrated Romanist in Leipzig." [This reference is found in Holl, *Luther*, 299, note 1, which is the likely source of Bonhoeffer's citation. Cf. above, page 164, editorial note 116.][CG]

[293.] See Holl, *Luther*, according to which the "grave misunderstanding" (343, note 3) is a proposition by Sohm who claims, based on his reading of Luther's statement, that the church could, if necessary, lack any external form.

[294.] Regarding the church-of-the-people [*Volkskirche*] and the voluntary church [*Freiwilligkeitskirche*], see Holl, *Luther*, 359. Concerning the origin of the German term *Freiwilligkeitskirche*, see Troeltsch, *Social Teachings*, 340 and 694ff.

historical nature.[295] Genuine love for the church will bear and love its impurity and imperfection too; for it is in fact this empirical church in whose womb grows God's sacred treasure, God's own church-community. Many presumptuous attempts have been undertaken to purify the church,[93] starting with the formation of the perfectionist sects in the ancient church, continuing with the Anabaptists, Pietism, the Enlightenment, and Kant's secularized concept of the Kingdom of God; we can further see it in the beginnings of Count Saint Simon's socialist expectation of the Kingdom of God, in Tolstoy, and finally in the contemporary religious-socialist Youth Movement. In all of these movements we find the attempt to have the Realm of God finally present not only by faith but by sight,[297] no longer veiled within the strange forms of a Christian church, but clearly manifested in the morality and holiness of human beings, and in a perfect solution to all historical and social problems.[298] The fact that God's revelation actually takes place in history, i.e., in a hidden way, that this world remains a world of sin and death, which also means a world of history, and that this history is itself sanctified by the fact that God created, entered, and uses it for God's own purpose—for all this there is a lack of understanding, a lack of love, which alone is capable of recognizing these things. No matter how serious the despisers of the historical nature of our church may act, they are merely playing games if they do not stay with the realities that God intends us to take seriously.[299] The church ought to let the weeds grow in its field, for where should it find the criterion for recognizing them?[300] In love it will thus perhaps tend many a budding life that later

151

---

93. Hirsch, *Die Reich-Gottes-Begriffe des neueren europäischen Denkens*, 1926.[296]

[295.] The phrase "by the despisers of its historical nature" is an allusion to Schleiermacher's *On Religion*. Regarding the context in question, see also Harnack, "Fifteen Questions to Those among the Theologians Who Are Contemptuous of the Scientific Theology" and Karl Barth's reply, "Fifteen Answers to Professor von Harnack" (1923).

[296.] Hirsch, *Die Reich-Gottes-Begriffe*, has the same comments on Saint Simon (17), Tolstoy (19), and the religious-socialists (19f., especially Karl Barth); see also Hirsch's critical conclusion that "according to Paul, the present orders must not be overturned as long as the awaited future of God has not yet arrived" (20).

[297.] See 2 Cor. 5:7. [CG]

[298.] Deleted from *SC-A*: (socialism, economy, war, etc.).

[299.] See above, page 126, editorial note 12.

[300.] See Mark 4:3ff. and parallels.

may become dangerous to it. However, the church will never condemn and judge but remain conscious of the limits of its historical nature.

Love coupled with a profound theological insight into the significance of the historical nature of the church made it difficult for Luther to break away from the church of Rome.[301] We should not allow our historical Protestant church to be easily stolen from us by resentment and theological thoughtlessness.

We have been speaking of *'the'* empirical church. But does this phenomenon exist at all? In a historical perspective, the church consists of many *individual congregations* [*Einzelgemeinden*], and an organization that encompasses them. But can these individual congregations be considered a unity? Unless it is equated completely with the organization, the 'empirical church' seems to be merely an abstraction, or the statistical composite of all individual congregations. The question arises whether such a composite fully exhausts the meaning of the concept of the empirical church. The answer to this question will tell us more about the structure of the sanctorum communio. 152

The New Testament calls individual congregations on the one hand, 'body of Christ', and on the other "regards them as the local actualization of the unity of God's church-community,"[94] since all who adhere to Christ are one body with him. The New Testament thus only poses the problem, but does not provide the answer.[302] Luther emphasized the individual congregation as church-community in the full sense. Nevertheless, he declared: "No one says, 'I believe in the Holy Spirit, one holy Roman church, the communion of Romans, so it is clear that the holy church is not bound to Rome; rather, it extends to the end of the earth. . . ."[95] Zwingli, after adopting Wycliffe's concept of the church and linking it with the Swiss concept of the local congregations [Kilchhöre], coined the term 'universal church' ['allgemeine Kirche'], which denotes

---

94. Von Hofmann, [*Schriftbeweis*, 2:]95.
95. *LW* 39:75 [*WA* 6:300].[303]

[301.] Regarding Luther, see the discussion in Holl, *Luther*, 324f.
[302.] For Bonhoeffer's earlier discussion of the New Testament concept of the church, see above pages 134ff. and 135ff., editorial note 29.
[303.] "Against the Papacy in Rome" (1520).

the church that comprises all individual congregations.[96] This corresponds to our concept of the empirical church, and is born from the insight that the numerous individual congregations do not exist atomistically as isolated units, but must themselves be considered a real unity. The concept of the empirical church as a whole corresponds to a reality, namely the church-community as a whole [Gesamtgemeinde]. This concept is necessary, for it alone is able to express the totality of God's historical will for redemption. In this church-community as a whole, as the 'sum' of all places in which the gospel is proclaimed, there is 'one Spirit', one word; it is one body, real community, sanctorum communio. This fact that all individual congregations belong together has always been more strongly emphasized by Roman Catholics than by us; although they have of course historicized this fact. We do not hold that the empirical church as a whole (e.g., council or general synod) is more than the individual congregations; this would be a complete contradiction of Protestant thinking.[97] But the body of Christ is indeed

153 Rome and Corinth, Wittenberg, Geneva, and Stockholm;[306] and the members of all individual congregations belong to the church-community as a whole, which is the sanctorum communio.[98]

---

96. [Zwingli,] "Ad Carolum imperatorum fidei ratio" (1530): "sumitur [. . .] ecclesia universaliter pro omnibus scilicet, qui Christi nomine censentur" ("For the term church is generally applied to all who belong to the name of Christ").[304]

97. The Eastern Orthodox Church in a distinctive way emphasizes the totality of the empirical church. It considers no individual congregation, and certainly no single individual, as infallible, but only the church as a whole. Thus the function of the pope in Roman Catholic theology is here assumed by the empirical totality of the church: unity and infallibility coincide.[305] The Protestant concept of the church also regards each individual congregation as body of Christ, and thus as infallible.

98. When our church constitution states in Article 4.1 that "the church

[304.] "An Account of the Faith of Huldrich Zwingli Submitted to the German Emperor Charles V, at the Diet of Augsburg, July 3, 1530," 44. The reference to Zwingli is found in Krauß, *Dogma von der unsichtbaren Kirche*, 19ff., esp. 23.

[305.] Regarding papal infallibility and the Roman Catholic concept of the church, see Denzinger, "Dogmatic Constitution 1 on the Church of Christ," 451–57.

[306.] This is an allusion to the International Christian Council for Life and Work, which was initiated by Archbishop Nathan Söderblom and convened in Stockholm in 1925.

Is the body of Christ as a whole thus primarily present in the universal church, so that all individual congregations would be members only of this body? The New Testament says nothing of the kind. The question is also theologically misguided since it understands *the concept of the body of Christ* simply in an organic and physical sense, whereas it in fact expresses the presence of Christ and the work of the Holy Spirit in his church-community. The concept of the body in this context is not a *concept referring to form* but to *function*, namely the work of Christ (concerning the 'body' of the collective person, see above). Christ is fully present in each individual, and yet he is one; and again he is not fully present in any one person, but only all human beings together possess the whole Christ.[99] In the same way, each individual congregation is the body of

---

[Kirche] is built up from the congregation [Gemeinde]," then this describes the relation between the unorganized and the organized corporate association. In this context church neither stands for the individual congregation [Einzelgemeinde] (this follows from 4.2), nor for the church-community as a whole [Gesamtgemeinde] throughout history. When 4.4 states that the congregation must cultivate its ties with the church, it follows that the church is conceived as separable in principle from the congregation;[307] it would be better to replace the very bland term 'cultivate' with a phrase that defines the situation clearly, by stating that the church becomes a meaningless organization wherever the congregation ceases to be its living and sustaining foundation (*Kirchenverfassung der Alten Preußischen Union*, 1922).[308]

99. Holl, *What Did Luther Understand by Religion?* 96f. See WA 20:336: "Fides, magna vel parva habet totum Christum" ("Faith, whether it be great or small, possesses the whole Christ"); and WA 4:401: "nunquam habet aliquis sanctorum totum Christum" ("None of the saints ever has the whole Christ") [*LW* 11:541].[309]

[307.] The preceding passage, "When our church constitution . . . in principle from the congregation," reads in *SC-A*:

But if, as Section 4.1 states, the church is actually built up from the congregation, and this is not intended merely to express its genetic origin, then Section 4.4 should speak not merely of ties—rather, in that case the church ceases to be church when it is not organically built on the congregation. The church constitution is in my view inadequate with respect to a clear definition of the concepts of church [Kirche] and church-community [Gemeinde].

[308.] Cf. [Evangelische Kirche der altpreußischen Union,] *Verfassungsurkunde für die Evangelische Kirche der altpreußischen Union: Amtlicher Text* (1924), section 4.6f.

[309.] "Predigt am Sonntag Quasimodogeniti," April 8, 1526, WA 20:366. *First Lectures on the Psalms* (1513–17), LW 11:541 [WA 4:401]. See Holl, *Luther*, 96f., notes 2 and 3, where both Luther statements are quoted.

Christ, and yet there is only one body; and again it is only the church-community as a whole that can actualize all the relationships within the body of Christ. If the concept of the body of Christ could only be applied to the individual congregation, we would immediately run into difficulties concerning its function as the *smallest sociological unit within the concept of the church*. For even a community of two people—for example, marriage—which has been placed under the word of God and is sustained by God, would doubtless fit this description of the smallest sociological unit, so that, strictly speaking, one would already have to apply to this the concept of the individual congregation; and this would mean that wherever even "two or three are gathered"[310] there would also be the body of Christ. And since the sanctorum communio exists wherever the body of Christ is, one has to regard marriage as its smallest sociological unit. Now, marriage can in fact be a full expression of the sanctorum communio. However, just as each collective person stands, without knowing and intending it, within another, more comprehensive collective person, so the smallest sociological unit of the sanctorum communio necessarily extends beyond itself and has its place within the 'whole' body of Christ; it is in fact merely an individual actualization of that body. It would, however, be wrong to subscribe either to the idea of a priority of the individual congregations over the church as a whole, and thus an atomistic structure of the whole body, or to assume the opposite; this follows from the general principles we derived earlier from social philosophy.

c) Sociological forms and functions of the empirical church

(1) Assembling for worship

A Christian church-community, whether a publicly visible congregation or a house-church [Hausgemeinde], is held together by its *assembling around the word*. The word constitutes the unity between essential and empirical church, between Holy Spirit and objective spirit. The concrete function of the empirical church, therefore, is *worship that consists of preaching and celebrating the sacraments*. Preaching is an 'office' of the church-community, so there must also be an *assembly* since both concepts imply one another. This was axiomatic from earliest Christianity up to the time of Pietism and Protestant Orthodoxy. Only when an indi-

154

[310.] Cf. Matt. 18:19.

vidualistic outlook began to transform this *obvious necessity* into a *psychological* one did it ask about the meaning of the assembly in terms of its usefulness and necessity for the individual. This question reveals a fundamental misunderstanding of the concept of the church-community.[311] It is therefore also completely useless to attempt to respond to it by listing a whole host of internal or external advantages, or moral obligations, which might lead the individual into the church; to do so would mean relinquishing from the very outset the right to have one's own basic premises. Instead, we submit that the very question is inappropriate to the subject matter. To justify this position we can only point to the concept of the church-community itself. Thus a justification for the purpose of the assembly is not lacking altogether; it is not simply an entrenched traditional habit, as one might assume. However, the justification simply lies on a completely different plane: preaching is a divinely ordained activity *of the church for the church.* Since I belong to the church-community, I come to the assembly; this is the simple rationale of those who are assembled. This act is not based on utilitarian considerations, or a sense of duty, but is 'organic' and obvious behavior. Max Weber[100] correctly emphasizes the importance of the congregational assembly in earliest Christianity (in contrast to the prophetic period in Israel). It is here alone that the Spirit is at work and dispenses the charismata [gifts of grace].[312] A Christian who stays away from the assembly is a contradiction in terms. The church-community, united by one word, hears this word again and again while assembled; conversely, *the word that created the church-community again and again calls it together* into concrete assembly. For it is the word *preached* according to the will of God and of the church-community that is the means through which this will is actualized.

Of course, this answer will not satisfy the individualistic inquirer. For cannot each member of the church-community read the Bible on their own, and in private profess that they belong to the church-community, namely the invisible church of the 'conscience' and the 'soul'? What is

155

---

100. *Ancient Judaism,* 291f.

[311.] Individualism is criticized also by Holl in *What Did Luther Understand by Religion?* 96ff., and *Luther,* 300. Holl especially criticizes the Luther interpretation of Ernst Troeltsch's *Social Teachings,* 477ff.

[312.] Cf. Rom. 1:11, 12:6; 1 Cor. 12:4. [CG]

the purpose of the deadly boredom of a publicly visible assembly in which one risks sitting in front of a narrow-minded preacher and next to lifeless faces?

There is no doubt that people who live apart from the assembled community can also belong to the sanctorum communio, namely the sick, or castaways for example. Thus we cannot claim that the assembly would be 'necessary for salvation' as far as the individual is concerned. However, the assembly retains its full significance for the church-community. For those who belong to it also received their faith through concrete contacts with others, through 'preaching' (Rom. 10:17). All other cases that might be conceivable in this context only prove that it is in principle also possible for God to bring human beings under the divine rule without the mediation of the concrete church-community. But this is something that falls outside the scope of this study. We regard the proclamation of the empirical church as the 'word of God' that we are able to hear. And this applies specifically to the historical, parish form of the empirical church. *The assembly of believers remains our mother.*[313] Thus the question why, psychologically,[314] one should stay with the assembly is first of all equivalent to the question why one should love one's mother; if need be, one might answer by pointing to the motive of gratitude. The decisive factor, however, is that Christians will never feel they have outgrown the place of their spiritual birth. They thus seek the assembly not merely out of gratitude for the gift they have already received, but are driven by the desire to receive it ever anew, to be born anew again and again (John 3:3; 2 Cor. 4:16). They know that it is in the assembly that the word of God is preached according to God's will, and that here they will also find God's church-community (Matt. 18:20).[315] In all their solitude as individuals they know themselves to be members of the good shepherd's flock; they know themselves to be part of the historical community of the church, the assembly, from which they have received life and continue to receive it, and in which alone they live. In the assembly *the church-community pledges itself to God*, according to God's

---

[313.] Regarding the image of the assembly of believers as mother, see Isa. 66:12f., 26f.; Luther, *Large Catechism*, 416; and Seeberg, *Dogmatik*, 2:332f.

[314.] Added to *SC-A*: psychologically.

[315.] Deleted from *SC-A*: Certainly it is in their personal, solitary encounter with the word that the individuals experience the storm of God's wrath and grace, of despair and assurance. It is in reverent solitude with the Lord that they bend their knees in adoration.

will; and here *God pledges to be present within the church-community*. The concrete assembly thus has a very specific significance of its own. First, it shows that church is something 'visible', a community of human beings consisting of body and soul; it is not a community of common convictions or based on kindred spirits, but a community of love made up of real human beings. This is what constitutes the historical import of the assembly. Its historical nature, however, is responsible for both *the weakness and the power* that are inherent in the assembly and carry over into personal life. The weakness is (1) the dullness of the assembly about which we could say just as much as the individualists. It is (2) the insight that we remain individuals, Greeks, Jews, Pietists, or liberals, that each of us is completely tied to our concrete condition. But this is also precisely the source of the assembly's strength. Other people next to me who may be completely immersed in their affliction, who may be quite different from me, strangers—they too are evidently willed by God. The utter dissimilarity of the individuals pales into insignificance before the sovereign[316] unity of the divine word. We become aware that one person cannot have anything in common with another, completely alien, unknown 'You', that they fundamentally differ even in the very core of their being. Yet this very insight makes it clear that divine action alone is able to intervene here, that what sustains the community can be nothing but the love given by God into our hearts. Thus one person reminds the other of the God who wants them both in the same church-community. Through the other concrete human being I recognize the glory[317] and power of God's kingship, and from the assembly thus springs adoration and confession of faith in God and God's church-community.

And there is yet another point: in the assembly I am not the one speaking and listening at the same time, as happens when I read the word of scripture on my own; rather, it is another who speaks, and this becomes an incomparable assurance for me. Total strangers proclaim God's grace and forgiveness to me, not as their own experience, but as God's will. It is in the others that I can grasp in concrete form the church-community and its Lord as the guarantors of my confidence in God's grace. The fact that others assure me of God's grace makes the

157

[316.] *SC-A* reads: majestic.
[317.] *SC-A* reads: Through the other human being shines the glory...

church-community real for me; it rules out any danger or hope that I
might have fallen prey to an illusion. The confidence of faith arises not
only out of solitude, but also out of the assembly.[318]

To summarize: *the assembly embodies God's will to use the social connections between human beings to extend God's rule. The objective spirit of the
church-community actualizes this will of God by establishing regular worship.
Assembling for worship belongs to the essence of the church-community.* This is
the objective side. Subjectively, individuals continue to be attached to
the assembly because they *accept that God wills to speak in the empirical
church, and because they are aware that they belong to the church-community
that bears the office of preaching, and is also the recipient of the preaching.*
There is an organic link between the assembly and the life of individuals. It originates from the *gratitude* of the latter toward the mother who
158   gave them their life; it is further based on their love for her, coupled
with the *trust* that she will time and again bestow her gifts upon them;
and finally it springs from the certain hope that in the assembly they
will again and again receive concrete and compelling assurance of
being members of God's church-community, which means being
embraced by God's grace.

Thus far we have understood the term 'assembly' ['Versammlung'] in
the general sense of an assembly for worship, whether *public or domestic.*
Both forms are manifestations of the sanctorum communio, and both
are of completely equal value; and yet we must stress that the former is
more important than the latter. *The local parish church [Kirchengemeinde]
is a piece of the world organized exclusively by the sanctorum communio;* as
such it is unlike the house-church, for example, in which a given form is
renewed by the church's objective spirit. In the *former*, the objective
spirit of the church-community must thus always be active in productive
and formative ways in order to find new forms and to preserve old ones;
in the *latter*, in contrast, there is no objective spirit of the church as such
for it coincides with the objective spirit of the household. The local
parish church will thus always serve as the model for the house-church.
It is also indispensable because, for all its imperfection, it is the guarantor of a relative unity of doctrine. The decisive reason, however, is that
the local parish church is independent of all familial and political ties.

[318.] Deleted from *SC-A*: The most intense struggles are certainly fought through in solitude; and yet it is the concrete assurance received in the assembly that alone provides the firmest
anchor in the storms of personal experience.

As such it is the direct "historical result of the work of Jesus,"[319] and also the source from which the house-churches spring. As such it aims to become universal, and has a commission that transcends every nationality. As such it becomes a serious concrete community, for it includes Jew and Greek, slave and free.[320] As such it stands not only in the world, but against the world as the power of an objective spirit that has a moral will and courageous determination. The public assembly is thus both God's will and act of the church-community, and therefore not only something that takes place between God and the church-community, but also something between the church-community and the world. It is a demonstrative act, 'pointing' to the power of the objective spirit of the church-community, which is borne by the will of God. "That they may become perfectly one, so that *the world* may know that you have sent me and have loved them even as you have loved me" (John 17:23).

It must be considered a backward step when house-churches increase in number at the expense of the local parish churches. This indicates a lack of creativity by the church-community, and a flight from the grav-   159
ity of the historical situation. The growth of both forms ought to go hand in hand.[321] Attempts at church renewal, such as the Pietist community movement,[322] ought to increase rather than sap the lifeblood from the institutional church.[323]

At the beginning we stated that assembly and office are intrinsically linked; now we will examine the meaning of the concept of office in the Protestant sense, and the sociological forms of the various assemblies established by it.

(2) The sanctorum communio as the bearer of the 'office'

The church [Kirche] is 'Christ existing as church-community' [Gemeinde]; Christ's presence consists in the word of justification. But since Christ's church-community is present where he is, the word of justification implies the reality of the church-community, that is, it

---

[319.] See Seeberg, *Dogmatik*, 2:319f.
[320.] Gal. 3:28. [CG]
[321.] Deleted from *SC-A*: and indeed this is what happens in a healthy situation.
[322.] See below, pages 277f.
[323.] Deleted from *SC-A*: Only by mutually enriching each other will both grow and develop healthy forms.

demands an assembly of the faithful. These are thoughts that have already been worked out.

The word is the word preached by the church-community. Is it not the Bible, then? Yes, it is the Bible also, but only in the church-community. Does this mean then that the Bible becomes the 'word' only through the church-community? That is indeed true, namely as the church-community is created only through the word and sustained by it.[101] The question as to what was first, the word or the church-community, is meaningless because the word inspired by the Spirit exists only where human beings hear it, so that the *church-community makes the word the word, as the word constitutes the church-community as church*.[325] The Bible is the word only in the church-community, that is within the sanctorum communio. The word, to be specific, is present in the church-community as the word of scripture and of preaching—essentially as the latter. There is no intrinsic difference between these two forms, for they remain a human word so long as they are not inspired by the Spirit of the church-community. The Spirit is not linked with the word of the Bible like a substance. Thus effective preaching is possible only within the sanctorum communio. Such preaching has the promise that the word shall bear fruit (Isa. 55:11).[326] Praedicatio verbi divini est verbum

---

101. Luther could say that he would invoke the dominus scripturae [Lord of the scripture], that is, Christ, against scripture, if others were to invoke scripture against Christ. *Disp.*, ed. Drews, 12, [thesis] 49.[324]

[324.] In February 1926 Bonhoeffer completed for Holl a paper on Luther's view of the Holy Spirit based on the Drews edition of Luther's disputations: "Luthers Anschauungen vom heiligen Geist nach den Disputationen von 1535–45 herausgegeben von Drews" (*DBW* 9:355–410). [CG]

[325.] Deleted from *SC-A*: This is in line with the principle of transcendentalism. Concerning transcendentalism, see Bonhoeffer, *AB* (*DBWE* 2) 83 and 93f.

[326.] Deleted from *SC-A*: (In the following we can disregard the reading of scripture, <<Luther frequently emphasized that the gospel was originally a "good shout," a viva vox [living word].>> for it entails no other aspects than preaching where the problems are more clearly defined). See, for example, *LW* 30:3 [*WA* 12:259] ("Sermons on the First Epistle of Peter"). The quote about preaching that follows in the published version is from the *Confessio Helvetica Posterior*, or "The Second Helvetic Confession," in *Reformed Confessions of the Sixteenth Century*, 225. [The quote is a heading given in Cochrane's translation, but without a Latin counterpart in Schaff's edition of the Latin text. Luther's description of the gospel as a "good shout" (*Geschrei*) evokes the image of a town crier.][CG]

divinum [The preaching of the word of God is the word of God].[102]
This is not self-evident, for obviously preaching is in essence a product
of the objective spirit of the church-community. And this not only happens to be so but it ought to be this way, because preaching does not
simply repeat the message but says it anew, does not recount the past
but addresses the present;[103] it is so because none of the church-community's members can leave the objective spirit behind. The attempt to
escape is futile. It only makes the situation more confusing; "serve the
moment" (Rom. 12:11) is the great motto of preaching.[104] The objective
spirit, fraught with so much contingency, imperfection, and sin, nevertheless has the promise that it can preach the word of God; it becomes
the *bearer of the social activity of the Holy Spirit*. Everybody who really
hears the word when listening to a sermon becomes acutely aware of the
clash between objective spirit (perhaps especially the 'theology') and
Holy Spirit; nevertheless the listener also recognizes that the Holy
Spirit deliberately seeks to use the objective spirit of the church as its
medium. Of course all this makes sense only on the basis of the *reality* of
the sanctorum communio; for the word has been entrusted to the sanctorum communio—it is both its creator and the instrument of its activity. Where it is present there the word is not without fruit.[329]

But who may preach? Surely only someone who belongs to the sanctorum communio? But how can we as human beings know what God
alone knows? "The Lord knows those who are his."[330] This is the point

---

102. *Confessio Helvetica Posterior*, chap. 1.[327] See K[arl] Barth, "Menschenwort
und Gotteswort in der Predigt," *Zw. d. Zeiten*, 3.2, 1925; "Das Schriftprinzip der
reformierten Kirche," *Zw. d. Z.*, 3.3, 1925; Thurneysen, "Schrift und Offenbarung," in *Zw. d. Z.*, no. 6, 1924.

103. See P[aul] Althaus, *Wesen des evangelischen Gottesdienstes*, 1926, 17ff.

104. I read καιρῷ [time], not κυρίῳ [Lord].[328]

[327.] Deleted from *SC-A*: This is the problem, in my view, which dialectical theology has
tackled most sucessfully. See the essays by K[arl] Barth which deeply penetrate into the subject
matter. The reference to *The Second Helvetic Confession* is found in Barth, "Menschenwort
und Gotteswort in der christlichen Predigt," 119.

[328.] By choosing the Greek for "time" rather than "Lord" Bonhoeffer follows the
Luther Bibel (1912), which reads "Schicket euch in die Zeit" ("Be appropriate to the
times"), and differs from the *NRSV* rendition, "Serve the Lord." [RK/CG]

[329.] *SC-A* does not start a new paragraph here.

[330.] See 2 Tim. 2:19; this phrase is also the title of a hymn by Philipp Spitta
(1801–59), "We Are the Lord's," *Lutheran Book of Worship*, no. 399 [*Evangelisches Kirchengesangbuch, Provinz Brandenburg*, no. 347].

where the church's task and its hope seem impossible. There appears to be only one way out: if the person is perhaps not holy, then it must be the office that is holy; and what follows is—the Roman Catholic concepts of priesthood and office.[331] But this is not a valid option either; for nothing is holy except God's holy will, and our will when it is touched by that divine will. Now we must assume[332] that at any given time there are practicing preachers who, at least at that moment, do not belong to the sanctorum communio. Is their preaching really doomed to bear no fruit? Luther already took comfort from the saying that the Spirit blows at will, and that to be able to preach effectively, that is, to be endowed by the Spirit with this charisma,[333] is something quite different from personally possessing the Holy Spirit internally and being justified and sanctified by the Spirit. Even a Judas[334] may have been able to preach most powerfully.[105] The Protestant church, first of all, trusts the promise in Isa. 55:11, and secondly is aware of the freedom of the Holy Spirit and the charismatic significance of preaching. It can therefore accord preaching the central place in its worship, without relying on the Roman Catholic understanding of office or a sectarian concept of personal holiness. Given the assumption that preaching has the purpose of exerting influence on individual spirits—of bringing them under God's rule and making them members of the sanctorum communio—and if we further assume that it is witness to Christ and not to one's own faith, then we must say that its effectiveness is mediated by the

---

105. Luther, *Disp.*, ed. Drews, 689, theses 41 and 42: "non est negandum miracula fieri posse per impios in fide mortua, praesertim si sunt in officio vel in coetu ecclesiastico, sicut verbum et sacramentum (id est, vita aeterna), quae superant omnia miracula, etiam per Judam Scharioth conferuntur" ["It cannot be denied that miracles can be done by impious men whose faith is dead, especially if they are in an ecclesiastical office or assembly, just as the sacrament and the word (i.e., life eternal), which surpass all miracles, were bestowed even by Judas Iscariot"] [*LW* 34:306]. Cf. [Luther, *Disp.*, ed. Drews,] 730, theses 9–12.

[331.] For the Roman Catholic concept of office, see Bartmann, *Lehrbuch der Dogmatik*, 2:150ff.

[332.] *SC-A* reads: Now it is certain . . .

[333.] *SC-RS*: "In what sense are *we* endowed with charismata?" Regarding the saying recorded in John 3:8 from which Luther took comfort, see "Predigten des Jahres 1535. Nr. 23: 16. Mai," *WA* 41:250.

[334.] "Even a Judas" reads in *SC-A*: These two are therefore not identical. Thus ruthless impostors and villains, even a Judas . . .

objective spirit; for it is obviously possible to achieve a purpose without the inner participation of the person promoting it. That person rather is the channel for two powers, namely the objective spirit of the church-community and that of the Holy Spirit. It is further possible to bear witness to the objective spirit that is alive within the church-community without personally participating in its source, the spirit of Christ. To summarize, it may be the case that a preacher does not belong to the sanctorum communio, and never will belong to it. The fact that this preacher uses, and must use, forms shaped by the objective spirit means that the Holy Spirit is able to use that person as an instrument of the Spirit's own work. The objective spirit not only consists of forms that have become fixed,[335] but, just as much consists of the living power of public opinion, which means, for example, theology, interest in certain problems, or a strong resolve to tackle some kind of practical project,[336] etc. Thus, there is no qualitative difference in this respect between preaching and administering the sacraments. These are the reasons why *the sanctorum communio is able to establish an 'office' of preaching and administration of the sacraments* that it *entirely sustains* by itself, but which is nevertheless *completely independent* from it as far as the actual people who hold it are concerned (this has nothing in common with the concept of office put forward by Stahl, Kliefoth, et al.).[337] On the other hand we can also find no fault with the formula used in the Augsburg Confession VII, "congregatio sanctorum, in *qua*" [communion of saints, in *which*]. It implies that Christian preaching is possible only within the sanctorum communio in which it is rooted.[106] *The*

162

106. Mulert, in his article "Congregatio sanctorum, in qua evangelium docetur," *Harnack Festschrift*, 292ff., has sought[338] to uncover contradictions in the "in qua" ["in which"] that allegedly go back to the very concept of the church put forward by the Reformation. In his view, preaching apparently does not take place within the sanctorum communio but within the empirical church; thus whereas the wording of the Augsburg Confession formula supposedly implies the sanctorum communio to be the more numerous group compared to the group of those who are addressed by the word, in Mulert's opinion it is in fact

[335.] Deleted from *SC-A*: (sacrament).
[336.] Deleted from *SC-A*: (mission).
[337.] See above, page 220, footnote 91. Stahl's concept of office is critcized by Ritschl, "Die Begründung des Kirchenrechts."
[338.] Deleted from *SC-A*: with unnecessary perspicacity it would seem to me . . .

church-community is the bearer of the office; this rules out any possibility of a special status of the office bearer. In the Protestant church there is no theurgy, and no magical authority invested in the office or its bearers. The concept of the *priesthood of all believers* is merely another way of expressing this. The reality of the church-community, which has only one head, namely Christ, protects us from the idea of a spiritual-earthly head, which, as Luther aptly states, cannot exist because he (that is, the pope) obviously would not know those whom he was governing.[107]

Having thus defined the Protestant meaning of the concept of office as it relates to the objective spirit, and having found it appropriate, we have gained a deeper understanding of the organized individual congregation, which is held together by orderly assemblies around the word and the administration of the sacraments. It became clear that empirical church-community, office, and assembly belong together, and thus that God wants to walk with God's holy people on a path that leads through the midst of history.[341]

---

just the reverse. Mulert is preoccupied with the idea of the coetus [assembly], which in fact is not at all applicable here. His later formulation, "congregatio, in qua" [community, in which], does not represent a theological advance.[339]

107. "On the Papacy in Rome," *LW* 39:71f. [*WA* 6:298].[340]

[339.] "does not . . . advance" reads in *SC-A*: does not represent a theological advance, but rather a more superficial conceptuality.

[340.] "How can a man rule something he neither knows nor recognizes? But who can know who truly believes or does not believe? Indeed, if papal power were to extend this far it could take faith away from Christian people and could guide, multiply, and change it as he pleases, just as Christ can" [See "Von dem Papsttum zu Rom, wider den hochberühmten Romanisten zu Leipzig" (1520)]. On this point, see also Holl, *Luther*, 315, note 6, and 337f.; here Holl criticizes the "neo-Lutheran 'concept of office' of the 19th century" (337, note 2).

[341.] In *SC-A* the remainder of the study is structured differently from the published version in the following way:

(3) The Sociological Connection Between the Official Ministerial Acts and the Assembly, the Three Concentric Circles

d) The Church as a Distinct Sociological Type and Its Place within the Sociological Typology—Church and Sect [see below, page 247, editorial note 371]

e) The Individual Form of the Objective Spirit in the Church today
   (1) Church and Proletariat
   (2) Sociology of Contemporary Worship and Pastoral Care [see pages 274ff., editorial note 430]

f) Faith in the Sanctorum Communio and the 'Experience' of the Church

4. Church and Eschatology

(3) The sociological meaning of the cultic acts   163
A more detailed analysis reveals that the various acts of the ministerial office, which are borne by the sanctorum communio, differ with

---

[341. *cont.*] Section 3, which follows at this point in the published version, reads in
SC-A:

**3. The sociological connection between the official ministerial acts and the assembly, the
three concentric circles**

It will now be our task to determine the sociological significance of preaching and sacrament, understood in the Protestant sense, for the assemblies in which they respectively
take place. In my view it seems important to begin this task with a brief analysis of sense
perceptions with regard to their sociological implications. Only the most basic aspects relevant for our purpose can be outlined here. We basically have to consider the aspects of
hearing and touch [SC-RS: "visual too"] since preaching and sacraments presuppose both of   281
these sense perceptions. The sense of hearing is the transmitter of the most profound and
most differentiated insights and emotions of the spirit; this takes place through the signs of
'word' and 'music' (Schopenhauer could describe music as pure idea). Each audible 'sign'
requires the attention of the human spirit. What develops is a system of cognitive relations
to the one who gives the signs. This stimulates the spirit of individuals to their own activity.
They know themselves to be in an exchange of spirit with the one who is speaking, either
disagreeing or approving what is said. The entire personal spirit of a human being is active
here. The tactile dimension—including the sense of taste—is, in contrast, confined to the
realm of sensory perceptions. Here the link between sense perception and mental content
is not essential and intrinsic but merely symbolic and accidental. A word is not symbol but
'sign'. It means something by itself, while tactile contact 'as such' does not mean anything; it
can only become the bearer or symbol of meaning. The former adequately expresses meaning while the latter has to be interpreted in some way in order to be intelligible. In the case
of tactile sense perceptions we experience ourselves to be completely alone with our
'body', which has this perception that it alone is the focus of the experience. In contrast
there is the objective fact that the spoken word is by its nature capable of gathering several
people around itself. Now, to make preaching the focal point in Protestant worship implies
above all that it creates a church-community, which consists of individual hearers and of
members who are to a certain degree intellectually active. Preaching is not captivating a
mass by cultic drama or magical touch. Rather it addresses all individuals in two ways: [SC-
RS: "not sufficient".] on the general intellectual level by demanding that they should mentally engage with what they have heard and thus make the intended intellectual connection,
and on the ethical level by demanding a decision 'for or against'. The Protestant church
addressed by preaching will always remain a church of ethical personalism. It can never
become a 'mass'.
But how is the church-community sociologically related to the preachers? Are they
drawn into its community as inquirers among other inquirers? Or are they bearers of ultimate truth, that is, do they address the members of the church-community as teachers
who answer their questions? Is preaching supposed to be a monologue or a dialogue? Is the
question-and-answer method used in catechesis appropriate not only pedagogically but also
theologically? The answer to this frequently discussed question, which is highly important
for a sociological understanding of the church-community, is unfortunately often one-sided.
It is a specific trait of preachers to be simultaneously inquirers and proclaimers. They have
to seek for answers together with the church-community, and have to form a 'Socratic'

regard to their effects on the sociological structure of the particular church-community in which they take place. We have to distinguish clearly between the community addressed by preaching [Predigt-gemeinde], the community celebrating baptism [Taufgemeinde], and the community celebrating the Lord's Supper [Abendmahlsgemeinde]. It is true that all of these stand first and foremost under the word, i.e., the word that originates within the church-community and is also intrin-sically addressed to it; it is that word which, if it is understood at all, is understood only within the church-community since outside of it it is not even the word of God.

All three modes of the church-community share the same basic socio-logical structure consisting of plurality of spirit, community of spirit, and unity of spirit; and each assembly for worship has to express all of these three modes. But this means that every assembly must in some way seek to express its confession of faith, whatever form this may assume. Nevertheless the sociological differentiation must not be over-looked.

The church addressed by preaching is the mode that depends solely on the word. According to what has been said, it can never be subsumed under the sociological category of audience, that is, an undifferenti-

---

[341. *cont.*] community with them—otherwise they could not provide answers. [*SC-RS*: "to provoke questions".] But they can and ought to provide answers because they know of God's declaration in Christ. They are in the pulpit in order to proclaim the truth, in order to be teachers who impart knowledge to their hearers. To use familiar sociological terms, preaching reveals God's claim to rule in God's church-community. The church is an associa-tion of authentic rule [Herrschaftsverband]. This is the reason why preachers as such do not possess the authority to rule; they have only the word that they speak. In his preaching Jesus combined the authority of his person with that of his message; but this is not the case with preachers. They are themselves members of the erring and sinful church-community, and this results in the sociologically dual nature of the church addressed by preaching. Just as the Christian assembly can only be an assembly of those who together seek answers, so it is its strength that all individuals can learn for themselves from the knowledge and truth that belong to the church-community, and thus become knowledgeable and, in faith, now also possess the truth. Here too it is true that it lies in the very nature of the knowledge of faith that one can possess it only in the continuous quest for the truth, and by continuously acquiring that knowledge anew. Question and answer belong together, not because ulti-mately there is no answer, as Barth suggests, <<See the articles by Barth listed above. Con-cerning this question, see also Lohmeyer, [*Vom Begriff der religiösen Gemeinschaft,*] 4ff.>> but because the concrete answer can be grasped only in faith.

In summary we can say that the church addressed by preaching is a church of ethical per-sonalism; it is a community of people who both question and know, a community that sub-mits to God's claim to authority.

ated, faceless mass [Masse]. It is characteristic of the word to address human beings who are intellectually adult, that is, who are able to make decisions, and to require them to make their own decision on the basis of the word's sovereignty, or that of Christ. The church addressed by preaching is thus personalist in nature; it comprises members who submit to the sovereign claim of the word and also those who reject it.

But what about the church-community in which the sacraments are administered? The Roman Catholic concept of grace leads to a magical concept of the sacraments; infant baptism must be understood as equal to the baptism of adults. But this implies that the Roman Catholic community administering the sacraments has become a 'mass', which formally[342] corresponds to the massa perditionis [mass of perdition], but now is united en bloc in salvation. The fate of original sin, understood in a naturalistic way, is eliminated by a similarly understood physically infused grace.[343] But the concept of the 'mass' is the sociological equivalent to the concept of a force in the physical sense. But is there also such a thing as a Protestant community constituted as a mass [Massengemeinde]?[344] Prompted by the well-founded sense that the 'spirit' withdraws from the masses, Tillich has attempted to uncover a direct relation between the two;[108] he sees the holiness of the formless mass in the fact that it can be given form by the revelation of the forming absolute. But this no longer has anything to do with Christian theology. We know only that holiness of God's church-community that is bound to and formed by the word in Christ. The word is received only by personal appropriation, which is why God's church-community is impelled away from the mass. But Tillich has nevertheless pointed out something important. The church-community must be engaged with the mass; it must hear when the masses are calling for community, such as in the Youth Movement or in sports, and must not fail also to proclaim its

164

---

108. [Tillich,] *Masse und Geist*, 1922.

[342.] Added to *SC-A*: formally. *SC-RS*: only formally.

[343.] Regarding the Roman Catholic concepts of grace and sacrament, see Bartmann, *Lehrbuch der Dogmatik*, 1:299ff.; 2:3ff. and 2:223ff. Concerning original sin, see also the Council of Trent's "Decree on Original Sin" in Denzinger, *Sources*, 246–48; on baptism see "Canons on the Sacrament of Baptism," in Denzinger, *Sources*, 263–64.

[344.] *SC-A* lacks the following reflections on Tillich's *Masse und Geist* up to the end of the paragraph.

word about the sanctorum communio within their very midst. The basic rule, however, remains unchanged: the Christian concept of the church-community is the criterion for evaluating the notion of the mass, and not the other way around.

The Protestant concept of sacrament is necessarily connected with the word, and this fact alone makes is impossible to employ the concept of the mass. Sacraments are acts of the church-community and, like preaching, they unite within themselves the objective spirit of the church-community and the Holy Spirit who is operating through it.[345]

[345.] The passage that follows, up to ". . . discussed above)" (see below, page 242), reads in *SC-A*:

Protestant and Roman Catholic 'baptism' are both infant baptism. <<Concerning the following, see Seeberg, [*Dogmatik,*] 2:433ff.>> But in the former case this cannot imply that the children would themselves receive faith in the sense of a personal appropriation or a naturalistic planting of a seed (as Frank maintains, who in this respect takes up thoughts of Hofmann and thus Schelling's nature philosophy). The act of baptism must be conceived as being effective in a purely objective way, at least in relation to the child. Since we cannot assume that the child is a subject with a will, we have to fall back once again on the concept of the objective spirit of the church-community as the subject that beseeches God's grace upon the child. By promising to serve as an instrument of God's will for the child as soon as the child has acquired mental faculties, the church can baptize the child and give the assurance of divine grace—and of subsequent justification and sanctification; this means practically that parents and godparents really must be serious about the idea that they as members of the church-community raise their children. God uses the objective will of the church-community for God's purposes. Baptism thus is a responsible objective act that the church-community does to the child; and it is effective because it is a means by which God organizes the objective spirit of the church-community according to God's own will, uses it as a means for God's purpose, and thus bestows grace upon the child. The church-community as the community of saints now carries its children like a mother, as its most sacred treasure. It can do this only by virtue of its 'communal life'; if it were a 'voluntary association' this act would be meaningless (see above on 'community'). In this context it even makes sense to speak of a gratia praeveniens [prevenient grace] in baptism, since the child is borne by the church-community according to God's will without knowing or consciously willing it. This means, however, that infant baptism ceases to be meaningful wherever the church can no longer envision 'carrying' the child, where it is internally broken, and where it is certain that baptism will be the first and last contact the child will have with it as a church-of-the-people. The church needs to be *open* for everybody, but must at the same time remain conscious of its responsibility. Only its responsibility before God can prompt it to close its doors; but here it must be recognized early enough where a church is no longer a church-of-the-people [Volkskirche], but has in fact become a missionary church [Missionskirche]. The charge to carry the children must be a serious admonition for the church-community with respect to its children's programs and Sunday school, and especially for confirmation classes. To understand baptism as an act of the church-community means challenging any Protestant use of the concept of the masses. Baptism incorporates the entire range of the empirical church since it defines that range. (The question whether

Protestant *baptism*, like the Roman Catholic ritual, is infant baptism. But since the children do not themselves receive faith, even as fides directa [direct faith], and the sacrament nevertheless demands faith, we must conclude that the subject that receives the sacrament in faith can only be the objective spirit of the church-community. Through baptism it incorporates the child in faith into itself; but since the whole church-community is present wherever one of its members is, it follows that the faith of the child is that of the whole church-community. Baptism is thus, on the one hand, God's effective act in the gift of grace by which the child is incorporated into the church-community of Christ; on the other hand, however, it also implies the mandate that the child remain within the Christian community. Thus the church-community as the community of saints carries its children like a mother, as its most sacred   165
treasure. It can do this only by virtue of its 'communal life'; if it were a 'voluntary association' the act of baptism would be meaningless.[346] This means, however, that infant baptism is no longer meaningful wherever the church can no longer envision 'carrying' the child—where it is internally broken, or where it is certain that baptism will be the first and last contact the child will have with it.[347] The church needs to be *open* for everybody, but must at the same time remain conscious of its responsibility. Only its responsibility before God can prompt it to close its doors; but here it must be recognized early enough where a church is no longer a church-of-the-people, but has in fact become a missionary church [Missionskirche].[109] To understand baptism as an act of the

---

109. It is against this background that confirmation instruction gains its special significance. For it—not the confirmation itself—is the means by which the church fulfills the responsibility that it took upon itself in baptism. But since confirmation classes essentially are held with confirmation in mind, the nature

[345. *cont.*] all those who have been baptized belong to the body of Christ has been discussed above.) As much as infant baptism is the means for making the church a church-of-the-*people* [*Volks*kirche], so, above all, it must be understood as preparation for a real *church*-of-the-people [*Volks*kirche], that is for a church-community that consists of persons who exercise their own will.

What follows in *SC-A* is the text that is now footnote 109: It is against this background . . . at the same time.

[346.] See above, page 90.

[347.] The views on infant baptism expressed here correspond almost literally to Seeberg, *Dogmatik*, 2:433ff., esp. 435.

church-community means to challenge a Protestant use of the concept of the mass. Baptism incorporates the entire range of the empirical
166 church since it defines that range. (The question whether all those who have been baptized also belong to the body of Christ has been discussed above.)[110]

Whereas *infant baptism* comprises *all those who potentially* belong to the church, *the sacrament of the Lord's Supper*[111] gathers all those who are[351] serious about submitting their will to God's rule in the Realm of Christ. The Lord's Supper is given to the sanctorum communio as an act that symbolizes God's effective will for community. Like the word, it

---

of both is, in my view, misunderstood. Both in the present and the past confirmation has been largely understood as the moment of a young person's commitment to the faith of the church. In my view, such an understanding of confirmation does not do justice to what the church-community as such can do. For in baptism it pledges to raise and instruct the children in the Christian faith, but it cannot pledge to bring them to a free profession of their own faith. Rather, in their confirmation the children attest to having been instructed by the church-community and thus express their gratitude toward it. The church-community, in turn, vows for a second time to accept them, now as members who have already been instructed and who carry within them the first beginnings of their own voluntary acceptance. It prays for them and knows itself to be fully responsible for their lives. They are *confirmandi* [to be confirmed], not *confirmantes* [confirming]. If one were to insist on a commitment by the children, one could find this only in the fact that they express their desire to stay in contact with the church-community. Confirmation is thus in essence the pledge and prayer of the church-community for those of its children it has instructed, and perhaps a commitment by the children to the church-community; for honesty's sake one cannot demand more at this stage. But this does not mean to surrender the *confessional character* of the church altogther. Rather, the first participation in the Lord's Supper should be seen as the act of the first voluntary profession of faith; and this is why it is inappropriate to celebrate confirmation and the Lord's Supper at the same time. (On this issue I agree with L[udwig] Thimme, *Kirche, Sekte und Gemeinschaftsbewegung*, 1925, 300.)[348]

110. See also Münchmeyer, *Das Dogma von der sichtbaren und der unsichtbaren Kirche*, 1854, 114. An excellent critical review of the book is provided by Ritschl, "Über die Begriffe."[349]

111. See Althaus, *Communio sanctorum*, 75ff.[350]

[348.] In *SC-A* this note follows the text cited above on page 240f., editorial note 345.
[349.] Also see above, pages 220f., footnote 92.
[350.] Footnote 111 has been added to *SC-A*.
[351.] Deleted from *SC-A*: really.

is real only 'within' the sanctorum communio (in qua [in which]),[352] which means it is part of the constitutive activity of the church-community and is of the greatest significance for its sociological structure. The efficacy of the Lord's Supper is secured like that of the word.

The Lord's Supper is (1) God's gift to every individual. Its sensory nature cannot be ignored. With the same clarity and vividness that it encounters a person, the Lord's Supper demands a decision and promises a gift.[353] The structure of the tactile sensory perception[354] assures individuals of the gift as well as the task being addressed to them personally—not only in spirit but also in body.

The Lord's Supper is (2) also, and to an even greater extent, a gift to the church-community. Christ's presence in spirit is not merely symbolic, but a given reality. Christ becomes alive in the believers as church-community. This means the gift has two aspects: *Christ gives community with himself,* i.e., his vicariously suffering unto death is my benefit; and *Christ gives the church-community,* i.e., he renews it, thus giving it to itself. Christ gives to each member the rights and obligations to act as priest for the other, and to each Christ also gives life in the church-community; it is Christ's gift that one member is able to bear the other and to be borne by the other. By the act of self-giving, Christ gives us the obligation and the strength to love one another. That Christ is present, and that the church-community is the body of Christ, already imply that Christian love is established as well. These two are not related as a sequence, even though from a temporal perspective it may appear that way. In substance Christ's presence means community with God through Christ and realization of the church-community as bearer of the individuals. Christ's priestly work becomes the basis for our own. 1 John 3:16 expresses this clearly, as does 1 Cor. 11:26: "as often as you eat this bread and drink this cup, you proclaim[112] the Lord's death." Just as the

167

---

112. Indicative! Καταγγέλλετε [you are proclaiming]; cf. Schmiedel's commentary on this verse.[355]

[352.] See the Augsburg Confession, Section 7: "The church is the assembly of saints in which the Gospel is taught purely and the sacraments are administered rightly" (*The Book of Concord*, 32).

[353.] Deleted from *SC-A*: It encompasses the totality of the gospel's demand and gift.

[354.] Regarding the structure of tactile sense perception, see above, page 236, editorial note 341.

[355.] See P. W. Schmiedel, "Die Briefe an die Thessalonicher," 160.

sacramental act combines both, so there is also an inner connection. Everything we said above about community of spirit[113] has its source in the Lord's Supper. In the writings cited above, Luther elaborates most clearly on the *gift and miracle of the church-community* in the Lord's Supper.[357]

But the sociological significance of administering the Lord's Supper is not fully grasped if it is not also understood as (3) *a human action before God*. A church-community confessing its faith comes before God and, symbolically expressing what happens to it, gathers as the most intimate kind of community[358] around one loaf and one cup. This free gathering together to eat from the table of the altar is not a self-chosen but rather an obedient symbolism, and *thus it has the warrant that God will act in it*. This obedient symbolic action of the freely participating community defines its difference from the church addressed by preaching. Here the decision brought about by preaching becomes a visible action, and a confession of faith not only in God's grace but also in God's holy church-community. The church-community addressed by preaching thus becomes the necessary precondition for the church-community celebrating the Lord's Supper; and the latter, as a church confessing its faith, is thus by nature smaller than the former. It is therefore not the case, as is often assumed, that the church-community is constituted only in the community celebrating the Lord's Supper; this already takes place in equal measure through the preached message. What is decisive in the Lord's Supper, however, is that here the church-community identifies itself as such by an obedient symbolic action in a publicly[359] visible form, and that God visibly recognizes it as such.

168   Two current problems call for our attention. First, there is talk about

---

113. Hollatz's notion that the influxus Christi [inflowing of Christ] upon the believers consists in creating the most intimate community is apparently based on the Lord's Supper. *Examen theologicum acroamaticum*, 4:1293.[356]

[356.] See the exposition of the theology of Hollatz by Seeberg, *Begriff der Kirche*, 154, where the reference just mentioned is also cited.
[357.] See above, pages 165ff. See esp. Luther, *LW* 35/1:49–73, "The Blessed Sacrament of the Holy and True Body of Christ" [*WA* 2:738ff.].
[358.] Deleted from *SC-A*: eating together as a community of brothers and sisters.
[359.] Added to *SC-A*: publicly.

core-communities [Kerngemeinden][114] whose members meet within the congregation on regular church occasions or informally, not least for the Lord's Supper; this practice claims as its basis Luther's famous Preface to the German Mass of 1526. Here Luther speaks of establishing small private gatherings for worship for those who "seek to be Christians in earnest";[115] these gatherings would include prayer, scripture reading, receiving the sacrament, as well as exercising church discipline including excommunication. Luther had already expressed similar ideas as early as 1522.[116] In both instances it is clear that Luther is not talking about the sanctorum communio becoming visibly manifest through such actions, but rather about seriously committed Christians, so that the idea of a core-community is not equated with that of the 'essential church'. This, however, is the grave danger that is almost inevitably inherent in this concept of a core-community. The core-community cannot be separated from the empirical community of the church [kirchlichen Gemeinschaft] but is, in fact, just that itself. If, in spite of this, one insists on a fundamental distinction, then this amounts to sectarianism [Rotterei].[362] We shall thus be well advised to use the concept of the core-community with caution, and likewise the practice itself, which religiously is just as important as it is dangerous.[363] A church celebrating the Lord's Supper is the empirical church and nothing else; it is not the sanctorum communio in its pure form.

¶Second, it has been deplored that urban congregations celebrating the Lord's Supper are faced with the unfortunate fact that participants

---

114. G[erhard] Hilbert, *Ecclesiola in ecclesia*, 2d ed., 1924. Thimme, [*Kirche, Sekte und Gemeinschaftbewegung,*] 254ff.

115. *LW* 53:61ff. [*WA* 19:72ff.][360]

116. *WA* 2:39.[361]

[360.] "The German Mass and Order of Service," *LW* 53:61–90 [*WA* 19:72–113].   284

[361.] "Appellatio F. Martini Luther ad Concilium" (1518).

[362.] Concerning the concept of sectarianism [*Rotterei*], see Luther, "The German Mass and Order of Service" (1526), *LW* 15:61ff. [*WA* 19:72ff.]: "However, I will not go beyond the two ways I have indicated, and will publicly before the people help to promote the kind of worship that includes teaching the youth, inviting and prompting others to faith, and preaching, so that Christians who take the word seriously will on their own accord come and also stay together; for if I were to try to implement it as my own idea, it might turn into sectarianism. For we Germans are a wild, uncultured, and chaotic people with whom it is not easy to do anything unless we are driven by the most severe hardship" (75). See also Luther, *Large Catechism*, Article 3 (*The Book of Concord*, 415ff.).

[363.] *SC-A* begins a new paragraph here. *SC-RS*: "see Luther himself".

do not know one another; this situation allegedly diminishes the weight placed on Christian community and takes away from the personal warmth of the ceremony.[364] But against this we must ask,[365] is this very kind of a church-community not itself a compelling sermon about the significance and reality of the community of saints, which surpasses all human community? Isn't the commitment to the church, to Christian love, most unmistakable where it is protected in principle from being confused in any way with any kind of human community based on mutual affection? Is it not precisely such a community that much better safeguards the serious realism of the sanctorum communio—a community in which Jew remains Jew, Greek Greek, worker worker, and capitalist capitalist, and where all are nevertheless the body of Christ—than one in which these hard facts are quietly glossed over? Wherever there is a real profession of faith in the community of saints, there strangeness and seeming coldness only serve to kindle the flame of the true fire of Christ; but where the idea of the sanctorum communio is neither understood nor professed, there personal warmth merely conceals the absence of the crucial element but cannot replace it. This is why celebrations of the Lord's Supper in an urban setting are so[366] beneficial, a fact that should not be ignored in the sermon preceding the sacrament. Only because the type of sermon currently still preached on such occasions was developed before the era of the large cities, because the sociological phenomenon of the large city is not understood, and because the pastor does not become an urbanite to the urbanites, are these sermons for the most part so appallingly out of touch with the contemporary situation.

To summarize, the word is the sociological principle by which the entire church is built up. It is the word by which the church is built up, both in numbers and in its faith. Christ is the foundation upon which, and according to which, the building (οἰκοδομή) of the church is raised (1 Corinthians 3; Eph. 2:20). And thus it grows into a "holy temple of God" (Eph. 2:21),[367] and "with a growth that is from God" (Col. 2:19), "until all of us come to maturity, to the measure of the full stature of

---

[364.] See Thimme, *Kirche, Sekte und Gemeinschaftsbewegung*, 261: "The danger of blurring the dividing line also becomes evident on church occasions when the Lord's Supper is celebrated en masse; this is nothing but a prostitution of what is most sacred."

[365.] "But against this we must ask" reads in *SC-A*: With this view I can agree only in part.

[366.] Deleted from *SC-A*: tremendously. *SC-RS*: "?"

[367.] *NRSV*: "holy temple in the Lord." [CG]

Christ" (Eph. 4:13), and in all this growing "into him who is the head, into Christ."[368] The entire building begins and ends with Christ, and its unifying center is the word. Whereas baptism signifies the will of the church-community in its most comprehensive form to spread God's rule, which for us implies the fact of a *church-of-the-people*,[369] the church addressed by preaching consists of those who are personally faced with the decision whether to accept or reject God's gift, and is thus both a *church-of-the-people and a voluntary church*. In the Lord's Supper the church-community manifests itself purely as a *voluntary* and as a *community confessing its faith*, and is summoned and recognized by God as such. It is not a manifestation of the pure sanctorum communio, however; rather it is the smallest of the three concentric, sociologically distinct circles, and is both the source from which all effectiveness of the church-community springs, and the focal point into which all its life flows. This duality is what constitutes its vitality, which is the vitality of the church, in that it is simultaneously the aim and the instrument of God's work.[370]

170

(4) The sociological problem of pastoral care[371]

Within the context of the empirical-historical church the relation of one member to another now appears in a new light; this means we must turn our attention from the problems of worship to the sociologically distinctive problem of pastoral care.[372]

[368.] Eph. 4:15. [CG]

[369.] In *SC-A* Bonhoeffer added and then crossed out the following footnote: <<The act of baptism also calls for a confession of faith; this is why it must be made on behalf of the child who is baptized.>>

[370.] In this context, see the exposition of Augustine's concept of church and sacrament by Seeberg, *Dogmengeschichte*, 2:437ff: "The *sanctorum communio* is the purpose and content, the *communio sacramentorum* the means and form" (470). Ritschl, "Über die Begriffe," 79, characterizes Zwingli's concept of the church as one of the concentric circles, even though he claims Zwingli's designation of these circles to be somewhat inconsistent. Concerning the relation between voluntary church and church-of-the-people in Luther's theology, see Holl, *Luther*, 358f.

[371.] *SC-A* continues with the section: *d)* The Church as a Distinct Sociological Type, and Its Place within the Sociological Typology—Church and Sect [see below, pages 267ff.]. The section entitled "(4) The Sociological Problem of Pastoral Care," which instead follows in the published version, was in *SC-A* originally part of the section entitled e) The Individual Form of the Objective Spirit in the Church Today, (2) The Sociology of Contemporary Worship and Pastoral Care [see below, pages 274ff., editorial note 430]. Regarding the original sequence of the contents in *SC-A*, see above, page 236, editorial note 341.

[372.] "Within the context . . . pastoral care" reads in *SC-A*: On the basis of the concept of

The relation of pastor (which means, of course, of every Christian) to church member is twofold. The pastor is, on the one hand, a member of Christ's church-community endowed with every priestly right and duty and, on the other hand, 'another believer', who in the last resort cannot know anything of significance about me. *Protestant pastoral care thus falls into two categories: 'priestly' and 'advisory'.*[373] The meaning and content of the former is evident from the concept of the church-community already discussed above.[117 [375]]

The concept of the advisory pastor, however, presents a new problem. To state the question in general terms: what does it mean for one Christian to have the example of another's faith? What help is the "cloud of witnesses" (Heb. 12:1) to individuals who have to fend for themselves? What use are the examples and role models? What is the significance of the history of the church, and the tradition? For a Protestant understanding, all of these questions are in a profound sense identical. It is not only Christ who is both donum [gift] and exemplum

---

117. It should be added that I consider it the most important task for today to make private confession once again a living source of strength for the church-community. In it one person encounters the other as a priest by virtue of Christ's priesthood, and as the church-community that intercedes and forgives sins. That such an act takes place not only in the setting of public worship, but amidst the distress and anguish of a concrete encounter between two persons, is of great importance for the understanding and experience of the Christian concept of community. In this regard it would be well to heed Löhe's urgent appeal in *Three Books Concerning the Church,* Book 3.[374]

[372. *cont.*] the church just developed, the problem of *pastoral care* now also proves to be sociologically unique.

[373.] The governing idea of this pastoral counseling is advice (*Rat*), not the nondirective psychological counseling widespread in twentieth-century America. On the type of advisory counseling done by Karl Bonhoeffer, see Clifford Green, "Two Bonhoeffers on Psychoanalysis." Also see Sabine Bobert-Stützel, *Dietrich Bonhoeffers Pastoraltheologie.* [CG]

[374.] See Löhe, *Three Books Concerning the Church,* 191ff.: "Above everything else, *the center of pastoral care was overlooked, namely personal confession.* Since personal confession, the examination connected with it, and personal absolution have been abandoned, the pastor is deprived not only of a dignified, quiet, secluded, and safe *place* for pastoral care, but also of a protected and sacred *relation* to the penitent" [trans. altered]. [See *LT (DBWE* 5):108–18 for Bonhoeffer's account of the theology and practice of personal confession at Finkenwalde].[CG]

[375.] *SC-A* continues with the text of footnote 117.

[example][376] for us human beings, but in the same way also one human being is so for another. Every role model and example, and all tradition   171 to which one might appeal, vanish the moment a human being stands before God; everyone must decide for themselves what they have to do.[377] How is it then that Luther again and again emphasized that, when faced with an important decision, it is necessary for one person to seek the 'counsel' of another?[118] And the same is true of Kierkegaard, who spoke like no other about the individuality of human beings.[119] Both men have remained mindful of the concrete social-historical context within which a human being is placed. We are in fact surrounded by role models, whom we ought to use, not by handing over to them the responsibility for our own actions, but by having them 'give us the facts' on the basis of which we then make our own free decision. God has made it possible for human beings to seek counsel from others; it would be presumptuous folly if one were not to accept this offer. Looking back on a history that testifies against them must give all individuals cause to think, unless they have no conscience. This is what made the struggle against Rome so difficult for Luther.[379] People ought to use all opportunities that can help them make the right decision; this is God's will. And to this end the community of the local congregation [die Kirchengemeinde], the 'counsel of the neighbor', in short, the fact that we live in sociality, is of the most momentous significance. The two types of pastoral care we mentioned must thus be sharply distinguished: the former expresses the *absolute significance of one person for the other*, as follows from the concept of the church. The latter speaks about the *relative significance of one person for the other*, as follows from the

---

118. *WA* 2:470.[378]

119. H[einrich] Barth, "Kierkegaard, der Denker," in *Zw. d. Z.*, 1926, no. 3, 204.

[376.] See, for example, Luther, *Disputationen*, 392: "Ita Christus proponitur ut donum seu sacramentum et exemplum" ["Thus Christ is set forth as gift or sacrament, and as example"].

[377.] Deleted from *SC-A*: Everything others recommend is merely of relative value.

[378.] Bonhoeffer seems to refer to Luther's "The Blessed Sacrament of the Holy and True Body of Christ" (1519) [*LW* 35:45–73 (*WA* 2:738–58)], not to Luther's "Lectures on Galatians" [*LW* 27:153–410 (*WA* 2:445–618)], which is cited in error (either Bonhoeffer's own or the typesetter's) in footnote 118 above.

[379.] Deleted from *SC-A*: (Here we once again encounter the concept of the relative value of history.) [See above, pages 219ff. and 269, editorial note 429.]

historicity of human beings. To overlook this distinction is to misunderstand the entire Protestant concept of the church. It once more reveals the difference between church and religious community.[380]

172   *d*) Authority and freedom in the empirical church[381]

The church rests upon the word.[120] It is the absolute authority that is present in the church. The word is of course present only within the word of the church; but in this form of a representative and relative authority it is nevertheless always the critical standard for the church, which now also serves as its guide. The absolute authority of the word demands absolute obedience, that is, absolute freedom; the relative authority of the church calls for relative obedience, which means relative freedom. What is irritating in this context, however, is merely the idea of the relative authority of the church, and the relative constraint and freedom of the individual in relation to it. This seems to threaten freedom of conscience and to run counter to Protestant thinking. And yet it is precisely acknowledging a theological necessity for the idea of the relative authority of the church that draws the line between the Reformation gospel and all kinds of unrestrained religious enthusiasm [Schwärmertum]. We hear the word of God through the word of the church, and this is what constitutes the authority of the church. The burden of the word laid upon the church forces it to assume responsibility not only for preaching but for speaking authoritatively, especially on all matters that concern preserving the purity of the word it preaches,

---

120. See K[arl] Barth, [*Die christliche*] *Dogmatik*, 1, secs. 21 and 22.

[380.] Deleted from *SC-A*:

How we might provide pastoral care in the church-community today is hard to imagine. At any rate it will become possible only when the Protestant concept of the church is understood. Especially the former type of pastoral care is not possible at all unless there is a recognition of Christ's presence within the community of saints. But on the other hand it is particularly the pastoral contact among church members through which the idea of the church-community is concretely grasped. It might perhaps help here to provide a regular opportunity for personal confession, but of course only if the church at large finally decides to clearly instruct the local church congregations about their own nature.

[381.] This passage is not found in *SC-A*. Bonhoeffer's papers include a three-page handwritten draft of this section that is almost identical to the published version; see *NL* A 17,1. See Barth, *Die christliche Dogmatik*, 473ff.

such as the creed, theology, exegesis, and liturgical order—there actually were synods at one time that talked about substance, and discussed theology! In addition, the church ought to speak authoritatively about its position on current events and the world at large; but of course only after these theological issues have been addressed clearly and unequivocally, for otherwise everything else would be without a foundation. If the church, however, is unable to speak authoritatively, then it still may have recourse to a qualified silence[382] that is fundamentally different from an unqualified disregard and inattention.[383] But once the church has spoken authoritatively on, let us say, what it considers to be legitimate Protestant doctrine, then I as a theologian—and every Protestant Christian is a theologian[384]—have only a relative freedom with respect to this matter, within the framework of what the church has declared; or conversely, I am relatively bound with respect to my thoughts on theology, my creed, and so on. I owe relative obedience to the church; it has the right to demand a sacrificium intellectus [sacrifice of intellect], and on occasion perhaps even a sacrificium conscientiae [sacrifice of conscience]. This relative freedom becomes absolute only when it is no longer my uncontrolled intellect, my insubordinate emotion and experience, but really the absolute authority of the word of God that confronts me and demands my absolute obedience, my absolute obligation. Then relative freedom becomes absolute, and only then can the relative obligation to the church be broken, that is, if it stands in the way of my absolute commitment to the word. If this were not so, the theologically justified principle of social equality would be invalidated, the Christian idea of the church-community would consequently be destroyed, and we would thus subscribe to Roman Catholic concepts of church and authority. The councils and synods do have relative authority and ought to prove and assert this authority most vigorously and emphatically. They ought to state plainly and clearly where they stand with regard to the Bible, doctrine, the creed, and Christian teaching; then there will

173

[382.] See Bonhoeffer's reference to the *disciplina arcani* (discipline of the secret) in his Finkenwalde lectures, *DBW* 14:549ff., and in *LPP*, 281, 286, 300. [CG]

[383.] See Barth, *Die christliche Dogmatik*, 489f., on the creed as a *qualified* effort to make contact, and 498f. on the concrete *authority* of the church's public profession as the exercise of its prophetic office.

[384.] See Bonhoeffer's graduation theses, Thesis 3, in *DBW* 9:477; see also the reference in footnote 9 on that page to notes from Barth's lectures. [CG]

no longer be any need for them to lament about the world's indifference. But the church must know that its authority remains derivative and representative. It remains for God alone to know when the moment has come when an individual within the church is forced to oppose its authority. This turning against the church's authority can at any rate only be an act of supreme obedience that is most deeply committed to the church and the word within it, but never a merely capricious act.

e) The church as a distinct sociological type,
and its place within the sociological typology[385]

The image of the church just outlined must now be related to our earlier definitions of the nature of sociological relations. What is at issue here is thus not the question of origin but the problem of essence.[386]

We found that two trains of thought converge in the concept of the church, namely that it is established by God, and yet is an empirical[387]

174   community like any other. This makes it more difficult to identify it as a sociological type. Such an identification seems nevertheless possible.

1. It would appear that the image of the church as an organized type of social formation can be classified sociologically under the concept of

---

[385.] Deleted from *SC-A*: —church and sect. Regarding the placement of this passage in *SC-A* see above, page 236, editorial note 341.

[386.] Deleted from *SC-A*:

We have already stated above that we are unable to say anything that could claim to be of more than hypothetical value about the question of how religious communities come into being. But we also felt that this kind of question, not being specifically sociological but rather historical, had to be excluded from our study.

'Religious community', understood as the community (in the general sense) which submits to the primordial will, is adequately defined by its typical practice of deriving all communal norms from the deity. It is by necessity an association of authentic rule [Herrschaftsverband], at least when viewed solely from a sociological perspective. But this does not yet assert anything about the social basic-relations, nor does the statement that religious community is based on social forms that are specifically communal in nature (such as the family). Frequently a genetic description approximates a portrayal of the phenomenological facts, as has already been indicated, so that it would seem safe to understand the religious house community also religiously as a community arising from a collective basis;

286   this is especially so in the case of primitive societies, since there the house community is in most cases valued more highly than the individual, and the public life of the community is also tied to religion. However, the social basic-relations are sociologically visible only in a concrete form of community, developed according to its own principles whether in *doctrine, cult,* or '*church*' *organization.*

[387.] *SC-A* reads: human.

'*society*' ['*Gesellschaft*']. A society, according to the definition above, is based on a multiplicity of atomistic wills. It is organized as a means directed toward an end. Admission to a society must be a formal act. Its constituitive element is the contract. The church as a sociological type can be conceived according to two subcategories within the society type, namely that of an *compulsory organization* [*Anstalt*] and that of *voluntary association* [*Verein*].[121] The sociological difference between these is the fact that the former, by its nature, is not dependent on those who attend, whereas the latter by definition ceases to exist when its members disperse.[388] If the church is conceived according to the second model, it would appear to be a voluntary association of people with a religious interest that they pursue in regular meetings, just like any music club that regularly gathers for concerts.[122] The church exists for the free enjoyment of each individual. The act of confirmation is the public testimony that the individuals being confirmed are really inter-

---

121. In their empirical expression both forms also usually contain some elements of a community [Gemeinschaft]. This can go so far as to make the designation 'association' sociologically inaccurate. See Spann, *Gesellschaftslehre*, 419, who, with reference to the Roman Catholic church, defines church as the institution of religious community life (420). Spann does not draw a sharp distinction between voluntary association and compulsory institution, as is evident from his definition of association as a "voluntary institution" (417). Concerning this issue as a whole, see Gierke, *Das deutsche Genossenschaftsrecht*, 1:143–46 (sec. 16), 1:844–65 (sec. 63), and 2:526–72 (secs. 19 and 20).

122. See above, page 94, footnote 28.[389]

[388.] Deleted from *SC-A*: An empty school classroom retains its institutional character, whereas a chess club without members ceases to exist.

[389.] This reference replaces the following footnote in *SC-A*:

<<Partly relevant in this context is Vierkandt's definition of the invisible church as an edifying community [Erhebungsgemeinschaft], which was classified above under the sociological concept of audience [Publikum]. Here Vierkandt lists side by side, as sociologically equal phenomena, the concepts of the invisible church, the republic of scholars [Gelehrtenrepublik], the *Kunstwart* community, and others. [*Kunstwart* was a periodical on art and literature that was very influential among bourgeois intellectuals from its founding in 1887 until World War I. It advocated "an elevating and purifying function of the arts," espoused a "decidedly nationalistic ethical idealism," and covered a wide range of topics including the Youth Movement. See Harald Olbrich, ed., *Lexikon der Kunst*, 4:160.][CG] In my view this is nothing but the result of a loose definition of the basic sociological concepts. Regarding these definitions, see Vierkandt, *Gesellschaftslehre*, 179ff.>>

ested, and declare that they follow the rules of the association. Once they have lost interest in the subject matter, however, they can declare at any time their resignation from membership, and thus be released from paying their 'dues' to the association (in the form of church taxes).[390] By the consent of all members the association ceases to exist. If we were to ask how the association theory accounts for the fact that the community of the church [kirchliche Gemeinschaft] understands itself as an instrument of God's will to rule, then we would receive an answer in which this claim is relativized by comparing it with the claim of other 175 religious communities; so this approach will get us nowhere. This model thus seems to make sense but still leaves quite a few loose ends from a purely sociological point of view: (1) What is the point of admitting infants into an association? No chess player, no matter how passionate, would enroll a small child in a chess club. (2) Every organized association is a closed society and can expel members. Church assemblies, on the other hand, are open on principle and accessible to everybody. There is no such thing as expulsion from the church.[123] (3) The forms of an association's objective spirit are conventional, goal-oriented, and propagandist; those of the church are symbolic and filled with meaning. Those of the association are discarded as soon as they are no longer useful; in the church there are dying forms that are deliberately preserved.[124] The association as such has no tradition whereas the church does.

Whereas the voluntary-association theory thus already fails with regard to the external organization, it breaks down completely when it comes to theology. A look at the Christian views on sin, grace, Christ,

---

123. It is true that the new church constitution speaks of an exclusion from the right to vote and of a suspension of that right ([*Kirchenverfassung der Alten Preußischen Union,*] par. 15, 2, 3), but it never mentions expulsion from the gathered congregation. Regarding excommunication, see below, page 258, footnote 130.

124. We do not judge here whether this is right or wrong. I do not consider this quality of the church as one of its frequently criticized weaknesses, but rather as an ability, rooted in its tradition, to bear those who went before even while running the danger of being outwardly unfashionable.

[390.] In Germany the state still collects a church tax (*Kirchensteuer*) and people who do not wish to pay can avoid it only by formally resigning from the church. [CG]

Holy Spirit, and the church reveals that the concept of the voluntary association is totally inapplicable to the concept of the church.

It would seem possible to overcome these difficulties with the idea, put forward by Max Weber[125] and Troeltsch,[126] of the church as a compulsory organization,[127] or as 'foundation'. Here the church is seen not 176 as a community of persons in essence but as an institution in which human beings are promised a certain efficacious gift if they render appropriate services in return. A parallel would be the university, for example, where the condition for receiving the gift is the payment of money, but where such things as 'cooperation' are required if that reception is to be effective. Likewise, within a church defined as a compulsory organization, all members are individually registered and liable to pay a tax, but are then also assured of eternal salvation provided they make regular use of the means of grace and submit to the rules of the

---

125. "Kirche und Sekte in Nordamerika," in *Christl. Welt*, 1906, 558ff., 578ff. See also "The Protestant Sects and the Spirit of Capitalism," *From Max Weber: Essays in Sociology*, 305f.: "Indeed, a church is a corporation which organizes grace and administers religious gifts of grace, like an endowed foundation. Affiliation with the church is, in principle, obligatory and hence proves nothing with regard to the member's qualities. One is born into it."[391]

126. *Social Teachings*, 331ff.

127. When using the concept of compulsory organization, one must distinguish between the relation of the individuals to the organization and the relation of the individuals to one another. The kind of contract involved here is different from that of a voluntary association, insofar as the individual only enters into a contract with the management of the organization, but not with its members. At first sight, it is thus only the contract between the compulsory organization and its member that has qualities typical of a 'society'. The relation of the individuals to one another remains undefined. From the organization's point of view it is purely accidental. Each individual has no other claim than to receive what the organization has to give; the individual wills run parallel. It would therefore seem possible, by seeing them as a unit, to consider the participants as a mass, which in the case of voluntary association would be sociologically unacceptable.

[391.] One of Max Weber's preliminary studies was his essay "The Protestant Sects and the Spirit of Capitalism," *From Max Weber*, 302ff. See also Weber's definition of voluntary association [*Verein*] and compulsory organization [*Anstalt*] in *Economy and Society*, 1:52f. For a critical view of Weber's distinction, see Holl, *Luther*, 243f., note 2, and 297, note 3. [Although included by Bonhoeffer in the quotation, the final sentence, "One is born into it," while stating Weber's view, is not found in the passage cited.][CG]

organization as well as to its mandates and disciplines. It is possible, appropriate, and advisable to make children, too, subject to the rules of the organization in order to provide them with salvation as early as possible. The requirements take into account the large number of people who attend the organization, and are consequently few. It would be possible to interpret baptism, confirmation, resignation from membership, church taxes, the meaning of the assembly, and perhaps even the forms created by the objective spirit within the framework of a compulsory organization, so that the view of Weber and Troeltsch would seem to be correct.

¶The weak point in their theory becomes apparent only when we ask about the authority that establishes the organization. If it is asserted as in Roman Catholicism that it is simply established by God, then the idea of the church being strictly a compulsory organization is preserved and carried through; when applied to the Roman Catholic church as an organized phenomenon the definition of Weber and Troeltsch is sociologically correct. Here spirit, organization, and office belong together without a necessary relation to the church-community. However, a look at theological issues reveals quite a few contradictions. It is impossible to understand the social basic-relations atomistically, if they indeed claim to have a Christian foundation. This is something that even Roman Catholicism has never forgotten. For here, in spite of the structural difference between compulsory organization and community,[128] both have been asserted side by side, as is already evident in Augustine.[392] The Protestant 'organization' is not established by God over and above the church-community but rather is an act of this church-community itself. For the church-community is also the bearer of the office, which must never be conceived in abstraction from it. This, however, dissolves the specifically sociological meaning of the concept of compulsory organization [Anstalt], insofar as there is no organization without church-community, as there is in Roman Catholicism, and insofar as the gifts the church promises are gifts that God gave to a specific community of persons, namely God's own church-community, by

---

128. Even an organization that promotes community starts out with an atomistic structure.

[392.] Regarding Seeberg's portrait of Augustine's concept of the church, see his *Dogmengeschichte*, 2:437ff., esp. 472ff., on Augustine's *City of God*.

entrusting and sustaining that community with the word of proclamation. In this respect the voluntary-association [Verein] concept makes a fundamentally valid point over against the concept of the compulsory organization [Anstalt], in that it understands the church as consisting of persons; and it is no accident that it emerged—apparently in connection with the study of Protestant sects—on Protestant soil.[393] To interpret the organizational forms of the Protestant church by means of the concept of compulsory organization is thus entirely mistaken.

2. Baptism, confirmation, resignation from membership, the assembly, and the judicial regulations (tax system) can, in their Protestant form, be understood only on the basis of the church being a community of persons [Persongemeinschaft];[129] it is also the foundation for an understanding of the structure of the church's objective spirit as it manifests itself in firmly defined forms. This must now be demonstrated, while at the same time pointing out the flaws of the association theory. The fact that the sociological concept of community [Gemeinschaft] is deficient, too, will become evident below.

Only a community [Gemeinschaft], not a society [Gesellschaft], is able to carry children (see above, page 90). Infant baptism within an association is an internal contradiction.[395]

---

129. See Althaus, *Communio sanctorum*, who, although using other terms, asserts (36) that the difference between the Roman Catholic and the Protestant concept of community is based on the distinction between what we have termed 'society' and 'community'; whether this interpretation is valid, however, still remains unclear to me. It presumably depends on whether one seeks to discover the identity of the Roman Catholic church in its deviant forms, or where it has preserved its original substance.[394]

[393.] Deleted from *SC-A*: Church is the community of persons that is nourished and grows through God's gifts, and only on this basis could one speak of an institutional church in a Protestant sense; but this would be sociologically confusing and incorrect.

[394.] *SC-A* lacks footnote 129. Footnote deleted from *SC-A*: <<Tönnies, *Soziologische Studien und Kritiken*, 2:271.>>

[395.] "Only a community . . . contradiction" reads in *SC-A*:

Baptism is a declaration of intent by the church-community to accept the child in order to prepare it for participation in the church-community in the future. Only a community, not a society, is able to carry children (see above). It is possible to be born into a community, provided the parents guide the child's will; they decide what happens to the child. The child is thus sanctified by the parents' will (1 Cor. 7:14). Such a statement makes sense because a community by its nature is not merely organized for a specific purpose, but rather makes a

178   The association theory considers either confirmation or first communion as the moment of admission into the association. Since we also
see the Lord's Supper as being such a first public act of professing allegiance to the church, we appear to concur with this theory, but only to
someone who confuses problems of origin with those of essence, a mistake upon which rests Troeltsch's whole distinction between church and
sect.[396] All genuine community, as community of will, presupposes the
voluntary affirmation of the community, and this is true also and above
all for the community of the church [kirchliche Gemeinschaft]. (Within
the human sphere there are no 'organic' communities in the sense of
purely vegetative growth.) The decisive element, therefore, is the object
of the social act of will. If it is really merely the pleasure of being
uplifted by preaching, etc., then the association theory is quite right.[397]
But this view fails to understand the heart of the matter. What is
affirmed is the church-community, within which I submit to God's rule,
to which I am grateful for baptism and instruction, and the value of
whose community I appreciate; and this understanding makes the association theory collapse. It will soon become clear, however, that this
does not yet fully describe the entity being affirmed.

Just as the Christian church-community, when accepting members,
does not impose any other condition but the affirmative act of will, so it
does not expel any of its members for any cause other than the rejecting
act of will. The Christian community has no control over the individual.
Not so the association: just as admission is dependent on certain
requirements (repectability as a citizen, money, etc.), so the loss of these
entails expulsion, even if the will to remain a member still exists. By its
nature the community of the church [kirchliche Gemeinschaft] does
not practice expulsion at all. Protestant excommunication,[130] if it

---

130. The answer to the question of Protestant excommunication will vary,
depending on the internal and external conditions in which the church finds
itself. Paul excommunicates (and perhaps even pronounces the death sentence)

[395. *cont.*] claim on one's entire attitude to life. Baptism is the affirmation by the church-
community of the child who is born into the community of saints. This insight is an argument against the idea that the church is a voluntary association [Verein] or compulsory
organization [Anstalt].

[396.] Regarding the distinction between church and sect, see below, pages 267ff.
[397.] Deleted from *SC-A:* and this is in fact largely the case today.

existed, would not be expulsion from the community, but temporary   178
exclusion from specific activities of the community. This is in the last

---

in order that the soul of the excommunicated person might be saved on the
Last Day (1 Corinthians 5). This is the only rule that can be discovered here. In
a purely confessional church-community [Bekenntnisgemeinde] excommunication is possible and meaningful, but of course only in accordance with the iudicium caritatis [charitable judgment] on who belongs to the church (cf. Luther's
hopes for a church of those confessing their faith, in which excommunication
might be possible. [*LW* 53:61ff., 36:265] [*WA* 19:72ff., 10/2:39.]).[398] According
to Calvin, however, those who prove themselves by attending church, participating in the sacraments, and leading a morally pure life can be considered church
members. For our church-of-the-people such a definition would be outright
meaningless. Today, unlike in Calvin's day, it is indeed no longer an ostentatious
act not to attend church, let alone the Lord's Supper. Within a church-of-the-
people excommunication is impossible to implement, and thus meaningless
from the outset. The iudicium caritatis will have to be more accommodating
today than it has been in the past, and include all those who have not consciously renounced the church.[399] It is acceptable for excommunication to be
practiced within 'core-churches', provided this happens in a Pauline manner.
"Non personam ipsam quae in manu atque arbitrio dei est in mortem abdica-
mus, sed tantum qualia sint cuiusque opera aestimemus ex lege dei, quae boni
et mali regula est" ("We do not condemn to death the person—that is in God's
hands and judgment; we are only called to determine the nature of each person's deeds according to the law of God, which is the measure of the virtuous
and the wicked") (Calvin, *Institutio [Institutes]*, 1536, chap. II, de fide IV).[400]
The New Testament saying that "the tree is known by its fruits" cannot be
reversed without qualification. Abraham and Hosea would certainly have been
excommunicated by a Calvinist church. Cf. Kierkegaard, *Fear and Trembling*.[401]

[398.] The quotations concerning Luther's "hopes for a church of those confessing
their faith" are from the preface to "The German Mass and Order of Service" (1526) (*LW*
53:61ff. [*WA* 19:72ff.]) and "Receiving Both Kinds in the Sacrament" (1522) (*LW* 36:264f.
[*WA* 10/2:39]). Both quotations are found in Holl, *Luther*, 359, esp. note 3, and 360ff.

[399.] Regarding church discipline in Calvin, see "Draft Ecclesiastical Ordinances,"   287
September and October 1541, Calvin: Theological Treatises, 58–72. Concerning the *iudicium caritatis* [charitable judgment] in Luther, see "Lectures on Galatians" (1519): "The
commonwealth of the church is built solely on the law of love" (*LW* 27:409 [*WA* 2:617]).

[400.] Calvin, *Institutes*, 62 [trans. altered] [*Institutio*, 1536 ed., 90]. In his own Latin
copy Bonhoeffer heavily marked the cited sentence with a thick underline.

[401.] See Kierkegaard, *Fear and Trembling*, where Kierkegaard, in reference to Abraham, characterizes faith as the paradox that "is able to turn murder into an act that is holy
and pleasing to God" (62f.). See also the idea of a "teleological suspension of the ethical"
(63ff.). Hosea is not mentioned by Kierkegaard; on this point, see Hosea 2:2ff. and 3:1ff.

resort due to the fact that God wants the church to be *historical*, which is the third argument against the voluntary-association theory.

The judicial forms are likewise not to be interpreted as being those of a society; rather, the community of the church [kirchliche Gemeinde] must sustain itself, and therefore pays its taxes, just as everyone in a family contributes to sustaining that community. All matters that are judicially regulated originated in the will of the community itself, and have the sole purpose of making its life possible.[402]

Finally, sociologists will have definitive proof that the church is a community when they consider that, like any other genuine community, it is an ethical collective person. It has its own culpability, just as a marriage does. It is addressed and judged by God as a whole and is one of many collective persons, even if it is larger and more powerful than most. Its uniqueness becomes apparent, however, only where it is understood as the community and church of God that is based upon and 180 brought about by the Spirit, in which capacity it is 'Christ existing as church-community', the presence of Christ. Both the theory of the voluntary association and the concept of the compulsory organization are rendered unacceptable by the Protestant understanding of the Spirit and the church-community, in the former because it does not take the reality of the Spirit into account at all, and in the latter in that it severs the essential relation between Spirit and church-community, thereby completely losing any sociological interest. An analysis of the concept of objective spirit will now reveal that the general concept of community [Gemeinschaft] also proves inadequate as a sociological category for interpreting the church.

The forms in which the objective spirit of the church has become embodied make it clear that its structure is obviously that of a community, i.e., expressive actions filled with symbolic meaning. This finds its primary expression in the cult.[403] However, as soon as we consider the distinctive acts of the church-community, which are preaching and administering the sacraments, we hesitate to call them purely expressive.[404] Merely looking at their forms, such a view would be possible

---

[402.] Deleted from *SC-A*: There is presumably general agreement that enforced collection of taxes by the state is an unhealthy practice.

[403.] Deleted from *SC-A*: Here one might think of the cross, the adorned altar, the entire church architecture, and a variety of cultic expressions.

[404.] Allusion to Schleiermacher, *Die christliche Sitte*, 502ff.: "II. Expressive acts."

and entirely consistent. Certainly, assembling around word and sacrament is a representation of the church-community, both before itself and before God. In that perspective, the means of grace are the forms with which the church-community adequately expresses itself. However, we already recognized earlier that this is only one part of the matter, and that the acts of preaching and the celebration of the sacraments must also be effective and purposeful. Taking up this train of thought once again here, we notice the church having the same internal antinomy that we already discovered in our discussion of the concept of the community of love. To understand the church as a community is not enough; it is indeed a community, but one that is concretely defined as a *community of spirit* [*Geistgemeinschaft*]. And as such it is not merely a modified or special version of the general category of 'community'; rather it constitutes an antinomic new basic-relation that we must now examine.[405]

Reflection on the theological nature of the concept of the church will thus provide correction and boundaries for the entire sociological construction. The issue is not religious community, but the empirical church as the present sanctorum communio, the community of Spirit extending beyond all community that is humanly possible. Community of Spirit is not identical with community of kindred spirits. The term   181 instead expresses the transcendent foundation of the community, thus identifying its nature not as an association of force [Gewaltverband], which is what dialectical theology seems inclined to think,[406] and which would preclude community altogether, but rather as an objective *association of authentic rule* [*Herrschaftsverband*]. This evidently means that the church-community is organized toward a certain end, namely the achievement of God's will. But this divine will is directed toward the church itself as a community of spirit, so that as a purposive society it is at the same time an end in itself, which corresponds with our earlier recognition that the *church is both a means to an end and at the same time an end in itself*. God, in seeking to implement the divine will, gives God's

---

[405.] The following two sentences up to "humanly possible" were added to *SC-A*. [The word "antinomic" (not "antinomian") is from "antinomy." By "antinomic new basic-relation" Bonhoeffer refers to the "duality" described below of "the will to community [*Gemeinschaft*] and will to embrace God's purpose [*Gesellschaft*]" that characterizes the community of spirit [*Geistgemeinschaft*], which is simultaneously a community of love [*Liebesgemeinschaft*].] [CG]

[406.] See above, page 169, footnote 28.

own self into our hearts and creates community; that is, God makes the divine self the means to God's own end.[407]

The construction of this mutual interconnection must neither be distorted into the idea of an existing community that has some communal purpose as well, nor that of a purposive society [Zweckgesellschaft] becoming a community, though both would be possible sociologically. In the concept of the church the one element is in fact connected with the other in such a way that any attempt to explain this relation genetically completely robs this concept of any meaning.

The objection that acts of will cannot simultaneously have the quality of a society and of a community if the distinction is to have any validity can be refuted only if both acts can be seen as being incorporated and transcended within another, new act. This is in fact the act of *love*, brought about by the Spirit, which is the very heart of community of spirit. I organize my relation to the other with a single end in mind, namely to fulfill God's will by loving the other. Now because it is the Holy Spirit who loves within me, I am assured that the end toward which I organize my relation to the other is this very relation itself. Only the Holy Spirit within me is able to tie both of these together. It is the Spirit's work that, by my seeking nothing but to be obedient to God, that is, by pursuing purely an end that as such is something other than the community, I completely surrender my will, so that simultaneously I truly love my neighbor. The Holy Spirit combines the claim to authority [Herrschaftsanspruch] with the will to establish purpose and to establish meaning by drawing the person into the Spirit's own course, thus being at once ruler and servant. The distinctive act among all the activities of the community of the church is that of love brought about by the Spirit in all the manifestations we described. Christian love is primarily not identical with a 'will to meaning'; it is not directed toward the acknowledgment of the value of community, but rather toward acknowledging God's will for the other, that is, toward the value God's will assigns to the other.[408] As has already been shown, it is precisely in complete surrender ("those who lose their life")[409] that community of the Holy Spirit is found. It would therefore be wrong to say that the

---

[407.] See Seeberg, *Dogmatik*, 2:522ff.
[408.] See Scheler, *Formalism in Ethics*, 503ff., esp. 506ff.
[409.] See Matt. 16:25 and parallels.

specifically sociological activity of the Christian church is that of a community [Gemeinschaft], understood as an ideal type. Rather, it transcends the activities characteristic of both community and society and combines both.[410] Nevertheless the church really is community, namely the community of spirit and the community of love. And this concept already expresses the one-sidedness of 'community' as a sociological type and goes beyond it. The basis from which to judge all empirical activity of the church is this duality and unity of the will to community and the will to embrace God's purpose, which means also that it is the foundation upon which a theory of the objective spirit of the church-community must be developed.[411]

As far as I can see, only the original patriarchal structure of the family is a sociologically comparable form, even if only approximately; this is then replicated in smaller circles, however. The object of the father's will is community between children and servants, and preserving community means being obedient. This is why the image of the family occurs most frequently in the Christian vocabulary, and furnished the most common name in the New Testament by which Christians called one another, namely 'brother'.[412] It is very significant when Paul in Eph. 3:15 says that all fatherhood on earth derives its name from God's fatherhood. This relation is also the reason why the idea of patriarchalism has played such a prominent role since earliest Christianity. Admittedly, the emphasis it received in the Middle Ages was also related to developments within the class structure and culture, but it also represents a recovery of one of the earliest sociological insights of Christianity. Troeltsch has forcefully focused our attention on this thought.[131] It indeed seems that here we have a structure similar[413] to that of the church, and yet it is not possible to define the patriarchal family as a

183

---

131. [*Social Teachings*,] 78, 99, 285ff.: "Repeatedly we are reminded that Christendom is a great family" (287). Cf. Th[eodor] Meyer, *Die christlich-ethischen Sozialprinzipien und die Arbeiterfrage*, 1904, esp. 70ff.

[410.] *SC-RS*: "Is it really necessary to bring the concept of society into this discussion? After all, belonging to a community satisfies all the needs we seek to communicate through love."

[411.] *SC-RS*: "Is this [illegible] understood?"

[412.] This is of course a historical reference to a specific term in the New Testament. [CG]

[413.] *SC-A* reads: identical.

pure union of purposeful obedience and true communal relation; it is either one or the other. The true interconnection of both elements within the church is brought about through the work of the Holy Spirit alone, so that one might call the church also a family moved by the Spirit. The reason for the distinctive sociological structure of the church is in fact to be found in the concept of the Spirit, that is, in the reality of it being based on the Spirit. This further means that this distinctive structure can be understood only theologically, and not in morphological and sociological terms alone. When seen as a religious community, the church, like most other social bodies, is an imperfect expression of an ideal type.[414] We saw that sociologically the church is to be described as community, and remain convinced that this conclusion is sociologically more accurate than any other.[415] The religious community, though, has no sociological structure sui generis; however, the empirical church brought about by the Spirit does. *In it community [Gemeinschaft], society [Gesellschaft], and association of authentic rule [Herrschaftsverband] are truly most closely intertwined.* Since this structure comes into being only through the Spirit, we speak of community of Spirit [Geistgemeinschaft]. Because of this we must also at this point reiterate that all community subsists in faith in the word, so long as we do not yet live by sight,[416] but only within the world of the eschatological signs of things to come.[417] Because love is now the life-principle of the community, the people in it no longer relate to one another like those in a society. With regard to content, however, the church's structure is based on the Christian idea of revelation. God's will to rule in love seeks to establish a Realm [Reich] of persons.[418] Love is the purpose of this Realm, and it seeks to rule and triumph. But the Realm itself consists in God's love being victorious, and is thus, as the Realm of the loving community, an end in itself. This means God's love is both a means for realizing the Realm and also rules within it. This whole discussion is basically nothing but a repeated elaboration of the peculiar

184

[414.] See Weber's definition of the ideal type in *Gesammelte Aufsätze zur Wissenschaftslehre*, 190ff.

[415.] Deleted from *SC-A*: even though it must still be developed considerably in the direction just outlined, if it is not only to encompass religious community but the church as well.

[416.] Cf. 2 Cor. 5:7. [CG]

[417.] *SC-A* lacks the following sentence.

[418.] *SC-RS*: "Good, but does this imply any society motifs?"

interconnection between *God's rule*[132] and *God's Realm*. We already encountered these same ideas earlier in the antithesis of the church-community as both an instrument and an end in itself, which also recurs in the actions of the church-community. In preaching the church-community makes itself the instrument with which it continually builds itself up. In preaching it confronts itself as a social formation [Vergesellschaftung] that is solely and exclusively organized according to God's will. On the other hand, however, this very act reveals that the goal of God's will is precisely the community of saints. According to the declaration in Matt. 16:18, both the means of grace and the organizational forms of church and doctrinal discipline reflect God's will to rule; and this applies not to the persons exercising these functions, but rather to the functions themselves insofar as they are sustained by the *sanctorum communio*. Mosheim[419] was already aware that within any commonwealth one has to distinguish between cives [citizens] and constitutio [constitution].[133] This idea proves immensely fruitful and sociologically perceptive. Even though Christ iura maiestatis regni sui sibi soli reservavit [reserved the rights of the majesty of his reign solely to himself], ordinatio [order] and gubernatio [governance] nevertheless also exist within the church. It did not occur to Mosheim[420] to extend

---

132. It is a mistake to equate the society type of association [Gesellschaftsverband] with an association of authentic rule [Herrschaftsverband], because the latter speaks about the relative strength of the wills, while the former is based on the direction of the wills. Of course, it is only through the association of authentic rule that the will of the community and that of the society coincide; the spirit of the association of authentic rule has the distinctive structure that it is the one who rules who sets in motion the wills of those who obey, thus serving them. All three forms are nevertheless preserved as fully distinct.

133. [Mosheim,] *Elementa theologiae dogmaticae*, 2d ed., 1764, sec. 2.

[419.] Deleted from *SC-A*: My insight that the sociological concept of the church has to do with authority is indebted not least to a suggestion by Mosheim.

[420.] See von Mosheim, *Elementa theologiae dogmaticae*, par. 2. 365: "In omni regno duo considerata sunt (1) cives regni, et (2) constitutio regni. Cives regni Christi sunt illi, qui eum pro domino et servatore habent, aut qui veritatem diligunt. . . . Visibilis tamen ecclesia non respuit externam quandam ordinationem seu gubernationem, atque hinc oritur ius ecclesiasticum, quod partim in supremo magistratu, partim in ipsa societate residet, quae ecclesia dicitur." ("Within any realm two elements must be considered: (1) the citizens of the realm and (2) its constitution. The citizens of Christ's Realm are those who acknowledge him as Lord and Savior, or who love the truth. . . . The visible church nevertheless does not reject a certain external order and governance; and this

the constitutio also to the means of grace, as we have done here in order to express their function as God's rule over the church-community. For us the church's entire claim to rule is derived solely from the rule of the word. The idea of the priesthood of all believers thus remains the foundational principle of the church.[421] No empirical body 'in itself' can claim to have authority over the church-community. Every claim derives from the word. In my view, it would thus seem a necessary conclusion that the church should become independent, that is, win its separation from the state, although this cannot be further elaborated here.[422]

185

Thus the *objective spirit* is on the one hand a will aiming toward an end,[423] seeking to subject individual spirits ever anew and ever more widely to itself and thus to God's rule; it is impelled to do so by God's unconditioned will to rule, which employs it as a means to its end. This inexhaustible will to subject people provides the basis for the idea of mission. God is one, and the whole world should be in God's Realm; thus the universality of the Christian message is established in principle. Mission is God acting through the church-community.[424] The objective spirit is, on the other hand, however, an *expression* of the community that is moved by the Holy Spirit, and is itself a will for community, precisely because it subjects itself to God's will to rule. With regard to its structure it is a novelty, for it springs from the need to achieve its end, and does so by being a community itself. Only from an internal perspective can this structure be understood not as an imperfect sociological type, but as the new phenomenon of the community of Spirit. *To summarize: church is a form of community sui generis, namely community of Spirit [Geistgemeinschaft] as community of love [Liebesgemeinschaft].* In it the basic sociological types of society [Gesellschaft], community [Gemeinschaft], and association of authentic rule [Herrschaftsverband] are combined and transcended. The objective spirit of the community

---

[420. *cont.*] gives rise to church law, which resides partly in the supreme magistrate, and in part within that society itself that is called the church.") See also Krauß, *Dogma von der unsichtbaren Kirche*, 97f., and Seeberg, *Begriff der Kirche*, 156, to whom Bonhoeffer most likely owes his remarks on Mosheim.

[421.] *SC-RS*: "Spirit within the word".

[422.] *SC-A* does not begin a new paragraph here.

[423.] *SC-A* reads: the objective spirit being a will purely aimed at an effect . . .

[424.] The views on mission expressed here are identical to those of Seeberg, *Dogmatik*, 2:386.

in all its effects must be understood as both representative and purposive. The relations of persons to each other are those of members of a community of spirit, not a society. From the society-type is derived only the trait that the church is objectively constituted by an ultimate purpose. There is no need here to repeat all that has been said earlier about the church's plurality and unity of spirit.

Church and sect

In light of these results the problem of church and sect simply disappears. We submit that the sociological definition of the concept of the church is equally applicable to the sect, which means that ultimately sociologically there is *no essential sociological difference between the two*. In this we disagree with the now famous distinction by Weber and Troeltsch. It holds that

> a sect is a voluntary association consisting (in its ideal type) exclusively of   186
> people who are religiously and morally qualified; they join by free choice
> and are accepted by free choice on the basis of having proven themselves
> religiously. [trans. altered][134]
> A sect is a voluntary association of serious and committed Christians,
> who come together as people truly born again, separate themselves from
> the world, remain confined to small groups, and emphasize the law rather
> than grace; within their own circle they establish, with varying degrees of
> radicalism, the Christian way of life governed by love, and do all this in
> preparation and expectation of the coming kingdom of God.[135]

Holl[136] has shown that this understanding of sect is derived exclusively from Protestant sectarianism, which already is one reason why it must be inaccurate. Weber and Troeltsch contrast the sect with the concept of the church as an organization of salvation [Heilsanstalt] into which a person is born, which is open to the world, adapting its requirements to the masses. This shows that they employ a genetic-sociological approach. The crucial difference, as they see it, is that the church develops historically and organically, whereas the sect is established and sustained only through voluntary association. However, both historically

---

134. Weber, "The Protestant Sects," *From Max Weber*, 306.
135. Troeltsch, [*Social Teachings,*] 993, 331.
136. [Holl,] *Luther,* 244.[425]

[425.] Holl, *Luther,* 244f., note 2.

and sociologically this distinction is inadequate and cannot be considered fundamental. It is not fundamental historically, since in the second and third generation large sects frequently become completely open churches-of-the-people [Volkskirchen]; nor is it fundamental sociologically since the community of the church is by its nature also a community of wills. The ultimate insight is lacking in Weber and Troeltsch; if it were present, the whole genetic question would disappear. For in that case the church also is church only insofar as it is actually willed by persons, that is insofar as it is a voluntary church [Freiwilligkeitskirche]. However, the social act of will as such, as long as it is guided by the word of God, that is, as long as it consists in love brought about by the Spirit, is the same in both church and sect. As long as it has the word, the sect too is community of Christ, *its community is the community of saints. In its basic sociological structure* it is identical with the church. Now the sociological structure of the church, as was shown, in fact essentially reflects the normative nature of these ontic basic-relations and their manifestations (infant baptism, openness of the church, community of those freely confessing their faith). The sect, on the other hand, has frequently placed an excessively one-sided emphasis on certain insights (personal holiness, conversion) that, in giving organizational shape to its sociological basic-relations, has led to one-sided forms. These are bound to be rejected by a church-of-the-people that is conscious of its own identity; they are not at all adiaphora.[426] However, as long the sect is judged by the criterion of the Christian social acts that are actually present within it, one has in principle no grounds for denying that in essence it is identical to the church.[137]

Earlier we drew a distinction between the Roman Catholic and the Protestant concepts of the church, in which the former sees a link between Spirit and office, whereas the latter assumes a connection

---

137. See Thimme, [*Kirche, Sekte und Gemeinschaftsbewegung,*] 250. Here Troeltsch's concept of sect is rightly rejected, although, it seems to me, without a sufficiently clear grasp of the sociological issues involved.

[426.] Literally 'indifferent things'; in the ethical teaching of the Stoics 'adiaphora' denotes acts or values that are mere means to achieve another end, but are not desirable for their their own sake. See the First Adiaphoristic Controversy (1549) between Lutheran Orthodoxy (Matthias Flacius) and Melancthon, who, during the Leipzig Interim of 1584, had conceded ground to the Roman Catholic camp on the issues of a church constitution and questions of worship.

between Spirit and church-community. Now this distinction apparently does imply a fundamental sociological difference. But we have to go even a step further. It is the miracle of the divine promise that wherever the word of God is proclaimed, it will create a church-community through its own power. Within the Roman Catholic church, as a place where God's word is proclaimed, we therefore must assume the existence of such a church-community that belongs together with the Protestant and sectarian church-communities. Not the 'word' but 'pure doctrine' is the point where the Roman Catholic church[427] fails; and it is only from this perspective that its sociological structure—church as compulsory organization—which is in fact completely different from the Protestant church, can be understood. There is no sociological structure that is holy as such, and equally there is no structure that would cut off all avenues for the word. That there is a quest for pure doctrine is just as self-evident as the fact that no church can claim to possess it fully. We must consider the Augsburg Confession to be in error when, in Article 7, it directly links recte docetur [being rightly taught] to the congregatio sanctorum [congregation of saints].[428] 'Pure doctrine' is not a necessary prerequisite for the existence of the community of saints (Isa. 55:11 is silent on this point). The community of saints will no doubt always strive for pure doctrine; but through historical circumstances this effort can remain ineffective. We are therefore bound to acknowledge and believe that in principle the sanctorum communio is present both in the Roman Catholic church and in the sect. We see the Protestant church as the 'true' church—which is not the same as defining it as the 'essential' church—and feel that in it God has chosen an exceptionally pure instrument for God's work. This leads us further to believe that it is in a special sense the womb of God's holy church-community.[429]

188

[427.] Regarding doctrine and doctrinal authority within the Roman Catholic church, see Bartmannn, *Lehrbuch*, 2:150ff.

[428.] See *Book of Concord*, 32; see also *Apology of the Augsburg Confession*, in *Book of Concord*, 168ff.

[429.] Deleted from *SC-A*:

One problem still remains. If the church is in essence a voluntary church [Freiwilligkeitskirche], how then is this related to its character as a church-of-the-people [volkskirchlich]? (1) The church-of-the-people expresses the church's theological purpose of offering the gospel to all; (2) however, it must be recognized as a special manifestation of God's gracious will. For as an organically grown, historical force it is more enduring and stable than a

To summarize, the sanctorum communio, the Christian community of love as a sociological type, is dependent upon the word of God, and it

[429. *cont.*] voluntary association; as such it can survive infertile periods in history, which are ruinous to an association. It is divine grace that we have a church deeply rooted in our nation's history; the power of the church's historical nature makes God's will for us relatively independent of the momentary situation in which we happen to find ourselves.

(3) The church-of-the-people is criticized for its conservatism, and often with good reason, to be sure. However, conservatism is not just a significant force, but is also justified by the Protestant view of history. Protestantism never rejects absolutely what has come into being historically; rather, it gives relative value to history, to tradition. History cannot be holy in an absolute sense, as Roman Catholicism would have it, but it is nevertheless in some sense God's will, even in its concrete form. This is the only reason why it was so difficult for Luther to break with history, and to 'make' history himself. This relative value given to historical tradition is the foundation for the conservatism of the Protestant church-of-

289   the-people. This conservatism is skeptical toward anyone proposing change. It makes the church appear old-fashioned, and runs the risk of canonizing the past. This is when its conservatism, which is appropriate as such and in superficial times preserves the healthy core, comes to endanger the church itself.

This conservatism also connects the church with the basic sociological conditions of the world, and the constitutions of the various states. It is the basis for the acknowledgment of the powers of the state in general; this acknowledgment rests on the idea of the priesthood of all believers. Internally, this has led the church, sociologically speaking, to justify patriarchy since the time of Paul. The dangers of conservatism are obvious, and the church has often succumbed to them, so that Troeltsch can even say that "the churches are shells that gradually fossilize the kernel they initially protected." <<*Social Teachings*, 993. [This corresponds to Bonhoeffer's citation from Troeltsch's *Soziallehren*, 967; but his citation is apparently erroneous, since this quotation is not found at this place in the text.][CG]>>

However, the Christian appreciation of history also gives rise to the principle of progress within the church. The church ought to be a contemporary church; it ought to accept and test all the forces it encounters in life today. Past history is in principle no more right than the present. As a contemporary Christian, I have the right and the obligation to wrestle with history and to shape the gospel for today; each individual congregation has this obligation toward the church as a whole. The Protestant view thus implies a balance between the *retarding and the progressive element*. In purely sociological terms, the progressive element in the church finds expression in the concept of organism. All vitality of the community derives from the cooperation between its members. Any specific case of rejecting something new, or of discarding a dead tradition, will have to be decided by the conscience of the church authorities [Kirchenleitung]. Their noblest task is to harness all kinds of innovative and invigorating forces for the benefit of the church's work. Part of this responsibility is to hand over certain offices of the church-community to charismatically gifted personalities, whether their charisma relates to the exposition of scripture, charitable work, or administrative skills. Another part of this task is to study continuously the interests of the younger generation, and to have the wisdom to seize opportunities wherever a cluster of related ideas emerges. Yet another aspect is to listen to the voices from outside the church. This kind of vitality essentially lives out the internal laws of the life of any community, the give-and-take between different parts of the church (for which there is no equivalent in the Roman Catholic church, understood as a compulsory organization or

alone. According to the promise in Isa. 55:11, it is present within every historical form in which the word is preached. The distinction between church and sect suggested by Weber and Troeltsch is untenable both historically and sociologically. Based on the efficacy of the word, we must believe the sanctorum communio to be present even within the sociologically unique type of the Roman Catholic church. Striving to attain the true church and pure doctrine is inherently necessary.[430]

[429. *cont.*] mass). Only when this give-and-take is fully encouraged, and when on the other hand the retarding element is sufficiently strong to reject what is inappropriate and to examine what is fruitful, can a congenial synergy between proper conservatism and proper progress take hold.

Now it is true that both forces are at work in every church-of-the-people and in every voluntary church, since they are both grounded in the Protestant view of history and historical life in general. It is also true that there are 'popular' churches with a strong desire for progress, and most certainly free churches that are governed by a most rigid conservatism. Nevertheless, it might be safe to say that in general the church-of-the-people type gravitates more toward historically established forms, whereas the voluntary-church type tends more toward what is new and progressive. If we now take into account everything we considered above, and especially what we said on purely theological grounds about the necessity of the church-of-the-people, then we can assert that the church-of-the-people and the voluntary church belong together. For today it is all too obvious that a church is in the gravest internal danger if, as a church-of-the-people, it does not again and again seek to become a community of those who freely confess their faith. There is such a moment when the church may no longer be a church-of-the-people; this moment has come when the church can no longer recognize its 'popular' form as the means for becoming a voluntary church (see above, on baptism and confirmation), but instead moves toward a complete rigidity and emptiness in the use of its forms that is harmful even to its living members. We have today reached a point where questions such as these must find their answer. Today, more than ever, we are grateful for the grace of having a church-of-the-people; but we are also more than ever attentive to the danger of its complete desecration.

[430.] Deleted from *SC-A*: As particular expressions of God's gracious will, the church-of-the-people and the voluntary church belong together. Regarding the original sequence of the material in *SC-A*, see above, page 236, editorial note 341. *SC-A* continues:

e) The individual form of the objective spirit in the Church Today

(1) Church and proletariat [*SC-RS*: "Does this really belong in the framework of this study? If so, only brief or rewrite."]

"What has become of . . . the question of the significance of Christianity for the solution of the social problem of the present day? This social problem is vast and complicated. It includes the problem of the capitalist economic period and of the industrial proletariat created by it; and of the growth of militaristic and bureaucratic giant states; of the enormous increase in population, which affects colonial and world policy; of the mechanical technique [Bonhoeffer writes *Tätigkeit*, or activity, where Troeltsch has *Technik.*][CG] that produces enormous masses of material and links up and mobilizes the whole world for purposes of trade, but also that treats people and labor like machines.

¶ Bearing in mind the whole trend of this book, we need only to formulate the question

f) Faith in the sanctorum communio and
the 'experience of the church'[431]

The purpose in exploring this question is threefold:

[430. *cont.*] in this way in order to recognize its most important reply: this problem is entirely new, a problem with which Christian social work has never been confronted until now" (Troeltsch). <<[*Social Teachings*,] 1010f.>> [Here Bonhoeffer had planned to include an introduction that he had drafted for the published version; it is found in *SC-A* on the facing page in handwritten form: The latter statement might no longer be true today in the same way. And yet the recognition needs to gain ground, that for the contemporary church everything depends on regaining access to the masses that have turned their back on her; and that this must happen in such a way that the church brings the gospel into genuine contact with the current condition of the proletariat, and that she pays increased attention to whatever seems to point in this direction within the masses that have turned away from her.]

291   The objective spirit of the church in its present historical form has basically not yet noticed this problem to any significant degree. Christian social work has accomplished admirable things; but where is the real discussion among gospel, church-community, and proletariat? [*SC-RS:* "Is this the business of the church?"] It cannot be denied, in my view, that the future and hope for our 'bourgeois' church lies in an infusion of new blood [*SC-RS:* "?"], and that this can happen only if the church is successful in winning the proletariat. [*SC-RS:* "?"] Should the church fail to recognize this, then it will have neglected a critically decisive moment. It is also not difficult to see that today the bourgeoisie's attachment to the church is threadbare, and that it has exhausted itself as a vital force within the church. [*SC-RS:* "?"] And, on the other hand, in spite of contrary appearance, and even protest by the proletariat itself, I would consider no other force in the present to be fundamentally more open to the Christian proclamation than precisely the proletariat. [*SC-RS:* "even now?"] The living proletariat knows only one affliction, namely its isolation, and only one cry, namely that for community. [*SC-RS:* "?"] Certainly, these ideas are still bound and restricted by their class background. [*SC-RS:* "The problem is even more general; all classes are connected to each other, especially with respect to the problem of the church."] The proletariat is after something, however, that was never sought with such intensity by the bourgeoisie. The church dare not let the proletariat proclaim 'peace for humanity' without speaking its own word on this subject. It must not let the socialist youth movements speak of community without addressing them loudly and clearly with its own word of the sanctorum communio. It must not shrug off the interest in sports, and the Americanization of modern youth (and not only the proletarians). Rather it must recognize that this desire for discipline and competitive sports is also a cry for community, and that here too its word of the sanctorum communio might fall on receptive ears. Certainly, this word is not heard, and it cannot be heard, if the church speaks in the way it frequently does today. For a first prerequisite is a concrete debate between the gospel with the present, which today means with the proletarian masses (τῷ καιρῷ δουλεύοντες [serve the moment,] Rom. 12:11). No apotheosis of the proletariat! It is neither the bourgeois nor the proletarian who is right, but the gospel alone. Here is neither Jew nor Greek. And yet, the gospel must be proclaimed concretely in history; and that is why it confronts us today with this very problem of the proletariat. [*SC-RS:* "But this certainly has to do not only with the proletariat."] It is rather difficult to offer proof for something that is better understood instinctively rather than by way of details, that is, in this case, for the fact that

1. to justify the underlying method of our investigation;

[430. *cont.*] our present church is 'bourgeois'. The best proof remains that the proletariat has turned its back on the church, while the bourgeois (civil servant, skilled worker, merchant) stayed. [*SC-RS:* "Really?"] Sermons are thus aimed at people who live relatively securely and comfortably, [*SC-RS:* "?"] in orderly family circumstances, who are relatively 'educated', and relatively stable morally. In this case the sermon serves the need to experience something beautiful, learned, and moral during the free hours of Sunday; hence the all too familiar type of sermon, the 'speech', in which proof is offered for the literary expertise of the preacher and the corresponding interest of the 'audience'. The danger of allowing the church to become a voluntary association is all too obvious here. (The same is true of the disgraceful habit of including individual artistic performances, such as a solo by a professional singer, in the worship.) [*SC-RS:* "But this is of course not something that has to do merely with the proletariat?"] One simply has to take a look at the pictures hanging in Christian-education facilities and church fellowship halls, or think about the architecture of churches of recent decades or the church music of Mendelssohn and others—it seems to me that all of this betrays a complete ignorance about the essentially social nature of the church. It would be an interesting task for a sociological study of the church to undertake a historical examination of what the church produced in the artistic field. I am convinced that it might perhaps be possible to gain some deeper insights in this arena than if one attempted to investigate the charitable work of the church in a similar way.

292

But we cannot pursue this matter further. Did all of this come about by mere accident? How can the present situation be any different if theological students are not required, parallel to their academic studies, to be engaged in one way or another with the current situation; if they never hear, in an encounter with another class such as the proletariat, the very specific criticism leveled at their own class? There is no Protestant proclamation without knowledge of the present situation. On yet another front I see possibilities for contemporary, engaged preaching. The attempt must be made, in my view, to bring proletarians into the ministry. I believe that the future of our church is not least dependent on our getting preachers from proletarian circles, [*SC-RS:* "but we already have them".] in the first instance, of course, for the working-class congregations in the large cities. I also consider it decisive that working-class children in Sunday school are trained to become teachers' assistants, and that then schools are established in which young working-class people who prove themselves are prepared for ministry in the church. [*SC-RS:* "this is already happening".] How this would look in detail cannot be discussed here. If only the need is recognized, then ways will be found. Serious reflection upon the gospel and a keen eye for the present are the forces from which the living church is born anew.

The coming church will not be 'bourgeois'. How it will look is today still unclear. It is certain, though, that it is not Thorwaldsen and Mendelssohn who are able to proclaim the importance of the church-community, but rather Dürer, Rembrandt, and Bach. [*SC-RS:* "they too belong to the 'bourgeoisie'."] We do not seek the proletarian spirit as such, nor to imprison freedom within socialist doctrine, [*SC-RS:* "What does that mean?"] but instead want to take the church-community [Gemeinde] to the proletariat, and to transform the 'masses' into 'church-communities' ['Gemeinden']. To be sure, the Christian church-community remains a community of individual persons [*SC-RS:* "Indeed!"] who experience God in judgment and grace. On this point one can never yield just to please the masses. Tillich's ideas about the "holiness of the masses" <<P[aul] Tillich, *Masse und Geist*, 1922.>> have nothing to do with Christian theology. We know only of the holiness of God's church-community; and we know that God has bound the church-community to God's own

2. to reach final clarity in defining the problem of 'church and religious community';

293

[430. *cont.*] word in Christ, and that this word must be personally appropriated. We know of no 'absolute' revealing itself in the formlessness of the masses. We do know about the concrete historical will of God; but we also know that we will not condemn the masses but leave it to the Deus absconditus [hidden God]—absconditus, that is, in his mercy!—to speak here a divine word that is unknown to us. In this sense we must affirm extra ecclesiam nulla salus [outside the church there is no salvation]. The criterion for judging the masses must be the concept of the church-community [Gemeinde], not vice versa. [*SC-RS:* "Good"]

It is incorrect to think that the idea of socialism as such would sociologically correspond to the Christian concept of community; and it is even less correct to equate the spread of socialism with God's Realm on earth, as the religious socialists often assume. Nevertheless there exists, in our view, a certain 'affinity' between socialism and the Christian idea of the church-community, [*SC-RS:* "?"] which we must not fail to use. Our earlier reflections on the problem already made it clear that the socialist idea of equality is theologically and sociologically untenable; and this is why the attempt to impose equality by force is not only bound to fail, but is also unchristian. The Christian community is based on the dissimilarity and inequality of persons that is part of creation. But the priesthood of all believers can nevertheless be considered its basic sociological principle, as was shown earlier. Those who are free remain free, and the servant remains a servant, and yet both are one in Christ.

But Christian community is also based on the freedom of the individuals. Enslavement by the majority is unchristian because there is no earthly court between the individual and God that would have authority over the former. Community and individual person are maintained only in mutual balance (recall the image of the monad). Genuine socialism and individualism belong together. That the Christian concept of the church-community ultimately cannot be realized in any political or economic organization reveals the dissimilarity between socialism and Christianity. But we must nevertheless take up the leads that are offered to us; and the church must dare, if only through honest engagement, to move into the proletariat, the masses.

(2) Concerning the sociology of worship and pastoral care
[*SC-RS:* "What is of basic importance has already been said?"]
We must take a brief look at the sociological structure of our contemporary worship. Doing so will require supplemental remarks, some critical and some positive. In principle this problem has already been discussed within the framework of the sociology of the assembly; so the following will deal only with the concrete form of our service.

Acts of worship must, on the one hand, allow the church-community to recognize the proper relation between expressive and purposive elements. On the other hand, the church-community must, with regard to its spirit, recognize itself as defined in a threefold way, namely as plurality of spirit, community of spirit, and unity of spirit. These are the nec-

294

essary foundations of every service of worship. The mutual interconnection of expressive and purposive elements has already been discussed.

The Protestant service begins with congregational singing, that is, with an essentially expressive act that presents the church-community to itself. It would be appropriate at this point, if this is possible, to choose hymns whose theme is the church-community, or for each congregation to sing the same hymn every Sunday. Compared to other countries we have very few hymns about the church-community. But this should only be an incentive to really know those few that we do have. The liturgy then clearly initiates the purposive

3. to warn against overly grand statements[432] about the 'experience of the church', and to point to theological reflection.

[430. *cont.*] emphasis of the worship service. In its course, through an exchange between pastor and congregation, the entire history between God and humanity is expressed: the praise of God's eternity, a joint confession of sin, the assurance of pardon, and the congregational response of praise, "Glory to God in the highest . . ." The congregation recognizes itself as both peccatorum and sanctorum communio [community who are both sinners and saints]. This implies that the confession of sin has to awaken not only the recognition of sin on an individual level, but also the universality of sin. The congregation, knowing that it is wholly united in sin with all humanity, consequently exclaims: "Lord have mercy on us." <<There is hardly a more moving sermon on Christ's church-community than the kyrie eleison in the B-minor Mass.>> The content of the assurance of pardon must be to constitute the church as the holy people of God; and through it the assembled congregation must experience and believe its rebirth as the church-community of Christ. As such it now gathers for the reading of scripture, and, in reciting the creed, knows itself as the one church of God, and the service might conceivably conclude. But in reality it is only now that the main element of the service, the sermon, begins, and it is still followed by a closing liturgy. But is all this appropriate just as it is? The main substantive problem, in my view, is raised by the question: Are our congregations mature enough to follow such a concentrated liturgy? It seems to me that we must deny this. This then leads us to the recognition that it would currently be much more important if the beginning part of the service were devoted, as in certain English churches, to the reading of scripture. This would accustom the congregations to the use of the book upon which they are built, and would assure them of their bond with it precisely as the church-community. The Bible is the book of the church-community, as was already recognized earlier (cf. above, pages 231ff.).

I also consider the current placement of the creed somewhat of a structural mistake in the liturgical design. If the church-community understands itself, through the opening liturgy, as peccatorum and sanctorum communio, then it is the task of the sermon to reinforce and interpret this awareness; this means, on the one hand, to assure the individuals of their individuality and their community before God, but, on the other hand, also to point clearly and explicitly to God's claim to rule, and to lead the church-community into all the experiences that were discussed earlier in connection with the problem of the assembly. It is not necessary for the sermon topic to be directly related to the church-community. Nevertheless, there cannot be any sermon that did not show that it grew out of the church-community and is originally linked to it, and that Christian life is possible only within the   295
church-community. Only the closing part of the liturgy can lead the church-community to the point where it professes its faith in its Lord as a unity, as a single I, in the unity of faith; this unity subjectively mirrors the unity of spirit of the church of Christ that is beyond our perception, namely 'Christ existing as church-community'. Here it is not the individual but the entire church who professes Jesus to be the Christ, and itself to be his elect church-community. The I of the Apostle's Creed represents the church, and is correctly translated by Luther in his hymn as: "We all believe in one true God" [*Evangelisches Gesangbuch*, no. 183 (Martin Luther, 1524) in *Lutheran Book of Worship*, no. 374.][CG] This, in my view, clearly settles in the affirmative the heated debate over whether to include the creed. [*SC-RS*: "Where is the creed to be placed now?"] [Some sentences from the following passage have been included in the published version; see above, page 200]. It is not possible for the Christian community to disperse without having come to God as a unity, without affirming with its faith the divinely established unity of spirit which is beyond our

In our discussion above we have not talked[433] about the experience
of sin and grace, but only about their theological meaning and the

[430. *cont.*] perception. In the church, community and unity necessarily go together. If God's
will that there be one Spirit, one Lord, one God is the decreed constitution (constitutio) of
the church-community (cives) then the creed is the 'Yes' of the church-community to this
constitution. Indeed, viewed purely from the outside, it is by the constitution itself that the
religious 'community' summarizes what its objective spirit knows about its own foundation,
meaning, and purpose, and by which it is held together. It is a second question whether the
Apostles' Creed lives up to this definition of creed; and this is incidentally something that I
would certainly deny, without being able to substantiate this view here. <<See only the
most recent literature on this issue: Mathews, "A Visible Church and Christian Unity," *The
construct. quart.* 10.504; Jörgensen, "Das Bekenntnis als eine unermeßliche Grundlage der
Kirche," *Allgemeine evangelisch-lutherische Kirchenzeitung* 56 (1923); J[ohannes] Kunze, "Wie
ist das Bekenntnis der lutherischen Kirche als ihre bleibende Grundlage zu bestimmen und
wirksam zu machen," [*Kirchenzeitung*]; O[tto] Schmitz, *Die Vorbildlichkeit der urchristlichen
Gemeinden*, 1922, 26ff. Schmitz favors the confession "Jesus is Lord." [See also] Althaus,
Erlebnis der Kirche, 24ff. (in favor of the Apostles' Creed); Seeberg, *Dogmatik* 2:361ff., 366ff.
(in favor of the Apostles' Creed in its Lutheran interpretation).>>
    As the church-community that lives one life, it prays the Great Intercessory Prayer and
the Lord's Prayer, <<Sociologists have also recognized the sociological significance of the
Lord's Prayer: "From a sociological point of view it is not possible to conceive of a more
genuine expression of religion." Schäffle, *Bau und Leben* 1:182.>> giving thanks for the gift
received, petitioning the Lord of the church to safeguard and protect it, and interceding in
priestly authority for God's grace on behalf of all people. To gather up all of this, it humbly
prays the prayer which, according to ancient tradition (Luke 11:1ff.), the Lord gave to his
church-community, the "Our Father." One of the most painful issues today is the fact that
we have to experience again and again how little the congregation understands that during
worship it is praying as the church-community. We must make every effort to have our congregations once again learn how pray. It is precisely the corporate prayer of the church-
community, as Luther never wearies of saying, that is one of the major sources of its
strength. <<It might be a good start if, when reciting the Lord's Prayer together, everybody
were to speak clearly and audibly instead of murmuring. More mature congregations should
be asked, at least when celebrating the Lord's Supper, to express their common bond by
joining hands; for this is not merely a common bond of the soul but something very concrete, which necessarily includes the duty of physical togetherness. Precisely the fright that
overcomes individuals when asked to join hands with the unknown other standing next to
them only serves to highlight the importance of this symbolic act.>> With the assurance
that God will remain with his church-community, the service concludes.
    This structure of the service not only would be in accord with the sociological nature of
the concept of the church-community, but also would correspond, provided the opening
liturgy is modified, to what the church-community is psychologically able to understand.
[*SC-RS:* "Actually only psychological considerations".] This is not to deny, of course, that
there are also a variety of other possibilities; the sociological principles must be respected,
however. (One might assume that the place for the creed might be at the very beginning of
the service. However, this would be possible only in congregations that are very alive and
mature.)
    Based on the concept of the church-community developed above, the problem of pas-
toral care now also presents itself in a characteristic sociological form.

296

social implications of this meaning. It is only because of this that we were able to show that the basic-relations are established in reality, and to arrive at a specifically Christian sociology. Without taking this route, it would not have been possible even to formulate the concept of the church as distinct from the religious community. The currently relevant problem, as to what extent faith and experience belong together, cannot be discussed here. What matters is the fact that in our discussion thus   189 far we have not dealt with faith as an experience, but only as something that perceives certain realities. We believe that in so doing we have done justice to the distinctive nature of the theological method. The church can in its essence be understood only *as a divine act, which means, through a statement of faith*;[434] and only on that basis can it then be seen as 'experience'.[435] Only through faith is the church perceived as a community that is established by God. The so-called 'experience of the church' is in principle identical to the experience of the religious community. And yet there is such a thing as a genuine experience of the church, just as there is an experience of justification. However, it is all too often forgotten today that it is not experience that makes the church. Whenever people talk about the church from the perspective of the Youth Movement, they always fail to take seriously enough that the church is a reality, which means that it is established by God, and fundamentally 'prior' to all experience. Especially characteristic in this regard are the writings of Erich Stange[138] and Paul le Seur.[139] [436] Church is not 'produced'

---

138. [Stange,] *Die kommende Kirche*, 3d ed., Dresden, 68f. See also the very characteristic phrase on page 29, that the state lacks the "serious will to become an expression of the kingdom of God."

139. [Le Seur,] *Die Meisterfrage beim Aufbau der evangelischen Kirche*, Berlin. All

---

[430. *cont.*] The section that follows was incorporated by Bonhoeffer in the published version under the title "(4) The Sociological Problem of Pastoral Care," starting with "The relation of pastor . . ." (see above, page 248).

[431.] *SC-RS*: "Is 'in' used deliberately? If so it must be addressed in the discussion (body of Christ, Spirit)."

[432.] *SC-A* reads: to warn the present age against overly grand statements . . .

[433.] *SC-A* reads: In our discussion above we have not employed social philosophy and sociology from a genetic perspective, but from a phenomenological and structural point of view; we are not talking essentially . . .

[434.] *SC-A* reads: . . . be understood through a statement of faith.

[435.] See Althaus, *Das Erlebnis der Kirche*, esp. 13ff.

[436.] Le Seur, *Die Meisterfrage*, 51. For Le Seur, important requirements of a future

through powerful community experiences. When they become conscious of it, people always find themselves already within the church. This is true not only historically but also from the perspective of faith. We have to rediscover and revitalize the lost insight that all who are moved by the Spirit stand within the church, and that this is something that is both a gift [Gabe] and a task [Aufgabe]. The 'will for the church' that has been frequently invoked most recently can be welcomed only insofar as it expresses not the will to produce the church, but the will to see oneself and to act as part of the church that is moved by the Holy Spirit.

190   It is very telling that the 'will for the church' and the 'experience' of the church are mixed up in most cases. We shall see in a moment why it is necessary to distinguish between them.

It is extremely dangerous to confuse community romanticism [Gemeinschaftsromantik] with the community of saints [Gemeinschaft der Heiligen]. For the latter must always be acknowledged as something that is already established by God. The community of saints is, of course, also something we ourselves must will. But it can be willed by us only once God wills it through us. *It is thus willed by God 'prior' to any human will for community, and at the same time is real only as human will for community. This antinomy is overcome only by the human will being subjected by God to God's own will.* In actuality this subjection always remains in its beginning stage. However, God considers as completed what here has only begun. This means that if we only speak of the present movement of our will, we fall short of a full account of what God does with us. The

---

emphasis is placed on the community movement [Gemeinschaftsbewegung]. The church [Kirche] is understood as an "essentially Roman Catholic" (417) phenomenon that has been superseded by the local congregation [Gemeinde]. See also the table on page 61 that seeks to illustrate the relationship between church [Kirche] and local congregation [Gemeinde]. Regarding both monographs, see also the article by Rich[ard] Karwehl, "Zur Diskussion über die Kirchenfrage," *Zw. d. Z.*, 1927, no. 2, 178ff.

[436. *cont.*] church are a *comprehensive evangelism program* [*Volksmission*], and introduction of the *office of Protestant bishop*; for the latter he intends to appropriate the idea of the leader [*Führergedanke*] that was developed by the Youth Movement [*Jugendbewegung*]. [English-language readers should note that here *Führer* (leader) is not identified with Adolf Hitler, but refers to leadership in general, in all its ambiguity, as in this instance.] [RK/CG]

fact is that the new will of the community of the church, which breaks down again and again, is considered as already holy in God's gracious judgment, but of course only because it is God's own will to make it holy. God establishes the church in Christ, and from then on it is at every moment already completed in God's sight. But to actualize it God makes use of human wills, which are both means to an end and ends in themselves. A community of will moved by the Spirit is always already church, when and because it is moved. Although the will for the church is necessary, it is genuine only in connection with, or when born from, faith in the church that has already been established by God and exists in reality. The '*experience of the church*' is something different. It supposedly allows us to experience the 'others' as members of God's church-community.[437] Against this claim, however, we must raise serious theological objections. "We live by faith, not by sight."[438] No one has insight into the election or the hardening of the heart of the other. In all their actions they remain completely opaque. This means not only that nothing is known about the presence of the donum preserverantiae [gift of perserverance],[439] but also that active Christian conduct can spring from a hypocritical, misguided heart that is driven by false enthusiasm. Only the opera [works] are perceptible but not the persona, quae in manu dei est [the person, who is in the hand of God] (Calvin);[440] "the Lord knows those who are his."[441] How then could it be possible actually to experience the church and not merely the religious community? The church is impalpabilis, insensibilis [beyond taste and sense], as Luther said;[442] it must be believed. Even where persons reveal their hearts to one another in love, none of them can state with certainty whether the other belongs to the church. It is only in faith that I perceive the church. And the experiences of community that necessarily arise can only be seen by faith as manifestations of the church.[443]

   191

[437.] Deleted from *SC-A*: This means we are not dealing with an impulse of our own will here, but with the question of whether we are able to experience the impulse of the other's will.

[438.] Cf. 2 Cor. 5:7.

[439.] See above, page 217, editorial note 284.

[440.] ". . . only the actions but not the person, who is in the hand of God." See Calvin, *Institutes* (1536), 62, regarding the relation between person and actions; see also Calvin, *Institutes*, (1559), 3.14, esp. 8 and 20, 775–76 and 786–87.

[441.] See above, page 233, editorial note 330.

[442.] See Luther, "Predigten des Jahres 1528," no. 78, November 1, *WA* 27:399.

[443.] Deleted from *SC-A*: It is popular to talk about 'feeling' the church. However, this is   297

Human beings 'experience' merely the religious community, but in faith they know this religious community to be 'church'.[444] Even when two or three encounter one another in Christian community and confess their faith in Christian unity they believe that they are the church, based on the promise (Isa. 55:11; Matt. 18:20). Only in faith does their experience become an experience of the church.

But then what does it mean 'to believe in the church'? We do not believe in an invisible church, nor in the Realm of God within the church as coetus electorum [company of the elect]. Instead we believe that God has made the concrete, empirical church [Kirche] in which the word is preached and the sacraments are celebrated to be God's own church-community [Gemeinde]. We believe that it is the body of Christ, Christ's presence in the world, and that according to the promise God's Spirit is at work in it.[445] We have faith that God is also at work in the others. We do not believe in the call of individuals, but rather in that of the church-community. We believe in the church as the church of God, as the community of saints, those who are sanctified by God. We believe, however, that this takes place always within the historical framework of the empirical church. Thus we believe the means of grace to be effective within the empirical church and hence have faith in the holy church-community created by these means of grace. We believe in the church as *una* [one], since it is 'Christ existing as church-community', and *Christ is the one Lord* over those who are all one in him; as *sancta* [holy], since the Holy Spirit is at work in it; as *catholica* [catholic], since as *God's church* its call is to the entire world, and wherever in the world God's word is preached, there is the church.[446] We believe in the church not as an ideal that is unattainable or yet to be fulfilled, but as a present reality.[140] Christian thinking, in contrast to all

---

140. See the excellent work by E. Vurpillot, *De la nécessité d'une 'doctrine' protestante de l'église*, Montbéliard, 1926, 11.

[443. cont.] such a mystical type of description that it makes this word completely unsuitable. Thus, if understanding the church requires faith as an essential component, then the experiences of community . . .

[444.] Deleted from *SC-A*: Only faith sees the experience as 'experience of the church'.

[445.] The understanding of the church as *coetus electorum* [assembly of the elect] became popular through Lutheran theology, especially the *Compendium* by Leonhard Hutter. See Seeberg, *Begriff der Kirche*, 144ff., and also his *Dogmatik*, 2:346.

[446.] Regarding the Apostles' Creed, see Seeberg, *Dogmatik*, 2:352ff.

idealist theories of community, considers Christian community to be God's church-community at every moment in history. And yet within its historical development it never knows a state of fulfillment. It will remain impure as long as there is history, and yet in this concrete form it is nevertheless God's church-community.[141]

¶If we now ask about where faith 'experiences the church' most purely, then the answer is that this certainly does not happen in communities that are based on romantic feelings of solidarity between kindred spirits.[448] It rather takes place where there is no other link between the individuals than that of the community that exists within the church [kirchliche Gemeinschaft]; where Jew and Greek, pietist and liberal, come into conflict, and nevertheless in unity confess their faith, come together to the Lord's Table, and intercede for one another in prayer.[449] It is precisely in the context of everyday life that church is believed and experienced. The reality of the church is understood not in moments of spiritual exaltation, but within the routine and pains of daily life, and within the context of ordinary worship. Everything else merely obscures the actual state of affairs. The communal impulses of the Youth Movement have been great.[450] Even where the attempt has been made, however, they have thus far not been able to contribute much to the experience of the church. In this regard, one can hardly judge too harshly.[451] First of all, it must be understood what the church is. According to its nature it is to be believed in spite of, or rather precisely within, all its visible manifestations. Otherwise, it is not only

192

---

141. Here it becomes clear once again that the concepts of the visible and the invisible church are inadequate. However in our view, according to the monadic model, this in no way justifies the conclusion, which some recent writers have drawn, that the empirical church would have absolute teaching authority, that its dogma would be absolutely binding, and that it alone, through its teaching authority, could establish the individual's assurance of faith. See the peculiar writings by Erik Peterson, "Was ist Theologie?" 1925, 22ff., and O[tto] Piper, *Theologie und reine Lehre*, 1926, 2ff.[447]

[447.] See above, page 126, editorial note 12.
[448.] Deleted in *SC-A*: such as those cultivated in the Youth Movement.
[449.] "Intercede" is a translation for *füreinander stehen*, which is probably an allusion to Bonhoeffer's important concept of *Stellvertretung*. [RK/CG]
[450.] *SC-A* reads: are beautiful and great.
[451.] Deleted from *SC-A*: and only by such a judgment is this matter well served.

dangerous but outright unscrupulous and a complete confusion of the Protestant understanding of the church when one speaks of experiences that can neither constitute the church, nor capture its essence in any way. Our age is not short on experiences, but on *faith*. But only faith creates a genuine experience of the church. Thus we think it more important for our age to be led into the faith in God's church-community than to have experiences squeezed out of it that as such are of no use, but that will come about of their own accord wherever faith in the sanctorum communio has been found.

193

4. Church and Eschatology [452]

"We walk by faith, not by sight."[453] This remains true as long as there is history. For us, this leads to the basic insight that history, and consequently even the end of history, is incapable of bringing the ultimate solution. It further follows that the meaning of history cannot consist in a progressive development, but that "every age is in direct relationship with God" (Ranke).[454] And this then also provides theological justification for our sociological method of asking about the essential structure of the church, rather than outlining its development based on a philosophy of history.[455] The course of church history basically teaches us no more about its eschatological meaning than does the understanding of each present moment.[456] Within history there are two basic conflicting tendencies, both of which will continue to gain strength and momentum. One is the impulse of the sanctorum communio to permeate the life of all communities and societies.[457] However, it would not be

---

[452.] See Bonhoeffer's seminar paper on this topic, written for Seeberg in the winter semester, 1925–26: "Kirche und Eschatologie (oder: Kirche und Reich Gottes)," *DBW* 9:336–54. [CG]

[453.] 2 Cor. 5:7.

[454.] See Leopold von Ranke, *The Theory and Practice of History*, 53.

[455.] Deleted from *SC-A*: This of course does not deny the legitimacy of a philosophy of church history, but only its potential claim to be eschatology.

[456.] *SC-RS*: "Insofar it is linked with x moments that are normatively shaped."

[457.] Deleted from *SC-A*:

The ultimate meaning of every marriage, family, or friendship is to become sanctorum communio, as has already been stated repeatedly. The relationship of the sanctorum communio to the world does not consist in a senseless hostility to culture, but in the struggle for the justification and sanctification of all human communal life through the word of God and the Holy Spirit. The sanctorum communio does not place its trust in culture, but it recognizes

correct to define the empirical church and the world as ultimate opposites. Rather, the rift goes right through the empirical church, and
within itself the struggle between good and evil must erupt. There will
never be a pure church, just as there never has been one. *Sanctorum communio and Antichrist* will remain the ultimate opposites in history.[142]

Christian eschatology is essentially *eschatology of the church-community
[Gemeindeeschatologie].*[458] It is concerned with the fulfillment[459] of the
church and of the individual within it. The concept of the Realm of
God, however, refers not merely to the fulfillment of the church, but
also to the problems of the 'new world', that is, the eschatology of culture and nature. In speaking only about the fulfillment of the church
and of the communities,[460] we are dealing with only a part of the whole
problem.

194

Within the problem as a whole we can distinguish two groups of
ideas, those of *judgment* and those of *eternal life*, which means perfect
community with God.

The question is,[461] how do we conceive of human community as

---

142. Regarding the arguments for a dual course of history, see the two most
recent major works on eschatology: Seeberg, *Dogmatik*, 2:606ff., and Althaus,
Die letzten Dinge, 3d ed., 1926, 119ff., which to a large extent are in agreement
on this point.

[457. *cont.*] culture as the ground on which it has to work. Thus we cannot of course concur with Rothe's eschatology, because we think that the polarities in the world, instead of
softening, will become more pronounced, and that the striving of the sanctorum communio
is opposed by the striving of the evil will. Consequently, a culture that had absorbed the
church into itself is therefore inconceivable. What is and remains central and basic for the
work of the sanctorum communio is the empirical church in history as willed by God. But
to define the empirical church and the world as ultimate opposites would also be wrong.

[458.] This sentence reads in *SC-A*:

Every study of eschatology is, by its subject matter, faced with the dual problem of an individual and a collective eschatology. The basic eschatological concept of earliest Christianity,
the kingdom of God, is collective. And it is very important to emphasize that Christian
eschatology is essentially *eschatology of the church-community*.

[459.] *Vollendung*, which we have translated "completion" at the beginning of chapter
5, is here appropriately translated "fulfillment" to convey completion in its full eschatological sense. [CG/RK]

[460.] Deleted from *SC-A*: namely essentially about the fulfillment of the community of saints
. . .

[461.] "The question is" reads in *SC-A*: Judgment takes place at every moment in history.
This implies two things for the last judgment. First, it must be understood as the revelation of this

298

undergoing judgment? Judgment applies to persons. But this obviously means that it applies not only to individual persons [Individual-personen], but also to collective persons [Kollektivpersonen]. This, in turn, entails the notion that the individual is judged not only in isolation, but also as a member of collective persons.[462] Nation, family, marriage—all undergo their judgment as undivided entities. What becomes significant in this context is what was said earlier about communities being at the limit of time [Grenzzeitlichkeit] and societies being limited in time [Zeitbegrenztheit].[463] The eternal judgment is passed on both. But it is passed only on the former as collective persons [Kollektiv-personen], and only on the latter as entities consisting of individual persons [Einzelpersonen]. Thus the community as a collective person can expect eternal life, whereas the society dissolves. It remains unclear how we are to imagine in detail a collective person being rejected or accepted, while the individual belonging to it may be treated according to a different verdict. But this must not lead us to reject the very idea of judgment being passed on the collective person. We learned that the community as a collective person exists from God to God (see above),[464] and that it must be conceived as being established through the will of God, and as such standing at the last judgment. This idea can also be found in the New Testament (Chorazin, Bethsaida, Capernaum, Matt. 11:21ff.; the address to the churches in Revelation 2 and 3, esp. 3:16 and 3:10). That God can condemn a collective person and at the same time accept individuals who are part of it, and vice versa, is an idea that is as necessary as it is incomprehensible.[465]

At the last judgment each one is consciously confronted—perhaps for the first time—with God's verdict. Here everyone becomes a 'person', recognizing God's holiness and their own sin; here everyone becomes 'solitary' [einsam]. However, there is a solitude [Einsamkeit] in the face

---

[461. cont.] judgment that takes place within history. But it nevertheless remains the final verdict that faith awaits. The question now is . . .

[462.] As Bonhoeffer has indicated above, by belonging to several communities—family, marriage, friendship, nation, church—one is ipso facto a member of several collective persons. [CG]

[463.] See above, page 101. [CG]

[464.] See above, page 119. [CG]

[465.] "That God . . . incomprehensible" reads in *SC-A*: However, this needs to be coupled with the other idea that God can condemn a collective person and at the same time accept individuals who are part of it, and vice versa.

of grace, and a solitude in the face of God's wrath. Eternal death means to exist in the solitude of God's wrath, that is to be alone in sin, without any ethical communication with the other spirits, and at the same time conscious of one's sin, and aware of what one is missing.[466] If one assumes that the spirit continues to live on apart from the body, then the possibility for communication provided by the body is entirely lost; in this case, the solitude [Einsamkeit] of the judgment of wrath is compounded by loneliness [Alleinsein].[143] Nevertheless, the gravity[467] of the divine judgment of wrath consists essentially in the 'solitude', and not so much in the general loneliness of the spirit. Solitude is an ethical category, and being under God's wrath is worse than the misery of loneliness. It is not the natural death of the human spirit, but death as being cut off from God's Spirit. And it is conceivable that it is felt most painfully precisely where it is not coupled with loneliness of the human spirit in general.

195

Luther, like Paul before him, assumed a resurrection and a new bodily existence even for unbelievers.[144] The fact that a resurrection is in principle possible only through Christ, and is thus conceivable only for those who believe, did not prevent both these men from teaching a general bodily resurrecton in order to preserve the idea of the last judgment.[468] However, the Christian concepts of person and of community are what give the idea of a new body its most profound meaning. In the Christian person soul and body are bound together in an

---

143. Seeberg, [*Dogmatik,*] 584ff.

144. See Althaus, [*Die letzten Dinge,*] 285ff., arguing against [Erich] Stange, [*Die kommende Kirche*].

[466.] Deleted from *SC-A*: Whether this solitude is seen, in addition, as accompanied by an eternal loneliness of the spirit in general depends on how one answers the problem of new bodily existence.

[467.] In *SC-A* "Nevertheless, the gravity" reads:

This state is indeed and with good reason conceived of as the death of the human spirit. <<Seeberg, [*Dogmatik,*] 2:584f.>> For sociality is not merely one among many human dispositions, but essential to being human, as we have shown above. How such survival of the human spirit could be conceived, however, remains a mystery. At any rate it is also important to emphasize that the gravity . . .

[468.] See Luther, "Confession Concerning Christ's Supper," *LW* 37:360ff. [*WA* 26:499ff.] and *LW* 28:144 [*WA* 36:596].

indissoluble unity.[145] [469] Concrete community is possible only because human beings are equipped with a body. Thus we must think of the body as being essentially connected with the soul. We assume that together with the body the sinful soul, too, will die, and that in the resurrection, together with the soul, God will also create a new body, and that this new spiritual [pneumatisch] body will be the warrant and condition for the eternal community between personal spirits. It cannot be explored here whether this idea necessarily also applies to unbelievers. Thus we can summarize by saying that God's judgment applies to both individual persons [Individualpersonen] and collective persons [Kollektivpersonen]. In the eternal judgment of wrath, God respects the freedom of the will that ultimately remains defiant. Those who only will themselves are granted what they desire, but at the same time will recognize that in so doing they have killed themselves spiritually [geistlich].[470] For human beings live only in community with other human beings and with God.

We define *the solitude of the judgment of grace* [Gnadengericht] as the judgment of those who believe. It is the final verdict and takes place in the eternal church-community. This moment implies that within the church-community solitude is totally overcome, and that individual personhood would exist only within the reality of the church-community. The very moment in which a human being must live in solitude through the unspeakable distress of painful repentance in God's sight—something that we must also assume for believers—is also the moment in which that person enters completely into the church-community of Christ that carries them.

We must not speak of a dual outcome here without at the same time emphasizing the inner necessity of the idea of apocatastasis.[471] We are unable to resolve this paradox.[146] On the one hand, the concept of the

---

145. C[arl] Stange, *Unsterblichkeit der Seele*, 121ff.

146. See Seeberg, [*Dogmatik*,] 625ff., and Althaus, [*Die letzten Dinge*,] 203ff.

[469.] Deleted from *SC-A*: This is an insight we gained in chapter 2. The body is not the prison of the soul, nor is the body the source of sin; the source of sin is rather the will of the person that holds body and soul together.

[470.] Deleted from *SC-A*: and perhaps also as far as the human spirit is concerned.

[471.] The Greek term for the doctrine of the salvation by grace of all creatures, also known as 'universalism'. [CG]

church, as Christ's presence in the world which calls for a decision, necessarily demands the dual outcome. The recognition that the gift of God's boundless love has been received without any merit would, on the other hand, make it seem just as impossible to exclude others from this gift and this love.[472] The strongest reason for accepting the idea of apocatastasis would seem to me that all Christians must be aware of having brought sin into the world, and thus aware of being bound together with the whole of humanity in sin, aware of having the sins of humanity on their conscience. Justification and sanctification are inconceivable for anyone if that individual believer cannot be assured that God will embrace not only them but all those for whose sins they are responsible.[473] But all statements in this regard only express a hope; they cannot be made part of a system.

God's judgment and grace apply to persons. This means that judgment and grace apply to all individual persons [Einzelpersonen] within the church-community—to the plurality of spirit [Geistvielheit] as described above—to marriages and friendships that have become part of the sanctorum communio, and finally to the unity of these, the collec- 197
tive person of the church-community, the unity of spirit [Geisteinheit]. Ultimately, however, these persons are persons only in community with each other, that is, in the community of spirit [Geistgemeinschaft]. This is something that in conclusion we must emphasize very clearly once again. However, community of spirit necessarily implies whole persons in their spiritual bodiliness, a bodiliness [Leiblichkeit] that must be understood as the direct expression of the new reality of spirit [Geistigkeit]. This precludes from the outset any mystical ideas such as a final assimilation into God's all-encompassing person, a fusion of our supposedly divine nature with that of God. Creator and creature remain as persons distinct from each other. And the creatures, too, are distinct from one another. Yet all of them together constitute the powerful unity of God's church-community. They are now 'entirely justified and sanctified', one in Christ and yet all individuals. Their community of spirit is based in and kindled by their mutual love for one another. They give themselves to each other and to God, thereby establishing

---

[472.] *SC-RS*: "Even within the church it must be assumed to have a *historical* form. As far as eternity is concerned, it is a different matter."

[473.] In *SC-A* the following sentence is lacking.

human community and community with God. Here that community is real and eternal, which in history is merely realized in a rudimentary way and disintegrates again and again. Whereas even in the church the I and the You still encountered each other as strangers, that is, in a strangeness that was overcome only in the eschatological foretaste of sanctification, here the revelation of one heart to the other is fulfilled in divine love. *The community of love becomes visible in hearts who, filled with the Spirit, reveal themselves to each other.* "I and I seek and find one another, and pour themselves into each other. . . . reality and truth become the same. . . ."[147] Here we see love is completed,[474] that is, that we only attain our 'self' when we no longer see our own person. And this takes place precisely in the most intimate community with the other, a community that may be described as blessedness. It remains a community of will [Willensgemeinschaft] between free persons, and its blessedness has nothing to do with mystical fusion. *It is the most powerful expression of personal life itself,* just as its loss means death. The mystic does not understand the power and glory of love. The dual condition of being under *God's rule* and in *God's Realm* has a dual result,[475] seeing the eternal truth—what was formerly faith—and loving with a love that is now perfect, the perfect service of spirit. The movement upwards must not be separated from that toward the neighbor. Both belong indissolubly together. Herein lies the fallacy of Ritschl's distinction.[476] To be under God's rule means to live in community with God and the church-community. God wants to be the king of his subjects, the father of his children, to rule over spirits whose will is free, and to have community with them—not to be the primordial ground of all being, thus becoming the death of all actual being. God is the God of living persons.

Now the objective spirit of the church really has become the Holy Spirit, the experience of the 'religious' community now really is the experience of the church, and the collective person of the church now really is 'Christ existing as church-community'. It is beyond what we are able to conceive now as to how it will come to pass that all become one and yet each keeps their own identity. All are in God, and yet each remains distinct from God.

198

147. Seeberg, *Ewiges Leben,* 1915, 33.

[474.] Deleted from *SC-A*: and profoundly mysterious.
[475.] Deleted from *SC-A*: of activity.
[476.] Regarding Ritschl, see above page 217, footnote 85.

All are united with each other, and yet distinct. Each possesses God totally and by themselves in the grace-filled dual solitude [Zweieinsamkeit] of seeing truth and serving in love, and yet never is solitary because they always really live only within the church-community. We walk by faith. But we shall see—not only God but also God's church-community. We shall no longer merely believe in its love and faith, but see it. At every moment we shall be aware of God's will to rule [Herrschaftswille] and implement it within the realm of the church-community. Here the realm of Christ has become the Realm of God. The ministerium Christi [ministry of Christ], of the Holy Spirit, and of the word have ceased.[148] Christ himself hands over his[477] church-community to the Father (1 Cor. 15:24), in order that God may be all in all. What has become reality here is not the ecclesia triumphans [church triumphant], but the Realm of God extending throughout the whole world. No longer repentance and faith, but service[478] and sight. Here the weeds are separated from the wheat; the age of the historical church in all its affliction has passed away. God will wipe away the tears from all eyes.[479] The victory is won, the Realm has become God's. "Καὶ ναὸν οὐκ εἶδον ἐν αὐτῇ. ὁ γὰρ κύριος ὁ θεὸς ὁ παντοκράτωρ ναὸς αὐτῆς ἐστιν καὶ τὸ ἀρνίον." ["I saw no temple in the city, for its temple is the Lord God the Almighty and the Lamb."][480]

199

This is the hope of the church, our present church,[481] the sanctorum communio. And it guards this hope as its most sacred treasure, but really only as a hope. It will refrain from premature attempts to transform this hope into a present reality. But in hope the church grows strong. It[482] knows "that the sufferings of this present time are not worth comparing with the glory about to be revealed to it."[483]

---

148. Luther, *Disp.*, ed. Drews, 116, Thesis 24.

[477.] Reading *seine* instead of the typographical error *seiner*. [RK/CG]

[478.] *SC-A* reads: love.

[479.] Cf. Isa. 25:8 and Rev. 7:12; 21:4.

[480.] The Greek citation of Rev. 21:22 replaces the following in *SC-A*: And the entire Realm is the new temple of God.

[481.] *SC-A* omits: our present church.

[482.] "It" replaces the following in *SC-A*: In the community of love and in the unity of faith it endures and it . . .

[483.] Cf. Rom. 8:18. [The *NRSV* reads "revealed to us."] [CG]

EDITOR'S AFTERWORD
TO THE GERMAN EDITION

I

In the meantime I have been thinking things over and came to the following conclusion. To have Holl or Harnack supervise the dissertation would really make no sense, since with a doctrinal-historical dissertation I should meet with no resistance from Seeberg either. So it makes very little difference whether I go to one or the other, as I think that on the whole Seeberg is also well-disposed toward me. Thus I decided to remain with Seeberg after all, and now have suggested a subject to him that is half historical and half systematic, and which he found very acceptable.[1]

Half historical and half systematic was the method by means of which the theme should be treated, according to the judgment of a young doctoral student in the mid-1920s. At the theological faculty in Berlin one ordinarily expected a work in church history, especially if the person concerned had studied with Adolf von Harnack, Reinhold Seeberg, or Karl Holl. After World War I, however, the questions arising in theology simply were too pressing, since theology was in a stage of intensive reexamination. Harnack as well as Holl assumed an approach which sought access, by way of historical criticism, to the past witness of faith. Such an approach refrains as long as possible from systematic-theological interpretation, which comes into play only after the historical-critical analysis. But precisely the systematic-theological premises implicit in this approach were seriously questioned by the postwar generation of students. Critical questions were addressed to the so-called liberal

---

[1.] *DBW* 9:156.

theology with a vehemence that the Berlin church historians must have found unsettling. This uneasiness is clearly apparent in Adolf von Harnack's address, delivered in June 1926 at the memorial commemoration for Karl Holl at the University of Berlin. Harnack spoke of "an age in which the intellectual heritage is in danger of disintegrating into visions, 307 inspirations, and paradoxes, and in which a clever person, through skillful combination and nimble style, is able to produce fragments of new worldviews without much effort."[2] Would Harnack's critical verdict have applied also to the young Dietrich Bonhoeffer? It might perhaps be admitted that Bonhoeffer's doctoral dissertation is a "skillfully combined piece" which, in spite of all the efforts to integrate the material, perhaps had to remain a fragment; but calling it a "new worldview" is something one cannot so easily concede. For it is very characteristic of Bonhoeffer's work that the results of historical research are not evaded, but taken into account. To a large extent Bonhoeffer's doctoral dissertation is based on the results of the hard work of the Berlin theologians, above all on the understanding of the theology of the young Martin Luther advanced by Karl Holl.

According to Bonhoeffer's account, the dissertation was supposed to be "half historical and half systematic."[3] This goal already reveals something of the tension implicit in the topic. Theology is unable and unwilling to remain on a historical level, especially if the historical approach itself is fraught with theological implications that require clarification; theology presses toward doctrinal theology, since the past witness of faith needs to be justified critically before one's own present. "Every Protestant Christian is a theologian" is the phrase formulated by Bonhoeffer in his graduation theses.[4] The tension in Bonhoeffer's work, however, is not caused merely by the historical-systematic formulation of the problem. It is also the result of a question that drives Bonhoeffer's theological enterprise as a whole: where within the reality of the world does the reality confessed by the Christian faith manifest itself and become concrete? From its very beginning, Bonhoeffer's theology is 308 informed by the conviction that the truth which is believed must have a concrete locus within the reality of the world. This is the leitmotif which he is to pursue throughout his entire life, and which in turn will always

---

[2.] Holl, *Briefwechsel mit Adolf von Harnack*, 84.
[3.] *DBW* 9:156.
[4.] "Thesis 3," in *NRS* 32 (*DBW* 9:477 [*GS* 3:47]). See also above, page 251.

remain an unsettling issue for him. This question of the reality of God in the world is evident in the programmatic statements with which Bonhoeffer concisely outlines the topic of his dissertation. "The church is God's new will and purpose for humanity. God's will is always directed toward the concrete, historical human being. . . ."[5] God's will must become visible and comprehensible at some point in history. But at the same point it must already be completed. Therefore, it must be revealed."[6] These concise statements contain both question and answer. God's church is where the divine will becomes concrete, visible, and comprehensible.

The concrete identification of the revealed will of God predetermines the method with which Bonhoeffer is to develop his theme. The theologian who desires to speak of the church cannot approach his subject from the outside but can only speak as one standing within, and coming from, the church. The programmatic title of the dissertation expresses this in significant fashion: *Sanctorum Communio*. The church as the subject matter of the confessional documents also determines the way one is to speak about the church. Bonhoeffer's method is characterized by the obligation to speak theologically about the church as an integral part of the third article of the creed. The entire book is informed by the desire to translate commitment to the church into theological terms.

Bonhoeffer's concentration on the reality of revelation grasped by faith is reminiscent of Karl Barth's early 'dialectical theology', which focuses all theological discourse on the divine revelation. This focus results in a critical stance toward Schleiermacher, Ritschl, and Troeltsch, whom Bonhoeffer severely castigates theologically. However, Bonhoeffer does not rest content with the dichotomy, as Barth had conceived it, between revelation and history. If revelation and history are related properly, then it is possible to move beyond understanding history merely as "crisis."[7] In his very approach Bonhoeffer already seeks to correct Barth's fundamental theological decisions, though out of basic sympathy for those decisions. It can be safely assumed, moreover, that Bonhoeffer consciously intends this controversy with Barth.[8] Barth, as

---

[5.] See above, page 141.

[6.] See above, pages 141f.

[7.] See Barth, *The Epistle to the Romans*, 55; esp. 226ff.

[8.] See the allusions to Barth's controversies with Peterson (page 126, editorial note 12) and Harnack (page 222, editorial note 295).

he specifically states, returns the doctrine of God to being a prolegomenon to theology.[9] Bonhoeffer's argument, however, runs strictly opposite. Only when one frees the doctrine of God from the constraint which confined it to the prolegomenon of theology can one escape the danger of failing to do justice theologically to the concept of the church. Bonhoeffer's proposal for the overall design of systematic theology can be understood as a direct criticism of Barth: "In order to establish clarity about the inner logic of theological construction, it would be good for once if a presentation of doctrinal theology were to start not with the doctrine of God but with the doctrine of the church."[10] We can presume that, at the time, Bonhoeffer's view of the church as a revelational reality established in Christ could only have been interpreted by Barth as "being homesick" for Roman Catholicism.[11] And it is even conceivable that Barth could have accused Bonhoeffer of a positivism of revelation [Offenbarungspositivismus].

Certainly, Bonhoeffer could have rebutted that criticism by referring to Martin Luther. For Bonhoeffer's position vis-à-vis Barth is not conceivable without the legacy he had inherited from the Berlin church historian Karl Holl, especially Holl's understanding of the theology of Martin Luther as taught in his seminar and presented to the scholarly community in his book on Luther. Two of Holl's basic insights guided Bonhoeffer in understanding Luther. Holl strongly emphasized the connection in Luther's theology between the doctrine of justification and ecclesiology. Holl's study "The Origin of Luther's Concept of the Church" is based on this central thesis.[12] A second thesis proposed by Holl, and taken up by Bonhoeffer without reservation, is that the church is to be seen primarily as community. According to Holl, a comprehensive view of Luther's understanding of the church must take into account this christological basis and communal structure of the church. In order to clarify this connection, Bonhoeffer himself now draws on Luther's own writings, in which this link between the christological basis and the social structure of the church-community is developed intensively. As a result, the importance of the sacrament and the related concept of vicarious representative action [Stellvertretung] now move into the center

310

[9.] See Barth, *The Word of God and the Word of Man*, 216f.
[10.] See above, page 134.
[11.] See Barth, "Das Schriftprinzip der reformierten Kirche," 215ff., esp. 229.
[12.] See Holl, *Gesammelte Aufsätze*, vol. 1, *Luther*, 288.

of Bonhoeffer's theology. Christ's vicarious representative action becomes the structural principle of the Christian church-community; this makes it possible for members of the church-community to be actively with-one-another [Miteinander] and for-one-another [Füreinander]. The principle of vicarious representative action "gives Christian basic-relations their substantive uniqueness."[13] It is consequently no longer possible to separate ecclesiology from Christology, since both are connected through the principle of vicarious representative action. This inseparable connection between ecclesiology and Christology, which already is present in Luther, can be pressed by Bonhoeffer to the point where the two become indistinguishable. It must be noted, however, that through this close connection both Bonhoeffer and Luther merely seek to establish the christological foundation of the concept of the church. In the unity between Christ and the church the relation of the former to the latter is therefore not reversible.

311   If Dietrich Bonhoeffer is seen as a student of Martin Luther, to whom he had been led by Karl Holl, then the title of his doctoral dissertation gains a new significance. The '*sanctorum communio*' is the community based on Christ's vicarious representative [stellvertretendes] suffering on our behalf, and it consists of Christians on earth who in turn stand up for-each-other [füreinander-eintreten]. The marks of the church [Kirche], if understood comprehensively, always imply the sociality of the church-community [Gemeinde]. The proclamation of the gospel and the celebration of the sacraments make Christ's vicarious representative action [Stellvertretung] present for us; and this vicarious representative action in turn finds expression in the church's social form. The social dimension of the concept of the church is, thus, not an external addition to this concept, but an original, constitutive element. This also implies then that all fundamental Christian concepts are fully understandable "only in reference to sociality,"[14] as Bonhoeffer, seemingly stating the self-evident, writes in his preface. In so doing, Bonhoeffer places the concept of the '*sanctorum communio*' back into the tradition of the Reformation from which it had become detached, because the question of the concrete social form of the church had been disconnected from the theological task of defining the marks of Christ's church.

[13.] See above, page 156.
[14.] See above, page 21.

Bonhoeffer encapsulated this connection in the pregnant phrase "Christ existing as church-community [Gemeinde]."[15] In the debate over Bonhoeffer's dissertation, this phrase has almost taken on a life of its own; consequently, its original meaning in Bonhoeffer has been almost totally obscured. To understand it one must keep two points in mind. On the one hand, Bonhoeffer can conceive of Christ 'existing as church-community' precisely because he defines Christ's vicariously representative action [Stellvertretung] as the structural principle shaping the life of the church-community. On the other hand, Christ can only become present and actualized within the witness of the church-community because the "unity of the church as a structure [is] established 'before' any knowing and willing of the members; it is not ideal, but real."[16] The unity of the church in and through Christ is a unity based on the person of Christ. This unity is perceived as already completed in Christ. Still present is Hegel's terminology, which had been so appealing to Bonhoeffer precisely because it conveys a close connection between Christ and the church-community. Within the bounds of this terminology, however, a decisive critique of Hegel is already visible. For with this phrase Bonhoeffer intends to take up Paul's concept of the church as the body of Christ,[17] and, going back to Paul's Adam-Christ typology, he also understands Christ as a "collective person."[18] Both of these notions, which are informed by the New Testament, are conceptually linked in the phrase "Christ existing as church-community."

Bonhoeffer himself senses the far-reaching implications of his christological-ecclesiological concentration, and this is why he runs into apparent difficulties in spelling them out in the language of systematic theology. He speaks about the "opposition of the concepts of revelation and time, completion and becoming."[19] In spite of the difficulties in explicating them precisely, Bonhoeffer insists emphatically on two points. First, God's revelation must be understood not only as a beginning, but also as a completion [Vollendung]. Second, revelation enters into time "not just apparently but actually," and precisely by doing so it "explodes" the category of time.[20] These definitions are based on an

312

[15.] See above, pages 189ff.
[16.] See above, page 199.
[17.] See above, pages 134ff.
[18.] See above, pages 192ff.
[19.] See above, page 143.
[20.] See above, ibid.

understanding of revelation whose silent implications point far beyond the theology of the early Bonhoeffer. For the underlying understanding of revelation has revolutionary consequences for the concepts of reality and time. Such a revision of basic categories follows inevitably from an approach that considers the church as being realized and completed in and through Christ. This makes it outright impossible to integrate the church philosophically into a historical process in which the world, by means of the church, moves toward the kingdom of God.

This evidently puts Bonhoeffer's approach in conflict with the basic notions of Reinhold Seeberg, in whose *Christliche Dogmatik* revelation and evolution remain essential concepts. The dissertation comprises several elements which are in tension with Reinhold Seeberg's theology. But there also are numerous themes that reflect Bonhoeffer's affinity to the theology espoused by his doctoral mentor. Especially reminiscent of Seeberg's history of doctrine is the close correspondence between Bonhoeffer's argument and Augustine's concept of the church. In his study Seeberg portrays Augustine's theology with great sympathy and places it at the center of his portrait of the ancient church. An additional factor contributing to Seeberg's positive assessment of the dissertation may have been Bonhoeffer's nearly continuous cross-references to the *Christliche Dogmatik*. These cross-references, however, have more than a merely tactical function. The most obvious themes which Bonhoeffer appropriates from Seeberg are a voluntaristic concept of God and Seeberg's insistence that the study have revelation as its starting point, thus making possible "positive theological knowledge."[21] Bonhoeffer also agrees with the consequences of Seeberg's voluntarism, as is evident by the fact that in the published version he retained Seeberg's illustrations of the 'ethical collective person'. Bonhoeffer clearly did not yet consider his own statements on people [Volk], history, and war to be problematic.[22] In Seeberg's view, Bonhoeffer's study quite clearly could be regarded as a contribution to "modern, positive theology."[23] We can assume that Seeberg was especially surprised and positively impressed by Bonhoeffer's use of social philosophy in his reflections on human sociality, with which he ventures to establish the link with 'formal sociology'.

[21.] See above, page 127.
[22.] See above, pages 119, editorial note 24.
[23.] See Seeberg, *Die Kirche Deutschlands im neunzehnten Jahrhundert*, 307.

One would expect that developing a theological definition of the concept of the church—one that seeks to steer a middle course between the two poles just described—would be a task large enough to demand all of 314 Bonhoeffer's theological skills. But Bonhoeffer considers his task to be even more comprehensive. In an absolutely unique and unprecedented venture for that time, he seeks to establish a relationship with sociology from within theology. Without any inhibition or theological resentment, he audaciously enters into a dialogue with the social philosophy and sociology of his time.

Bonhoeffer defines the criteria for this dialogue with social philosophy and sociology. A study in systematic theology that seeks to interpret theological concepts in social terms, and at the same time intends to be a "Study of the Sociology of the Church" as its subtitle reads, can only enter into dialogue with a sociology that for its part is able to provide a foundation and sociological interpretation of sociality. Here, Bonhoeffer's "theological method"[24] becomes once again the compass for the way through the challenging terrain of sociology and social philosophy.

The crucial link with sociology is established through a concept of reality which Bonhoeffer develops in critical dialogue with German idealist philosophy. This dialogue with philosophy, which precedes the sociological discussion proper, is necessary because sociology, whether consciously or implicitly, is based upon insights gained through social philosophy. Through this dialogue Bonhoeffer adopts a number of ideas which are extremely important for his thinking even beyond his early theology.

First, Bonhoeffer adopts the critique of Kant's understanding of the subject that Max Scheler had developed in his study, *Formalism in Ethics and Non-formal Ethics of Values*. In contrast to the epistemological inquiry that had dominated modern philosophy, Bonhoeffer finds himself attracted to the 'phenomenological method' which no longer has the cognitive self as its center. The other who confronts the self as a You guarantees that reality cannot be deduced from the cognitive self, according to Bonhoeffer, who thus already moves beyond Scheler's 315 thought. The I-You-relation serves as a countermodel to modernity's subject-object scheme. Among the phenomenologists it is especially

---

[24.] See above, page 65.

Theodor Litt, in his study *Individuum und Gemeinschaft*, who for Bonhoeffer becomes the chief proponent of an understanding of reality
based on a reciprocity between the self and the other. With remarkable
intensity Bonhoeffer enters the thought-world of the I-You-philosophy
which in the 1920s developed as a broad philosophical as well as cultur-
al movement in opposition to the philosophy of German idealism. The
dispute between Eberhard Grisebach and Friedrich Gogarten in Jena
also had an impact on the shape of Bonhoeffer's theology.

Another strong impulse came from the philosophically inclined theologian Emanuel Hirsch. Through a criticism of idealist philosophy, particularly Fichte's generative idealism [Erzeugungsidealismus], Hirsch, in
his studies on idealistic philosophy and Christianity, sought to establish
a "Christian philosophy of history."[25] Its aim was to overcome the limitations of idealist philosophy, and to provide a more solid foundation
for the concepts of person and community by relating them to the concept of God. In Hirsch's view, this required moving away from the epistemological question that had been the primary focus of idealist
philosophy and instead giving first priority to the question of ethics.
And it is this point that Bonhoeffer adopts from Hirsch. Hirsch's argument, too, leads to an I-You-philosophy.

If the I-You-relation is now applied to the concept of the church, then
the church can be understood in terms of social philosophy as the reality of persons encountering one another. Such a definition of the relational structure of reality provides the basis for the substantive concept
of the *humanum*; this concept does not permit treating human beings
only as means to an end without regarding them "always as ends in
themselves too."[26] "A person can never be only a means to an end,"
writes Bonhoeffer.[27] Precisely this apodictic statement, distinctly reminiscent of Kant, is the source of the empathetic concept of community
which runs as a thread through Bonhoeffer's entire study. In community "being-with-one-another [Miteinander] can be willed as a end in
itself."[28] However, Bonhoeffer then weakens such statements again by
placing the general concept of community within the differentiating
typology of 'community [Gemeinschaft] and society' [Gesellschaft];

316

[25.] See Hirsch, *Die idealistische Philosophie*, 1ff.
[26.] Kant, *Groundwork of the Metaphysic of Morals*, 101.
[27.] See above, page 104.
[28.] See above, page 88.

even as originally proposed by Ferdinand Tönnies, this typology appears to be a somewhat static distinction. Bonhoeffer's statements, however, must be read against the background of the categorical claim that the personal dignity of a human being can be preserved only if that person never merely serves as a means to an end. If Bonhoeffer's statements are understood in this light, then his final conclusion becomes inevitable, namely that the church is a distinct sociological type. For what is characteristic of Bonhoeffer's concept of the church, as we have found, is that the underlying notion of sociality is defined structurally by vicarious representative action [Stellvertretung], both with regard to the christological foundation of sociality and the ecclesiological form it requires. An ecclesiology thus defined, however, calls for a sociological typology which can be found neither in Max Weber nor in Ferdinand Tönnies.

Having established such a close link between theology and sociology, Bonhoeffer casts an interesting verdict on the contemporary empirical church. He explicitly does not want to be seen as a "despiser of the historical nature"[29] of the church. Do his statements therefore amount to an ecclesiological 'positivism'? Strong evidence in support of this hypothesis can be found particularly in Bonhoeffer's defense of the so-called formal sociology,[30] which explicitly separates the basic structures of social formation [Vergesellschaftung] from their historical context, and is more concerned with the question of the 'essence' of sociality than with its historical form. However, viewing the church-of-the-people [Volkskirche], the gathered congregation [Personalgemeinde], and the voluntary church [Freiwilligkeitskirche] as different types of church that are arranged concentrically around Christ as their center, as does Bonhoeffer, makes it clear that his verdict on the empirical church is derived by critically measuring it against a specific criterion. It is therefore not inappropriate to classify Bonhoeffer's study as a critical affirmation of the reality of the church. Bonhoeffer responds to questions about the locus and form of the church by examining the theological foundations of definitions that seek to answer these questions. And this is why his study does not in fact amount to a blank justification of the given reality of the church-of-the-people; rather it contributes to a critical view. The unity between Christ and his church-community, that is, the body of

317

[29.] See above, page 222.
[30.] See above, pages 24ff. and 25ff., editorial note 1.

Christ, entails an irreversible movement which compels the church continually to reexamine its foundation.

Bonhoeffer's position thus calls for a 'theory of the church' which, while preserving the inseparable link between Christology and ecclesiology—and precisely because it is fundamentally informed by that link—is at the same time able to provide a proper description of the place and form of the church within the reality of the world. *Sanctorum Communio*, Bonhoeffer's earliest theological study, forcefully demonstrates why theological, sociological, philosophical, and legal arguments must not be considered in isolation from one another. A comprehensive 'theory of the church', as programmatically envisioned in *Sanctorum Communio*, still waits to be written, in spite of a number of monographs on the subject. Although it will certainly not be possible to adopt all of Bonhoeffer's conclusions, he must be considered a significant starting point. Any 'theory of the church' must ask about the conditions under which the church takes shape within the world, and also what might hinder the realization of an authentic form. The dialogue between theology and sociology which is necessary to answer that question must to a large extent be rewritten. What Bonhoeffer can teach us is that such a dialogue is, at its core, a debate about the concept and understanding of reality itself. This self-imposed standard was almost more than Bonhoeffer was able to cope with in his first work. His persistence in holding to that standard—as late as the fragments of his ethics and his letters from prison—is therefore all the more remarkable.

The conclusions Bonhoeffer reached in *Sanctorum Communio* are preliminary and certainly must not be given undue weight. But they also do more than simply providing hints for a 'theory of the church'. Most important, they possess an internal dynamic by which Bonhoeffer himself will be driven to go beyond his earliest work.

II

Comparing Bonhoeffer's dissertation with his later writings discloses the tendency of *Sanctorum Communio* toward over-systematization. This makes certain parts of it very difficult to understand, but later this systematizing clearly decreases and the content of Bonhoeffer's arguments comes to the fore. In the later writings Bonhoeffer's language becomes more simple, dense, and concise; with the power of succinct expressions,

Bonhoeffer skillfully carries his thoughts into the center of a given theological debate. In retrospect, he himself assessed his academic writings rather critically.[31] Boldly and without fear he began tackling the systematic problems in his doctoral dissertation, and without fear he continues to think, write, and act. Bonhoeffer's expressions often condense a broad and complex theological issue into an intensely concentrated concept and address the issue in a way that already fascinated the students attending his lectures.[32] But it was during Bonhoeffer's own lifetime that this density of expression also became a source of misunderstanding. Nevertheless, this density must not be allowed to conceal the complexity of his intellectual constructs, which Bonhoeffer continually develops and expands step by step. Above all, the large number and broad variety of challenges are what will force Bonhoeffer to continue to develop his theology. The internal dialogue between his personal existence and theological reflection again and again causes Bonhoeffer to begin anew, to rethink, and to come to new conclusions.

During Bonhoeffer's pastoral internship in Barcelona, the characteristic tension between the Berlin teachers, the early dialectical theology, and the Lutheran tradition still lies largely dormant. Especially his congregational address, "Basic Questions of a Christian Ethic,"[33] still reveals elements of Reinhold Seeberg's voluntarism. It is also influenced by a decisionist contextual ethic, such as Barth and Bultmann had advocated at the time, and it bears the mark of a Lutheran theology of orders of creation as advocated by Paul Althaus or Emanuel Hirsch. The strained marriage of these heterogeneous elements apparently did not begin to break up until the postdoctoral study at Union Theological Seminary after September 1930. It is significant that Bonhoeffer, upon returning to Berlin in July 1931, immediately travels on to Bonn so that he might still reach Karl Barth for a conversation during the final weeks of the semester.

Is it a surprise that Bonhoeffer sought Barth's company? In his *Habilitationsschrift*, written in 1929 and submitted to the Berlin faculty in 1930, he had ventured to criticize Barth and Bultmann explicitly. Although Seeberg had encouraged him to tackle a historical study,[34] Bonhoeffer

[31.] See *DBW* 10:169f. and *DBW* 11:63.
[32.] Zimmermann and Smith, eds., *I Knew Dietrich Bonhoeffer*, 60f.
[33.] See excerpts in *NRS* 39–48 (*DBW* 10:323–45 [*GS* 5:156–80]).
[34.] See *NRS* 36 (*DBW* 10:105 [*GS* 3:17f.]).

nevertheless took up his systematic theme again, and continued to develop it on a theological and epistemological level. The continuity with
Sanctorum Communio lay in the question as to how revelation becomes
concrete. God's unconditional commitment to us—"God is free not from
human beings but for them"[35]—led to a debate with Barth regarding the
implications of the Lutheran *finitum capax infiniti* versus the *extra Calvi-
nisticum*. And for Bonhoeffer the church is once again the concrete manifestation of God's commitment to us and for us. In addition to this
theological leitmotif, *Act and Being* is characterized by the fact that Bonhoeffer carries on the dialogue between theology and philosophy.
Although *Act and Being* was written in a brief period of time, it is nevertheless still somewhat enigmatic. In his conversation with Barth in
Bonn, however, Bonhoeffer wasted no time in coming to the point.
Since *Sanctorum Communio*, the debate between Bonhoeffer and Barth
was characterized by a fundamental affinity. "Rarely, I think, have I
regretted an omission in my theological past more than the fact that I
did not visit him earlier,"[36] wrote Bonhoeffer in a letter from Bonn.
Bonhoeffer's ironic reference to his own "illegitimate theological pedigree"[37] showed how much he was attracted to Barth. However, this
closeness did not become an uncritical theological allegiance. Rather,
Barth and Bonhoeffer remained in intense conversation from a characteristic distance, and both forced each other to spell out their own positions more clearly. Barth questioned Bonhoeffer on those points which
presumably he would also have criticized in Bonhoeffer's doctoral dissertation, had he then known it.[38] And to alert Bonhoeffer to the dangers involved in linking Christology and ecclesiology too closely, Barth
suggested that he write "the little study about what distinguishes contemporary Protestant theology from Roman Catholicism."[39] The impa-
tience with which Bonhoeffer pursued the concreteness and specificity
of theological statements appeared indeed somewhat 'catholic' to Barth.
In his conversation with Barth, Bonhoeffer raises the "problem of
ethics" and asks about the "possibility of the church proclaiming the

---

[35.] *AB (DBWE* 2) 90f.
[36.] *NRS* 120 (*DBW* 11:19 [*GS* 1:19]). See also Eberhard Bethge, *Dietrich Bonhoeffer*, 131ff.
[37.] *DBW* 11:18 (*GS* 1:19).
[38.] See Barth's remarks in the *Church Dogmatics*, 4/2:641 and 4/3:754ff.
[39.] *NRS* 121 (*DBW* 11:20 [*GS* 1:20]).

320

321

concrete commandment."[40] Such a comment alone made it clear how, on his part, Bonhoeffer was determined to press Barth on the issue of concreteness.

The main theme around which the conversation between Bonhoeffer and Barth revolved was the necessity of concrete obedience in Christ's church. This became Bonhoeffer's central theme in the years that followed, years which were a time of decision for the church. In his lectures on "The Essence of the Church"[41] in the summer semester of 1932 and on "Christology"[42] in the summer semester of 1933, Bonhoeffer provided the theological tools that enabled him to deal with the questions of the foundation, locus, and form of Christ's church in the world. Here Bonhoeffer still used the phrase "Christ existing as church-community" [Christus als Gemeinde existierend], which he developed in his doctoral dissertation. However, in these lectures the concept of vicarious representative action [Stellvertretung] becomes even more central than in *Sanctorum Communio*. In 1933 the young university teacher in Berlin posed the question as to which challenges a student of theology must face "today."[43] And the way he answered this question indicates just how urgent it had become—in the midst of the scuffle of the emerging confrontation between the church and the National Socialist state—to deal with the questions of the appropriate locus, form, and action of the church.

One of the recurrent theological leitmotifs dominating Bonhoeffer's work after his doctoral dissertation was the concept of vicarious representative action [Stellvertretung]. It is this concept that provided him with the theological foundation for connecting Christology, ecclesiology, and ethics. An example is Bonhoeffer's detailed evaluation of the church's different options for its actions in the face of increasing discrimination against the Jews in 1933. This evaluation is rooted in the idea, adopted from Luther, of a vicarious representative witness of the church by which the church manifests itself as the body of Christ in the reality of world. Thus, a grasp of the true nature of the church indeed 322

[40.] *DBW* 11:100 (*GS* 1:33f.).
[41.] *DBW* 11:239–303 (*GS* 5:227–75).
[42.] *CC*.
[43.] *DBW* 12:416–19 (*GS* 3:243–47).

does not permit an uninvolved stance in which the church remains focused on itself. Instead it raises the "question" about the responsibility of the state to administer justice, places the church under the obligation to "care for the victims" of the state's injustice, and finally—in the face of unrestrained violation of basic human rights—requires as a last resort "direct political action" by the church.[44] On the one hand, Bonhoeffer strictly insists that the true church of Jesus Christ exists only where the vicarious representative witness of faith takes on a concrete form. On the other hand, however, this witness—precisely because as witness to Christ it has a universal content—points beyond any boundaries, rifts, and divisions imposed by human beings. Thus, Bonhoeffer wrote in *Discipleship* that the brother or sister protected by divine law includes "not only another Christian in the church-community."[45] Where the church in its discipleship is called to issue its vicarious representative witness, there it can no longer remain unrelated to the world and concerned only with itself. Who the neighbor is, the suffering other for whom Christians must care and whom they must defend, is determined solely by the One whom the Christian obediently follows in faith. The church in its walk of discipleship shows its real nature precisely in its critical stance toward the separations and exclusions that confront it, but which it cannot accept if its witness is to remain credible.

Bonhoeffer's rejection of Max Weber's typology of 'institution' and 'sect', and his insistence in *Sanctorum Communio* that the church be considered a distinctive sociological type, has direct consequences for the way the church acts. This certainly becomes apparent at this point, if not before. A church which is governed structurally by the principle of vicarious representative action embodies an ethic of neighborliness [Brüderlichkeitsethik] that transcends the dualism of an in-group and out-group morality, an ethic of conscience [Gesinnungsethik], and an ethic of responsibility [Verantwortungsethik].[46] It is therefore no accident that in Bonhoeffer's sketches for his *Ethics*, the concept of vicarious

323

[44.] Bonhoeffer, "The Church and the Jewish Question," *NRS*, 225 (*DBW* 12:353 [*GS* 2:48]).

[45.] *CD* 127.

[46.] See Max Weber, "Religious Rejections of the World and Their Directions," in *From Max Weber*, 329f., and "Politics as a Vocation," ibid., 119ff. See also Bonhoeffer, *E* 220ff. (*DBW* 6:256ff.).

representative action stands at the center of his reflections on responsibility. If one further considers that the *Ethics* fragments should be understood as a theological account of the journey leading to resistance against the Hitler regime, then the idea of vicarious representative action becomes the center of Bonhoeffer's justification of his conspiratorial activities. The phrase "the church is church only if it exists for others,"[47] which Bonhoeffer uses as late as his prison letters, testifies to the continuity of this motif in his theology. However, in prison Bonhoeffer interprets the concept of vicarious representative action in a context that is based on a radical theology of the cross. This theology of the cross even leads to a theological criticism of religion that undermines the metaphysical concept of God. It is the most radical expression of the idea that God's truth, although already real, can and even must become true only in the reality of the world through the witness of persons who in vicarious representative action mutually stand-up-for-each-other [*Füreinandereintreten*]. Only thus can this truth be expressed "nonreligiously."[48]

Bonhoeffer's theology continuously revolves around a core of questions that have already been raised in his first major theological work. The tension that was already present in *Sanctorum Communio* was maintained until the end. In his letters from prison, Bonhoeffer describes himself as a "modern theologian who still carries within himself the legacy of liberal theology."[49] The debate with Karl Barth also is continued in these letters.[50] And again and again it is Martin Luther—as already in *Sanctorum Communio*—who in this tension was consulted, who posed questions, and who precisely as such was the mediating theologian. The truth of God's reality, which is the subject of theological discourse, is not beyond time. Rather, for us human beings it must always take shape within time. Bonhoeffer therefore subscribed to Luther's phrase that Christians prove their identity not in what they have become, but by always remaining in the process of becoming.[51] It is not

324

[47.] *LPP* 382.
[48.] *LPP* 328.
[49.] *LPP* 378.
[50.] *LPP* 280, 286, 317, and 328f.
[51.] Luther, "Annotationes in aliquot capita Matthaei" (1538), *WA* 38:568: "Christianus enim non est in facto, sed in fieri" ["A Christian is not so in fact, but in becoming"].

particular answers that we ought to adopt from Bonhoeffer. Rather, it is the question as to how the reality of God becomes concrete in the here and now of this world, and also the question of the permanent becoming into which everyone is drawn who dares to address this question. For these are the questions that again and again force us to listen.[52]

[52.] For further perspective on the afterword see Joachim von Soosten, *Die Sozialität der Kirche: Theologie und Theorie der Kirche in Dietrich Bonhoeffers "Sanctorum Communio."*

CHRONOLOGY OF
SANCTORUM COMMUNIO

February 4, 1906
Dietrich Bonhoeffer and his twin sister, Sabine, born in Breslau, Germany

1912
Dietrich's father, Karl Bonhoeffer, called to the Friedrich-Wilhelm University, Berlin

1913
Bonhoeffer begins gymnasium studies

1921
Bonhoeffer is confirmed at Grunewald Church, Berlin

1922
Publication of the second edition of Karl Barth's *Der Römerbrief*

1923
First issue of *Zwischen den Zeiten* published

Summer semester 1923
Bonhoeffer begins year of theological study at the University of Tübingen; attends inter alia lectures by Schlatter on the Gospel of John and courses by Groos on philosophy, including seminar on Kant's *Critique of Pure Reason*

1924
Publication of Eberhard Grisebach's *Die Grenzen des Erziehers und seine Verantwortung*

Summer 1924
Bonhoeffer begins theological studies at the Friedrich-Wilhelm University,
Berlin; attends lectures by Karl Holl on church history, Adolf von Harnack on
the history of doctrine, and Heinrich Maier on epistemology

Winter semester 1924–25
Attends Harnack's special seminar on *1 Clement*

June 8, 1925
Seminar paper for Karl Holl, "Luthers Stimmungen gegenüber seinem Werk in
seinen letzten Lebensjahren"

July 31, 1925
Paper for Reinhold Seeberg, "Läßt sich eine historische und pneumatische
Auslegung der Schrift unterscheiden, und wie stellt sich die Dogmatik hierzu?"

Winter semester 1925–26
Attends Harnack's special seminar on Augustine's *De Civitate Dei*

January 22, 1926
Paper for Reinhold Seeberg, "Kirche und Eschatologie (oder: Kirche und Reich
Gottes)"

February 22, 1926
Paper for Karl Holl, "Luthers Anschauungen vom Heiligen Geist"

Winter semester 1926–27
Attends Spranger's course on the philosophy of culture

July 18, 1927
Sanctorum Communio accepted by Reinhold Seeberg for Bonhoeffer's licentiate
in theology

December 17, 1927
Bonhoeffer's oral defense of his promotion theses; degree awarded *summa cum
laude*

February 15, 1928–February 1929
Bonhoeffer serves as curate for German congregation in Barcelona

1929
Beginning with the summer semester, Bonhoeffer serves as *Voluntärassistent* in
systematic theology to Professor Wilhelm Lütgert at the Friedrich-Wilhelm
University, Berlin

July 31, 1930
Bonhoeffer's inaugural lecture at the Friedrich-Wilhelm University, Berlin

September 2, 1930
Abridged first edition of *Sanctorum Communio* published by Trowitzsch und Sohn, Berlin

September 5, 1930
Bonhoeffer departs for postgraduate year at Union Theological Seminary, New York

September 1931
Publication of *Akt und Sein*

November 11, 1931
Bonhoeffer's ordination at St. Matthias Church, Berlin

1954
Second edition—a reprinting—of *Sanctorum Communio* published by Chr. Kaiser Verlag, Munich

1955
Karl Barth's praise for *Sanctorum Communio* in *Die kirchliche Dogmatik*, 4/2

1960
Third edition of *Sanctorum Communio* published by Chr. Kaiser Verlag, including an appendix containing much material which had been omitted from the first edition

1963
First English translation of *Sanctorum Communio* published by Collins, London, incorporating in the body of the text some material from the appendix to the German third edition

1964
American edition published by Harper & Row, New York, as *The Communion of Saints*

1986
German critical edition of *Sanctorum Communio* published as volume 1 of the Dietrich Bonhoeffer Werke

BIBLIOGRAPHY

1. Literature Used by Bonhoeffer

Adam, Karl. *Das Wesen des Katholizismus*. 2d ed. Düsseldorf, 1925. English translation: *The Spirit of Catholicism*. Translated by Dom Justin McCann. Introduction by Robert A. Krieg. New York: Crossroad, 1997.

Althaus, Paul. *Communio sanctorum: Die Gemeinde im lutherischen Kirchengedanken* (Communion of saints: The congregation in the Lutheran idea of the church). 3d ed. Munich, 1926.

———. *Das Erlebnis der Kirche* (The experience of the church). 2d ed. Leipzig, 1924.

———. *Die letzten Dinge* (The last things). 3d ed. Gütersloh, 1926.

———. *Das Wesen des evangelischen Gottesdienstes* (The nature of Protestant worship). Gütersloh, 1926.

Anselm of Canterbury. *Liber De Fide Trinitatis et De Incarnatione Verbi*. In Migne, *Patrologia Latina*, 158:259B–84C. English translation: "On the Incarnation of the Word." In *Trinity, Incarnation, and Redemption: Theological Treatises*, 5–36. Edited by Jasper Hopkins and Herbert Richardson. Revised edition. New York: Harper & Row, 1970.

———. *Opera Omnia* (Complete works). Edited by Franciscus Salesius Schmitt. 6 vols. Stuttgart-Bad Cannstatt, 1968.

Die Apologie der Konfession [*Confessio Augustana*]. See the *Bekenntnisschriften der evangelisch-lutherischen Kirche*, 141–404. English translation: *Apology of the Augsburg Confession*. See *The Book of Concord: The Confessions of the Evangelical Lutheran Church*.

Arsenev, Nikolaus S. *Die Kirche des Morgenlandes: Weltanschauung und Frömmigkeitsleben* (The church of the East: Worldview and devotional practices). Berlin: W. de Gruyter, 1926.

Augsburg Confession. See *The Book of Concord,* 23–96.

Augustine, Bishop of Hippo. *De Baptismo contra Donatistas.* In Migne, *Patrologia Latina,* 43.9. English translation: *On Baptism, against the Donatists.* Translated by J. R. King. Vol. 4 of *Nicene and Post-Nicene Fathers,* first series. Grand Rapids: Eerdmans, 1956.

———. "De bono conjugali." In Migne, *Patrologia Latina,* 40.373–96. English translation: "The Good of Marriage." In *Treatises on Marriage and Other Subjects,* 9–51. Vol. 27 of *Fathers of the Church.* Edited by Roy J. Deferrari. New York: Fathers of the Church, 1955.

———. *De Civitate Dei.* In *Corpus Christianorum: Series Latina,* vols. 47–48. Turnhout, Belgium, 1955. English translation: *The City of God.* New York: Modern Library, 1993.

———. *Enarrationes in Psalmos.* In *Corpus Christianorum: Series Latina,* vols. 38–40. Turnhout, Belgium, 1956. English translation: *Saint Augustine on the Psalms.* Translated by Scholastica Hebgin and Felicitas Corrigan. In *Ancient Christian Writers,* vols. 29–30. Edited by Johannes Quasten and Walter J. Burghardt. Westminster, Ind.: Newman Press; London: Longmans, Green, 1961.

———. "Epistola CCVIII" (Letter 208). In Migne, *Patrologia Latina,* 33:950f.

———. *De peccatorum meritis et remissione.* In Migne, *Patrologia Latina,* 44. English translation: *A Treatise on the Merits and Forgiveness of Sins, and on the Baptism of Infants.* Vol. 5 of *Nicene and Post-Nicene Fathers,* first series. Grand Rapids: Eerdmans, 1956.

Baader, Franz von. *Schriften zur Gesellschaftsphilosophie* (Writings on social philosophy). Edited by Johannes Sauter. Vol. 14 of *Die Herdflamme.* Edited by Othmar Spann. Jena, 1925.

Ballanche, Pierre Simon. *Essai sur les institutions sociales* (Essay on social institutions). Paris, 1818.

Barth, Heinrich. "Kierkegaard der Denker" (Kierkegaard the thinker). *Zwischen den Zeiten* 4/3 (1926):194–234.

Barth, Karl. *Die Auferstehung der Toten: Eine akademische Vorlesung über 1. Kor 15.* Munich: Chr. Kaiser, 1924. English translation: *The Resurrection of the Dead.* Translated by H. J. Stenning. London: Hodder and Stoughton, 1933. Reprint. New York: Arno Press, 1977.

———. *Die christliche Dogmatik im Entwurf* (Christian dogmatics in outline). Vol. 1, *Die Lehre vom Worte Gottes: Prolegomena zur christlichen Dogmatik* (The doctrine of the Word of God: Prolegomena to Christian dogmatics). Munich, 1927. *NL* 3 B 9.

——. "Menschenwort und Gotteswort in der christlichen Predigt" (The human word and the word of God in Christian proclamation). *Zwischen den Zeiten* 3/2 (1925):119–40.

——. *Der Römerbrief.* 2d ed. of the new, revised edition of 1922. Munich, 1923. English translation: *The Epistle to the Romans.* Translated from the sixth German edition by Edwin C. Hoskins. London, 1933, 1960.

——. "Das Schriftprinzip der reformierten Kirche" (The scriptural principle in the Reformed church). *Zwischen den Zeiten* 3/3 (1925):215–45.

Barth, Paul. *Die Philosophie der Geschichte als Soziologie* (Philosophy of history as sociology). 2d rev. ed. Leipzig, 1897, 1915.

——. *Die Stoa* (The Stoics). 2d ed. Stuttgart, 1908.

Bartmann, Bernhard. *Lehrbuch der Dogmatik* (Textbook of dogmatics). 6th ed. Vol. 2. Freiburg im Breisgau, 1923. *NL* 6 B 3.

Die Bekenntnisschriften der evangelisch-lutherischen Kirche. Edited by Heinrich Bornkamm. Published in the anniversary year of the Augsburg Confession, 1930. Göttingen, 1930. *NL* 2–3. English translation: *The Book of Concord: The Confessions of the Evangelical Lutheran Church.* Edited and translated by Theodore G. Tappert, in collaboration with Jaroslav Pelikan, Robert H. Fischer, and Arthur Piepkorn. Philadelphia: Fortress Press, 1959.

Beyschlag, Willibald. *Neutestamentliche Theologie oder geschichtliche Darstellung der Lehren Jesu und des Urchristenthums nach den neutestamentlichen Quellen* (New Testament theology or historical presentation of the teaching of Jesus and original Christianity according to New Testament sources). 2 vols. Halle, 1891.

Biedermann, Aloys Emanuel. *Christliche Dogmatik* (Christian dogmatics). 2d ed. Vol. 2. Berlin, 1885.

Bonald, Louis-Gabriel-Ambroise de. *Essai analytique sur les lois naturelles de l'ordre social; ou, du pouvoir, du ministre et du sujet dans la société* (Analytical essay on the natural laws of the social order; or, concerning power, the minister, and the subject in society). Paris: A. Le Clerc, 1800.

The Book of Concord. See above, *Die Bekenntnisschriften der evangelisch-lutherischen Kirche.*

Bousset, Wilhelm. "Der zweite Brief an die Korinther" (The second letter to the Corinthians). In *Die Schriften des Neuen Testaments* (The writings of the New Testament). Edited by J. Weiss, W. Bousset, and W. Heitmüller. Vol. 2, *Die paulinischen Briefe und die Pastoralbriefe* (The

Pauline letters and the pastoral epistles), 167ff. 3d ed. Göttingen, 1917ff.

Brouwer, Luitzen Egbertus Jan. *Begründung der Mengenlehre unabhängig vom logischen Satz vom ausgeschlossenen Dritten* (Establishment of set theory independent of the logical premise of the excluded middle). Amsterdam: J. Müller, 1919.

Brunner, Emil. *Die Mystik und das Wort: Der Gegensatz zwischen moderner Religionsauffassung und christlichem Glauben dargestellt an der Theologie Schleiermachers* (Mysticism and the Word: The opposition between the modern interpretation of religion and Christian faith as exemplified in Schleiermacher's theology). Tübingen: Mohr, 1924.

Buber, Martin, ed. *Die Gesellschaft: Sammlung sozialpsychologischer monographien* (Society: Social-psychological monographs), 40 vols. Frankfurt: Rutten & Loening, 1906–.

Bultmann, Rudolf. *Glauben und Verstehen*, vol. 1. 6th ed. Tübingen: J. C. B. Mohr, 1966. English translation: *Faith and Understanding*, vol. 1. Edited and introduced by Robert W. Funk. Translated by Louise Pettibone Smith. New York: Harper & Row, 1969.

———. *Jesus.* Berlin: Deutsche Bibliothek, 1926. English translation: *Jesus and the Word.* Translated by Louise Pettibone Smith and Erminie Huntress Lantero. New York: Scribner, 1962, 1989.

Burn, Andrew Ewbank. *Niceta of Remesiana: His Life and Works.* Cambridge: Cambridge University Press, 1905.

Busch, Joseph Hubert. *Das Wesen der Erbsünde nach Bellarmin und Suarez* (The nature of original sin according to Bellarmine and Suarez). Paderborn, 1909.

Calvin, Jean. *Christianae Religionis Institutio.* Vol. 1 of *Opera Selecta.* Edited by P. Barth. Basel, 1536; Munich, 1926. English translation: *Institutes of the Christian Religion,* 1536 edition. Translated and annotated by Ford Lewis Battles. London: Collins; Grand Rapids: Eerdmans, 1986.

Catharinus, Ambrosius. *De casu hominis et peccato originali* (The fall of humanity and original sin). Dresden, 1524.

Comte, Auguste. *Cours de philosophie positive.* Vol. 4: *La partie dogmatique de la philosophie sociale.* Paris, 1839–. English translation: *The Positive Philosophy.* 2 vols. Freely translated and condensed by Harriet Martineau. London: John Chapman, 1853, and G. Bell, 1913.

———. *The Essential Comte: Selected from Cours de philosophie positive.* Edited by Stanislav Andreski. London: Croom Helm; New York: Barnes and Noble, 1974.

——. *Soziologie* (Sociology). [Selections of *Cours de philosophie positive* translated into German by Valentine Dorn]. 2d ed. Jena, 1923.

Confessio Augustana. See *Die Bekenntnisschriften,* 44–137.

Confessio Helvetica Posterior. Latin text in Philip Schaff, *The Creeds of Christendom,* vol. 3, 233–306. New York: Harper and Brothers, 1877. English translation: "The Second Helvetic Confession." In *Reformed Confessions of the 16th Century,* 220–301. Edited by Arthur C. Cochrane. London: SCM, 1966.

Corpus Christianorum: Series Latina [series]. Turnholt: Typographi Brepols, 1953–.

Cremer, Hermann. "Ekklesia." In *Biblisch-theologisches Wörterbuch der neutestamentlichen Gräcität,* 458ff. 4th ed. Edited by H. Cremer. Gotha, 1886. English translation: "Church." In *Biblico-theological Lexicon of New Testament Greek,* 332–35. Translated by William Urwick. 3d ed. Translated from second German edition. Edinburgh: T. & T. Clark, 1883; New York: Charles Scribner's Sons, 1895.

Deissmann, Gustav Adolf. *Die neutestamentliche Formel "in Christo Jesu"* *untersucht* (An investigation of the New Testament formula "in Christ Jesus"). Marburg, 1892.

Delitzsch, Franz. *Vier Bücher von der Kirche: Seitenstück zu Löhe's drei Büchern von der Kirche* (Four books on the church: Companion to Löhe's three books on the church). Dresden, 1847.

Denzinger, Henry. *Enchiridion Symbolorum.* Freiburg: Herder, 1967. English translation: *The Sources of Catholic Dogma.* Translated by Roy J. Deferrari. St. Louis and London: Herder, 1957.

Dorner, August Johannes. *Grundriß der Dogmengeschichte* (Outline of the history of dogma). Berlin: G. Reimer, 1899.

——. *Kirche und Reich Gottes* (The church and the realm of God). Gotha: Perthes, 1883.

Durkheim, Emil. *Les formes élémentaires de la vie religieuse.* Paris, 1912. English translation: *The Elementary Forms of the Religious Life.* Translated and with an introduction by Karen E. Fields. New York: Free Press, 1995.

——. *Die Methode der Soziologie.* Leipzig, 1908. English translation: *The Rules of Sociological Method.* Edited by Stephen Lukes. Translated by W. D. Halls. New York: Free Press, 1982.

Espinas, Alfred Victor. *Die thierischen Gesellschaften.* 2d ed. Braunschweig, 1879. Translated by W. Schloesser from the second enlarged French edition, *Des sociétés animales* [Animal society]. Paris: G. Bailliaere, 1878. Reprint. New York: Arno Press, 1977.

Feine, Paul. *Theologie des Neuen Testaments* (Theology of the New Testament). Leipzig, 1910; 4th ed., 1922.

Fichte, Johann Gottlieb. *Darstellung der Wissenschaftslehre aus dem Jahre 1801* (Outline of the classification of academic disciplines from the year 1801). In *Werke,* vol. 2. Edited by Immanuel Hermann Fichte. Bonn: Marcus, 1834. Second edition newly edited by Fritz Medicus. Leipzig: Felix Meiner, 1922.

——. *Rechtslehre* (Jurisprudence). From the handwritten manuscript edited by Hans Schulz. Leipzig: F. Meiner, 1920. Also published in *Fichtes Werke,* 10:493ff. Edited by I. H. Fichte. Berlin: W. de Gruyter, 1971. Reprint of *Das System der Rechtslehre.* In *Fichtes nachgelassene Werke,* 3:493ff. Bonn: Adolf-Marcus, 1834–35.

Freyer, Hans. *Theorie des objektiven Geistes: Eine Einleitung in die Kulturphilosophie* (Theory of objective spirit: An introduction to the philosophy of culture). Leipzig and Berlin, 1923.

Gierke, Otto Friedrich von. *Das deutsche Genossenschaftsrecht* (The German law of associations), vols. 1 and 2. Berlin: Weidmann, 1868–73.

Giles of Rome. *De regimine principum.* In *Opera Omnia.* Edited by F. del Punta et al. Florence: Leo S. Olschki, 1985-. English translation: *The Governance of Kings and Princes.* Edited by David C. Fowler et al. New York: Garland Publishers, 1997.

Gloel, Johannes. *Der heilige Geist in der Heilsverkündigung des Paulus* (The Holy Spirit in Paul's proclamation of salvation). Halle, 1888.

Gogarten, Friedrich. *Ich glaube an den dreieinigen Gott: Eine Untersuchung über Glauben und Geschichte* (I believe in the triune God: An investigation into faith and history). Jena, 1926. *NL 3 B 29.*

Grisebach, Eberhard. *Die Grenzen des Erziehers und seine Verantwortung* (The limits of educators and their responsibility). Halle, 1924.

Häring, Theodor. *Der christliche Glaube: Dogmatik.* 2d ed. Calwer, 1912. English translation: *The Christian Faith: A System of Dogmatics.* Translated by John Dickie and George Ferries from the second revised and enlarged German edition. New York: Hodder and Stoughton, 1912, 1913.

Harnack, Adolf von. *Das apostolische Glaubensbekenntnis* (The apostolic confession of faith). Berlin: 2d. ed., 1892; 3d. ed., 1896. [Cited by Bonhoeffer as "Das apostolische Symbol."]

———. *Die Mission und Ausbreitung des Christentums*. Vol. 1, *Die Mission in Wort und Tat*. 2d ed. Leipzig, 1924. English translation: *The Mission and Expansion of Christianity in the First Three Centuries*. Translated and edited by James Moffat. Second revised and enlarged edition. New York: Harper, 1962.

Hase, Karl August von. *Gnosis oder protestantisch-evangelische Glaubenslehre für die Gebildeten in der Gemeinde wissenschaftlich dargestellt* (Knowledge or Protestant-evangelical doctrine for the cultured in the congregation, academically presented). 2 vols. Leipzig, 1869–.

Hegel, Georg Wilhelm Friedrich. *Grundlinien der Philosophie des Rechts oder Naturrecht und Staatswissenschaft im Grundrisse*. Edited by Georg Lasson. In *Sämtliche Werke*, vol. 6. Leipzig: Felix Meiner, 1921. (Theorie-Werkausgabe, vol. 7.) [Cited by Bonhoeffer as *Rechtsphilosophie*.] English translation: *Elements of the Philosophy of Right*. Edited by Allen W. Wood. Translated by H. B. Nisbet. Cambridge, New York: Cambridge University Press, 1991.

———. "Die Philosophie des Geistes." Pt. 3 of *Enzyklopädie der philosophischen Wissenschaften im Grundrisse* (1830). Edited by G. Lasson. Leipzig, 1905. English translation: "The Philosophy of Spirit." In *Encyclopedia of the Philosophical Sciences in Outline*. Translated by Steven A. Taubeneck. In *Encyclopedia of the Philosophical Sciences in Outline, and Other Philosophical Writings*. Edited by Ernst Behler. New York: Continuum, 1990.

———. *Vorlesungen über die Philosophie der Geschichte*. Edited by F. Brunstäd. Leipzig, 1925. English translation: *Lectures on the Philosophy of History*. Translated by John Sibree. London: George Bell and Sons, 1914.

———. *Vorlesungen über die Philosophie der Religion*, vol. 2. In *Sämtliche Werke*, vol. 16. Edited by P. Marheineke. Berlin, 1832. English translation: *Lectures on the Philosophy of Religion*. 3 vols. Edited by Peter C. Hodgson. Translated by R. F. Brown, P. C. Hodgson, and J. M. Stewart with the assistance of J. P. Fitzer and H. S. Harris. Berkeley: University of California Press, 1985.

Heiler, Friedrich. *Das Gebet: Eine Religiongeschichtliche und religionspsychologische Untersuchung*. 4th ed. Munich, 1921. English translation: *Prayer: A Study in the History and Psychology of Religion*. Abridged. Translated and edited by Samuel McComb with the assistance of J. Edgar Park. New York: Oxford University Press, 1932, 1958.

Heim, Karl. *Leitfaden der Dogmatik: Zum Gebrauch bei akademischen Vorlesungen* (Guide to dogmatics: For use in academic lectures). Halle, 1912; 3d ed., 1925.

Hilbert, Gerhard. *Ecclesiola in ecclesia: Luthers Anschauungen von Volkskirche und Freiwilligkeitskirche in ihrer Bedeutung für die Gegenwart* (The church within the church: Luther's views on the church of the people and the voluntary church, and their importance for the present). Leipzig and Erlangen, 1924.

Hirsch, Emanuel. *Die idealistische Philosophie und das Christentum: Gesammelte Aufsätze* (Idealist philosophy and Christianity: Collected essays). Gütersloh, 1926. *NL* 3 B 37.

———. *Die Reich-Gottes-Begriffe des neueren europäischen Denkens: Ein Versuch zur Geschichte der Staats- und Gesellschaftsphilosophie* (The idea of the realm of God in recent European thought: Toward a history of the philosophy of the state and society). Göttingen, 1926.

Hobbes, Thomas. *Leviathan.* Vol. 3 of *Opera Latina.* Edited by William [Gulielmi] Molesworth. London: J. Bohn, 1839–. Reprint. Aalen, Germany: Scientia, 1961. English translation: *Leviathan.* Edited by Richard Tuck. Cambridge: Cambridge University Press, 1991.

Hofmann, Johann Christian Konrad von. *Der Schriftbeweis: Ein theologischer Versuch* (Scriptural proof: A theological experiment). 2 vols. Nördlingen, 1852–56; 2d ed., 1857–.

———. *Schutzschriften für eine neue Weise, alte Wahrheit zu Lehren* (Writings in defense of a new way to teach old truth). 4 vols. Vol. 1, *Die Versöhnung Gottes und die Rechtfertigung des Menschen betreffend* (Concerning God's reconciliation and human justification). Nördlingen, 1856.

Holl, Karl. *Augustins innere Entwicklung* (Augustine's inner development). Berlin, 1922. Reprinted in *Gesammelte Aufsätze zur Kirchengeschichte,* 3:54ff. Tübingen: J. C. B. Mohr, 1928.

———. "Der Kirchenbegriff des Paulus in seinem Verhältnis zu dem der Urgemeinde" (Paul's concept of the church in its relation to the understanding of the church in the earliest church community). In *Sitzungsberichte der preußischen Akademie der Wissenschaften* (December 1921):920ff.

———. *Luther.* Vol. 1 of *Gesammelte Aufsätze zur Kirchengeschichte.* (Collected essays on church history). See above.

———. "Was verstand Luther unter Religion?" In *Gesammelte Aufsätze zur Kirchengeschichte,* 1:1–110. English translation: *What Did Luther Under-*

stand by Religion? Edited by James Luther Adams and Walter F. Bense. Translated by Fred W. Meuser and Walter R. Wietzke. Philadelphia: Fortress Press, 1977.

Hollatz, David. *Examen theologicum acroamaticum universam theologiam theticopolemicam complectens* (A consideration of theological issues including polemical theology). [1707]. Leipzig, 1763. Reprint. Darmstadt, 1971.

Holtzmann, Heinrich Julius. *Lehrbuch der neutestamentlichen Theologie* (Textbook of New Testament theology), vol. 2. Freiburg in Breisgau, 1897; 2d ed., 1911.

Hus, Jan. *Tractatus de ecclesia* (Treatise on the church). Edited by S. Harrison Thomson. Boulder: University of Colorado Press, 1956. English translation: *The Church.* Translated by David S. Schaff. New York: Scribner, 1915.

Husserl, Edmund. *Logische Untersuchungen.* 3d ed. Vol. 2, *Elemente einer phänomenologischen Aufklärung der Erkenntnis.* Halle, 1922. Also in *Gesammelte Werke,* vol. 19/1, bk. 2, pt. 2, 544ff. Edited by U. Pauzer. English translation: *Logical Investigations.* Translated by J. N. Findlay. London: Routledge and Kegan Paul; New York: Humanities Press, 1970.

Ignatius of Antioch. "Ad Smyrna." In *Die Apostolischen Väter.* Edited by Franz X. von Funk and Karl Bihlmeyer. Tübingen: Mohr, 1956. English translation: "To the Smyrnaeans." In *The Apostolic Fathers,* vol. 1. Edited and translated by Kirsopp Lake. London: William Heinemann; Cambridge: Harvard University Press, 1949.

Irenaeus, Bishop of Lyons. *Adversus haereses.* In *Sources chretiennes,* vols. 210–11. Edited and translated by A. Rousseau and L. Doutreleau. Paris, 1974. English translation: *Irenaeus Against Heresies.* Vol. 1 of the *Ante-Nicene Fathers.* Edited by Alexander Roberts and James Donaldson. Grand Rapids: Eerdmans, 1956.

Jerome, Saint. "Epistola 17" (Letter 17). In Migne, *Patrologia Latina,* 22:359ff. English translation: *Select Letters of St. Jerome, with an English Translation.* Translated by Frederick A. Wright. London: Heinemann; New York: Putnam's Sons, 1933.

Jörgensen, Alfred Theodor. "Das Bekenntnis als eine unermeßliche Grundlage der Kirche" (The confession as an inexhaustible foundation of the church). *Allgemeine evangelisch-lutherische Kirchenzeitung* (Leipzig) 56 (1923):706ff., 722ff., 738ff., 755ff.

Kaftan, Julius Wilhelm. *Dogmatik* (Dogmatics). Vol. 1. Tübingen, 1901.

Kant, Immanuel. *Idee zu einer allgemeinen Geschichte in weltbürgerlicher Absicht.* English translation: "Idea for a Universal History from a Cosmopolitan Point of View." In *On History*, 11–26. Translated by Lewis White Beck. Indianapolis and New York: Bobbs-Merrill, 1963.

———. *Die Metaphysik der Sitten.* Vol. 7 of *Werke.* Edited by Wilhelm Weischedel. Darmstadt: Wissenschaftliche Buchgesellschaft, 1968. English translation: *The Metaphysics of Morals.* Translated and edited by Mary J. Gregor, with an introduction by Roger J. Sullivan. New York: Cambridge University Press, 1996.

———. *Die Religion innerhalb der Grenzen der blossen Vernunft.* Edited by K. Kehrbach. Leipzig, 1919. English translation: *Religion within the Limits of Reason Alone.* Translated by Theodore M. Greene and Hoyt H. Hudson. New York: Harper & Row, 1960.

Karwehl, Richard. "Zur Diskussion über die Kirchenfrage" (On the discussion of the church question). *Zwischen den Zeiten* 5 (1927):178–96.

Kattenbusch, Ferdinand. *Das apostolische Symbol* (The Apostolic Creed). Vol. 2, *Verbreitung und Bedeutung des Taufsymbols* (The extent and meaning of the baptismal creed). Leipzig: J. C. Hinrichs, 1900.

———. "Der Quellort der Kirchenidee" (The origin of the idea of the church). *Festgabe von Fachgenossen und Freunden: A. von Harnack zum 70. Geburtstag dargebracht* (Commemorative volume from faculty colleagues: For Adolf von Harnack on his 70th birthday), 143–72. Edited by Karl Holl. Tübingen, 1921.

Khomiakov, Alekse Stepanovich. "Die Einheit der Kirche." In *Östliches Christentum*, vol. 2, 1ff. Edited by Nicolai von Bubnoff and Hans Ehrenberg. Munich, 1925. English translation: *The Church Is One.* London: Fellowship of St. Alban and St. Sergius, 1968.

Kierkegaard, Søren. *Furcht und Zittern* and *Wiederholung.* 2d. ed. Vol. 3 of *Gesammelte Werke.* Edited by Hermann Gottsched and Christoph Schrempf. Translated by H. C. Ketels. Jena: Diederichs, 1909. English translation [from the Danish]: *Fear and Trembling* and *Repetition.* Vol. 6 of *Kierkegaard's Writings.* Translated by Howard V. Hong and Edna H. Hong. Princeton: Princeton University Press, 1983.

———. *Leben und Walten der Liebe.* Vol. 3 of *Erbauliche Reden.* Translated by Albrecht Dorner and Christoph Schrempf. Jena: Diederichs, 1924. English translation: *Works of Love.* Vol. 16 of *Kierkegaard's Writings.* Edited and translated by Howard V. Hong and Edna H. Hong. Princeton: Princeton University Press, 1995.

Kirchenverfassung der Alten Preußischen Union (Church constitution of the Old Prussian Union). 1922.

Kirsch, Johann Peter. *Die Lehre von der Gemeinschaft der Heiligen im christlichen Alterthum.* Mainz: Franz Kirchheim, 1900. English translation: *The Doctrine of the Communion of Saints in the Ancient Church: A Study in the History of Dogma.* Translated by John R. M'Kee. London: Sands and Company; St. Louis: B. Herder, 1911.

Kistiakowski, Theodor. *Gesellschaft und Einzelwesen: Eine methodologische Untersuchung* (Society and individual: A methodological investigation). Berlin, 1899.

Kliefoth, Theodor. *Acht Bücher von der Kirche* (Eight books concerning the church). Schwerin, 1854.

Köstlin, Julius. "Kirche." In *Realenzyklopädie für protestantische Theologie und Kirche* 10 (1901):315–44. English translation: "Church, the Christian." In *The Schaff-Herzog Encyclopedia of Religious Knowledge,* 3:77–85. Edited by Samuel M. Jackson et al. New York and London: Funk and Wagnalls, 1908.

Kracauer, Siegfried. *Soziologie als Wissenschaft: Eine erkenntnistheoretische Untersuchung* (Sociology as academic discipline: An epistemological investigation). Dresden: Sibyllen Verlag, 1922. New edition in *Schriften,* vol. 1. Frankfurt: Suhrkamp, 1971.

Krauß, Alfred. *Das protestantische Dogma von der unsichtbaren Kirche* (The Protestant doctrine of the invisible church). Gotha: Perthes, 1876.

Kunze, Johannes. "Wie ist das Bekenntnis der lutherischen Kirche als ihre bleibende Grundlage zu bestimmen und wirksam zu machen?" (How can the confession of the Lutheran church be seen and used as its abiding foundation?). *Allgemeine evangelisch-lutherische Kirchenzeitung* (Leipzig) 56 (1923):354ff., 370ff., 386ff.

Le Bon, Gustave. *Psychologie des Foules.* Paris: F. Alcan, 1895. German translation: *Psychologie der Massen.* 2d ed. Leipzig: W. Klinkhardt, 1912. English translation: *The Crowd: A Study of the Popular Mind.* New York: Penguin Books, 1977.

Leo XIII, Pope. "Satis cognitum" (June 29, 1896), or "De unitate Ecclesiae qua Corporis Christi Mystici." In Denzinger, ed., *Enchiridion Symbolorum,* 643–47. English translation: "The Unity of the Church." In Denzinger, ed., *The Sources of Catholic Dogma,* 494–96.

Le Seur, Paul. *Die Meisterfrage beim Aufbau der evangelischen Kirche: Ein Wort an die Treuen unter den Freunden und an die Frommen unter den*

Verächtern der Kirche (The key question for building up the Protestant churches: A word to the faithful among its friends and to the pious among its despisers). Berlin, 1925.

Lipsius, Richard Adalbert. "Briefe an die Galater, Römer, Philliper" (Letters to the Galatians, Romans, Philippians). In *Hand-Commentar zum Neuen Testament* (Commentary on the New Testament), vol. 2, pt. 2. Freiburg im Breisgau, 1891.

Litt, Theodor. *Individuum und Gemeinschaft* (Individual and community). 3d ed. Leipzig and Berlin, 1926.

Löhe, Wilhelm. *Drei Bücher von der Kirche*. Stuttgart, 1845; 6th ed., 1928. English translation: *Three Books Concerning the Church*. Translated by Edward T. Horn. Reading, Pa.: Pilger, 1908.

Lohmeyer, Ernst. *Vom Begriff der religiösen Gemeinschaft* (On the idea of religious community). Leipzig and Berlin, 1925.

Luther, Martin. "Auslegung des 15. Kapitels der 1. Epistel St. Pauli an die Korinther, von der Auferstehung der Todten" (1534). *WA* 36:478ff. [Cited by Bonhoeffer from the *Sämtliche Werke (Erlanger Ausgabe)* 51:70ff., 1852.] English translation: "The Fifteenth Chapter of St. Paul's First Letter to the Corinthians." *LW* 28:57–213.

———. *Disputationen Dr. Martin Luthers in den Jahren 1535–1545 an der Universität Wittenberg gehalten* (Dr. Martin Luther's disputations in the years 1535–45 held at the University of Wittenberg). [Cited by Bonhoeffer as *Disp.* Drews.] Edited by Paul Drews. Göttingen, 1895. English translation: Some disputations translated in *LW* 34.

———. *In epistolam Pauli ad Galatas commentarius* (1519). *WA* 2:436–618. English translation: "Lectures on Galatians" (1519). *LW* 27:151–410.

———. *Die erste Predigt am Sonntag Invocavit* (1522). *WA* 10/3:1–13. English translation: "The First Sermon, March 9, 1522, Invocavit Sunday." *LW* 51:70–75.

———. "Predigt am Sonntag Quasimodogeneti" (Sermon on Low Sunday, April 8, 1526). *WA* 20:363–68.

———. *Sämtliche Werke* (Complete works) [cited as *Erlanger Ausgabe*]. 56 vols. Erlangen: Heyder, 1826, 1857.

———. "Sermo die Resurrectionis Domini habitus" (A sermon held on the day of the resurrection of the Lord). *WA* 1:53–58.

———. "Ein Sermon von dem hochwürdigen Sakrament des heiligen wahren Leichnams Christi und von den Brudershaften" (1519). *WA* 2:738–58. English translation: "The Blessed Sacrament of the Holy and True Body of Christ, and the Brotherhoods" (1519). *LW* 35/1:49–73.

———. "Tesseradecas consolatoria pro laborantibus et oneratis," (1520). *WA* 6:104–34. English translation: "Fourteen Consolations for Those Who Labor and Are Heavy Laden." *LW* 42:121–66.

———. "Vom dem Papsttum zum Rom, wider den hochberühmten Romanisten zu Leipzig" (1520). *WA* 6:285–324. English translation: "On the Papacy in Rome against the Most Celebrated Romanist in Leipzig." *LW* 39:49–104.

———. *Vorlesung über den Römerbrief 1515/1516.* Vol. 1 of *Anfänge der reformatorischen Bibelauslegung.* Edited by J. Ficker. Part 1: Die Glosse; Part 2: Die Scholien. Leipzig: Dieterich'sche Verlagsbuchhandlungen, 1908; 3d ed. 1925 [used by Bonhoeffer]. *NL* 1 D 24. The definitive version of Ficker's edition was published as vol. 56 of Luther's *Werke: Kritische Gesamtausgabe* in 1938. English translation of *WA* 56: *Lectures on Romans, LW* 25. Edited by Hilton C. Oswald. "Glosses": chaps. 1–2, trans. Walter G. Tillmanns; chaps. 3–16 trans. Jacob A. O. Preus. "Scholia": chaps. 1–2 trans. Walter G. Tillmanns; chaps. 3–15, trans. Jacob A. O. Preus.

———. *Vorrede auf die Offenbarung S. Johannis [2].* WA (*Die Deutsche Bibel*) 7:406–21. English translation: "Preface to the Revelation of St. John [2]." *LW* 35:399–411.

———. *Werke: Kritische Gesamtausgabe.* Weimar: H. Böhlau, 1883–. English translation: *Luther's Works,* 55 vols. Vols. 1–30 edited by Jaroslav Pelikan. St. Louis: Concordia, 1958–67. Vols. 31–55 edited by Helmut Lehmann. Philadelphia: Muhlenberg Press and Fortress Press, 1957–67.

Das Martyrium des Polykarp. Translated and edited by Gerd Buschmann. Göttingen: Vandenhoeck & Ruprecht, 1998. English translation: "The Martyrdom of Polycarp." In *The Apostolic Fathers,* vol. 2. Translated by Kirsopp Lake. London: William Heinemann; Cambridge: Harvard University Press, 1959.

Mathews, Shailer. "A Visible Church and Christian Unity." *The Constructive Quarterly: A Journal of the Faith, Work and Thought of Christendom* 10 (1922):72ff.

Maurenbrecher, Max. *Thomas von Aquino's Stellung zum Wirtschaftsleben seiner Zeit* (Thomas Aquinas's attitude to the economic life of his time). Leipzig, 1898.

Mauthner, Fritz. *Die Sprache* (Language). Vol. 9 of *Die Gesellschaft: Sammlung sozialpsychologischer monographien* (Society: Social-psychological monographs). Frankfurt: Rutten & Loening, 1907. See above, Buber.

McDougall, William. *Social Psychology: An Introduction to Social Psychology.* 13th ed. London, 1918.

Meyer, Theodor. *Die christlich-ethischen Sozialprinzipien und die Arbeiterfrage* (Christian-ethical social principles and the worker question). 4th ed. Freiburg im Breisgau, 1904.

Migne, Jacques-Paul, ed. *Patrologiae cursus completus* (The complete works of church patrology) [*Series Latina*]. [Cited as *Patrologia Latina.*] 221 vols. Paris: Apud Garniere Fratres, 1844–64.

Mosheim, Johann Lorenz von. *Elementa theologiae dogmaticae* (Elements of dogmatic theology). Edited by C. E. de Winheim. Nuremberg, 1758; 2d ed. 1764.

Mulert, Hermann. "Congregatio sanctorum, in qua evangelium docetur" (The community of saints in which the gospel is taught). In *Harnack-Ehrung: Beiträge zur Kirchengeschichte. Ihrem Lehrer Adolf von Harnack zu seinem siebzigsten Geburtstage dargebracht* (In honor of Harnack: Contributions to church history, for their teacher Adolf von Harnack on his seventieth birthday), 292ff. Leipzig: J. C. Hinrichs, 1921.

Müller-Lyer, Franz Carl. *Die Phasen der Kultur und Richtungslinien des Fortschritts.* Vol. 2 of his *Entwicklungsstufen der Menschheit.* Munich, 1908. English translation: *The History of Social Development.* Translated by Elizabeth Coote Lane and Hilda Amelia Lake. London: Allen and Unwin, 1935.

Münchmeyer, August Friedrich Otto. *Das Dogma von der sichtbaren und unsichtbaren Kirche* (The dogma of the visible and invisible church). Göttingen, 1854.

Natorp, Paul. *Sozialpädagogik: Theorie der Willenserziehung auf der Grundlage der Gemeinschaft* (Social pedagogy: The theory of educating the will on the basis of the community). 2d ed. Stuttgart, 1904.

Niceta of Remesiana. "An Explanation of the Creed." In *Niceta of Remesiana: Writings*, 43–53. Vol. 7 of *Fathers of the Church.* Translated by Gerald G. Walsh. New York: Fathers of the Church, 1949.

Oppenheimer, Franz. *System der Soziologie* (System of sociology). 3 vols. Jena, 1922–35.

"'Pastor aeternus' de Ecclesia Christi." Vatican Council I, Session 4, July

18, 1870. In Denzinger, ed., *Enchiridion Symbolorum*, 595–60. English translation: "Dogmatic Constitution 1 on the Church of Christ." In Denzinger, ed., *The Sources of Catholic Dogma*, 451–57.

Peterson, Erik. "Was ist Theologie?" (What is theology?) [pamphlet]. Bonn, 1925. Reprinted in Peterson, *Theologische Traktate* (Theological treatises), 11–43. Munich: Kösel Verlag, 1951. Also in *Theologie als Wissenschaft* (Theology as an academic discipline), 232ff. Edited by Gerhard Sauter. Munich, 1971.

Piper, Otto. *Theologie und reine Lehre: Eine dogmatische Grundlegung von Wesen und Aufgabe protestantischer Theologie* (Theology and pure doctrine: Dogmatic principles on the nature and task of Protestant theology). Tübingen, 1926. *NL* 3 B 56.

Pius IX, Pope. "Officii ad episcopos Angliae" (September 16, 1864), "De unicitate Ecclesiae, contra theoriam ramorum." In Denzinger, ed., *Enchiridion Symbolorum*, 573–76. English translation: "The Unity of the Church." In *The Sources of Catholic Dogma*, 428–29. See Denzinger.

Ritschl, Albrecht. "Die Begründung des Kirchenrechts im evangelischen Begriff von der Kirche" (The foundation of canon law in the Protestant concept of the church). *Zeitschrift für Kirchenrecht* 9 (1869):220ff. Reprinted in *Gesammelte Aufsätze*, 100ff. Freiburg and Leipzig, 1893.

———. *Die christliche Lehre von der Rechtfertigung und Versöhnung.* Vols. 1 and 2, 2d rev. ed., Bonn, 1882. Vol. 3, 2d rev. ed., Bonn, 1883. English translation: Vol. 1, *A Critical History of the Christian Doctrine of Justification and Reconciliation.* Translated by John S. Black. Edinburgh: Edmonston and Douglas, 1872. Vol. 3, *The Christian Doctrine of Justification and Reconciliation: The Positive Development of the Doctrine.* Edited by H. R. Mackintosh and A. B. Macaulay. Edinburgh: T. & T. Clark; New York: Charles Scribner's Sons, 1900.

———. "Über die Begriffe sichtbare und unsichtbare Kirche" (On the concepts of visible and invisible church). *Theologische Studien und Kritiken* 32 (1859):189ff. Reprinted in *Gesammelte Aufsätze*, 68ff. Freiburg and Leipzig, 1893.

Rosenstock-Huessy, Eugen. *Soziologie* (Sociology). Vol. 1, *Die Kräfte der Gemeinschaft.* Berlin and Leipzig: W. de Gruyter, 1925.

Rousseau, Jean Jacques. *Du contrat sociale, ou, Principes du droit politique.* Amsterdam: Marc Michel Rey, 1762. English translation: *On the Social Contract.* Translated and edited by Donald A. Cress. Introduction by Peter Gay. Indianapolis: Hackett, 1988.

Rückert, Leopold Immanuel. *Ein Büchlein von der Kirche* (A little book concerning the church). Jena, 1857.

Schäffle, Albert Eberhard Friedrich. *Abriß der Soziologie* (Outline of sociology). Edited by K. Bücher. Tübingen, 1906.

———. *Bau und Leben des sozialen Körpers* (The structure and life of the social body). 4 vols. Tübingen, 1875–.

Scheel, Otto. *Die Kirche im Urchristentum* (The church in earliest Christianity). Tübingen, 1912.

Scheler, Max. *Der Formalismus in der Ethik und die materiale Wertethik.* Vol. 2 of *Gesammelte Werke.* 4th ed. Bern: Francke Verlag, 1954. English translation: *Formalism in Ethics and Non-formal Ethics of Values: A New Attempt toward the Foundation of an Ethical Personalism.* 5th rev. ed. Translated by Manfred S. Frings and Roger L. Funk. Evanston, Ill.: Northwestern University Press, 1973.

———. *Zur Phänomenologie und Theorie der Sympathiegefühle und von Liebe und Hass.* Halle, 1913. Second edition, enlarged, as *Wesen und Formen der Sympathie.* Bonn, 1923. English translation: *The Nature of Sympathy.* Translated by Peter Heath. Introduction by W. Stark. 2d ed. London: Routledge and Kegan Paul, 1954. Reprint. Hamden, Conn.: Archon Books, 1970.

Schilling, Otto. *Die christlichen Soziallehren* (Christian social teachings). Cologne, Munich, and Vienna, 1926.

Schleiermacher, Friedrich Daniel Ernst. *Der christliche Glaube–nach den Grundsätzen der evangelischen Kirche im Zusammenhange dargestellt.* 2 vols. 2d ed. Berlin, n.d. [Cited by Bonhoeffer as *Glaubenslehre.*] English translation: *The Christian Faith.* Edited by H. R. MacKintosh and J. S. Stewart. 2d ed. Edinburgh: T. & T. Clark; Philadelphia: Fortress Press, 1976.

———. *Die christliche Sitte nach den Grundzügen der Evangelischen Kirche.* Pt. 2, vol. 12 of *Sämmtliche Werke.* Edited by Ludwig Jonas. Berlin, 1843; 2d ed. Berlin: G. Reimer, 1884.

———. *Entwurf eines Systems der Sittenlehre.* Pt. 3, vol. 5 of *Sämmtliche Werke.* Edited by A. Schweitzer. Berlin, 1835. [Cited by Bonhoeffer as *Ethik.*]

———. *Reden über die Religion.* Critical edition edited by G. C. B. Pünjer. Braunschweig, 1879. English translation: *On Religion: Speeches to Its Cultured Despisers.* Translated and with an introduction by Richard Crouter. Cambridge and New York: Cambridge University Press, 1988.

Schmidt, Traugott. *Der Leib Christi: Eine Untersuchung zum urchristlichen Gemeindegedanken* (The body of Christ: An investigation of the earliest Christian ideas of the church-community). Leipzig and Erlangen, 1919.

Schmiedel, Paul Wilhelm. "Die Briefe an die Thessalonicher und an die Korinther" (Letters to the Thessalonians and Corinthians). In *Hand-Commentar zum Neuen Testament* (Commentary on the New Testament). Vol. 2. Freiburg im Breisgau, 1892.

Schmitz, Otto. *Die Vorbildlichkeit der urchristlichen Gemeinden für die kirchliche Lage der Gegenwart* (The earliest Christian congregations as model for the church situation of the present). 2d ed. Berlin, 1922.

Scholz, Heinrich. *Religionsphilosophie* (Philosophy of religion). 2d ed. Berlin, 1922.

Schumann, Friedrich Karl. "Zur Grundfrage der Religionssoziologie" (On the fundamental question of sociology of religion). *Zeitschrift für Systematische Theologie* 4 (1927):662ff.

Seeberg, Reinhold. *Der Begriff der christlichen Kirche* (The concept of the Christian church). Erlangen, 1885.

———. *Christliche Dogmatik* (Christian dogmatics). Vol. 1, *Religionsphilosophisch-apologetische und erkenntnistheoretische Grundlage* (Philosophy of religion, apologetic, and epistemological foundation); vol. 2, *Die spezielle christliche Dogmatik* (Specifically Christian doctrines). Erlangen and Leipzig, 1924–25.

———. *Ewiges Leben* (Eternal life). Leipzig, 1915.

———. *Lehrbuch der Dogmengeschichte.* Vol. 2, *Die Dogmenbildung in der Alten Kirche.* Leipzig, 1923 [reprint: Darmstadt, 1974]; vol. 3, *Die Dogmengeschichte des Mittelalters.* Leipzig, 1913 [Reprint: Darmstadt, 1974]. English translation: *Textbook of the History of Doctrines.* Abridged translation by Charles E. Hay. Grand Rapids: Baker Book House, 1956. [Note: The English translation was made in 1905 from a modified version of the German first edition; it does not correspond in organization and pagination to the German third edition of vols. 2 and 3 used by Bonhoeffer.]

Sigwart, Christoph. *Logik.* Vol. 2, *Die Methodenlehre.* 2d ed. Tübingen, 1893. English translation: *Logic.* Translated by Helen Dendy. Second edition, revised and enlarged. 2 vols. London: Sonnenschein; New York: Macmillan, 1895. Reprint. New York and London: Garland, 1980.

Simmel, Georg. "Die Erweiterung der Gruppe und die Ausbildung der Individualität." In *Soziologie: Untersuchungen*, 527–73. English translation: In *On Individuality and Social Forms: Selected Writings*, sections 4, 14, and 18. Edited by Donald N. Levine. Chicago: University of Chicago Press, 1971.

——. *Grundfragen der Soziologie (Individuum und Gesellschaft)*. Berlin and Leipzig: G. J. Göschen, 1917, 2d ed. 1920. English translation: "Fundamental Problems of Sociology (Individual and Society)." In *The Sociology of Georg Simmel*, 1–84. Translated, edited, and with an introduction by Kurt H. Wolff. New York: Free Press, 1967.

——. "Die Kreuzung sozialer Kreise." See *Soziologie: Untersuchungen*, 305–44. English translation: "The Web of Group Affiliations." Translated by Reinhard Bendix. In *Conflict* and *The Web of Group Affiliations*, 125–95. (See below, *Soziologie: Untersuchungen*.)

——. *Philosophie des Geldes*. 2d ed. Leipzig, 1907. English translation: *The Philosophy of Money*. Edited by David Frisby. Translated by Tom Bottomore and David Frisby. Second enlarged edition. London and New York: Routledge, 1990.

——. *Die Religion*. Vol. 2 of *Die Gesellschaft: Sammlung sozialpsychologischer monographien* (Society: Social-psychological monographs). [See above, Buber.] English translation: *Sociology of Religion*. Translated by Curt Rosenthal. New York: Philosophical Library, 1959. Reprint. Arno Press, 1979.

——. *Soziologie: Untersuchungen über die Formen der Vergesellschaftung* (Sociology: Studies in the forms of sociation). Leipzig: Duncker & Humblot, 1908; 3d ed. 1923. English translation of selections from the 3d edition. In *Conflict* and *The Web of Group Affiliations*. New York: Free Press, 1964; *The Sociology of Georg Simmel*. Edited by Kurt H. Wolff. New York: Free Press, 1967; and *On Individuality and Social Forms: Selcted Writings*. Edited by Donald N. Levine. Chicago: University of Chicago Press, 1971.

——. "Der Streit." See *Soziologie: Untersuchungen*, 186–255. English translation: "Conflict." Translated by Kurt H. Wolff. In *Conflict and The Web of Group Affiliations*, 1–123.

Sohm, Rudolf. *Kirchenrecht* (Canon law). Vol. 1, *Die geschichtlichen Grundlagen* (The historical foundations). Leipzig, 1892.

Spann, Othmar. *Gesellschaftslehre* (Theory of society). 2d ed. Leipzig, 1923.

Spencer, Herbert. *Einleitung in das Studium der Soziologie.* Edited by H. Marquardsen from second edition of the original. Leipzig, 1875. English edition: *The Study of Sociology.* New York and London: D. Appleton, 1924.

——. *Die Principien der Soziologie.* Vols. 1–4. German translation by Benjamin Vetter. Stuttgart, 1877–. [Cited by Bonhoeffer as *Soziologie.*] English edition: *The Principles of Sociology.* London: Williams and Norgate, 1876–96. Reprinted in 3 vols. Westport, Conn.: Greenwood Press, 1975.

Spranger, Eduard. *Lebensformen: Geisteswissenschaftliche Psychologie und Ethik der Persönlichkeit.* 2d ed. Halle, 1921. English translation: *Types of Man: The Psychology and Ethics of Personality.* Translated by Paul J. W. Pigors. Halle: M. Niemeyer, 1928.

Stahl, Friedrich Julius. *Die Kirchenverfassung nach Lehre und Recht der Protestanten* (The church constitution according to Protestant doctrine and law). 2d ed. Erlangen, 1862.

Stange, Carl. *Die Unsterblichkeit der Seele* (The immortality of the soul). Gütersloh, 1925.

Stange, Erich. *Die kommende Kirche* (The coming church). Dresden, 1925.

Steffen, Gustaf. *Die Grundlage der Soziologie: Ein Programm zu der Methode der Gesellschaftswissenschaft und Naturforschung* (The foundation of sociology: A design for the methodology of the social and natural sciences). Jena, 1912.

Stein, Edith. "Individuum und Gemeinschaft" (Individual and community). *Jahrbuch für Philosophie und Phänomenologische Forschung* 5 (1922):116ff.

Stern, William. *Die menschliche Persönlichkeit* (The human personality). Leipzig, 1919.

Süssmilch, Johann Peter. *Beweis daß der Ursprung der menschlichen Sprache göttlich sei* (Proof of the divine origin of human language). Berlin, 1766.

Symeon the New Theologian. "Homilie 54." *Catecheses.* In *Sources Chretienne*, vols. 96, 104, and 113. Edited by Basile Krivocheine. Paris: Editions du Cerf, 1963–65. English translation: *The Discourses.* Translated by C. J. Catanzaro. Introduction by George Maloney. Mahwah, N.J.: Paulist Press, 1980.

Tarde, Gabriel de. *Les lois de l'imitation: Étude sociologique.* Paris, 1890. English translation: *The Laws of Imitation.* Translated from the second

French edition by Elsie Clews Parsons, with an introduction by Franklin H. Giddings. New York: H. Holt, 1903. Reprint. Gloucester, Mass.: Peter Smith, 1962.

Thimme, Ludwig. *Kirche, Sekte und Gemeinschaftbewegung vom Standpunkt einer christlichen Soziologie aus* (Church, sect, and the church renewal movement from the perspective of a Christian sociology). Schwerin: Friedrich Bahn, 1925.

Thomas Aquinas. *Summa Theologiae.* 42 vols. Cambridge: Blackfriars; New York: McGraw-Hill, 1964–.

Thurneysen, Eduard. "Schrift und Offenbarung" (Scripture and revelation). *Zwischen den Zeiten* 6 (1924):3–30.

Tillich, Paul. *Masse und Geist: Studien zur Philosophie der Masse* (Mass and spirit: Toward a philosophy of the masses). Berlin, 1922.

Tönnies, Ferdinand. "Comte's Begriff der Soziologie." See his *Soziologisches Studien und Kritiken* 2.

———. *Gemeinschaft und Gesellschaft: Grundbegriffe der reinen Soziologie.* English translation: *Community and Society.* Translated and edited by Charles P. Loomis. New York: Harper & Row, 1963. Reprint. New Brunswick, N.J.: Transaction Books, 1988.

———. *Soziologische Studien und Kritiken.* 3 vols. Jena, 1925–.

———. "Spencer's soziologisches Werk." See his *Soziologisches Studien und Kritiken* 1.

Troeltsch, Ernst. *Die Soziallehren der christlichen Kirchen und Gruppen.* Vol. 1, first half of *Gesammelte Schriften.* Tübingen, 1912. English translation: *The Social Teachings of the Christian Churches,* 2 vols. Translated by Olive Wyon, with a foreword by James Luther Adams. Louisville: Westminster/John Knox, 1992.

———. "Zum Begriff und der Methode der Soziologie" (On the concept and method of sociology). *Weltwirtschaftliches Archiv* 8 (1916):259ff. Also published in *Gesammelte Schriften,* 4:705ff. Tübingen, 1925.

Tyconius. *Tyconius: The Book of Rules.* Latin and English texts. Translated by William S. Babcock. Atlanta: Scholars Press, 1989.

Vierkandt, Alfred. *Gesellschaftslehre: Hauptprobleme der philosophischen Soziologie* (The theory of society: Major problems of philosophical sociology). Stuttgart, 1923. Reprint of completely revised second German edition (1928). New York: Arno Press, 1975.

Vilmar, August Friedrich Christian. *Dogmatik: Akademische Vorlesungen* (Dogmatics: Academic lectures). 2 vols. Posthumously edited by K. W. Piderit. Gütersloh, 1874–75.

Vurpillot, E. *De la nécessité d'une doctrine protestante de l'Église* (Concerning the necessity of a Protestant doctrine of the church). Montbéliard, 1926.

Wallau, René. *Die Einigung der Kirchen vom evangelischen Glauben aus* (The unification of the churches from the perspective of the Protestant faith). Berlin, 1925.

Walther, Georg. "Zur Ontologie der sozialen Gemeinschaften" (Toward an ontology of social communities). *Jahrbuch für Philosophie und Phänomenologische Forschung* 5 (1922):116ff.; 6 (1923):1ff.

Weber, Max. *Gesammelte Aufsätze zur Religionssoziologie.* 3 vols. Tübingen, 1920f. English translation: Volume 1: (a) *The Protestant Ethic and the Spirit of Capitalism.* Translated by Talcott Parsons. New York: Charles Scribner's Sons, 1976, c1958. (b) *From Max Weber: Essays in Sociology.* Translated, edited, and introduced by Hans H. Gerth and C. Wright Mills. New York: Oxford University Press, 1958, c1946. (c) *The Religion of China. Confucianism and Taoism.* Translated and edited by Hans H. Gerth. New edition, with an introduction by C. K. Yang. New York: Macmillan, 1964, c1951. Volume 2: *The Religion of India: The Sociology of Hinduism and Buddhism.* Translated and edited by Hans H. Gerth and Don Martindale. Glencoe, Illinois: Free Press, 1858. Volume 3: *Ancient Judaism.* Translated and edited by Hans H. Gerth and Don Martindale. New York: Free Press, 1967, c1952.

————. "'Kirchen' und 'Sekten' in Nordamerika: Eine Kirchen- und sozialpolitische Skizze" ('Churches' and 'sects' in North America: A sketch of church and social politics). *Die christliche Welt* 20 (1906):558ff. and 577ff. Revised version published as "Die protestantischen Sekten und der Geist des Kapitalismus." In *Gesammelte Aufsätze zur Religionssoziologie,* 1:207–36. English translation: "The Protestant Sects and the Spirit of Capitalism." In *From Max Weber: Essays in Sociology.* Translated, edited, and with an introduction by Hans H. Gerth and C. Wright Mills. New York: Oxford University Press, 1946, 1958.

————. "Religionssoziologie." In Weber, *Wirtschaft und Gesellschaft.* English translation: "Religious Groups (The Sociology of Religion)." Translated by Ephraim Fischoff. In Max Weber, *Economy and Society,* 1:399–634.

————. "Über einige Kategorien der verstehenden Soziologie" (On some categories of interpretive sociology). *Logos: Internationale Zeitschift für*

Philosophie und Kultur 4 (1913):253ff. Also published in *Gesammelte Aufsätze zur Wissenschaftslehre*, 403–50. Tübingen, 1922. English translation: "Basic Sociological Terms." In Max Weber, *Economy and Society*, 1:3–62.

———. *Wirtschaft und Gesellschaft*. Pt. 1. Vol. 3 of *Grundriß der Sozialökonomik*. 2d ed. Tübingen: Mohr, 1925. English translation: *Economy and Society: An Outline of Interpretive Sociology*. Vol. 1. Edited by Guenther Roth and Claus Wittich. Berkeley: University of California Press, 1978.

Weiss, Bernhard. *Lehrbuch der biblischen Theologie des Neuen Testaments.* Berlin, 1868; 2d ed., 1873. English translation: *Biblical Theology of the New Testament.* Translated from third revised edition; vol. 1 by David Eaton, vol. 2 by James E. Duguid. Edinburgh: T. & T. Clark, 1883, 1888–89.

Wiese, Leopold von. *Allgemeine Soziologie als Lehre von den Beziehungen und Beziehungsgebilden der Menschen.* Vol. 1, *Beziehungslehre.* Munich and Leipzig, 1924. English translation: *Systematic Sociology.* Translation and adaptation by Howard Paul Becker. New York: J. Wiley; London: Chapman and Hall, 1932; New York: Arno Press, 1974.

Windelband, Wilhelm. *Einleitung in die Philosophie.* 2d ed. Tübingen: J. C. B. Mohr, 1919. English translation: *An Introduction to Philosophy.* Translated by Joseph McCabe. London: Unwin, 1921.

———. *Die Geschichte der neueren Philosophie in ihrem Zusammenhange mit der allgemeinen Kultur und den besonderen Wissenschaften* (The history of recent philosophy in its relationship to general culture and the particular academic disciplines). 8th ed. 2 vols. Leipzig, 1922. *NL* 7 A 93.

———. *Lehrbuch der Geschichte der Philosophie.* Edited by E. Rothacker. 11th ed. Tübingen, 1924. English translation: *A History of Philosophy.* Second revised and enlarged edition. 2 vols. Translated by James H. Tufts. New York: Harper, 1958.

Wycliffe, John. *Trialogus cum supplemento trialogi.* Oxford: Clarendon Press, 1869.

Zahn, Theodor. *Das apostolische Symbolum: Eine Skizze seiner Geschichte und Prüfung seines Inhalts.* Leipzig, 1893. English translation: *The Apostles' Creed.* London: Hodder and Stoughton, 1899.

Zwingli, Huldrich. "Ad Carolum Romanorum Imperatorem Fidei ratio" (1530). In *Corpus Reformatorum, Huldrych Zwinglis Sämtliche Werke.* Berlin and Zurich, 1904ff. English translation: "An Account of the

Faith of Huldreich Zwingli Submitted to the German Emperor Charles V, at the Diet of Augsburg, July 3, 1530." In *On Providence and Other Essays*. Edited by William J. Hinke. Reprint. Durham, N.C.: Labyrinth Press, 1983.

2. Literature Consulted by the Editors

Abel, Theodore. *Systematic Sociology in Germany*. New York: Columbia University Press, 1929.

Ancient Christian Writers [serial]. New York and various places: Newman Press, 1946–.

Annals of the American Academy of Political Science 6/3 (1895).

Anselm of Canterbury. *Cur Deus Homo*. In *Opera Omnia*, 2:37–133. Edited by F. S. Schmitt. English translation: *Why God Became Man*. In *A Scholastic Miscellany: Anselm to Occam*. Edited by Eugene R. Fairweather. Philadelphia: Westminster Press, 1981.

———. *De conceptu virginali et de originali peccato*. In *Opera Omnia*, vol. 2, 135–173. Edited by F. S. Schmitt. English translation: In *Why God Became Man, and the Virgin Conception and Original Sin*. Edited and translated by Joseph M. Colleran. Albany, NY: Magi Books, 1969.

Aristotle. *The Basic Works of Aristotle*. Edited by Richard McKeon. New York: Random House, 1941.

Arnauld, Antoine, and Pierre Nicole. *La logique ou l'art de penser*. Paris, 1662. English translation: *Logic, or, the Art of Thinking*. Edited by Jill Vance Buroker. Cambridge and New York: Cambridge University Press, 1996.

Aron, Raymond. *German Sociology*. New York: The Free Press of Glencoe, 1954.

Baader, Franz von. *Sätze aus der erotischen Philosophie* (Theses from an erotic philosophy). Vol. 4 of *Sämtliche Werke*. Edited by Franz Hoffmann. Aalen, Germany: Scientia, 1987.

Barth, Karl. "Fünfzehn Antworten an Herrn Professor von Harnack." *Die christliche Welt* 37/5–6 (February 8, 1923): cols. 89–91. English translation: "Fifteen Answers to Professor von Harnack." In *The Beginnings of Dialectic Theology*, 167–70. Edited by James M. Robinson. Translated by Keith R. Crim and Louis De Grazia. Richmond: John Knox Press, 1968.

———. "Kirche und Theologie." *Zwischen den Zeiten* 4/1 (1926):18–40.

English translation: "Church and Theology." In *Theology and Church: Shorter Writings, 1920–1928,* 286–306. Translated by Louise Pettibone Smith. London: SCM, 1962.

——. *Die kirchliche Dogmatik.* Vol. 4, *Die Lehre von der Versöhnung.* Zurich: Evangelischer Verlag, 1955 (4/2); 1959 (4/3). English translation: *Church Dogmatics.* Vol. 4, *The Doctrine of Reconciliation.* Translated by G. W. Bromiley. Edinburgh: T. & T. Clark, 1958 (4/2); 1961–62 (4/3).

——. "Not und Verheißung der christlichen Verkündigung." *Zwischen den Zeiten* 1 (1923):3–25. English translation: "The Need and Promise of Christian Preaching." In *The Word of God and the Word of Man,* 97–135. Translated by Douglas Horton. London: Hodder and Stoughton, 1928; New York: Harper & Row, 1957.

——. *Das Wort Gottes und die Theologie.* Munich: Chr. Kaiser Verlag, 1929. English translation: *The Word of God and the Word of Man.* Translated by Douglas Horton. London: Hodder and Stoughton, 1928; New York: Harper & Brothers, 1957.

Becker, Carl Heinrich. *Gedanken zur Hochschulreform* (Thoughts on university reform). Leipzig: Quelle and Meyer, 1919.

Die Bekenntnisschriften der evangelisch-lutherischen Kirche. Edited by Hans Lietzmann, Heinrich Bornkamm, Hans Volz, and Ernst Wolf. Göttingen: Vandenhoeck & Ruprecht, 1986. English translation: *The Book of Concord: The Confessions of the Evangelical Lutheran Church.* Edited and translated by Theodore G. Tappert, in collaboration with Jaroslav Pelikan, Robert H. Fischer, and Arthur C. Piepkorn. Philadelphia: Fortress Press, 1959.

Below, Georg von. "Soziologie als Lehrfach" (Sociology as an academic subject). *Schmollers Jahrbuch* 43 (1919):271ff.

Bernard of Clairvaux. "In dedicatione ecclesiae: Sermo Primus" (In dedication of a church: First sermon). In *Sancti Bernardi Opera,* 5:370ff. Edited by J. Leclerq and H. Rochais. Rome: Editiones Cistercienses, 1957–77.

Bethge, Eberhard. *Dietrich Bonhoeffer: Theologe–Christ–Zeitgenosse: Eine Biographie.* 8th ed. Munich: Chr. Kaiser Verlag, 1994. English translation: *Dietrich Bonhoeffer: Man of Vision, Man of Courage.* Abridged from the third German edition. Translated by Eric Mosbacher, Peter and Betty Ross, Frank Clarke, and William Glen-Doepel, under the editorship of Edwin H. Robertson. London: William Collins; New York: Harper & Row, 1970.

Bobert-Stützel, Sabine. *Dietrich Bonhoeffers Pastoraltheologie.* (Dietrich Bonhoeffer's pastoral theology). Gütersloh: Chr. Kaiser/Gütersloher Verlagshaus, 1995.

Bonhoeffer, Dietrich. "Christologie." *GS* 3:166–242 [also published in *DBW* 12:279–348]. English translation: *Christ the Center.* A new translation [from the *GS*] by Edwin H. Robertson. London: Collins; San Francisco: Harper & Row, 1978. [U.K. Title: *Christology.*]

——. *The Communion of Saints: A Dogmatic Inquiry into the Sociology of the Church.* Translated and edited by Ronald Gregor Smith. London: Collins, 1963; New York: Harper & Row, 1964. [U.K. title: *Sanctorum Communio: A Dogmatic Inquiry into the Sociology of the Church.*]

——. *The Cost of Discipleship.* Translated by Reginald H. Fuller, revised by Irmgard Booth. New York: Macmillan, 1963.

——. Dietrich Bonhoeffer Werke. 16 vols. Edited by E. Bethge et al. Munich, 1986–. English translation: Dietrich Bonhoeffer Works. 16 vols. Edited by Wayne Whitson Floyd, Jr. Minneapolis: Fortress Press, 1996–.

2: *Akt und Sein: Transzendentalphilosophie und Ontologie in der systematischen Theologie.* Edited by Hans-Richard Reuter. Munich: Chr. Kaiser Verlag, 1988. English translation: *Act and Being: Transcendental Philosophy and Ontology in Systematic Theology.* Edited by Wayne Whitson Floyd, Jr. Translated by H. Martin Rumscheidt. Minneapolis: Fortress Press, 1996.

4: *Nachfolge.* Edited by Martin Kuske and Ilse Tödt. Munich: Chr. Kaiser Verlag, 1989, 1994.

6: *Ethik.* Edited by Ernst Feil, Clifford Green, and Heinz Eduard Tödt. Munich: Chr. Kaiser Verlag, 1992.

8: *Widerstand und Ergebung.* Edited by Christian Gremmels, Eberhard Bethge, and Renate Bethge, assisted by Ilse Tödt. Munich: Chr. Kaiser Verlag, 1998.

9: *Jugend und Studium 1918–1927* (Youth and education, 1918–27). Contains "Luthers Stimmungen gegenüber seinem Werk in seinen letzten Lebensjahren" (Luther's feelings toward his work in the last years of his life), 271–305; "Lasst sich eine historische und pneumatische Auslegung der Schrift unterscheiden, und wie stellt sich die Dogmatik hierzu?" ("Can a historical and a spiritual interpretation of scripture be distinguished, and what is the attitude of dogmatics to this issue?," 305–23; and "Luthers Anschauungen vom

Heiligen Geist nach den Disputationen von 1535–45 herausgegeben von Drews" (Luther's views on the Holy Spirit according to the disputations of 1535–45 edited by Drews), 355–410. Edited by Hans Pfeifer, with Clifford Green and Carl-Jürgen Kaltenborn. Munich, 1986.

12: *Berlin: 1932–1933.* Includes "Christologie," 279–348, and "Die Kirche vor der Judenfrage," 349–58. Edited by Carsten Nicolaisen and Ernst-Albert Scharffenorth. Munich: Chr. Kaiser Verlag, 1997.

———. *Ethics.* Translated by Neville Horton Smith. New York: Macmillan, 1965; Simon and Schuster, 1995.

———. *Gesammelte Schriften* (Collected works). 6 vols. Edited by Eberhard Bethge. Munich, 1958–74.

———. "Die Kirche vor der Judenfrage." *GS* 2:44–53 [also published in DBW 12:349–58]. English translation [from the *GS*]: "The Church and the Jewish Question." In *No Rusty Swords,* 221–29. Edited by Edwin H. Robertson. New York: Harper & Row, 1965.

———. *Letters and Papers from Prison.* London: SCM, 1971; New York: Macmillan, 1972; New York: Simon and Schuster, 1997.

———. *No Rusty Swords: Letters, Lectures, and Notes, 1928–1936.* From the *Collected Works of Dietrich Bonhoeffer,* vol. 1. Edited and with an introduction by Edwin H. Robertson. Translated by Edwin H. Robertson and John Bowden. London: Collins; New York: Harper & Row, 1965.

Bonhoeffer, Dietrich, and Maria von Wedemeyer. *Love Letters from Cell 92. The Correspondence Between Dietrich Bonhoeffer and Maria von Wedemeyer, 1943–45.* Translated by John Brownjohn. Nashville: Abingdon, 1995.

Buber, Martin. *I and Thou.* Translated by Ronald Gregor Smith. New York: Scribner, 1937. Translated by Walter Kaufmann. New York: Scribner, 1970.

Bultmann, Rudolf. "Welchen Sinn hat es von Gott zu reden?" *Theologische Blätter* 4 (1925):129–35. Also published in his *Glauben und Verstehen,* 1:26–37. Tübingen, 1933. English translation: "What Does It Mean to Speak of God?" In *Faith and Understanding,* 53–65. Edited by Robert W. Funk. Translated by Louis Pettibone Smith. Philadelphia: Fortress Press, 1987.

Calvin, Jean. *Institutio,* 1559. Edited by P. Barth and G. Niesel. English translation: *Institutes of the Christian Religion.* Vols. 20–21 of *The Library of Christian Classics.* Edited by John T. McNeill. Translated by Ford Lewis Battles. Philadelphia: Westminster Press, 1960.

——. "Projet d'Ordonnances ecclésiastiques" (1541). In *Ioannis Calvini opera quae supersunt omnia*, cols. 15ff. Vol. 38 of *Corpus Reformatorum*. Edited by Guilielmus Baum, Eduardus Cunitz, and Eduardus Reuss. Brunsvigae: C. A. Schwetschke, 1871; New York, Johnson Reprint, 1964. English translation: "Draft Ecclesiastical Ordinances," September and October 1541. In *Calvin: Theological Treatises*, 58–72. Vol. 22 of the *Library of Christian Classics*. Translated with introductions and notes by J. K. S. Reid. Philadelphia: Westminster Press, 1977.

"Canones de sacramento baptismi" (March 3, 1547). Council of Trent, Session 7. In Denzinger, *Enchiridion Symbolorum*, 383–84. English translation: "Canons on the Sacrament of Baptism." In Denzinger, *Sources*, 263–64.

"Catechismus Romanus" (1566). In *Quellenschriften zur Geschichte des Protestantismus*, 1:656ff. Leipzig, 1904–32. English translation: *Catechism of the Council of Trent*. Translated by J. Donovan. Dublin: James Duffy, 1914.

Cyril of Jerusalem. *The Works of St. Cyril of Jerusalem*. Translated by Leo P. McCauley and Anthony A. Stephenson. Washington: Catholic University of America Press, 1969–70.

"Decretum de peccato originali" (June 17, 1546). Council of Trent, Session 5. In Denzinger, *Enchiridion Symbolorum*, 366–68. English translation: "Decree on Original Sin." In Denzinger, *The Sources of Catholic Dogma*, 246–48.

Denzinger, Heinrich, and Adolf Schönmetzer, eds. *Enchiridion Symbolorum Definitionum et Declarationum de Rebus Fidei et Morum*. Freiburg, 1965. English translation: *The Sources of Catholic Dogma*. Translated by Roy J. Defarrari. St Louis: Herder, 1957.

Deutschen Gesellschaft für Soziologie. *Die Verhandlungen des Deutschen Soziologentages* (Proceedings of the German congress of sociologists). Vols. 1–24. Frankfurt and Tübingen, 1910/11–1988/89.

Durkheim, Emile. *Die elementaren Formen des religiösen Lebens*. Translated by L. Schmidts. Frankfurt: Suhrkamp, 1981. English translation (from the original French edition; see above, page 314, *Les formes élémentaires de la vie religieuse*): *The Elementary Forms of Religious Life*. Translated and with an introduction by Karen E. Fields. New York: Free Press, 1995.

Epicurus. *Epicurus, the Extant Remains*. Translated and edited by Cyril Bailey. Oxford: Clarendon Press, 1926. Reprint. Westport, Conn.: Hyperion Press, 1979.

Evangelische Kirche der altpreußischen Union. *Verfassungsurkunde für die evangelische Kirche der altpreußischen Union: Amtlicher Text* (Constitution of the Evangelical Church of the Old Prussian Union: Official Text). Berlin: Evangelischer Pressverband für Deutschland, 1924.

Evangelisches Gesangbuch, Provinz Brandenburg (Protestant Hymn Book for the Province of Brandenburg). Berlin, 1903.

Evangelisches Kirchengesangbuch (Protestant Hymn Book). Munich, n.d.

Fathers of the Church [series]. New York: Cima Pub. Co., 1947-.

Fichte, Johann Gottlieb. *Grundlage der gesamten Wissenschaftslehre.* 1794; 2d ed., 1802. Reprint. Hamburg: Meiner, 1970. English translation: *The Science of Knowledge: With the First and Second Introductions.* Translated by Peter Heath and John Lachs. Cambridge: Cambridge University Press, 1982.

——. *Reden an die deutsche Nation.* Vol. 7 of *Werke.* Edited by Fritz Medicus. Leipzig: F. Meiner, 1919-. In *Philosophische Bibliothek,* vols. 127-32, 163. English translation: *Addresses to the German Nation.* Translated by R. F. Jones and G. H. Turnbull. London and Chicago: Open Court, 1922. Reprint. Westport, Conn.: Greenwood Press, 1979.

——. *Zweite Einleitung in die Wissenschaftslehre.* Vol. 1 of *Werke.* Edited by Immanuel Hermann Fichte. Berlin, 1971. English translation: *Introductions to the Wissenschaftslehre and Other Writings, 1797-1800.* Translated and edited by Daniel Breazeale. Indianapolis: Hackett, 1994.

Geiger, Theodor, and Hans Lorenz Stoltenberg. "Soziologie" (Sociology). In *Handwörterbuch der Soziologie* (Dictionary of sociology), 568ff. and 579ff. Edited by Alfred Vierkandt. Stuttgart, 1931.

Goethe, Johann Wolfgang von. *Wilhelm Meisters Lehrjahre.* Edited by Ehrhard Bahr. Stuttgart: Reclam, 1982, 1990. English translation: *Wilhelm Meister's Apprenticeship.* Edited and translated by Eric A. Blackall in cooperation with Victor Lange. Princeton: Princeton University Press, 1995.

——. *Wilhelm Meisters theatralische Sendung.* 1771. English translation: *Wilhelm Meister's Theatrical Calling.* Edited and translated by John Russell. Columbia, S.C.: Camden House, 1995.

Gogarten, Friedrich. "Nachwort" (Afterword) to *Vom unfreien Willen* (On the bondage of the will), by Martin Luther. Munich: Chr. Kaiser, 1924. English translation: "Protestantism and Reality: Epilogue to Martin Luther's *Bondage of the Will.*" In *The Beginnings of Dialectic Theology,* 359-80. Edited by James M. Robinson. Richmond: John Knox, 1968.

Green, Clifford James. "Two Bonhoeffers on Psychoanalysis." In *A Bonhoeffer Legacy: Essays in Understanding,* 58–75. Edited by A. J. Klassen. Grand Rapids: Eerdmans, 1981.

——. *The Sociality of Christ and Humanity: Dietrich Bonhoeffer's Early Theology, 1927–1933.* Missoula, Mont.: Scholars Press, 1975. Reprint. *Bonhoeffer: A Theology of Sociality.* Grand Rapids: Eerdmans, 1999.

Hamann, Johann Georg. "Zwo Recensionen . . . den Ursprung der Sprache betreffend" (Two reviews . . . concerning the origin of language). In *Schriften über Sprache, Mysterien, Vernunft* (Writings on language, mysteries, and reason), *1772–1788.* Vol. 3 of his *Sämtliche Werke.* Edited by Joseph Nadler. Vienna: Verlag Herder, 1951.

——. *Schriften zur Sprache.* Edited by Josef Simon. Frankfurt am Main: Suhrkamp, 1967.

Harnack, Adolf von. "Apostles' Creed." In *The New Schaff-Herzog Encyclopedia of Religious Knowledge,* 1:240–43. Edited by Samuel M. Jackson et al. New York and London: Funk and Wagnalls, 1908.

——. "Apostolisches Symbolum." In *Protestantische Realencyklopädie für protestantische Theologie und Kirche,* 1:741–55. 3d ed. Edited by Johann J. Herzog and Albert Hauck. Leipzig, 1896–1913. English translation: *The Apostles' Creed.* Edited by Thomas Bailey Saunders. Translated by Stewart Means. London: A. & C. Black, 1901.

——. "Funfzehn Fragen an die Verächter der wissenschaftlichen Theologie unter den Theologen." *Die christliche Welt* 37/1–2 (January 11, 1923): cols. 6–8. English translation: "Fifteen Questions to Those Among the Theologians Who Are Contemptuous of the Scientific Theology." In *The Beginnings of Dialectic Theology,* 165–66. Edited by James M. Robinson. Richmond: John Knox Press, 1968.

Hegel, Georg Wilhelm Friedrich. *Phänomenologie des Geistes.* Vol. 3 of *Werke in Zwanzig Bänden* (Works in twenty volumes). Theorie-Werkausgabe (Scholars work edition). Frankfurt: Suhrkamp, 1969–. English translation: *Phenomenology of Spirit.* Translated by Arnold V. Miller. New York: Oxford University Press, 1977.

——. *Wissenschaft der Logik.* Vol. 2; appears as vol. 6 of *Werke in Zwanzig Bänden* (Works in twenty volumes). Theorie-Werkausgabe (Scholars work edition). Frankfurt: Suhrkamp, 1969–. English translation: *Hegel's Science of Logic.* Translated by Arnold V. Miller. Foreword by J. N. Findlay. New York: Humanities Press, 1969.

Holl, Karl. *Briefwechsel mit Adolf von Harnack* (Correspondence with

Adolf von Harnack). Edited by Heinrich Karpp. Tübingen: Mohr, 1966.

Huber, Ernst Rudolf, and Wolfgang Huber, *Staat und Kirche im 19. and 20. Jahrhundert* (State and church in the 19th and 20th centuries), vol. 3. Berlin: Duncker und Humblot, 1976.

Humboldt, Wilhelm von. *Schriften zur Sprachphilosophie* (Writings on the philosophy of language). Vol. 3 of *Werke.* Edited by A. Flither and K. Giel. Stuttgart, 1963.

Hutter, Leonhard. *Compendium locorum theologicorum, ex Scripturis Sacris et libro concordiae.* Wittenberg, 1609. English translation: *Compend of Lutheran Theology: A Summary of Christian Doctrine, Derived from the Word of God and the Symbolical Books of the Evangelical Lutheran Church.* Translated by H. E. Jacobs and G. F. Spieker. Philadelphia: Lutheran Book Store, 1868.

Jerome, Saint. *Sancti Hieronymi . . . Commentarioli in Psalmos* (St. Jerome . . . Commentary on the Psalms). Vol. 3 of *Anecdota Maredsolana.* Edited by Germain Morin. Maredsous, Belgium, 1897.

Kant, Immanuel. *Critique of Pure Reason.* Translated by Norman Kemp Smith. New York: St. Martin's Press, 1929, 1965.

———. *Grundlegung zur Metaphysik der Sitten.* Vol. 6 of *Werke.* [See below.] English translation: *Groundwork of the Metaphysic of Morals.* Translated by H. J. Paton. New York: Harper & Row, 1964.

———. "Über den Gemeinspruch: Das mag in der Theorie richtig sein, taugt aber nicht für die Praxis" (On the saying: That may be correct in theory but is no use in practice). Vol. 9 of *Werke.* [See below.]

———. *Werke in zehn Bänden.* Edited by Wilhelm Weischedel. Darmstadt, 1956–64. English translation: *The Cambridge Edition of the Works of Immanuel Kant.* New York: Cambridge University Press, 1992–.

Kierkegaard, Søren. *Der Begriff der Angst.* Vols. 11 and 12 of *Gesammelte Werke.* Edited by Emanuel Hirsch and Hayo Gerdes. Translated by Emanuel Hirsch. Düsseldorf: Diederichs Verlag, 1952. English translation from the Danish original: *The Concept of Anxiety.* Edited and translated with introduction and notes by Reidar Thomte, in collaboration with Albert B. Anderson. Princeton: Princeton University Press, 1980.

———. *Der Liebe Tun.* Vol. 19 of *Gesammelte Werke.* Edited by Emanuel Hirsch and Hayo Gerdes. Jena: Diederichs, 1966. English translation from the Danish original: *The Works of Love.* Edited and translated by

340   Bibliography

Howard V. Hong and Edna H. Hong. Princeton: Princeton University Press, 1995.

———. *Philosophische Brocken*. Vol. 10 of *Gesammelte Werke*. Edited by Emanuel Hirsch and Hayo Gerdes. Düsseldorf: Diederichs Verlag, 1952. English translation from the Danish original: *Philosophical Fragments*. Edited and translated by Edna H. Hong and Howard V. Hong. Princeton: Princeton University Press, 1985.

Kölner Vierteljahreshefte für Sozialwissenschaften. Leipzig, 1921ff.

Lake, Kirsopp, ed. *The Apostolic Fathers*. Vol. 1. Cambridge: Harvard University Press, 1949.

Leibniz, Gottfried Wilhelm. *Disputatio Metaphysica de Principio Individui* (Metaphysical disputation concerning the principle of the individual). Vol. 4 of *Die philosophischen Schriften*. Edited by C. Gerhardt. Berlin: Weidmann, 1880.

———. *Monadologie*. Published with *Vernunftprinzipien der Natur und der Gnade*. Edited by Herbert Herring. Hamburg: Felix Meiner, 1982. English translation: "The Principles of Philosophy, or, The Monadology." In *Discourse on Metaphysics*. Edited and translated by Daniel Garber and Rofer Ariew. Indianapolis: Hackett, 1991.

Luther, Martin. "Annotationes in aliquot capita Matthaei" (1538) (Notations on several chapters of Matthew). *WA* 38:443–667.

———. "Appellatio F. Martini Luther ad Concilium" (1518) (Appeal of Martin Luther to the Council). *WA* 2:34–40.

———. "Deutsche Messe und Ordnung Gottesdiensts" (1526). *WA* 19:44–113. English translation: "The German Mass and Order of Service." *LW* 36:51–90.

———. *Dictata super Psalterium* (1513–16). *WA* 4:1–462. English translation: *First Lectures on the Psalms*. *LW* 11:3–553.

———. "Epistel in der Früh-Christmess, Titus 3:4-7." *WA* 10/1:95–128. English translation: "Second Christmas Sermon: Early Christmas Morning Service." In *Sermons of Martin Luther*, 6:142–65. Edited by John Nicholas Lenker. Grand Rapids: Baker Book House, 1983.

———. "Epistel S. Petri gepredidgt und ausgelegt: Erste Bearbeitung" (1523). *WA* 12:249–399. English translation: "Sermons on the First Epistle of Peter." *LW* 30:1–145.

———. "Fastenpostille" (1525). *WA* 17/2:1–247. English translation: "Second Sunday after Epiphany." In *Luther's Epistle Sermons*, vol. 2. Vol. 8 of *Luther's Complete Works*. Edited by John Nicholas Lenker. Minneapolis: The Luther Press, 1909.

————. *Grosser Katechismus.* In *Bekenntnisschriften der evangelisch-lutherischen Kirche.* Deutsche evangelische Kirchenausschuss. Göttingen, 1930; 6th ed., 1967. English translation: *The Large Catechism.* See *The Book of Concord.*

————. *In Epistolam Pauli ad Galatos Commentarius* (1519). *WA* 2:443–618. English translation: *Lectures on Galatians. LW* 27:151–410.

————. *Operationes in Psalmos* (1519–20). *WA* 5:20–74. English translation: "Preface from Works on the First Twenty-two Psalms" (1519–22), "Commentary on Psalm 1," and "Commentary on Psalm 2." *LW* 14:280–349.

————. "Predigt am Pfingsttage" (Sermon on Pentecost). No. 23, May 16, 1535. *WA* 41:248–52.

————. "Ein Sermon am grünen Donnerstag" (A sermon preached on Maundy Thursday) (1523). *WA* 12:476–93.

————. "Vom Abendmahl Christi, Bekenntnis" (1528). *WA* 26:261–509. English translation:"Confession Concerning Christ's Supper." *LW* 37:151–372.

————. *Vom unfreien Willen.* Munich, 1924. English translation: *The Bondage of the Will.* Translated by Philip S. Watson with Benjamin Drewery. In *LW* 33:3–295.

————. "Von beider Gestalt des Sakraments zu nehmen" (1522). *WA* 10/2:11–41. English translation: "Receiving Both Kinds in the Sacrament." *LW* 36:231–67.

————. "Von den guten Werken" (1520). *WA* 6:196–276. English translation: "Treatise on Good Works." *LW* 44:15–114.

————. "Vorrede zum 1. Band der Gesamtausgabe der lateinischen Schriften." *WA* 54:175–87. English translation: "Preface to the Complete Edition of Luther's Latin Writings." *LW* 34:323–38.

————. "Wider die himmlischen Propheten, von den Bildern und Sakrament" (Against the heavenly prophets, on images and the sacrament) (1525). *WA* 18:37–214.

Lutheran Book of Worship. Minneapolis: Augsburg Publishing House; Philadelphia: Board of Publication, Lutheran Church in America, 1978.

Nietzsche, Friedrich. *Jenseits von Gut und Böse.* In *Werke,* 7:1–274. Edited by Giorgio Colli and Mazzino Montinari. Berlin: W. de Gruyter, 1967–. English translation: *Beyond Good and Evil.* Translated, with commentary, by Walter Kaufman. New York: Random House, 1966.

Novum Testamentum Graece et Germanice. Edited by D. Eberhard Nestle and Erwin Nestle. 13th ed. Stuttgart, 1929.

Olbrich, Harald, ed. *Lexicon der Kunst* (Encyclopedia of art). 7 vols. Leipzig: E. A. Seemann, 1987–94.

Plato. *The Collected Dialogues of Plato, Including the Letters.* Princeton: Princeton Univ. Press, 1961.

Ranke, Leopold von. "Preface to the First Edition of Histories of the Latin and Germanic Nations." [See next entry, *The Theory and Practice of History.*]

———. *Über die Epochen der neueren Geschichte.* Darmstadt, 1982. English translation: "On Progress in History." In *The Theory and Practice of History.* Edited by Georg G. Iggers and Konrad von Moltke. New York: Irvington, 1993.

Robinson, James M. *The Beginnings of Dialectical Theology.* Richmond: John Knox Press, 1968.

Rothe, Richard. *Theologische Ethik.* 2d ed. Vols. 1–5. Wittenberg: Zimmermann, 1869–71. *NL* 4 41.

———. *Zur Dogmatik.* 2d ed. Gotha: F. A. Perthes, 1869. *NL* 3 B 59a.

Schaff, Philip, et al., eds. *A Select Library of the Nicene and Post-Nicene Fathers of the Christian Church* [1st series]. 14 vols. Grand Rapids: Eerdmans, 1956. [Cited as *Nicene and Post-Nicene Fathers.*]

Schelling, Friedrich Wilhelm Josef. *Philosophie der Offenbarung.* Vol 6 of his *Werke.* Edited by Manfred Schröte. Munich: Beck, 1946–.

Schleiermacher, Friedrich Daniel Ernst. *Der Christliche Glaube.* 7th ed. 2 vols. Edited by Martin Redeker. Berlin: W. de Gruyter, 1960. English translation: *The Christian Faith.* Translation of second German edition. Edited by H. R. MacKintosh and J. S. Stewart. Edinburgh: T. & T. Clark; Philadelphia: Fortress Press, 1976.

Scholder, Klaus. *The Churches and the Third Reich.* 2 vols. Translated by John Bowden. Philadelphia: Fortress Press, 1988.

Seeberg, Reinhold. *Die Kirche Deutschlands im neunzehnten Jahrhundert* (The German church in the nineteenth century). Leipzig, 1903.

Sombart, Werner. "Die Anfänge der Soziologie" (Beginnings of sociology). In *Hauptprobleme der Soziologie: Erinnerungsgabe für Max Weber* (Chief issues in sociology: presented to Max Weber as a commemorative gift), 1:3ff. Edited by Melchir Palyi. Munich and Leipzig, 1923.

Spinoza, Benedict. *Die Ethik.* Edited by C. Gebhardt. Hamburg: Felix Meiner, 1976. English translation: *Ethics and Treatise on the Correction of the Intellect.* Translated by Andrew Boyle and George H. R. Parkinson. London: J. M. Dent; Rutland, Vt.: Charles E. Tuttle, 1993.

———. *Kurze Abhandlung von Gott, dem Menschen und seinem Glück.* Edited by C. Gebhardt. Hamburg: Felix Meiner, 1959. English translation: *Short Treatise on God, Man, and his Well-Being.* Translated and edited by Abraham Wolff. New York: Russell and Russell, 1963.

Tacitus. *The Annals of Imperial Rome.* Translated with an introduction by Michael Grant. Rev. ed. New York: Dorset Press, 1956, 1984.

Tatian. *Diatessaron.* Edited by August Pott. Heidelberg, 1926. English translation: "The Diatessaron of Tatian." In *The Ante-Nicene Fathers,* 9:35–138. Grand Rapids: Eerdmans, 1951. Reprint. Peabody, Mass.: Hendrickson, 1994.

Tönnies, Ferdinand. "Soziologie und Hochschulreform" (Sociology and university reform). In *Weltwirtschaftsliches Archiv* 16 (1920–21):212ff.

Tyconius. *Tyconius: The Book of Rules.* Edited and translated by William S. Babcock. Atlanta: Scholars Press, 1989.

Weber, Max. *Gesammelte Aufsätze zur Wissenschaftslehre* (Collected essays on the philosophy of the academic disciplines). Edited by Johannes Winckelmann. Tübingen, 1968.

———. "Politik als Beruf." In *Gesammelte Politische Schriften.* Edited by Johannes Winkelmann. 2d ed. Tübingen: J. C. B. Mohr, 1958. English translation: "Politics as Vocation." In *From Max Weber: Essays in Sociology,* 77–128. Translated, edited, and with an introduction by Hans H. Gerth and C. Wright Mills. New York: Oxford University Press, 1946.

Wiese, Leopold von. "Die Soziologie als Einzelwissenschaft" (Sociology as a distinct discipline). *Schmollers Jahrbuch* 44 (1920):347ff.

Zimmermann, Wolf-Dieter, ed. *Begegnungen mit Dietrich Bonhoeffer.* Munich: Chr. Kaiser Verlag, 1965. English translation: *I Knew Dietrich Bonhoeffer.* Edited by Wolf-Dieter Zimmermann and Ronald Gregor Smith. London: Collins; New York: Harper & Row, 1966.

3. Other Literature Related to *Sanctorum Communio*

Ahlers, Rolf. "Hegel and Bonhoeffer: Community and Return." In *The Community of Freedom: Barth and Presuppositionless Theology,* 148–88. New York: Peter Lang, 1989.

Berger, Peter L. "The Social Character of the Question Concerning Jesus Christ: Sociology and Ecclesiology." In *The Place of Bonhoeffer:*

Problems and Possibilities in His Thought, 51–80. Edited by Martin E. Marty. New York: Association Press, 1963.

Bethge, Eberhard. "Nachwort" (Afterword) to *Sanctorum Communio*, 4th ed. Munich: Chr. Kaiser Verlag, 1963.

———. "Zur dritten Auflage" (On the third edition) of *Sanctorum Communio*. Munich: Chr. Kaiser, 1960.

Brocker, Mark. "The Community of God, Jesus Christ, and Responsibility: The Responsible Person and the Responsible Community in the Ethics of Dietrich Bonhoeffer." Ph.D. diss., University of Chicago Divinity School, 1996.

Champion, Maxwell Lloyd. "Knowledge of God as the Transformation of Human Existence in the Theology of Dietrich Bonhoeffer." Th.D. diss., Princeton Theological Seminary, 1988.

Clements, Keith. "The Freedom of the Church: Bonhoeffer and the Free Church Tradition." In *Bonhoeffer's Ethics: Old Europe and New Frontiers*, 155–72. Edited by Guy C. Carter et al. Kampen: Kok Pharos, 1991.

Day, Thomas I. *Dietrich Bonhoeffer on Christian Community and Common Sense*. Lewiston, N.Y.: Edwin Mellen Press, 1982.

de Lange, Frits. "Grond onder de voeten: Burgerligkheid bij Dietrich Bonhoeffer. Ein theologische studie" (Ground under one's feet: Civic responsibility according to Dietrich Bonhoeffer—a theological study). Diss. (theology), Kampen, 1984.

Duchrow, Ulrich. "Dem Rad in die Speichen fallen—aber wo and wie? Luthers und Bonhoeffers Ethik der Institution im Kontext des heutigen Weltwirtschaftssystems" (Putting a spoke in the wheel—but where and how? The ethic of institutions in Luther and Bonhoeffer in the context of the global economic system). In *Bonhoeffer und Luther*. Edited by Christian Gremmels. Munich, 1983.

Dumas, André. *Dietrich Bonhoeffer: Theologian of Reality*. Translated by Robert McAfee Brown. New York: Macmillan, 1971.

Feil, Ernst. *Die Theologie Dietrich Bonhoeffers: Hermeneutik, Christologie, Weltverständnis*. 3d ed. Munich and Mainz, 1979. English translation: *The Theology of Dietrich Bonhoeffer*. Translated by Martin Rumscheidt. Philadelphia: Fortress Press, 1985.

Feil, Ernst, with Barbara Fink. *Internationale Bibliographie zu Dietrich Bonhoeffer* (International bibliography of Dietrich Bonhoeffer). Gütersloh: Chr. Kaiser/Gütersloher Verlagshaus, 1998.

Floyd, Wayne Whitson, Jr. *Theology and the Dialectics of Otherness: On*

Reading Bonhoeffer and Adorno. Lanham, Md.: University Press of America, 1988.

Floyd, Wayne Whitson, Jr., and Clifford J. Green. *Bonhoeffer Bibliography: Primary Sources and Secondary Literature in English.* Evanston, Ill.: American Theological Library Association, 1992. [Annual updates of this bibliography are published in the *Newsletter* of the International Bonhoeffer Society, English Language Section.]

Godsey, John D. *The Theology of Dietrich Bonhoeffer.* Philadelphia: Westminster Press; London: SCM, 1960.

Green, Clifford James. "Human Sociality and Christian Community." In *The Cambridge Companion to Dietrich Bonhoeffer.* Edited by John W. de Gruchy. Cambridge: Cambridge University Press, forthcoming.

Hase, Hans Christoph von. "Begriff und Wirklichkeit der Kirche in der Theologie Dietrich Bonhoeffers" (The concept and reality of the church in the theology of Dietrich Bonhoeffer). *Evangelische Theologie* 15 (1955):164ff.

Honecker, Martin. *Kirche als Gestalt und Ereignis* (Church as form and event). Munich: Chr. Kaiser, 1963.

Huber, Wolfgang. "Wahrheit und Existenzform: Anregungen zu einer Theorie der Kirche bei Dietrich Bonhoeffer" (Truth and form of existence: Toward a theory of the church in Dietrich Bonhoeffer). In his *Folgen Christlicher Freiheit.* Neukirchen-Vluyn: Neukirchener Verlag, 1983. Also in *Dietrich Bonhoeffers Kirchenverständnis heute.* Edited by Ernst Feil and Ilse Tödt. Munich: Chr. Kaiser, 1980.

Hyun, Yo-han. "The Holy Spirit and the Problem of the Cor Curvum in Se in Dietrich Bonhoeffer's Early Theology." Ph.D. diss., Princeton Theological Seminary, 1992.

Kaltenborn, Carl-Jürgen. *Adolf von Harnack als Lehrer Dietrich Bonhoeffers* (Adolf von Harnack as a teacher of Dietrich Bonhoeffer). Berlin: Evangelische Verlagsanstalt, 1973.

Lange, Ernst. "Kirche für andere: Dietrich Bonhoeffers Beitrag zur Frage einer verantwortbaren Gestalt der Kirche in der Gegenwart" (The church for others: Dietrich Bonhoeffer's contribution to the question of a responsible form of the church today). In *Kirche für die Welt: Aufsätze zur Theorie kirchlichen Handelns.* Edited by R. Schloz. Munich: Gelnhausen, 1981.

Lehel, Ferenc. *Dietrich Bonhoeffers Hegel Seminar 1933: Nach den Aufzeichnungen von Ferenc Lehel* (Dietrich Bonhoeffer's 1933 Hegel seminar according to the notes of Ferenc Lehel). Edited by Ilse Tödt. Munich: Chr. Kaiser Verlag, 1988.

Marsh, Charles. *Reclaiming Dietrich Bonhoeffer: The Promise of His Theology.* New York: Oxford University Press, 1994.

Mayer, Rainer. *Christuswirklichkeit: Grundlagen, Entwicklung und Konsequenzen der Theologie Dietrich Bonhoeffers* (Christ-reality: Foundations, development, and consequences of the theology of Dietrich Bonhoeffer). Stuttgart: Calwer, 1969.

Moltmann, Jürgen. *Herrschaft Christi und Soziale Wirklichkeit nach Dietrich Bonhoeffer.* Munich: Chr. Kaiser, 1959. English translation: "The Lordship of Christ and Human Society." In *Two Studies in the Theology of Bonhoeffer,* by Jürgen Moltmann and Jürgen Weissbach. New York: Charles Scribner's Sons, 1967.

Mottu, Henri. "'Christ existant comme communaute': Le sens de la formule du premier ouvrage de Dietrich Bonhoeffer" ("Christ existing as community": The meaning of the formula in Dietrich Bonhoeffer's first work). *Recherches de science religieuse* 79 (1991):221–22.

Müller, Gerhard Ludwig. *Bonhoeffers Theologie der Sakramente* (Bonhoeffer's theology of the sacraments). Frankfurt am Main: J. Knecht, 1979.

Müller, Hanfried. *Von der Kirche zur Welt: Ein Beitrag zu der Beziehung des Wort Gottes auf die societas in Dietrich Bonhoeffers theologische Entwicklung* (From the church to the world: A contribution to the relation of the word of God to society in Dietrich Bonhoeffer's theological development). 2d ed. Hamburg: H. Reich, 1966.

Oettingen, Alexander von. *Kirchliche Gemeinwesenarbeit–Konflikt und gesellschaftliche Strukturbildung: Eine empirische Untersuchung im Kontext der Ekklesiologie Dietrich Bonhoeffers* (The work of the church in the public arena—conflict and formation of social structures: An empirical study within the framework of Dietrich Bonhoeffer's ecclesiology). Frankfurt: Lang, 1979.

Ott, Heinrich. *Reality and Faith: The Theological Legacy of Dietrich Bonhoeffer.* Translated by Alex A. Morrison. London: Lutterworth; Philadelphia: Fortress Press, 1972.

Pangritz, Andreas. *Karl Barth in der Theologie Dietrich Bonhoeffers: Eine notwendige Klarstellung* (Karl Barth in the theology of Dietrich Bonhoeffer: A necessary clarification). Berlin: Alektor, 1989.

Peters, Tiemo Rainer. "Der andere ist unendlich wichtig: Impulse aus

Bonhoeffers Ekklesiologie für die Gegenwart" (The other is infinitely important: Impetus from Bonhoeffer's ecclesiology for the present). In *Die Präsenz des verdrängten Gottes: Glaube, Religionslosigkeit und Weltverantwortung*, 166–84. Edited by Christian Gremmels and Ilse Tödt. Munich: Chr. Kaiser, 1987.

———. *Die Präsenz des Politischen in der Theologie Dietrich Bonhoeffers: Eine historische Untersuchung in systematischer Absicht* (The presence of the political in the theology of Dietrich Bonhoeffer: A historical inquiry with a systematic intention). Munich and Mainz: Chr. Kaiser, 1976.

Pfeifer, Hans. "Das Kirchenverständnis Dietrich Bonhoeffers: Ein Beitrag zur theologischen Prinzipienlehre" (Dietrich Bonhoeffer's understanding of the church: A contribution to the theory of theological principles). Diss., Heidelberg, 1963.

Pinner, Michael R. "The Responsible Community: Ecclesiology in the Thought of H. Richard Niebuhr and Dietrich Bonhoeffer." Ph.D. diss., Florida State University, 1990.

Prenter, Regin. "Jesus Christus als Gemeinde existierend: Ein Beitrag zum Verständnis Dietrich Bonhoeffers" (Jesus Christ existing as church-community: A contribution to understanding Dietrich Bonhoeffer). *Lutherische Monatshefte* 4 (1965):262–67.

Rades, Jörg Alfred. "Bonhoeffer and Hegel: From *Sanctorum Communio* to the Hegel Seminar with Some Perspectives for the Later Works." Unedited manuscripts, University of St. Andrews, 1988. Available in the Bonhoeffer Archive, Union Theological Seminary, New York. Also including "Kierkegaard and Bonhoeffer," "Luther and Bonhoeffer," and "Nietzsche and Bonhoeffer."

Schollmeyer, Matthias. "Die Bedeutung von 'Grenze' und 'Begrenzung' für die Methodologie und Grundstruktur der Theologie Dietrich Bonhoeffers" (The significance of 'limit' and 'limitation' for the methodology and fundamental structure of Dietrich Bonhoeffer's theology). In *Die Aktualität der Theologie Dietrich Bonhoeffers*, 55–79. Edited by Norbert Müller. Halle-Wittenberg: Martin-Luther-Universität, 1985.

———. "Bonhoeffers Theologie zwischen Geheimnis und Rationalismus: Untersuchung zur Struktur eines Fragments" (Bonhoeffer's theology between mystery and rationalism: Analysis of the structure of a fragmentary corpus). Diss., Halle, 1987.

Schönherr, Albrecht. "Sanctorum Communio: Dietrich Bonhoeffer als

Theologe der Kirche" (The community of saints: Dietrich Bonhoeffer as a theologian of the church). *Monatsschrift für Pastoraltheologie* 45 (1956):327–39.

Schroeder, Steven. "Ecclesiogenesis: Leonardo Boff and Dietrich Bonhoeffer on the Church." Conference paper, 1988. Bonhoeffer Archive, Union Theological Seminary.

Schwarz, Joachim. "Christologie als Modell der Gesellschaft: Eine Untersuchung zu den ersten Schriften Dietrich Bonhoeffers" (Christology as model of society: An inquiry into the first writings of Dietrich Bonhoeffer). Diss., Vienna, 1968.

Smit, Dirk J. "Dietrich Bonhoeffer and 'The Other'." *Journal of Theology for Southern Africa* (1995):3–16.

Smith, Ronald Gregor. "A note on the translation [of *Sanctorum Communio*]." [See above, Bonhoeffer, Dietrich. *The Communion of Saints.*]

Soosten, Joachim von. *Die Sozialität der Kirche: Theologie und Theorie der Kirche in Dietrich Bonhoeffers "Sanctorum Communio"* (The sociality of the church: Theology and the theory of the church in Dietrich Bonhoeffer's *Sanctorum Communio*). Munich: Chr. Kaiser Verlag, 1992.

Staats, Reinhard. "Adolf von Harnack im Leben Dietrich Bonhoeffers" (Adolf von Harnack in the life of Dietrich Bonhoeffer). *Theologische Zeitschrift* (1981):94ff.

Umidi, Robert Gerhard. "Imaging God Together: The Image of God as 'Sociality' in the Thought and Life of Dietrich Bonhoeffer." Ph.D. diss., Drew University, 1993.

Weinrich, Michael. *Der Wirklichkeit begegnen: Studien zur Buber, Grisebach, Gogarten, Bonhoeffer und Hirsch* (Encountering reality: Studies in Buber, Gogarten, Grisebach, Bonhoeffer, and Hirsch). Neukirchen-Vluyn: Neukirchener Verlag, 1980.

Weizsäcker, Carl Friedrich von. "Gedanken eines Nichttheologen zur theologischen Entwicklung Dietrich Bonhoeffers" (Thoughts of a nontheologian on the theological development of Dietrich Bonhoeffer). In *Genf 1976: Ein Bonhoeffer Symposion. Internationales Bonhoeffer Forum 1*. Edited by Hans Pfeifer. Munich: Chr. Kaiser, 1976. Also published in *Der Garten des Menschlichen: Beiträge zur geschichtlichen Anthropologie*, 454–78. Munich and Vienna: C. Hanser, 1977. English translation: *The Ambivalence of Progress: Essays on Historical Anthropology*. New York: Paragon House, 1988.

Woelfel, James. *Bonhoeffer's Theology: Classical and Revolutionary.* Nashville: Abingdon Press, 1970.

Wolf, Ernst. "Vorwort" (Foreword) to the second edition of *Sanctorum Communio.* Munich: Chr. Kaiser Verlag, 1954.

Wüstenberg, Ralf Karolus. *Glauben als Leben: Dietrich Bonhoeffer und die nightreligiöse Interpretation biblischer Begriffe.* Frankfurt: Peter Lang, 1996. English translation: *A Theology of Life: Dietrich Bonhoeffer's Religionless Christianity.* Translated by Douglas Stott. Grand Rapids: Eerdmans, 1998.

INDEX OF
SCRIPTURAL REFERENCES

INDEX OF NAMES

INDEX OF SUBJECTS

EDITORS AND TRANSLATORS

WAYNE WHITSON FLOYD, JR. (Ph.D., Emory University) is visiting professor and director of the Dietrich Bonhoeffer Center at the Lutheran
Theological Seminary at Philadelphia, an Associate Fellow in the Religion Department of Dickinson College, and serves as Canon Theologian
for the Episcopal Cathedral of St. Stephen in Harrisburg, Pa. He is the
author of *Theology and the Dialectics of Otherness: On Reading Bonhoeffer
and Adorno* (University Press of America, 1988); he co-authored with
Clifford Green the *Bonhoeffer Bibliography: Primary Sources and Secondary
Literature in English* (American Theological Library Association, 1992);
and he co-edited with Charles Marsh *Theology and the Practice of Responsibility: Essays on Dietrich Bonhoeffer* (Trinity Press International, 1995). Dr.
Floyd's articles on Bonhoeffer have appeared in *Union Seminary Quarterly Review, The Lutheran, Modern Theology, Religious Studies Review,
Dialog,* and *The Christian Century.*

CLIFFORD J. GREEN (Ph.D., Union Theological Seminary, New York) is
Professor of Theology at Hartford Seminary. A native of Australia, his
early education was at Sydney University and Melbourne College of
Divinity. Founding president of the International Bonhoeffer Society,
English Language Section, he now serves as Executive Director of the
Dietrich Bonhoeffer Works Translation Project. He is the author of
Bonhoeffer: The Sociality of Christ and Humanity, co-editor of *Ethik* and
Jugend und Studium in the German Dietrich Bonhoeffer Werke, editor of
the English translation of Bonhoeffer's *Fiction from Prison,* and author of
numerous articles and bibliographical works on Bonhoeffer. His other

371

publications include *Karl Barth: Theologian of Freedom* (Collins, 1989; Augsburg Fortress, 1991); *Churches, Cities, and Human Community* (Eerdmans, 1996); and chapters on Tillich, Marx, Cone, and Gutiérrez in *Critical Issues in Modern Religion* (Prentice-Hall, 1973, 1990).

REINHARD KRAUSS (Ph.D., University of St. Andrews) began his theological education at the universities of Tübingen and Bonn. His doctoral research on Karl Barth's concept of religion and its indebtedness to nineteenth-century liberal theology was published as *Gottes Offenbarung und Menschliche Religion: Eine Analyse des Religionsbegriffs in Karl Barths Kirchliche Dogmatik mit besonderer Berücksichtigung F. D. E. Schleiermachers* (Edwin Mellen, 1992). Dr. Krauss's interest in Dietrich Bonhoeffer's life and thought is rooted in his own German background and the experience of growing up in postwar Germany. His appreciation for Bonhoeffer's theology has deepened over time both through translating Bonhoeffer texts and through seeking to apply Bonhoeffer's insights in parish ministry. Since 1986 Dr. Krauss has lived and worked in the United States and has served several Presbyterian parishes. He is also a member of the Dietrich Bonhoeffer Works Editorial Board and of the translation teams for Bonhoeffer's *Discipleship* and *Ethics*.

NANCY LUKENS (Ph.D., University of Chicago) is Professor of German and Women's Studies at the University of New Hampshire, Durham, N.H. She is co-editor and translator of *Daughters of Eve: Women Writers of the German Democratic Republic*. Her translations of Bonhoeffer's prison poems appeared in *A Testament to Freedom: The Essential Writings of Dietrich Bonhoeffer* and in *Sojourners* magazine; she also created the subtitles for the film *Dietrich Bonhoeffer: Memories and Perspectives*. She is a member of the Dietrich Bonhoeffer Works Editorial Board and translator of *Fiction from Tegel Prison*.